1,80

THE WORLD'S CLASSICS

THE ATTACK ON THE MILL
AND OTHER STORIES

ÉMILE ZOLA was born in Paris in 1840, the son of a Venetian engineer and his French wife. He grew up in Aix-en-Provence where he made friends with Paul Cézanne. After an undistinguished school career and a brief period of dire poverty in Paris, Zola joined the newly-founded publishing firm of Hachette which he left in 1866 to live by his pen. He had already published a novel and his first collection of short stories. Other novels and stories followed until in 1871 Zola published the first volume of his Rougon-Macquart series with the sub-title *Histoire naturelle et sociale d'une famille sous le Second Empire*, in which he sets out to illustrate the influence of heredity and environment on a wide range of characters and milieux. It was, however, not until 1877 that his novel *L'Assommoir*, a study of alcoholism in the working classes, brought him wealth and fame. The last of the Rougon-Macquart series appeared in 1893 and his subsequent writing was far less successful, although he achieved fame of a different sort in his vigorous and influential intervention in the Dreyfus case. His marriage in 1870 had remained childless but his extremely happy liaison with a young laundress in later life gave him a son and a daughter. He died in 1902.

DOUGLAS PARMÉE now lives in Adelaide, South Australia, after retiring as Director of Studies in Modern Languages at Queens' College, Cambridge. He has written widely on French authors, edited two anthologies of nineteenth- and twentieth-century French poetry, and is a prize-winning translator from French, German, and Italian.

D1550174

THE WORLD'S CLASSICS

ÉMILE ZOLA

The Attack on the Mill
and Other Stories

Translated with an Introduction by
DOUGLAS PARMÉE

Oxford   New York
OXFORD UNIVERSITY PRESS

Oxford University Press, Walton Street, Oxford OX2 6DP

Oxford New York

Athens Auckland Bangkok Bombay
Calcutta Cape Town Dar es Salaam Delhi
Florence Hong Kong Istanbul Karachi
Kuala Lumpur Madras Madrid Melbourne
Mexico City Nairobi Paris Singapore
Taipei Tokyo Toronto

and associated companies in
Berlin Ibadan

Oxford is a trade mark of Oxford University Press

Translation, Introduction, Note and editorial matter
© Douglas Parmée 1984

First published 1984 as a World's Classics paperback

British Library Cataloguing in Publication Data
Zola, Emile
The attack on the mill and other stories
(The World's classics)
I. Title
843'.8[F] PQ2493
ISBN 0-19 281599 7

Library of Congress Cataloging in Publication Data
Zola, Emile, 1840 1902.
The attack on the mill and other stories.
(The World's classics)
1. Zola, Emile, 1840 1902 — Translations, English.
I. Parmée, Douglas. II. Title.
PQ2493.P36 1984 843'.8 84 7890
ISBN 0-19-281599-7

5 7 9 10 8 6 4

Printed in Great Britain by
BPC Paperbacks Ltd
Aylesbury, Bucks

CONTENTS

INTRODUCTION

THE relative or sometimes complete unavailability of texts has been the major factor in depriving non-French admirers of Zola's novels of the rewarding and exciting literary experience of reading his tales and short stories. The present volume is unique in providing a conspectus of these works, ranging from his first collection, *Contes à Ninon*, published in 1864, to his last story, 'The Haunted House' (*Angeline*), which appeared more than thirty years later. The stories provide many pleasures of recognition: readers will find a variety of theme, a dramatic power, a minute observation of physical detail, the narrative invention, the social scope, which bring a whole epoch of French life into vigorous relief, and with which his novels have made them familiar. There are also, however, stimulating differences: they will be spared the irritation they may have felt at the novelist's occasional jejune determinism and his tendency to over-play (though not, thank God, in his best novels) the importance of so-called laws of heredity and environment. They will meet in the short stories no attempt to apply his half-baked and totally misplaced theories as to the possibility of turning the novel into a sort of experimental research laboratory to observe and deduce the laws of human behaviour. They will even find the novelist's dramatic sense enhanced by the enforced concision of the short story form. And they will discover an accuracy of details that owes more to experience and intuition than to documentation, as the more anecdotal nature of the stories gives them an added liveliness.

But above all, from the very first tale (which is, significantly, in the first-person narrative), readers will become aware of a new dimension, a noticeable difference in tone, which may best be described as a sort of wry playfulness, used variously to mitigate or heighten an underlying seriousness. This different tone covers a wide range. It takes the form, for instance, of broad, even farcical humour, in 'Coqueville on the Spree' (*La Fête à Coqueville*)—a particularly interesting example, since Coqueville, as the epitome of the closed society, isolated in space and time, could have lent itself excellently to a painstaking study of the influence of heredity and environment, whereas Zola chooses to treat the village and its inhabitants largely as a huge joke. Mainly, however, this playfulness finds expression in a wide range of irony: the savage irony of 'The Attack on the Mill' (*L'Attaque du moulin*); the cruellest irony of all, with 'Captain Burle' (*Le Capitaine Burle*), perhaps the only story where the tone is almost unrelievedly tragic; and, more frequently, a gentler irony, as in the story of Monsieur Chabre (*Les Coquillages de Monsieur Chabre*), or in 'The Girl Who Loves Me' (*Celle qui m'aime*). The irony is sometimes blatant: sections of 'Priests and Sinners' offer good examples of this; at other times far subtler, as in 'Absence Makes the Heart Grow Fonder' (*Jacques Damour*), which ends on at least two different levels. Whatever form it takes, the irony is rarely unadulterated, and here again, I think, readers of Zola's short stories will have a further advantage over someone who knows only his novels, where irony is generally in rather short supply, and often obtrusive when it does appear. The eponymous anti-hero Burle, for example, excites compassion at the same time as he evokes an ironical smile of contempt, and the same can be said of Jacques Damour. Indeed pity, aroused, be it noted, obliquely in accordance with Zola's tenet of realistic impartiality, by ostensibly objective depiction rather than direct appeal to the reader's emotions, is a predominant element in many of these stories, and this skilful blending of contrasting suggestions arouses a similarly ambiguous reaction in the reader, a reaction more complex than that provoked by most of his novels, and which for many readers will more than adequately compensate for the lack of the epic quality of the better novels, well-nigh impossible to produce in a short story—although the spree at Coqueville is a binge of epic proportions, albeit on a mock-heroic scale.

Quite apart from the differences inherent in the genres, there is a deeper underlying distinction to be drawn between the novels and the short stories. For Zola the novelist, ambition and fame are the spur and the epic tone clearly forms part of the grand manner which will enable him to challenge a giant such as Balzac; but the charm of the short stories springs from the more urgent spur of economic necessity, the need to survive. The majority of these stories, in fact, form an important part of Zola's considerable and sometimes feverish production as a journalist, most of which falls between 1864 and 1880.

In 1865, when he left his job as head of the publicity department
of the newly formed publishing firm of Hachette which he had
joined two years before, Zola had to support his mother as well as
himself, for his father had died when Émile was only seven years
old; and incidentally, it should be mentioned that being the only
son of a widow proved to have compensations: he was exempted
from military service and had the additional bonus—his war
stories make it plain that he must have considered this a bonus—
that he escaped the servitudes and hardships and dangers of
soldiering during the Franco-Prussian war. It is interesting to
reflect that his numerous writings on the subject of war were
based on hearsay and imagination, not on experience, which may
explain why he fails to realize, in 'The Attack on the Mill', that in
modern warfare, shells had replaced cannon-balls . . .

Zola's economic straits, already bad enough, were shortly to
become even worse when, very soon, a further mouth was added
to the two he had to feed: that of his mistress Gabrielle-Alexandrine
Meley, whom he was to marry in 1870. Something had to be
done; it had to be done quickly; but it takes a long time, weeks or
months, even for someone of Zola's methodical and industrious
routine, to write a novel. It can take even longer to reap any
considerable benefit from royalties, even if, with luck, you have the
good fortune to have your novel accepted for publication in serial
form, a method which Zola was able to adopt in later life. But as
an unknown writer, there was only one possibility: journalism.
Articles and short stories can be dashed off in a few days or even
hours and, with luck and a reliable editor, you'll be paid on the
nail: the problem of cash flow is solved; you can eat and drink.

Zola's journalistic output never consisted solely of short stories;
throughout his career as a journalist, a large part of his time and
energy was devoted to criticism and reviews, not only of literary
and dramatic works but also of painting, as we are reminded
when reading 'Fair Exchange' (*Madame Sourdis*); and Zola, like
young Ferdinand Sourdis, was a modernist, not surprisingly
since he was a schoolmate of Paul Cézanne whom he continued to
frequent for many years. One of his earliest public controversies
arose from his support of the unfashionable and 'iconoclastic'
painter, Édouard Manet.

Zola is today, however, best known as a journalist for his short
stories and tales, some barely a couple of pages long, others of

thirty pages or more, of which he wrote more than eighty over a period of more than thirty years, although of this number only 'The Haunted House' was written after 1880. The reason for the cessation of his activity after this date was simple: the resounding success of his proletarian novel *L'Assommoir* in 1877 brought him fame overnight and proportionate wealth shortly afterwards. The spur of financial necessity had gone; the contract which he had secured in 1875 through the good offices of the friendly Turgenev to provide articles and stories to the Russian periodical *Vestnik Evropy* (*European Messenger*) was to expire in 1880. The years of grinding poverty which Zola had experienced in the mid-sixties were now but a memory; they had, however, been useful in providing personal knowledge of a way of life which appeared in both his novels and his short stories. Henceforth his novels were to bring him enduring fame of a magnitude that he could never have expected as a critic or a short story writer. All the same, as a journalist, Zola obviously learned many of his skills during this period and it could be argued that he might even have done well to carry some of them over more fully into his novels. If journalism has disadvantages, it can also bring benefits.

The potential disadvantages are obvious. Paid by the word or by the page, a journalist can easily sacrifice quality to quantity. A very stern critic might, I fancy, find some *longueurs* in parts of Zola's short stories; but we should not forget that a more leisurely age than ours would be happy to linger over charming descriptions of Guérande and Piriac (in 'Shellfish for Monsieur Chabre') or of L'Estaque, in 'A Flash in the Pan' (*Naïs Micoulin*), all the more willingly if such descriptions have the charm of exoticism as well, since many of these short stories were written for Russian readers. Furthermore, as a realist, Zola is concerned to create as complete an atmospheric background as possible. And the occasional lengthy description, far from being purely decorative, serves to prolong our suspense and even, as in a good detective story (I think again of 'A Flash in the Pan'), the trivial, apparently unnecessary detail can provide a clue to the dramatic dénouement.

Another danger facing the journalist is that topicality is often expected to be one of his ingredients: especially in his earlier works, Zola takes his starting point from a contemporary event or a matter of current interest. Here again, Zola manages to survive relatively unscathed, and in any case, his output was sufficiently considerable to enable a selection to be made which avoids ephemerae unlikely to interest a modern reader. In much of his later work, Zola avoids any such danger by deliberately choosing a topic of general import (as in 'Priests and Sinners') and inventing a dramatic framework to illustrate his point.

But the benefits of journalism are so considerable, at least for someone of Zola's temperament, as to outweigh the disadvantages. Writing quickly, you will find yourself writing briskly and crisply; you will seek to be lively. Writing for different editors and different reading publics gives you practice in flexibility: Parisian readers have different attitudes from those of the provincials, while Russian readers—for most of the stories here collected were written under contract to a Russian periodical—require a good deal of background information, a requirement which admirably suits Zola's technique; and they have their special expectations and preconceptions with regard to French society: could this perhaps explain some of the flippancy—'French sauciness' is perhaps the better word—of 'Coqueville on the Spree'? But, above all, people will not, I suggest, read short stories to be preached at or indoctrinated, even if they are not averse to having their prejudices flattered: so didacticism, that scourge of Zola's criticism and his later novels, has no place in his short stories, although he has his own methods of inferring a moral. In fact, the best way of entertaining males—and more females than they may perhaps care to admit—is by the slightly scabrous or the quasi-erotically suggestive. However, from what we know of Zola, such a tone was not one which represented his own inclinations and here again this sort of constraint can only have furthered his development as an artist: he has to be careful to avoid too forthright an expression of strongly held personal views; artistry is more important than outspoken sincerity. It is, of course, an attitude which squares very well with the realist's avowed aim of depicting people and society in their everyday life, however dull and even hateful, people as they are and not as we would have them be. Such suppression of personal feelings is bound to have its limits, of course: particularly as a young man, Zola was much given to sentimentality which can sometimes sink to mawkishness and he had a strong melodramatic tendency which he never threw off. The sentimentality diminished with age and self-discipline but he never seemed able to accept Hardy's dictum that while nothing is too strange to have happened, there is a good deal that is too strange to be believed. Once again, we have been saved by the quantity of Zola's output: with over eighty stories to choose from, it is easy to weed out the mawkish or over-melodramatic, which might, indeed, have appealed to a Victorian reader but would now be found unacceptable.

Zola's short story writing falls into two easily distinguishable periods, with 1875 as the dividing line, when he was, in fact, at thirty-five, *nel mezzo del cammin*, though his life was to be forcibly abridged. The first period contains largely very short pieces, some little more than a couple of pages long; the majority are mere sketches illustrating Parisian life (one of the collections of this typically journalistic production, first published in 1866, was called *Esquisses Parisiennes*). These sketches were a very prevalent genre at the time, a chronicle, and its author, the *chroniqueur*, writes of his personal impressions, usually basing his story on a *fait divers*, an anecdote, real or imagined, a genuine or fictitious personal memory; he strolls through Paris noting things that strike his fancy or people who seem perhaps odd or even 'typically Parisian'; topics on which he can talk out loud, personally, inviting the reader's complicity. Occasionally, the tale will invite the expression of a hope or a non-censorious moral, although we should beware of accepting any such expression of emotion or judgement at its face value. It is pleasant chat and much of it, where Zola's contribution to the genre is concerned, is now read only by critics in search of influences or anxious to find in it the seeds of his future novels. These *chroniques* were largely published in the many newspapers and magazines which proliferated in Paris in the declining years of the Second Empire; and they tend to have a sameness of tone, a sort of slickness which quickly palls. All the same, some have a sufficiently strong ironic edge and an observation of permanent human foibles accurate enough to amuse a modern reader. Five have been included here, out of a total of over fifty.

The second period of Zola's activity as a short story writer is very different; no longer sketches, the stories all have a plot and characters. Although still writing for a periodical, he is relieved of the need to crave the suffrage of the French reading public and can avoid any direct editorial pressure; the obligation to provide slick entertainment and instant dramatization is lifted. On his much broader canvas of more than ten thousand words, he can exercise his realistic technique of detailed observation, he is free to develop situations in accordance with views that from other evidence we know to be closer to his heart but which he has learned to express with artistic discretion. All except one of the remaining translations of the present selection are taken from this collaboration: ten stories in all, exactly half of Zola's total output of short stories for the Russian periodical (he also wrote more than forty other pieces, articles on literary and other topics). One or two of the stories have retained the impressionistic stamp of his earlier journalism, not surprisingly since he occasionally borrowed from earlier sketches to put his Russian pieces together; and one or two of them are too essentially topical for inclusion here, for instance, a series of short sketches recounting some of the electioneering and voting in the important French general election of 1878, which are of greater interest for the historian than for the general reader.

We have mentioned the importance of drama in the short story to offer the reader an unexpected twist, a surprising turn of events or a sudden striking revelation of character. Zola well understood the desirability of this technique and in many of these stories he keeps the reader on tenterhooks. What exactly is going to become of the sexually obsessed Captain Burle? Who is going to be shot—or is anyone going to be shot—in 'The Attack on the Mill'? In 'Absence Makes the Heart Grow Fonder', what possible solution can be found for Jacques Damour's agonizing problem? Is that rather unpleasant young Frédéric Morand, so perfectly adapted to his rich middle-class background, none the less riding for a serious, if not fatal, fall? These are a few of the major dramas which combine with interlocking minor dramas to provide complex suspense for the reader. But it would be underestimating Zola's inventive narrative talent to assume that he places exclusive reliance on what are, after all, fairly ordinary basic skills which, if indulged in to excess, can turn into mannered devices. Zola has other strings to his bow and in all his full-length stories the questions are more subtly posed: it is not so much *what* is going to happen, as *when* and *how* is what we can expect to happen *actually going to happen*. Far less common is the question *why* something happens. Zola rarely probes motives nor, indeed, does he generally need to do so, for the mainsprings of most characters' behaviour are plain, although not necessarily simple. All the same, in one or two of these stories, there is greater ambiguity: Jacques Damour's final resolution, in 'Absence Makes the Heart Grow Fonder', is not explained. When Zola does choose thus to respect the uncertainty of human motive, his realistic technique stands him in good stead, relying as it does on the external recording of behaviour rather than on omniscient authorial probing: here actions or even gestures speak louder than words and the reader can ponder the motives at leisure.

But there is no doubt that the question of *how* something happens is most important for Zola and is worth examining in some greater detail. 'Shellfish for Monsieur Chabre' is as good an example as any. Now, it is surely not necessary to be particularly sophisticated or cynical to realize very early in the story that Monsieur Chabre's balding head is going to be adorned with horns and we know quite well who is going to put them there. The main suspense thus centres on the question of *how*, and this is where Zola shows his artistry. We see in great detail the physical background and contributory events which foster the growth of a relationship between a shy young man, becoming progressively and charmingly less shy, and a respectable and spirited young wife, becoming progressively less respectable; a relationship which not only unites two bodies—both equally beautiful bodies— but reveals a marriage of minds which share the same feeling for nature and a similar sense of beauty as well as the same sense of fun, the same interest in life's oddities. All these aspects of the links between the two young people are observed with careful and selective realistic detail, never over-explicit: the reader is not taken into the exact workings of the protagonists' minds or the minute development of their feelings but is left to surmise and deduce—and to be amused. Woven into the tale are Zola's own holiday impressions of a specific district of France which is realistically portrayed in considerable detail for the foreign Russian reader, no doubt fascinated—as English readers may well also be—by a glimpse into an excitingly beautiful landscape or a charmingly picturesque old town. More importantly, the impact of such joint impressions on the young couple in creating a stimulating bond between them is central to the plot; it seems clear that here is no description for the sake of description and even the long drawn out account of the shrimping expedition has an important functional role: it increases our suspense as well as suddenly revealing a breakthrough in the couple's relationship. The net result is that what could have been a banal and sordid adultery, a quick seaside 'petticoats up and trousers down' on the beach, becomes a lyrical celebration of the beauty of natural forces set in a convincing and fascinating specific French background, in a specific French milieu. Even the chief victim is not entirely a caricatural black-and-white character. Paunchy and absurd though he is, Monsieur Chabre is a living person and not really a bad sort of fellow—he's mannerly and considerate towards his wife; and, in the end, Zola lets him come to no harm. He's nobly eaten his loathsome shellfish and the reader is delighted when he gets his reward in the shape of a bouncing son and heir; it's a sort of nineteenth-century form of *in vitro* fertilization. And quite apart from the sexual problem, we may feel that, through his truth to life, Zola has, as it were incidentally, given us an intriguing and plausible glimpse into a perennial mystery: how can rich businessmen, so shrewd and expert in their particular sphere, prove so ineffectual and stupid outside these activities?

I have spent time on 'Shellfish for Monsieur Chabre' because it is an excellent example of Zola's narrative technique, albeit one of many, whereby he succeeds in turning a relatively predictable *what* into a far more uncertain *how*. Beyond simple comedy or drama, we are taken into more enriching regions of the mind while at the same time our attention is constantly held by the convincing and accurate depiction of many different milieux. By the manner of their telling, we are persuaded to overlook the familiarity or even banality of the events being told; the realist Zola has, strangely, achieved a sort of classicism, the classicism of 'what oft was said but ne'er so well expressed'.

Zola's stories extend through a very wide range of French society, almost as wide as his novels, though the typical *nouveau riche* parvenu of the period is not well represented; Durandeau in 'Rentafoil' (*Les Repoussoirs*) is the nearest approach to the crafty Second Empire speculator lavishly depicted in the novels. Apart from this, we see specimens from the aristocracy down to the peasantry and proletariat: indeed, in two of the stories here reproduced, 'The Way People Die' (*Comment on meurt*) and 'Priests and Sinners', there is a deliberate juxtaposition of the attitudes of different classes, although in the second of these, the emphasis is placed more on a particular type of priest rather than on the class of society to which he was ministering. If realism is deemed to depend exclusively on observation, there must be some difficulty in considering such works as realistic: Zola had no direct or personal experience of most of the milieux he was depicting, the aristocracy, the upper- and lower-middle classes, the proletariat or the peasantry. His own frequentations were largely of journalists, of literary and artistic Parisian bohemians. However, in his years of poverty in the early and mid-sixties, he would certainly have rubbed shoulders with the working and poorer artisan classes and he would have seen something of provincial life and peasantry in his boyhood in Provence. The life of the aristocracy and the upper-middle classes must have remained a closed book to him, to be learnt about from other writers' works or from other people's conversation. Critics have taken Zola to task over this. However, Zola had very sensitive antennae and a lively imagination; he was to need less than a week 'in the field' in Beauce when gathering material for his superb peasant novel *La Terre* and since both Balzac and Proust, in their different ways, seem to have overcome similar shortcomings in their novels, it would be prudent to let readers judge for themselves as to the authenticity of Zola's portrayal of classes of which he had limited direct knowledge.

From our knowledge of Zola's strong feelings about social injustice, we might have expected the aristocracy to have suffered harshly at his hands; in fact, they do not come off too badly. True, they appear as heartless, hypocritical and sexually promiscuous but they are shown as possessing good manners, decorum and a certain panache, a conventional picture, of course, but Zola's invention of incident, the *petit fait vrai* of Stendhal, and the accurate background detail make perfectly plausible and interesting stories out of this unoriginal material. The middle classes at all levels had been the butt of most of the important poets and novelists of the nineteenth century in France and Zola similarly belabours them for their materialistic greed, their snobbery and, particularly the women, for their bigotry; again, it is the manner rather than the matter that is original. Predictably, the lower-middle classes, harder pressed by economic circumstances, are treated more sympathetically, although Monsieur Rousseau, the stationer in the third section of 'The Way People Die', however sincerely he may mourn his wife, still has a nagging grievance against her: what a pity she had to die on a day which forced him to close the shop! It is far easier to arouse compassion for the wretched working classes and Zola does so; nonetheless, his code of impartiality leads him to show a few warts: the working-class inhabitants of the tenement block in the fourth section of 'Priests and Sinners' are notably uncharitable in their judgements as well as drunk and disorderly in their communal lives. On the whole, the peasantry come out best; they have a simple fatalistic dignity springing from their close contact with natural forces; but this does not prevent Zola from drawing a devastating picture of their appalling superstitiousness in the first section of 'Priests and Sinners'.

In a word, Zola's view of mankind is unflattering but it must be said that if there are few wholly admirable characters, there are also not many really despicable ones. Indeed, it could be argued that his characterization in his short stories, because of his frequent humorous or ironic touches, is more rounded than in his novels; and the narrower canvas still gives him room to etch in some convincing, often slyly funny vignettes of minor characters.

As we might expect, one of the major characters of his short stories is the carefully drawn environment. Zola invites the readers' close attention to the influence of social and other circumstantial conditioning on our behaviour; and this condition-ing not only helps to explain our complexities, it also serves as an extenuating circumstance. In 'A Flash in the Pan' (*Naïs Micoulin*), for instance, Naïs' father is a wife-beater, a harsh father who knocks his daughter about, and a would-be murderer; yet this sort of uncouth savagery is shown as rooted in the desperate struggle to survive in a pitiless drought-ridden region, as well as in the still living tradition of a Latin paterfamilias whose pride in family honour is the mainstay of his existence. Similarly, the stupid Father Pintoux in the first part of 'Priests and Sinners' is as much a victim of circumstance as his pathetically superstitious flock of Breton peasantry; his life is almost as hard as theirs and his belief in hell fire as strong; and if the Monsignor of the fifth section of the same group is ruthlessly ambitious, it is his early military training which is partly to blame for his insensitivity. Zola obviously considers professional military training as one of the most pernicious environments. It results in a besetting sin which incurs his ultimate condemnation of any human being: lack of imagination. No amount of courage or loyalty can make up for this failure: the jaunty, gallant French officer in 'The Attack on the Mill' as well as the dour, pathetic, doggedly courageous and strictly honourable Major Laguitte in 'Captain Burle' are both ultimately condemned, in so far as Zola allows anyone to be condemned, as blinkered automata.

A further reason for Zola's distaste for the military is that, through their association with war, which he views as a deplorable but inevitable human infirmity, they are closely associated with death. Zola had a streak of morbidity which finds explicit expression in 'Dead Men Tell No Tales' (*La Mort d'Olivier Bécaille*), and which no doubt will find an echo with many a reader. We know from other sources not only of his fear, which proved to be prophetic, of meeting an untimely death but also of being buried alive; and the story plainly owes much of its initial impact to this autobiographical element. However, as always, Zola constructs a plot and a situation which go far beyond any personal feelings. Fear of death and of burial alive turn out to be the most superficial, if perhaps the most dramatic, of the levels at which the story works; the real subjects are the fragility of the marriage vows, the pressure of economic necessity, the portrayal of women as creatures possessing habits and customs rather than morals, and finally, a favourite theme in Zola's short stories, the justification of sexual desire, an interesting contrast to the depressing view of sexuality revealed in the novels of the *Rougon-Macquart* cycle; it seems almost as if in this portrayal of the successful fulfilment of young love, a vein of sentimentality persists from the early *Contes à Ninon* which was ruthlessly excised from the later novels. Let it be noted, by the way, that if women are sternly treated at times, the men have nothing to crow about: the motives of men's actions are usually social advancement or material gain, with love as a secondary commodity.

In later life, Zola became a very active political figure in his support for Dreyfus; but politics and politicians are sceptically viewed in his stories. The political Monsignor of 'Priests and Sinners' is a rabidly reactionary self-seeker while, at the other end of the spectrum, the left-wing Berru of 'Absence Makes the Heart

Grow Fonder' is a rascally rabble-rousing firebrand who takes good care of his own skin. Big Michu's father, in 'Big Michu' (*Le grand Michu*), is mentioned as a brave and honest 1848 Republican; but Jacques Damour, in 'Absence Makes the Heart Grow Fonder', also brave and honest, is shown as a credulous simpleton whose Communard activity is closely linked to the few francs a day which he receives as a National Guardsman. Politics are in fact largely the preserve of a corrupt aristocracy and a conservative and ambitious upper-middle class and Zola shows us no evidence to suggest that any of the lower-class aspirants to political power are likely to be very different. In a word, politicians are members of the human race, of which someone wrote:

> I wish I liked the human race,
> I wish I liked its silly face,
> And when I'm introduced to one
> I wish I thought: What jolly fun!

Such indeed, here expressed in humorous Anglo-Saxon terms, which need not exclude a hidden anguish, is a sentiment that can be seen to run through Zola's short stories. It is a cry from the heart of many French writers, from Molière and La Rochefoucauld, Chamfort and Voltaire, Flaubert and Céline. In Zola, it is no isolated disenchantment, for his picture is very complete. He takes us into aristocratic bedrooms and dining-rooms, into drawing-rooms in Paris and in the provinces, into little shops and wretched garrets, into a garrison town, seaside resorts, the Faubourg Saint-Germain and Ménilmontant, a Lorraine village and an assortment of cemeteries. He peoples his accurate backgrounds with convincing characters: men-about-town, middle-class money-makers, petty bourgeois, soldiers, fishermen, peasants, bricklayers, shopkeepers, artisans and other manual workers, not forgetting the odd kept woman; conservative reactionaries as well as uneasy liberals and opportunistic republicans; and they are all seen in action, often dramatically and frequently ironically. We see a well-composed and authoritative fresco, of a wide range in full colour, of French society in the second half of the nineteenth century. But this is not just a period piece: Zola's themes—love, young and fierce or tired and disillusioned, maternal, paternal, filial, married or adulterous; death, natural or violent; money (or lack of it); religion (or lack of it);

work (or lack of it)—are always with us and to many of them he gives a strikingly modern, even prophetic, slant. His general theme is, after all, various forms of recognizably modern conflict: the dilemma of the tormented Abbé de Villeneuve is similar to that of the worker-priest; fundamentalist religious fanatics, in the line of poor Father Pintoux, are today, in many parts of the world, a commonplace; we can all think of gifted men destroying themselves through drink and dissipation; the lures of high-pressure salesmanship are familiar bogies; and many people have an uneasy suspicion that there may still exist those who hope to be able to cry, like the French captain in 'The Attack on the Mill', 'We've won! We've won!' on piles of corpses and flattened buildings. It would seem very likely therefore that, having survived for a century, these brilliant stories, so varied in theme and tone, will continue to engross and entertain readers for a long time to come.

D.P.
Adelaide, South Australia

NOTE ON THE TEXTS

THE first five of the stories selected here appear in the chrono-logical order of their publication in periodicals. Of the remaining stories, those eventually published in volume form appear in the chronological order of the publication of the various volumes, and in the sequence in which they are grouped within a particular volume. Publication details and general notes on each story will be found in the Explanatory Notes.

Zola's titles are often rather unenlightening, and the translator has ventured, here and there, to provide English versions that may be found more stimulating. The original French titles are to be found in the Introduction or the Notes.

SELECT BIBLIOGRAPHY

MANY of the original manuscripts of the short stories have been lost (see 'Les "Manuscrits perdus" d'Émile Zola' in *Les Cahiers naturalistes*, no. 39, 1970, pp. 84–6). Printed texts of the stories, either in their various versions in periodicals or in volume form are available in the Bibliothèque Nationale in Paris, and, in part, in the British Museum Library in London.

Three of the main twentieth-century editions of the short stories are: *Contes et Nouvelles*, ed. Maurice le Blond (2 vols, Bernouard, Paris, 1928); *Contes et Nouvelles*, ed. H. Mitterand, vol. 9 of *Oeuvres complètes* (Cercle du Livre Précieux, Paris, 1970); *Émile Zola, Contes et Nouvelles*, ed. R. Ripoll (Gallimard, Bibliothèque de la Pléiade, Paris, 1976).

Zola's short stories have received remarkably little critical attention either in French or English. Readers should consult *Les Cahiers naturalistes, passim*, and H. Mitterand and H. Suwala, *Émile Zola Journaliste: Bibliographie chronologique et analytique* (Les Belles Lettres, Paris, 1968) and H. Mitterand, *Zola journaliste* (Armand Colin, Paris, 1962).

The standard critical biography of Zola is by F. W. J. Hemmings (Oxford University Press, rev. edn, 1964). See also in English, J. C. Lapp, *Zola before the Rougon-Macquart* (University of Toronto Press, 1964).

Articles specifically on Zola's short stories include: D. Baguley, 'Maupassant avant la lettre? A study of a Zola short story, *Les Coquillages de M. Chabre*' (Nottingham French Studies, 6, October 1967, pp. 77–86); J. Christie, 'The Enigma of Zola's *Madame Sourdis*' (Nottingham French Studies, 4, May 1968, pp. 21–2); R. J. Niess, 'Autobiographical elements in Zola's *Joie de Vivre* and *La Mort d'Olivier Bécaille*' (Modern Language Notes, 57, no. 3, March 1942, pp. 205–7); R. Ricatte, 'Zola conteur' (*Europe*, April–May 1968, pp. 209–17); J. Triomphe, 'Zola collaborateur du *"Messager d'Europe"*' (Revue de Littérature comparée, 17, no. 4, 1937, pp. 754–65).

A CHRONOLOGY OF ÉMILE ZOLA

1840 Émile Zola born 2 April, in Paris, of French mother and Italian father

1843 Family settles in Aix-en-Provence

1847 Émile's father dies

1859 Zola twice fails school-leaving Baccalauréat

1861 Destitute in Paris. Zola obtains post in shop of newly-founded firm of Hachette. Already writing poetry and short stories

1864 In charge of Hachette's publicity. Publishes first collection of short stories, *Contes à Ninon*

1865 Publication of first novel, *La Confession de Claude*. Liaison with Gabrielle-Alexandrine Meley; leaves Hachette, and embarks on writing career, at first largely as a journalist (reviewer, critic, short story and feature article writer)

1867 Favourable article on Manet's painting. As friend of Cézanne, frequents artistic circles, including many Impressionists. Publication of *Thérèse Raquin*

1870 Marries Mlle Meley. Publication in serial form of *La Fortune des Rougon*, which becomes the first of the twenty-volume cycle of novels concerning the Rougon-Macquart family, published over the next twenty-three years. Takes refuge in Marseilles to avoid invading Prussian army; later becomes Parliamentary correspondent to French government, which had retreated to Bordeaux

1871 Returns briefly to Paris but leaves to avoid Commune uprising

1874 Publication of *Nouveaux Contes à Ninon*

1875 Beginning of collaboration with St Petersburg periodical *Vestnik Evropy* (*European Messenger*). Holiday in Saint-Aubin, on Normandy coast (c.f. 'Coqueville on the Spree')

1876 Holiday in Piriac (c.f. 'Shellfish for Monsieur Chabre')

1877 Success of *L'Assommoir*, seventh volume of *Rougon-Macquart* series, brings fame and financial security. Holiday in L'Estaque (c.f. 'A Flash in the Pan')

1878 Buys property in Médan, village on outskirts of Paris

1880 Publication of *Soirées de Médan* (see notes on 'The Attack on the Mill'). End of collaboration with *Vestnik Evropy*

1882 Publication in France in one volume of six of Zola's *Vestnik Evropy* stories, under collective title of *Le Capitaine Burle*

1883 Publication in one volume of further six of Zola's *Vestnik Evropy* stories, under collective title of *Naïs Micoulin*

1885   Publication of *Germinal*, twelfth in the *Rougon-Macquart* series

1888   Starts lifelong liaison with Jeanne Rozerot

1889   Birth of Denise, daughter of Jeanne and Zola

1891   Birth of Jacques, son of Jeanne and Zola

1893   *Le Docteur Pascal* ends *Rougon-Macquart* series

1894   Extended trip to Italy

1898   Publication of Zola's article *J'Accuse* in Paris newspaper in favour of Dreyfus leads him to take refuge in England to avoid imprisonment. Writes his last story, 'The Haunted House' (*Angeline*)

1902   Death of Zola by asphyxiation in his Paris flat; suspicion that his bedroom chimney may have been deliberately blocked

THE GIRL WHO LOVES ME

Is the Girl Who Loves Me a fine lady dressed in silk and lace and jewels, reclining on a sofa in her boudoir, dreaming of our love? Is She a marchioness or duchess, as light-footed and dainty as a dream, langorously trailing her long flowing white gown over sumptuous rugs with a charming pout, softer than a smile, on her lips? Is the Girl Who Loves Me a smart little grisette skipping along the pavement, lifting her skirts as she hops over the gutter and glancing sideways to make sure that the slimness of her legs is receiving its due appreciation? Is She an easy-going sort of girl who is not very particular whose glass She's drinking out of, wearing satin one day and coarse calico the next, with a capacious heart able to find a little corner for everybody?

Is the Girl Who Loves Me the fair-haired young girl kneeling down to pray beside her mother or the Foolish Virgin hailing me at night from a dark little side street? Is She the nut-brown peasant wench who looks at me as I walk by and who still keeps thinking of me amidst her wheatfields and vineyards? Or the poor woman who thanks me when I give her alms? The woman belonging to some other man, husband or lover, whom I followed one day and never saw again?

Is the Girl Who Loves Me a European, pale as the dawn, an Asian, golden yellow like the setting sun, or a daughter of the desert, black as the starry sky?

Is the Girl Who Loves Me hidden behind that partition or is She over the Ocean? Is She further than the stars?

Is the Girl Who Loves Me not yet born? Or did She die a hundred years ago?

2

Yesterday I went in search of her on a fairground. There was a celebration in one of the suburbs and the populace, all dressed up in their Sunday best, was noisily thronging the streets.

The fairy-lights had just been lit. Spaced out along the avenue there were blue and yellow posts decorated with shallow cups in

A.O.M.—2

which wicks were burning, smoking and fluttering in the wind.
Venetian lanterns were swaying to and fro in the trees. The
pavements were lined with canvas booths whose red-fringed
curtains were trailing in the gutter. Gilded pieces of china, bright-
coloured sweetmeats and garish stall displays were glittering in
the harsh light of the flares.

The air was heavy with the smell of dust, gingerbread and crisp
waffles. Hurdy-gurdies were grinding out their tunes; clowns
with powdered faces were laughing and crying as they were
showered with kicks and blows. Over all this gay spectacle a
warm haze was hanging.

Above the haze and the noise, the summer sky stretched out,
vast and pure and sad. An angel had just lit up its azure depths in
honour of some divine festivity, a celebration of infinity, serene
in its sovereign majesty.

Lost in the crowd, I became aware of the loneliness of my
heart. As I walked along, following with my eyes the girls who
smiled at me as I went by, I said to myself that I should never see
them again. The thought of all these warm, tender lips, glimpsed
for a brief second and then lost for ever, filled my heart with deep
distress.

With these thoughts, I reached a crossing in the middle of the
avenue. On the left, leaning against an elm tree, there stood a
solitary booth. In front, a few planks roughly nailed together
formed a stage and the entrance, screened by a strip of canvas,
was lit by two lanterns. I stopped to look at a man dressed in a
long black magician's gown and a star-spangled pointed hat
standing on the platform haranguing the crowd.

'Roll up! Roll up!' he was shouting. 'Come along, all you fine
ladies and gentlemen! I've just come hotfoot from darkest India to
gladden your hearts, risking my life to bring back for your
pleasure the Mirror of Love which was guarded by a dreaded
dragon. And now, you fine ladies and gents, I can offer you the
realization of all your dreams. Walk up, walk up, ladies and
gentlemen, and see the Girl Who Loves You! Yes, the Girl Who
Loves You, for only two sous!'

An old woman dressed as a nautch girl pulled aside the canvas
strip. She gaped at the crowd and shouted in a hoarse voice: 'Roll
up! Roll up! Only two sous for the Girl Who Loves You! Come
along and see the Girl Who Loves You!'

3

The magician beat a lively tattoo on the big drum, with a vigorous accompaniment from the nautch girl on a bell.

The public was undecided. A trained donkey playing cards is fascinating; a strong man lifting hundred-pound weights is a sight not to be missed; nor can it be denied that a half-naked giant woman offers attractions for all ages. But to see the Girl Who Loves You is something of little interest to anyone and hardly offers much of a thrill.

I had been listening spellbound to the invitation of the man in the long black robe. His promises struck a chord deep in my heart; it was surely Providence which had chanced to lead my steps here and my amazement at hearing this miserable little man reading my innermost thoughts raised him considerably in my estimation. As he beat away with truly diabolical fury on his big drum and shouted in a voice that completely drowned the sound of the bell, his blazing eyes seemed to be boring into me.

I was just about to place my foot on the first step leading up to the platform when I felt someone holding me back. I turned round and saw a man standing at the foot of the stage who had caught me by the sleeve. He was tall and thin and his large hands were covered in still larger gloves. He was wearing a hat that had turned a reddish colour, a black frockcoat rubbed white at the elbows and twill breeches in a deplorable state, yellow with mud and stained with grease. He made a long, superb bow that bent him double and addressed me in a high-pitched voice, in these words:

'I am deeply unhappy, my dear sir, to see a young man of good upbringing setting such a bad example to the populace. It is extremely frivolous on your part to encourage that impudent rogue who is trading on our baser instincts, for I find it profoundly immoral of him to be publicly inviting, so vociferously, young men and young girls to indulge in visual and mental debauchery of this sort. Oh, my dear sir, the people are weak but men like us, fortified by the benefits of a good education, we, sir, I beg you to remember, have a solemn and compelling duty: let us not give way to our sinful curiosity, let us be worthy citizens in every respect. The morality of our society, sir, depends on us.'

I listened to his words. He had continued to hold on to my sleeve and seemed unable to bring himself to stop bowing. Hat in hand, he was pontificating in so gentle and obliging a manner that the thought never entered my head to become annoyed. When he had finished speaking, I merely looked him straight in the eyes without attempting to reply. He took my silence to be a question.

'I am, dear sir,' he went on, with yet another bow, 'I am the Friend of the People* and my mission is to bring happiness to mankind.'

He pronounced these words with an air of modest pride and suddenly drew himself up to his full height. I turned on my heels and climbed up on to the platform. Before going in, as I pulled the canvas strip aside, I looked back at him for the last time. With his right hand he had delicately caught hold of the fingers of his left and was trying to smooth out the wrinkles of his glove, which seemed in danger of slipping off.

Then, folding his arms, the Friend of the People tenderly contemplated the nautch girl.

4

I let the canvas fall behind me and found myself in the inner sanctum. It was a kind of long narrow room, chairless, with canvas walls, and lit by a single lamp. A few people were already gathered there: some girls, all agog with curiosity, and a number of noisy young men. Everything was highly proper: the sexes were segregated by means of a rope stretched across the room.

To tell the truth, the Mirror of Love was nothing more than a pair of two-way mirrors, one in each compartment, tiny round panes of glass looking into the inside of the booth. The promised miracle was being performed with admirable simplicity: all you had to do was to place your eye against the pane of glass and your Loved One appeared on the other side, without any assistance from fire and brimstone. How could anyone fail to believe in such a natural vision!

I didn't feel ready to undergo the ordeal immediately on going in: the nautch girl had given me a heart-chilling look as I went by. How could I know what was awaiting me on the other side of that pane of glass? It might be a horrifying face with lifeless eyes and purple lips; or a centenarian thirsting for young blood, one of those misshapen creatures whom I used to see in my nightmares. I was no longer able to believe in those lovely fair-haired ladies whom I charitably invent to colonize my private desert. I thought of all those ugly women who show some fondness for me and asked myself with dismay whether it might not be one of them who would be appearing before my eyes.

I went away into a corner and urged myself on by watching those people, braver than I, who were prepared to consult their fate without so much heart-searching. I soon found myself taking a strange pleasure in watching their different expressions as they peered with their right eye wide open and two fingers covering their left one, each with a particular smile according to the extent of their enjoyment at what they saw. The pane of glass was fairly low and they had to bend down slightly; nothing seemed to me more ludicrous than the sight of these men lining up to peep at their soulmate through a hole a few inches in size.

Two soldiers led the way: a sergeant tanned by the African sun and a young conscript, a farm-hand still smelling of the land, his arms floating awkwardly in a greatcoat three sizes too large for him. The sergeant gave a scornful laugh. The conscript remained bending forward for a long time, uncommonly pleased with himself at having found a girl-friend.

Then a stout man with a white jacket and a bloated red face looked through the hole, calmly and without showing either pleasure or displeasure, as if it was perfectly natural for someone to love him.

He was followed by three schoolboys, cheeky-looking young scamps of fifteen or sixteen, jostling each other to make believe that they had achieved the distinction of being drunk. All three swore blind that they recognized their aunt.

So all these people satisfied their curiosity by peeping through the pane of glass one by one and I can no longer remember now all the different expressions on their faces which struck me at the time. Oh, that vision of the Loved One! What hard truths you forced those peering eyes to admit! Those eyes were the real Mirrors of Love, mirrors in which feminine charm was reflected in a squalid glint in which lust vied with stupidity.

At the other window, the girls were enjoying themselves in a more seemly way. The only expression on their faces was one of great curiosity, with not the slightest trace of nasty thoughts or lewdness. They were coming up and peeping through the hole one by one with a surprised look and then going away, some pensively, others laughing and giggling.

In point of fact, I couldn't really imagine what they were doing there. If I were a woman with the slightest claims to be called pretty, I'd never be so silly as to bother to go and look at the Man Who Loved Me. On days when I felt sad and lonely, that is on fine sunny days in the spring, I'd go for a walk along a lane full of blossom and I'd make every passer-by adore me. In the evening I'd come home with a great store of love.

True, these inquisitive girls were not all equally pretty. The beautiful ones obviously didn't give a damn for the magician's arts; they'd long since ceased to have need of them. The plain ones on the other hand had never enjoyed themselves so much. One such, with a large mouth and sparse hair, found it hard to tear herself away from the Magic Mirror; she still had on her face the bright heart-breaking smile of a beggar eating his fill after a long fast.

I asked myself what romantic notions were being aroused in their foolish heads. It was not an easy question to answer. They had all, certainly, seen a prince falling at their feet in their dreams and they all felt the need to become better acquainted with the sweetheart whom they could still vaguely remember when they woke up. No doubt many of them were disappointed; princes are in short supply and the mind's eye has a glimpse of a better world at night and is kinder than the one we use during the daytime. There were also girls who seemed very happy; their dream was coming true: their lover had the silky moustache and dark hair of their dreams. These naive romances, as shortlived as hope, could all be deduced from the blush on their cheeks and the gentle heaving of their breast.

Yet after all, these girls were perhaps just silly and I was being silly myself to have seen so much where there was no doubt nothing to see. However, on closer inspection, I felt completely reassured: both men and women seemed in general extremely well satisfied with what they saw. The magician would surely not have been so hardhearted as to give honest folk who'd paid their two sous to see his show the slightest cause for disappointment.

I went over and trying hard to remain calm put my right eye to the little peep-hole. Resting her elbows on the back of an armchair placed between two long red curtains was a woman. Brilliantly lit by concealed lamps, she was standing in front of a painted canvas backcloth, somewhat tattered, which must originally have represented a lovers' arbour, with blue trees.

Like any well brought up vision, the Girl Who Loves Me was wearing a long white dress, slightly waisted, with a long train trailing in a cloud of muslin on the floor. A wide veil, also white and held by a crown of may blossom, covered her forehead. Thus attired, the dear little angel was all whiteness and innocence. She was leaning forward in a saucy pose, with a tenderly caressing look in her large blue eyes. Behind her veil, I thought she looked exquisite: long fair curls glimpsed through the muslin, a brow of childlike purity, delicately curved lips and the most kissable dimples you could possibly imagine. At first sight she seemed to me a saint; a second look gave me the impression of an easy-going sort of girl, far from prudish and extremely accommodating.

She put three fingers to her lips and blew me a kiss with a curtsy that had nothing otherworldly about it at all. Seeing that she showed no sign of levitating, I fixed her features in my mind and walked away.

As I was going out, I saw the Friend of the People coming in. This solemn preacher did not seem anxious to meet me; he hurried over to the peep-hole and set a bad example of sinful curiosity. Bent double, his long back squirmed with desire; then, unable to go any further, he kissed the magic mirror.

6

I went down the three steps and found myself once more caught up in the crowd. Now that I had seen her smile, I was determined to go in search of the Girl Who Loves Me.

The lamps were smoking, the bustle was growing more and more frantic and the jostling throng was threatening to overturn the booths. The festivity had reached that apogee of joy when you face the happy fate of being crushed to death.

Craning my neck, I could see an horizon of linen bonnets and silk hats. I walked along, pushing past the men and making my way circumspectly round the ladies' voluminous skirts. Perhaps it was that pink cape; perhaps that tulle coiffe adorned with mauve ribbons; perhaps that delightful straw toque with its ostrich feather? Alas, the cape was sixty years old; the coiffe was disastrously ugly and leaning lovingly against the shoulder of a sapper in uniform; the toque was in fits of laughter and her big round eyes were the loveliest you ever saw, but not the ones I was looking for.

Over all crowds there seems to float a vague distress, an atmosphere of pervasive melancholy, as if any large gathering of people creates an aura of terror and pity. I've never found myself in any large group without feeling a kind of unease. It always seems to me as if this assembled mass of men and women is threatened by a dreadful doom, that one single flash of lightning will suffice to freeze their frenzied gestures into immobility and still their raucous cries forever...

As I watched this heartrendingly festive mood I gradually slowed my pace. I saw an old beggar standing in the yellow glare of the fairy-lights, his crooked body paralysed with arthritis. His face was ghastly pale and he was looking piteously up at the passers-by, blinking his rheumy eyes to soften their hearts. He kept making sudden twitches with his limbs so that they trembled like a dry branch. The sprightly young girls were walking past this hideous spectacle laughing and blushing.

Further on, two workmen were having a fight outside a tavern. In their struggle they had overturned their drinks and the wine was flowing over the pavement like blood pouring out of a wound.

The laughter seemed to change into sobs, the fairy-lights into a blazing fire and the crowd went spinning round, gripped by horror. As I walked along, peering questioningly at all these young faces, I felt sad unto death as I vainly sought the Girl Who Loves Me.

7

I saw a man standing in front of one of the posts to which the fairy-lights were attached, contemplating it with rapt attention. From his weary look, I realized that he was seeking the solution

to some weighty problem. I recognized the Friend of the People.
He turned his head and saw me.

'The oil used in these festivities, my dear sir,' he said to me, 'is priced at one franc a litre. A litre of oil will fill twenty of these cups that you see here, that is to say, it costs five centimes for each. Now this post here has sixteen rows, each comprising eight cups. Furthermore, if you can follow my calculation, I have counted sixty identical posts along this avenue, thus making seven thousand six hundred and eighty cups, which brings us to a total of seven thousand six hundred and eighty sous, in other words three hundred and eighty-four francs.'

As he spoke, the Friend of the People was waving his arms in the air to emphasize each figure and bending forward from the waist as if to place himself within reach of my limited intelligence. As soon as he had finished talking, he straightened up with an air of triumph, folded his arms and looked at me solemnly.

'Three hundred and eighty-four francs worth of oil!' he exclaimed, stressing every syllable. 'And the poor haven't enough bread to eat, my dear sir. I ask you—and I ask this with tears in my eyes—would it not be more decent, for the love of humanity, to distribute those three hundred and eighty-four francs to the three thousand poor and indigent persons numbered in this suburb alone? Such an act of charity would provide each of them with approximately twelve and a half centimes worth of bread. This reflection should give all sensitive people serious food for thought, my dear sir.'

He saw that I was looking at him with curiosity and his voice took on a dying fall as he smoothed his gloves over his fingers.

'Poor people should not enjoy themselves, dear sir. It is quite unseemly for them to forget their poverty for a single hour. Who indeed would shed tears for the sufferings of the people were the government to provide such saturnalia frequently?'

He wiped away a tear and left me. I saw him go into a wine-shop where he drowned his sorrows in five or six small glasses of wine which he gulped down in quick succession at the bar.

8

The last fairy-lights had just gone out. The crowd had departed. In the flickering light of the street lamps, there were now only a few dark shapes to be seen wandering under the trees, belated loving couples, drunks and melancholy patrolling constables. The drab and silent lines of booths stretched on both sides of the avenue, like the tents of a deserted encampment.

The morning breeze, damp with dew, set the leaves of the elm trees quivering. The pungent effluvia of the evening had given way to a delicious freshness. Fondly, the infinite silence and limpid shadows of the fathomless sky sank slowly down to earth as the festive stars succeeded the festive fairy-lights. At last respectable folk would be able to take their pleasure in their own way.*

I felt reinvigorated. The time had come for me to enjoy myself. I stepped out at a brisk pace, walking up and down the tree-lined alleys, when I saw a grey shadow slipping along beside the houses. The shadow was coming quickly towards me and from her light step and swinging dress, I realized that it was a woman.

Just as she was about to bump into me, she looked up. In the light of a street lamp, I recognized the face of the Girl Who Loves Me; not the Goddess in her cloud of white muslin but a poor earthbound girl in a faded cotton frock. Poverty-stricken as she looked, she still seemed charming to me, even if pale and tired. There was no possible doubt: there were those same large eyes and caressing lips of my vision; and in addition, seen more closely, she had that softness of expression that comes from suffering.

As she stopped for a second, I seized her hand and kissed it. She looked up at me with a vague smile and made no attempt to pull her fingers away. Seeing me standing there without saying a word, for I was overcome by emotion, she gave a little shrug and began to go on her way as quickly as she had come.

I ran after her and put my arm round her waist. She gave a quiet laugh and then shivered, saying in a low voice:

'Let's walk faster, I'm cold.'

My poor little angel was cold! Under her thin black shawl, her shoulders were trembling in the cool wind. I kissed her on the forehead and asked her gently:

'Do you know me?'

She looked up at me for the third time and replied without hesitation:

'No.'

A sudden thought came into my mind and it was my turn to shiver.

'Where are we going?' I asked her.

She shrugged her shoulders and, with a little pout of indifference, said in her childlike voice:

'Wherever you like, to my place or yours, I don't mind.'

9

We were still walking down the avenue.

I saw two soldiers sitting on a bench. One of them was gravely holding forth while the other was listening respectfully. It was the sergeant and the conscript. The sergeant seemed to me to be in a state of great emotion: he gave me a derisive look and said in an undertone:

'Sometimes the rich are willing to lend to those worse off, sir.'

The conscript, a naive and sensitive soul, said to me miserably:

'She was the only girl I had, sir. You're taking the Girl Who Loves Me away from me.'

I crossed the road and went down the other side.

Three young lads were coming towards us, holding on to each other and singing at the tops of their voices. I recognized the schoolboys. The young rascals no longer had any need to pretend to be drunk. They stopped, burst out laughing and then followed me for a few steps, shouting in unsteady voices:

'Hi there, sir, that lady's having you on, she's the Girl Who Loves Me!'

I felt a cold sweat breaking out on my forehead. I started walking faster, anxious to get away from them, no longer thinking of the young woman whom I was dragging along beside me. At the end of the avenue, just as I was about to escape from this diabolical spot, stepping off the pavement I collided with a man sitting comfortably in the gutter. He seemed demented. His head was propped against a stone and with his face turned towards the sky, he was doing a very complicated sum on his fingers.

He turned to look at me and, without raising his head from its pillow, he said, speaking with some difficulty:

'Ah, it's you, my dear sir. You really should help me to count the stars. I've already discovered several million but I'm afraid I may have missed one or two. The happiness of mankind, dear sir, is strictly a matter of statistics.'

He hiccuped and went on in a tearful voice:

'Do you know the cost of a star? Surely the good Lord must have spent a great deal of money up there, while down here the people are going short of bread, my dear sir! What's the good of all those fairy-lights? Can you eat them? What, I ask you, is their practical application? I can't think that we needed this eternal festivity. No, God has never had the slightest notion of social economics.'

He had managed to sit up completely and was looking round him in bewilderment, shaking his head indignantly. At that moment he caught sight of my companion. He gave a start and turned red in the face as he greedily stretched out his arms.

'Good gracious me!' he exclaimed. 'It's the Girl Who Loves Me.'

10

'Well, that's how it is,' she said to me. 'I've got no money so I do what I can to earn a living. Last winter I spent fifteen hours a day embroidering and there were still days when I went hungry. So in the spring, I chucked away my needle, because I'd found a less tiring and more lucrative job.

'Every evening I dress up in white muslin. Then I stand leaning over the back of an armchair, all alone in a tiny room, and the only thing I have to do is to smile from six o'clock till midnight. Now and again I drop a curtsy or throw a kiss into empty space. I get paid three francs a session.

'All the time I can see an eye watching me through a little pane of glass in the partition. Sometimes it's blue, sometimes it's brown. If it wasn't for that eye I'd be perfectly happy. It spoils my job for me. There are times, as I watch that solitary eye staring at me, when I feel quite terrified and I'm tempted to cry out and run away.

'But you've got to work to stay alive and so I smile, wave my hand and throw kisses. At midnight I remove my make-up and put on my cotton frock. Ah well, there's lots of women who, like me, put on airs and graces in front of a wall without even being obliged to do so.'

RENTAFOIL

IN Paris, everything's for sale: wise virgins, foolish virgins, truth and lies, tears and smiles.

You must certainly be aware that in such a commercially-minded place, beauty is a commodity and the object of an obnoxious trade. People buy and sell big bright eyes and charming little mouths; noses and chins are all quoted at their exact valuation. A particular dimple or beauty-spot can command a steady income. And since there's always fraud somewhere or other, at times you have to copy nature's handiwork, so that eyebrows drawn with burnt matchends, and false hairpieces fetch better prices than the real article.

This is quite fair and reasonable. We're a civilized people and what's the good of being civilized if it doesn't help us to take other people in and be taken in ourselves, thereby making life less tedious.

But I must confess to being really astonished yesterday when I learnt that old Durandeau, that businessman known to all and sundry, had come up with the astoundingly ingenious idea of finding a market for ugliness.

Selling beauty is something I can understand, even selling false beauty seems perfectly natural, it's a sign of progress. But I think the businessman I mentioned really has deserved well of his country by putting into circulation such a hitherto unsaleable article as ugliness. Don't misunderstand me, I'm talking about real ugliness, ugly ugliness, sold on the open market.

I'm sure you've occasionally seen women in couples, walking slowly along the pavement, stopping in front of shop-windows, giggling and swishing their long skirts in a very fetching way. They go along arm-in-arm like good friends, talking as if they have known each other for ages. They're about the same age and both smartly dressed. But one of them is always relatively good-looking, not the sort of face you'd write home about or turn round to examine more closely, but had you caught sight of it accidentally, you'd have viewed it without displeasure. The other woman is always hideous, the sort of ugliness that grates on your nerves but which you can't take your eyes off; it forces the passer-by to draw comparisons between her and her companion.

Own up: you've sometimes been taken in and started to follow
the couple. In isolation, the hideous one would have disgusted
you and the moderately good-looking one would have left you
cold. But together, the ugliness of the one has magnified the good
looks of the other.

Well, let me explain to you that the hideously ugly one, the
monstrosity, belongs to Durandeau's agency. She's on the staff of
Rentafoil. The great Durandeau had hired her out to the ordinary-
looking one at five francs an hour.

2

Let me tell you the full story.

Durandeau is an imaginative and original entrepreneur, a
multi-millionaire who has succeeded in turning business into an
art. For many years he had been bewailing the fact that no one
had hitherto been able to make money out of ugly girls. As for
pretty ones, trading in them is a tricky matter and I can assure
you that the idea of such a thing has never crossed his mind; he's
rich enough to be able to afford scruples.

One day he received a sudden illumination from heaven. As
with all great inventions, this brainwave sprang quite unexpectedly into his head. He was walking along the boulevard one day
when he saw two girls tripping along in front of him. One was
pretty and one was ugly and as he looked the realization dawned
on him that the ugly one was an adornment worn, as it were, by
the pretty one. Just as you buy ribbons and face-powder and false
plaits, it was only right and proper, he said to himself, that the
pretty one should buy the ugly one as a suitable embellishment, a
foil.

Durandeau went home to ponder over the matter. The commercial operation that he had in mind needed to be conducted
with great care. He didn't want to launch out rashly into an
enterprise which would be a stroke of genius if it succeeded and
preposterous if it failed. He spent the night doing his sums and
reading up those philosophers who have written most wisely
about the stupidity of men and the vanity of women. When dawn
came, his mind was made up: his arithmetic had made sense and
the philosophers had shown such a low opinion of mankind that
he felt able to rely on a large number of prospective clients.

3

If my Muse were more inspired, I'd produce a splendid epic on the creation of Durandeau's agency. It would be farcical and sad, full of tears and full of laughter.

Durandeau had greater difficulty than he had anticipated in acquiring his stock-in-trade. At first, using the direct approach, he had little hand-written notices stuck on rainwater-pipes, on trees and in out-of-the-way corners. These notices read as follows: 'Ugly girls required. Undemanding work.'

He waited a week and not a single ugly girl came forward. Five or six pretty ones turned up who were facing the desperate alternative of starving to death or a life of vice but still hoping to find work to rescue themselves. Durandeau was dreadfully embarrassed and assured them repeatedly that they were pretty and of no use to him. They insisted that they were ugly and that it was pure gallantry and callousness on his part to describe them as anything else. Since they were unable to sell their non-existent ugliness, I expect by now they'll have found buyers for their undoubted beauty.

By now Durandeau had realized that only pretty women have the courage to make a false confession of ugliness. The ugly ones would never admit of their own free will that their mouths were too big and their eyes ludicrously small. You could put up notices all over Paris offering ten francs to every ugly woman who cared to apply without the slightest risk of becoming impoverished.

So Durandeau gave up his idea of notices and commissioned half-a-dozen agents to scour the city in search of female monstrosities: a general mobilization of the ugly women of Paris. The agents—men of tact and taste—had a tricky assignment, needing to take into account temperament and situation. Thus, when the person concerned needed money urgently, they didn't beat about the bush; when they were dealing with girls not yet on the point of starving, they had to show greater subtlety. It's not easy for someone polite to go up to a woman and say: 'Madame, you're ugly; I'll pay you so much per day for your ugliness.'

This hunt for girls who dare not face their mirrors without bursting into tears led to many memorable moments. Sometimes the agents would see passing in the street an ideally ugly woman and were so keen to show her to Durandeau that they could barely restrain themselves. Indeed, some of them stopped at nothing.

Every morning Durandeau held court to inspect the goods that had been rounded up the day before. Sprawling in his armchair in a yellow dressing-gown and black satin skull cap, he had the new recruits parade in front of him, each accompanied by her agent. He would lean back and scrutinize them through half-closed eyes, with the air of a satisfied or disappointed connoisseur; he would slowly take a pinch of snuff and reflect; then, to get a better look, he'd make the article turn round and examine it from every angle; sometimes he would even stand up and feel the hair or peep into the face like a tailor stroking a piece of cloth or a grocer checking the quality of a lump of tallow or some pepper. When the ugliness was blatant, when the face was stupid and heavy, Durandeau would rub his hands together and congratulate the agent. He would almost have liked to embrace the monstrosity herself. But he mistrusted any signs of singularity in a woman: eyes that were bright or lips with an ironical twist would make him scowl and he would say to himself that an ugly woman like that might not excite love but could well excite passion. He would give the agent a black look and tell the woman to come back again later—when she was old.

It's not as easy as you might think to be an expert in ugliness and gather a collection of really ugly women unlikely to spoil the chances of pretty ones. Durandeau's deep knowledge of the human heart and its passions made him a collector of genius. For him, the expression was the essential, and he chose only faces that were intimidating by reason of their appalling dullness and stupidity.

The day he felt in a position to offer beautiful women past their prime a full selection of ugly ones to match their colouring and their particular brand of beauty, he opened his agency with the following prospectus:

RENTAFOIL
L. Durandeau   Paris, May 1st, 18. .
  18, Rue M . . .
    in Paris
Office hours: 10 a.m. to 4 p.m.

  Dear Madame,
    I have the honour to inform you that I have recently established a firm with the express purpose of providing a unique service for the

preservation of a lady's beauty. I have invented an article of fashion which will add new lustre to your own natural beauty.

Hitherto the means of enhancing a lady's beauty have been painfully obvious. Jewels and other finery are clearly visible and it is also well known that false hairpieces exist and rosy cheeks come out of a box.

I have endeavoured to confront this apparently insoluble problem of making ladies even lovelier while hiding from any indiscreet eye the origin of their adornment. The question was this: could we find some infallible method of ensuring that she should attract favourable attention and avoid wasteful expenditure of time and energy without recourse to one single extra ribbon or facial adornment.

I think that I may flatter myself that I have completely mastered this thorny problem.

Today, any lady prepared to honour me with her patronage will, for a derisory sum, attract the eyes of an admiring public.

My article of fashion is extremely simple and its effect is guaranteed. I need only describe it to you, Madame, for you to understand immediately how it operates.

Have you not ever seen a beggar-woman being given alms from the elegantly gloved hand of a fine lady dressed in silk and other finery? Did you not notice how splendid the sheen of her silk looked against the beggar-woman's rags and how her wealth stood out with even greater elegance by comparison with the other's poverty?

Madame, I have the pleasure and privilege of providing your lovely countenance with the richest collection of ugly faces to be found anywhere. Tattered rags emphasize the chic of new clothes: my ugly faces bring out the full charm of pretty ones.

Away with false teeth, false hair, false busts! Away with expensive cosmetics and costly toiletries, away with make-up and lace! Simply *Foils* whose arm you can take, with whom you can walk through the streets to bring out your beauty and attract the fond gaze of the gentlemen!

I invite you, Madame, to honour me with your custom. You will find in my agency the greatest possible variety of ugly creations. You will be able to select the exact type of ugliness most suitable to your particular style of beauty.

My charge for this unique service is a paltry five francs an hour or fifty francs for the whole day.

I remain, Madame, your humble and devoted servant,

Durandeau

N.B. My agency also has a stock of Mothers and Fathers, Uncles and Aunts at extremely reasonable prices.

4

The venture was a great success. When the agency opened the very next morning, the office was crowded with female customers each choosing her own foil and carrying it off with a tigerish delight. You can't imagine the pleasure of a pretty woman leaning on the arm of an ugly one. Not only was she enhancing her own beauty, she was enjoying someone else's ugliness. Durandeau is a great philosopher.

However, don't imagine that organizing this service was an easy matter. There were innumerable hitches. It had been difficult enough to organize the supply; it was far worse trying to satisfy the demand.

When one lady appeared and asked for a foil, they displayed the goods and invited her to make her choice, contenting themselves merely with offering a few helpful hints. The lady then went disdainfully from one foil to the next, finding all the poor girls either too ugly or not ugly enough, on the grounds that not one of them had the right kind of ugliness to suit her own special sort of beauty. The assistants did their best by pointing out a splendidly crooked nose here, an enormous slit of a mouth there: they might have saved their breath.

At other times the lady herself was appallingly ugly and if he happened to be present, Durandeau would be itching to take her on to his staff at any price. This lady wanted a foil to set off her beauty, she declared; she wanted a young one, not too ugly, since her beauty needed little embellishment. The despairing assistants placed her in front of a large mirror and paraded their whole stock beside her. She still took the prize for ugliness and flounced off indignantly, furious that they had dared to offer her such inferior articles.

Gradually, however, a regular clientele became established and each foil had her regular customers. Durandeau was able to relax with the inner satisfaction of having achieved a new breakthrough in civilization.

I don't know if you can realize what it is like to be a foil; they have their joys and public triumphs but they also have their very private sorrows.

Foils are ugly; they're slaves and they suffer since their money comes from being slaves and ugly. On the other hand, they're well-dressed, they wear jewellery, they walk arm-in-arm with the upper crust of the ladies of the town, go everywhere by carriage, eat in the best restaurants and spend their evenings at the theatre. They're on familiar terms with fashionable cocottes and the simple-minded think they belong to the high society of race-goers and first-nighters.

They spend all day in a whirl of gaiety. At night, they fret and fume and sob. They've had to take off their fine dress which belongs to the agency, they're all alone in their attic, sitting in front of a bit of broken mirror which tells them the truth. Their ugliness is staring them mercilessly in the face and they're quite aware that nobody will ever love them. They may help to excite desire but never will they know the joy of being kissed themselves.

5

I've tried to tell you here the story of the creation of Durandeau's agency and make his name known to posterity. Such men have their special niche in the hall of fame.

One day I may write the *Secret Memoirs of a Foil*. I knew one such unfortunate girl whose sad tale was heartrending. Her customers were ladies of the town known to everyone in Paris and they treated her quite shamefully. Please, ladies, don't misuse your foils, be kind towards the ugly ducklings without whose help you wouldn't even be pretty at all!

This foil I knew was an emotional sort of girl whom I suspect of reading too much Walter Scott.* I know nothing sadder than a hunchback in love or an ugly woman full of romantic ideals. The wretched girl kept falling in love with all the young men whose eyes were caught by her unfortunate face, which then led their attention on to her employer. It was like a mirror being in love with the larks which it lures down within the range of the huntsman's gun.

She had many harrowing experiences. She was terribly jealous of those women who bought her like a skin-cream or a pair of boots. She was an object hired for so much an hour and it so happened that this object had feelings. Can you imagine her resentment while she had to smile and joke familiarly with the women who were depriving her of her share of love? Those

20 *Rentafoil*

professional Beauties who took malicious pleasure in using honeyed words in public and treating her like a skivvy in private, whom they would have smashed with no more concern than they would have broken a china figure in their display-cabinet.

But what importance has a tormented soul when progress is at stake? Mankind marches on. Durandeau will be blessed by future generations because he has created a market for a hitherto unsaleable commodity and invented a fashion article which makes love easier.

DEATH BY ADVERTISING

I ONCE knew a very nice young man. He died last year. His life had become a sheer martyrdom. Let me tell you the story of a man killed by advertising. Pierre Landry was born in the Rue St Honoré, near the Central Markets; a paradise for idle loafers. His first reading lessons were given him by his nurse who made him spell out the signs and billposters in the streets. He grew to like those large oblong yellow and blue pieces of paper so conveniently displayed on the walls and later on, as a young lad roaming the streets, he fell in love with some of the posters—the ones printed in enormous characters in queer shapes, on which there is a lot to read. His father, a retired hosier, had completed his son's education by letting him have the advertisement page to read—everyone knows that the large print of the advertisements is easier for children to make out.

At the age of twenty, Pierre Landry was orphaned and found himself quite well-off. He decided to live entirely for his own pleasure and to exploit every aspect of modern progressive civilization for his own personal benefit. His father had been a worker; he was going to relax and enjoy the fantastic luxury of the Golden Age promised him by the advertisements on page four of his paper and on the hoardings. 'What a marvellous age we live in!' he mused, 'an age of enlightenment and benefits without end. Where can you see anything more moving than those men who devote themselves night and day to the happiness of mankind by producing a constant stream of inventions to provide us with a more peaceful and happy life and who are even so generous as to put all these delightful things within reach of the most modest purse? And to think that these benefactors of mankind even take the trouble to draw our attention to all these wonderful things, great and small, tell us where to find them, and even how much we'll have to pay for them! Some of them we really ought to thank on bended knees for being willing even to lose money on our behalf; and others are quite satisfied merely to cover their expenses. They're working purely in the service of mankind, so that we can live richer, peaceful lives. Well, I've already planned how I want to live. I intend to keep up with progress and enjoy all the advantages of the modern world without any further question. I want a blissfully happy life and for that, all I need is to consult the newspapers and posters, night and morning, and do exactly what they tell me. It's an infallible guide to true wisdom and happiness is guaranteed!'

From then on, Pierre's guideline in life was the advertisements in the papers and on the hoardings. He followed them blindly whenever he had a decision to make and he would never buy or do anything that hadn't been warmly recommended by the publicity men. Every morning he would religiously scan the papers, conscientiously noting down the new discoveries and products. As a result his home became a repository of every crackbrained invention or shoddy article on sale in Paris. Indeed, his basic reasoning was not without logic. By keeping abreast of the times, and choosing the products most enthusiastically praised and recommended in rhapsodic terms by the publicity men, he could claim, with legitimate pride, that he was using the most advanced products of the most highly developed civilization in the world and had thus solved the problem of attaining perfection. However, this was only the theory, and unfortunately the reality became more unpleasant every day. Although everything should have been for the best, in fact it all went from bad to worse and the drama now began which was to make his life a hell on earth.

He had bought a plot of filled-in swampland, into which his house slowly sank. The house itself had been built according to the latest modern principles; when the wind blew, it shook and when rainstorms came, it gently crumbled. The fireplaces, equipped with ingenious smokeless hoods, belched forth asphyxiating fumes; the electric bells remained obstinately silent; the carefully planned modern lavatories turned out to be noisome cesspits; cupboards provided with special mechanical locks would neither open nor shut properly.

In particular, there was a splendid pianola which sounded like a rather inferior hurdy-gurdy, and a burglar-proof and fireproof safe which was quietly removed, bodily, by burglars one fine winter's night. There was also the country cottage that Pierre had bought at Arcueil, which was quite a different story. Here, he experimented with trees cut out of sheet metal and tried cultivating rare plants which, when they grew, looked like rather poor couchgrass. His architect-designed water tank, widely advertised, collapsed and he was nearly drowned as well as almost crushed to death.

Amidst all these trials and tribulations, Pierre continued to smile blandly, his faith quite unshaken. On the contrary, his confidence grew stronger. 'Everything isn't yet for the best in the best of all possible worlds,'* he said to himself, 'and the most logical way to avoid all these misfortunes is to follow the march of progress even more closely. The reason my water tank collapsed was that my architect wasn't warmly enough recommended. I must find one recommended more strongly. If I watch the newspapers, I'm bound to achieve perfection and perfect happiness.'

Poor Pierre suffered not only in his possessions but in his person.

His clothes would split at the seams as he was walking down the street: he had bought them from firms offering vast discounts on stocks being cleared, either because of stock-taking or a takeover. He would seek out such bargains not through meanness but solely in order to enjoy all the benefits of the modern world.

One day when I met him, he'd gone completely bald. In his tireless pursuit of progress, he had hit on the odd idea of changing the colour of his hair from blond to dark. He'd applied a liquid which made all his hair fall out, to his great delight, since he could now, he claimed, employ a certain hair lotion guaranteed to give him a head of brown hair twice as thick as his previous one. Incidentally, his cheeks and chin were perpetually covered in gashes from the superior modern razors he used. His hats went out of shape after a week's wear and the clever little springs designed to open his umbrella never worked when it was raining.

I won't mention all his patent medicines. He had always been strong and healthy; he became emaciated and short of breath. And now advertising really started to destroy him. Thinking he was ill, he began to try out all the wonder-cures advertised in such glowing terms, and to increase their effectiveness, since he was quite at a loss to distinguish between their conflicting claims, all couched in equally highflown language, he took all the medicines at once. He also consumed enormous quantities of chocolate, unable to resist the blandishments of the various manufacturers. He used toiletries in great abundance and several times went to have teeth pulled out in order to provide work for numerous philanthropic dentists who swore blind that their extraction would be painless, nearly breaking your jaw in the process.

Advertising attacked his mind as well as his body. He had bought an extendable bookcase into which he crammed all the books recommended in newspaper reviews. He invented a very ingenious classification system: he arranged books according to their order of merit, that is to say, according to the degree of enthusiasm displayed by the reviewers, all subsidized by the publishers. His shelves groaned under the weight of his collection of rubbish recording all the stupidity and corruption of the age. On the back of each volume, Pierre carefully stuck the blurb which had caused him to buy it, so that each time he opened it he knew in advance how he ought to react: he could laugh or weep according to the instructions.

The outcome of all this was to turn him into a moron, although, having become more selective and difficult to please, in the end he bought only those books described as 'outstanding masterpieces', thereby reducing his purchases to some twenty books a week.

We now reach the last act of this harrowing drama. Having heard of a clairvoyante claiming to cure all ills, he rushed round to consult her about his own non-existent diseases. The clairvoyante obligingly offered to restore his youth. All he had to do was to drink a certain liquid and take a bath. Pierre Landry was convinced that such a potion must be the acme of civilization. He swallowed the drug, jumped into his bath and regained his youth to such good effect that two hours later he was discovered there, dead. He had a smile on his lips and the look of ecstasy on his face suggested that he had died worshipping the Great God Advertising. This was no doubt the radical remedy for all ills promised him by the clairvoyante.

Even in death, Pierre Landry remained the humble devotee of advertising. In his will, he had asked to be embalmed in a casket in accordance with a recently patented instant chemical process. At the cemetery, the coffin burst open, tipping his wretched corpse into the mud. He had to be buried higgledy-piggledy with the broken bits of plank. Next winter, the rains rotted the papier-mâché of his imitation marble tombstone, and his grave was left an anonymous heap of mouldering refuse.

STORY OF A MADMAN

ISIDORE-JEAN-LOUIS MAURIN was a worthy middle-class citizen, the owner of several blocks of flats in Belleville* and residing on the first floor of one of them. He had grown up in the back rooms of this old house, tending his garden and idling away his days like many a Parisian with time on his hands. At the age of forty he was foolish enough to marry the daughter of one of his tenants, an eighteen-year-old blonde whose grey eyes with their occasional sparkle were as shining and gentle as a cat's.

Six months later she had found her way upstairs to the flat of a young doctor who lived on the floor above. This happened as naturally as anything, one evening during a thunderstorm while Maurin had gone out for a stroll along the fortifications of Paris. Their love grew into a devouring passion. They soon found that the few odd minutes they were able to steal together in secret were not enough; they dreamt of living together as man and wife. Their close proximity, the fact that they were separated from each other by nothing more than the thickness of a ceiling, sharpened their desire still more. At night, the lover could hear the husband coughing in bed.

Mind you, Maurin was a decent sort, known in the district as a model husband; he didn't pry and he was as kind and tolerant as anyone could be. But that was exactly what made him such an exasperating obstacle; with his contented nature, he hardly ever left the flat and the very simplicity of his tastes meant that his young wife was a prisoner in the house. After a few weeks, she had run out of excuses for visiting the second floor and so the lovers decided that the old fellow must be got rid of.

*

They were reluctant to resort to violence or crime. How could you possibly slit the throat of such a tame sheep? Besides, they were afraid of being found out and sent to the guillotine. In any case, the doctor, who was an ingenious young man, hit on a less risky but equally effective method, the bizarre nature of which fired the young woman's romantic imagination.

One night the whole house was aroused by dreadful screams coming from the owner's flat. They forced open the door and found the young woman in a terrible state, kneeling on the floor, all dishevelled and shrieking, her shoulders covered in red weals. Maurin was standing in front of her, trembling and quite bewildered. His speech was slurred like that of a drunken man and when pressed he was quite incapable of replying coherently.

'I can't understand it,' he stammered, 'I didn't go near her, she suddenly started screaming.'

When Henriette had somewhat recovered her composure, she herself stammered something, giving her husband a strange look full of a kind of frightened pity. The neighbours went away greatly intrigued and even rather horrified, muttering to themselves that 'it wasn't at all clear'.

Similar scenes recurred regularly and the whole house was soon living in a state of constant alarm. Every time the screams were heard and the neighbours forced their way into the flat, they saw the same scene: Henriette was lying on the floor in a state of collapse and trembling like someone who had just been mercilessly beaten, while Maurin was running round the room in a state of bewilderment, unable to offer any explanation.

*

The poor man became careworn. Every evening he would go to bed trembling with the secret fear that he would be awakened by Henriette's screams. He could not make head or tail of her strange fits: she would suddenly leap out of bed, hit herself violently round the shoulders, tear her hair and roll about on the floor without giving him the slightest idea as to the cause. He concluded that she must be mad and he made a vow to himself not to answer any questions and to keep this private drama to himself. But his easygoing way of life had vanished with his peace of mind; he lost weight and looked pale and ill; his self-satisfied smile had gone for good.

Meanwhile a rumour—the source of which no one quite knew—was spreading in the neighbourhood that almost every night the poor man was subject to an attack of fever during which he thrashed the unfortunate Henriette to within an inch of her life. His pale, stricken face and his evasive answers, as well as his sad and embarrassed demeanour, served only to confirm this rumour.

From then onwards Maurin could not do anything that was not interpreted as the action of a madman. As soon as he went out, he became the focus of everyone's eyes, monitoring his every move and leading to strange interpretations of every word he uttered: nobody more resembles a madman than someone who is perfectly sane. If his foot slipped, if he looked up at the sky, if he blew his nose, people would laugh and shrug their shoulders in pity. Street urchins followed him about as though he were some strange animal. At the end of a month, everyone in Belleville knew that Maurin was mad, stark, staring mad.

People would whisper extraordinary things about him. One woman said she had met him on one of the outer boulevards walking in the rain without a hat. It was quite true: it had just been blown off his head by a gust of wind. Another woman declared that he used to walk round his garden at midnight every night, carrying the sort of candle used in churches and chanting the funeral service. This seemed quite terrifying. The truth was that the woman had seen Maurin on one occasion using a lamp to discover the slugs which were eating his lettuces. Gradually they pieced together a whole indictment of queer actions, an overwhelming dossier of mad behaviour. Tongues were busily wagging: 'Such a nice, kind, gentle man! What a shame! But that's how it is!. . . . All the same, we'll have to get him put away in the end!. . . He's killing his poor dear wife, such a wonderful well-bred little woman. . .'

*

They went to the police and one fine morning, after a dreadful scene, played to perfection by Henriette, Maurin was bundled into a cab on some pretext or other and taken off to Charenton.* When he reached there and realized what was happening, in his rage he bit a warder's thumb right off. They put him into a strait-jacket and dumped him among the violent madmen.

The young doctor had arranged for the poor man to be kept shut up in a cell as long as possible. He claimed to have been following Maurin's illness and observing such strange symptoms in him that his colleagues thought they had discovered a new form of madness. Moreover, the whole of Belleville was there to provide circumstantial details. Mental specialists conferred and learned articles were written. The lovers slipped away to enjoy their honeymoon in a leafy retreat in Touraine.

*

It took Henriette eleven months to become tired of her young doctor. Often, in between kisses, her thoughts had turned to her poor wretch of a husband screaming in his mad-cell. She began to feel a growing affection for him now that such a dreadful fate had overtaken him and he was no longer able to go out and look at his lettuces or take his stroll along the fortifications. Women with grey cat's eyes tend to be subject to such whims. She left her lover and went post-haste to Charenton, determined to make a full confession.

She had often felt surprised that the doctors were taking so long to discover that Maurin was not mad. At best, she had relied on enjoying only a few weeks' freedom. When they took her to her husband she saw in a shadowy corner of his cell a pale, thin, filthy, animal-like figure, more ghost than man, who stood up and looked at her with eyes full of mindless, imbecilic horror. The poor man failed to recognize her. And as she stood there in terror, he began to sway to and fro with an idiotic laugh. Suddenly he burst out sobbing and stammered: 'I can't understand it, I can't understand it... I didn't go near her!...'

Then he hurled himself flat on the floor, exactly as Henriette had done, and kept hitting himself on the shoulders as he screamed and rolled around on the ground.

'He does that trick twenty times a day,' said the warder who had accompanied the young woman.

With her teeth chattering with fear and almost fainting, she covered her eyes to avoid looking at the man she had reduced to this brute beast.

Maurin was mad.

BIG MICHU

ONE afternoon, during the four o'clock recess, Big Michu took me aside in a corner of the playground. He looked serious and that made me feel rather scared because Big Michu was sturdy and broad-shouldered, with enormous fists, and I should have hated to have him as an enemy.

'Listen to me,' he said, in his broad country accent which he had never quite succeeded in losing: 'Tell me, are you prepared to join in?'

I didn't hesitate for a moment. 'Yes,' I said, pleased to be able to join in something with Big Michu. Then he explained to me what the plot was. The fact that he was letting me into his confidence gave me a thrill of delight that I've never felt since. At last I was going to keep a secret and wage a battle; I was going to participate in life's wild adventures and indeed it was the sneaking fear I felt at the idea that I was becoming compromised in this way that contributed greatly to the thrill of becoming his accomplice.

So I listened in silent admiration as he unfolded his plan. He did so in a somewhat abrupt tone, like an officer addressing a conscript whose keenness and initiative are rather suspect. However, my eagerness and the ecstatic look of enthusiasm that I must have shown while listening must eventually have given him a better opinion of me.

As the second bell rang and we went to line up to go back to our classrooms: 'It's agreed, then,' he whispered to me. 'You'll join in. And you won't be afraid, will you? You'll not let us down?'

'Oh no, you'll see . . . I promise.'

His grey eyes looked me straight in the face, with all the gravity of a grown-up man and he added:

'Otherwise, you know, I won't give you a hiding but I'll let everyone know that you're a traitor and nobody will ever want to speak to you again.'

I can still recall the strange effect that this threat had on me. It made me feel tremendously brave. 'All right,' I said to myself, 'I don't mind if they give me 2000 lines, I'm damned if I let Michu down.' I waited for dinner-time to come with great excitement and impatience: our revolt was due to break out that evening in the dining-hall.

2

Big Michu came from the Var.* His father was a small peasant farmer who had taken up arms during the insurrection against Napoleon III's *coup d'état* in 1851. During the fighting he had been left for dead and had then gone underground. When he re-emerged, he had been left in peace, but the authorities, the big-wigs and all those of independent means henceforth never referred to him as anything but 'that thug Michu'.

This 'thug', this decent, illiterate man, sent his son to the lycée in Aix, doubtless wanting him to have the education needed to bring about the triumph of the cause which he himself had tried to defend by force of arms. At school we had a vague idea of all this which made us look on Michu as a very formidable person.

Big Michu was in any case much older than we were, but at the age of nearly eighteen he was still only in the third form. He had one of those inflexible minds which lack imagination and learn slowly; but once he knew something, he knew it thoroughly and for good. Immensely strong and built like an oak, he ruled the roost in the playground, although he was extremely gentle. Only once did I ever see him lose his temper, when he nearly throttled an assistant master who was telling us that republicans were all thieves. He was nearly expelled.

It was not until later, when looking back at my recollections of my schoolmate, that I came to understand his combination of strength and gentleness: his father must have taught him early on to be a man.

3

Not the least of our surprises was that Big Michu liked school. There was only one thing that plagued him, although he never dared to mention it: he was perpetually hungry.

I can't recall anyone with an appetite like his. Proud though he was, he would still sometimes invent humiliating stories in order to scrounge a piece of bread, a lunch or a dinner. He had been brought up in the mountain air of the Maures* and still suffered more cruelly from the meagre school fare than the rest of us.

The food was one of our main topics of conversation in the welcome shade of the long wall of our playground. Most of us tended to be fussy and I particularly remember a certain cod with melted butter and haricot beans in white sauce which had become the special subject of general loathing. On the days these appeared, the discussion was never-ending. Not wishing to appear different, Big Michu would join in the chorus of complaints, although he would willingly have guzzled all the six portions served at each table.

Almost the only thing that Big Michu complained about was the amount of food. A further cause of exasperation was that he happened to have been placed at the end of a table beside a young whipper-snapper of an assistant master, who allowed us to smoke during our walks. Now the rule at mealtimes was that masters were allowed a double portion so that when sausages were served you could see poor Michu casting hungry eyes on the pair of sausages lying side-by-side on the assistant's plate.

'I'm twice his size,' he said to me one day, 'and he has twice as much to eat as me. And he doesn't leave a single scrap. *He* doesn't find two sausages too much!'

4

So the big boys had decided that we should finally rise in revolt against the cod with melted butter and the beans in white sauce.

The conspirators naturally asked Big Michu to be their leader. The young gentlemen's plan was heroically simple: it would, they thought, be sufficient to go on hunger strike and refuse to eat any food until the Principal should announce, officially, that the school meals would be improved. Michu's acceptance of this plan was one of the finest and most courageous acts of unselfishness that I have ever met. He agreed to be the leader of the movement with the quiet heroism of an ancient Roman sacrificing himself for the republic.

Remember that he could not have cared less about the disappearance of the cod and beans from the menu; all he wanted was to have more of them, as much as he could eat! And the last straw was that he was being asked to go without food altogether. He confessed to me later that all those republican virtues taught him by his father—solidarity, the individual sacrifice of one's own interests to those of the community—had never been put to a sterner test.

That evening in the dining-hall—it was the cod and melted butter day—the strike began with a really splendid *tutti*. Only bread was to be eaten. When the dishes were served, we left them untouched and ate our dry bread. And it all took place with due solemnity, without any of our normal whispered conversations. Only some of the younger ones laughed.

Big Michu was superb. That evening he even went so far as not to eat his bread. With his elbows on the table, he was contemptuously watching the little assistant master, who was greedily stuffing himself.

Meanwhile the senior master had gone off to fetch the Principal who now came storming into the dining-hall and delivered a vigorous harangue, demanding to know what was wrong with the meal, which he tasted himself and pronounced exquisite.

Then Big Michu stood up.

'The truth is, sir, that the cod has gone off and we just can't get it down.'

'That's odd,' exclaimed the assistant, without giving the Principal time to reply. 'The other evening you ate almost the whole lot on your own, didn't you?'

Big Michu went very red. That evening, they merely sent us to bed saying that no doubt we would think better of it tomorrow.

5

Next day and the next, Big Michu was awe-inspiring. The assistant's words had stung him to the quick. He urged us on and said we would be cowardly to give in. He was determined now, as a matter of personal pride, to prove to us that, when it came to the point, he could go without food.

It was real torture. All those of us who could manage it were hiding chocolate, jars of jam and even ham or sausage in our desks so that we might at least have something to go with our dry bread which we were stuffing into our pockets. But Big Michu, who had no relatives in town and in any case refused to indulge in such luxuries, stuck steadfastly to the few crusts of bread which he managed to collect.

On the second day, when the Principal announced that since the pupils were so stubborn as not to touch the food provided, he was going to refuse to issue any more bread, open revolt broke out at lunchtime. It was beans and white sauce day.

Big Michu, whose mind must have become confused by his agonizing pangs of hunger, suddenly leapt to his feet, took hold of the plate of the assistant master, who was greedily tucking in, no doubt to provoke us, threw it into the middle of the room and started loudly singing the 'Marseillaise'. It was like a spark in a keg of gunpowder. Plates and glasses and bottles hurtled from all sides while the assistants hastily scrambled through the wreckage, leaving us in complete control of the dining-hall. As he rapidly took to his heels, our whipper-snapper received a plate of beans, with their white sauce, fairly and squarely between his shoulder-blades, leaving him with a large white collar-band round his neck.

The question now was how to fortify our stronghold. Big Michu was appointed commanding general. He had the tables carried up and piled in front of the doors. I well remember that we had all picked our knives up and were holding them in our hands. And the 'Marseillaise' thundered on: revolt was turning into a revolution. Fortunately, they decided to leave us to our own devices for a good three hours while they went off to fetch the police. Those three rowdy hours were enough to cool us down.

At the end of the dining-hall there were two large windows overlooking the playground. The more timorous of us, scared by the long reprieve that we were being granted, quietly opened one of the windows and slipped out. Gradually they were followed by others. Soon Big Michu was left with less than a dozen insurgents to support him. Gruffly he said to them: 'Off you go and join the others, there's no need for more than one of us to take the blame.'

Then, seeing that I was hesitating, he spoke to me directly:

'I'm letting you off your promise, all right?'

When the authorities broke down one of the doors, they found Michu on his own, quietly sitting on the end of a table amidst the broken crockery. He was sent home in disgrace that very same evening. As for the rest of us, we didn't get much benefit from our revolt. They took care not to serve cod or beans for a few

weeks. They then made their reappearance, but this time the cod
was in a white sauce and the beans in melted butter.

6

Long afterwards I met Michu again. He had not been able to
continue his studies and he was farming the few bits of land left to
him by his father on his death.

'I'd've made a rotten lawyer or doctor,' he said, 'because I was
a bit thick. I'm better as a farmer. It suits me. All the same, you
certainly did let me down, all of you. And to think that I was
really mad on cod and beans!'

THE ATTACK ON THE MILL

I

IT was a lovely summer's evening and old Merlier's mill was in festive mood. In the courtyard three tables had been placed end to end, to await the guests. Everyone in the district knew that today Merlier's daughter Françoise was to be betrothed to Dominique, a young man who, although often accused of being rather idle, was so good-looking that the eyes of all the women for miles around would light up each time they saw him.

Set in the very heart of Rocreuse, where the main road makes a bend, Merlier's old mill was as blithe as a lark. The village consisted of the one street, lined on each side by a row of tumbledown cottages; but at the bend there were broad meadows and tall trees following the course of the Morelle and forming a magnificently shady corner at the head of the valley. There was no more charming beauty spot in the whole of Lorraine. On both sides of the valley there were dense woods of century-old forest giants sloping gently upwards to the skyline in a sea of greenery while towards the south the marvellously fertile plain, cut up into hedge-lined fields, stretched out as far as the eye could see. But, apart from its greenness, the great charm of Rocreuse lay in its refreshing coolness during the hottest days of July and August. As the Morelle came down from the Gagny woods it seemed to bring with it the chill of the leafy boughs beneath which it had flowed for mile after mile; and it brought with it, too, the rustle of forest glades. Nor was this the only source of coolness: all kinds of babbling brooks flowed gaily through the undergrowth and at every step you took a new stream seemed to be welling up. As you walked through the narrow paths you could feel underground lakes surfacing beneath the moss and taking advantage of every little gap at the roots of the trees or between rocks to gush out in streams of crystal-clear water; and so numerous and so loud were the whispering voices of these springs that they drowned the chirping of the bullfinches. It was like being in a magic park surrounded by hundreds of tiny waterfalls.

Down below there were water-meadows on which the tall sweet chestnut trees cast their giant shadows and along which long rows of poplars formed their rustling screens. An avenue of enormous plane trees led up through the fields to the old ruined castle of Gagny. In this perpetually well-watered spot, grasses of all sorts shot up to astounding heights. Between the wooded slopes, it was like a park in which the meadows were the lawns and the giant trees formed colossal round flowerbeds. When the midday sun was at its height the shadows took on a bluish tinge, and the grass lay drowsing in the scorching summer heat; but a cold shiver still ran through the undergrowth.

And in the heart of this lush greenery there could be heard the cheerful clatter of old Merlier's mill. Half sunk in the Morelle which at this point formed a limpid pool, the old building, made of wood and plaster, seemed to date from the beginning of time. There was a small mill-race and the water fell several yards down on to the mill-wheel which creaked as it turned, wheezing like an asthmatic old servant who has grown old in her faithful service to the family. When people advised old Merlier to get a new one, he would shake his head and say that a younger wheel would be lazier and wouldn't know the work so well; and he would repair the old one with any makeshift materials he could lay hands on, staves of wine-barrels, pieces of rusty iron and odd bits of lead or zinc. This treatment made the wheel, in fact, look all the more cheerful, with its new queer shape and its plumes of grass and moss. When the silvery water cascaded down on to it, it seemed to be covered in sparkling jewels and its quaint old framework spun round under a glittering string of pearls.

The part of the mill which stood half sunk in the Morelle had the look of some primitive ark left stranded by the passage of time. More than half of the ramshackle old building was supported on piles. The water came in under the floor and there were deep pools in the river, well known throughout the district for the eels and crayfish that could be caught there. Underneath the fall, the mill-pond was as limpid as a sheet of glass and when the wheel was not stirring it up into foam, you could see shoals of big fish swimming slowly round like squads of manoeuvring soldiers. A broken-down staircase led down to a boat moored to a pile in the river; a wooden gallery with irregular window-openings spanned the space above the mill-wheel. The building was, in fact, a conglomeration of tiny recesses, low walls, beams and roofs built on as afterthoughts, creating the impression of some old dismantled citadel. But ivy had grown up and all sorts of climbing plants had covered over the larger cracks in the old house with a green mantle. Young ladies would always stop to sketch old Merlier's mill.

On the side facing the road, the building was much more solid. A stone gateway led into the main courtyard, with stables and sheds on either side. Next to a well there stood an enormous elm, shading half the yard. At the far end you could see the four first-floor windows of the house, with a dovecote above. Old Merlier's only concession to public opinion was to have the front of the house whitewashed every ten years; this had just been done and in the light of the midday sun, the villagers were quite dazzled by its whiteness.

Old Merlier had been mayor of Rocreuse for the last twenty years. People admired him for the way in which he had become so rich: he had built up his wealth sou by sou and it was now thought to amount to some eighty thousand francs. When he had married Madeleine Guillard, with the mill as her dowry, he had himself possessed not much more than his two strong arms. But Madeleine had never regretted her choice. Now his wife was dead and he had been left a widower with a daughter, Françoise. Doubtless he could by this time have relaxed and let the mill-wheel drift round clogged with moss; but he would have been bored and the old house would have seemed dead, so he still kept on working, for pleasure. Merlier was now an old man, tall, with a long taciturn face, who never laughed but who seemed full of an inner joy. He had been elected mayor because of his money and also because he was superb at officiating at weddings.

Françoise had just celebrated her eighteenth birthday. She was considered as one of the local beauties because she was delicate. Until the age of fifteen she had even been thought ugly and the villagers could never understand how such a sturdy couple as the Merliers could possibly have produced such a weakling of a daughter. However, at the age of fifteen, while still remaining delicate she had suddenly blossomed out and her tiny face was as pretty as a picture. Her hair was black and she had dark eyes, but with a peaches-and-cream complexion, lips that were always laughing, dimpled cheeks and a white forehead that looked like a halo of sunshine. Although hardly plump by country standards, she was not thin either, far from it; people merely thought that she could not have managed to lift a bag of flour; but as she grew older, she became rounder and she had ended up as plump and juicy as a young partridge. However, her father's dourness had made her from an early age into a sensible, self-reliant girl. If she was always laughing, it was in order to please other people; at heart, she was rather an earnest sort of girl.

She was, of course, much courted in the district, even more for her money than for her pleasant nature. Her final choice had recently scandalized everyone. On the other side of the Morelle, there lived a tall young man called Dominique Penquet. He was not from Rocreuse; ten years before, he had come down from Belgium, having inherited a small property from an uncle, situated right on the edge of the forest of Gagny, exactly opposite the mill and only a few gunshots away. He said that he was intending to sell up the property and go back home. However, it would seem that he had found the district to his liking for he stayed on. He farmed his little plot, grew a few vegetables for his own table and went fishing and shooting. On a number of occasions he was nearly caught by gamekeepers and sent up before the magistrates. Such an independent way of life, from sources which the locals found a trifle mysterious, finally brought him a bad reputation. People referred to him as something of a poacher. Be that as it might, he was certainly lazy, for he would be found sleeping in the grass at times when he should have been working. He lived in a sort of a shack tucked away amongst the last trees at the edge of the wood and this hardly seemed a proper place for a respectable young man to live. The old women of the village would not have been surprised to learn that he had dealings with the wolves which prowled round the ruins of the old castle. But the girls would sometimes venture to spring to his defence because this young man was a superb specimen of manhood, tall and athletic, very white-skinned, with blond hair and beard that gleamed like gold in the sunshine. And then, one fine day, Françoise had told old Merlier that she loved Dominique and would never marry anyone else.

You can imagine that old Merlier felt that he'd been pole-axed. However, as was his wont, he said nothing. He looked thoughtful and his eyes had lost their normal cheerful glint. For a whole week, they sulked; she too had a solemn look on her face and old Merlier was plagued by a disturbing thought: how on earth had this rogue of a poacher managed to cast his spell over his daughter? Dominique had never visited the mill. The miller kept his eyes open and caught a glimpse of the young swain lying in the grass on the opposite bank of the Morelle, pretending to be asleep. Françoise could have seen him from her window. The conclusion was obvious: they must have fallen in love while making sheeps' eyes at each other across the mill-wheel.

Meanwhile, another week went by. Françoise was looking more and more solemn. Old Merlier was as tight-lipped as ever. Then one evening, without saying a word, Merlier himself brought Dominique into the room where Françoise was just laying the table. She showed no surprise and merely laid another place; but the little dimples in her face had reappeared and her laughter as well. That morning, old Merlier had gone off to Dominique's shack on the edge of the forest and the two men had spent three hours talking behind closed doors and windows. Nobody ever found out what they might have said to each other. The only certainty was that when old Merlier came out he was already treating Dominique as his son. No doubt, in this idle young fellow-me-lad who would lie in the grass making girls fall in love with him, the old man had found what he had been looking for: a decent young man.

There was much tongue-wagging in Rocreuse. The old women talked at length on their doorsteps of old Merlier's madness in introducing this ne'er-do-well into his house like that; but he let them talk. Perhaps he'd remembered his own marriage. When he'd wedded Madeleine and her mill, he himself hadn't had two pennies to rub together either; but that hadn't prevented him from being a good husband. Moreover, Dominique put a stop to all the gossip by buckling down to work with an energy that astounded everyone. It so happened that the mill-hand had just been called up for military service and Dominique refused to listen to any suggestion that Merlier should take on another one. He carried the sacks, drove the cart and struggled with the old mill-wheel when it showed signs of giving up the ghost, and all with such vim and vigour that it was a pleasure to come and watch him. Old Merlier chuckled to himself. He was very proud at having detected this young man's hidden qualities. And there's nothing like love to give young men a boost.

Amidst all this hard work, Dominique and Françoise walked about idolizing each other. They might not have said very much but all the time they kept exchanging fond smiles. Till now, Merlier had made no mention of marriage and they both respected his silence and awaited the old man's decision. Finally, one day towards the middle of July, he had three tables set up in the courtyard under the old elm tree and invited his friends in Rocreuse to come and have a drink with him that evening. When the yard was full of people with their glasses in their hands, old Merlier raised his own and said:

'I've great pleasure in announcing that Françoise will be marrying this young fellow here in one month's time, on the feast of St Louis.'

Everyone enthusiastically drank the young couple's health; they were all laughing and smiling. Then old Merlier raised his voice and spoke again:

'Now kiss the bride, Dominique, that's what you've got to do!'

And so they kissed each other, all red in the face, while everyone laughed even more loudly. It was a real celebration and a whole barrel of wine was drunk. Then, when only the close friends were left behind, they all chatted together more quietly. Night had fallen, clear and full of stars. Dominique and Françoise sat silently side by side on a bench while one old peasant started talking about the war which the Emperor had just declared on the Prussians. All the lads of the village had already been called up. Troops had still been going through Rocreuse the day before. Hard knocks were going to be exchanged.

'Ah well,' said old Merlier with the selfishness of any happy man, 'Dominique's a foreigner, he won't have to fight... And if the Prussians ever get as far as here, he'll be on the spot to defend his wife.'

The idea that the Prussians could possibly come to Rocreuse seemed nothing more than a joke. The French were going to give them a thrashing and it would all be over in next to no time.

'I've already seen them,' said the old peasant in a hollow voice, 'I've already seen them.'

Nobody spoke. Then they all clinked glasses and drank again. Françoise and Dominique had not heard a single word; they had gently caught hold of each other's hands, behind the bench so that no one could see, and it seemed such a nice thing to do that they just sat there gazing blankly into the darkness.

What a lovely warm night it was! In their houses on both sides of the road the villagers were quietly dropping off to sleep like children. The only sound was the crowing of some cock who had woken up too soon. The cooler air was drifting gently down from the thick woods nearby, caressing the roofs of the cottages as it passed slowly over the village. The dark pensive shadows on the meadows assumed majestic and mysterious proportions while the cool brooks and springs gushing in the gloom seemed like the rhythmic breathing of the drowsing countryside. Every so often the sleepy old mill-wheel seemed to rouse itself from its dreams like a sleeping watchdog barking as it stirs; then there were creakings and clatterings as it communed with itself, lulled by the rippling Morelle which spread out and murmured like soft organ music. Never had so charming a little beauty spot bathed so happily in the peace of nature.

2

One month later to the day, in fact on the eve of the festival of St Louis, Rocreuse was living in the shadow of terror. The Prussians had defeated the Emperor and, in forced marches, were rapidly advancing towards the village. For the past week, the people passing through along the main road had been warning of their progress: 'They've reached Lormière; they've reached Novelles'; and when they were told how swift their advance was, the villagers of Rocreuse expected to see the Prussians sweeping down from the Gagny woods and when they did not appear, it was even more frightening. They would swoop down on the village in the night and slit everyone's throat.

The previous night, shortly before dawn, there had been an alert. The inhabitants had been woken up by a great noise of men on the road. The women were already flinging themselves on their knees and making the sign of the cross when, as they peered cautiously out of their windows, the villagers recognized the red trousers of a detachment of French soldiers. The captain commanding them had immediately asked to see the mayor and, after a word with old Merlier, he had decided to remain down at the mill.

Day dawned bright and clear; by noon it would be hot. The woods were bathed in a golden light and in the distance a pale haze drifted up from the meadows. The neat little village awoke, cool and pretty, and with its streams and springs the whole countryside looked like a dainty bunch of flowers sparkling in the dew. But this lovely day brought no answering smile to the villagers' lips. They had just seen the captain walking round the mill, looking at the nearby houses, crossing over to the other bank of the Morelle and studying the lie of the land through his field-glasses; old Merlier, who was accompanying him, seemed to be supplying him with information. Then the captain had posted soldiers behind walls and trees and down in hollows. The main body of troops were bivouacking in the courtyard of the mill. Would there be fighting? When old Merlier came back, they questioned him. He nodded without speaking: yes, they were going to fight.

Françoise and Dominique were in the courtyard watching him. Finally he took his pipe out of his mouth and said simply:

'It's a sad day for you, my loves. There'll be no wedding for you tomorrow!'

Dominique sat scowling with clenched lips, occasionally springing to his feet to peer up towards the Gagny woods, as though trying to see the Prussians arriving. Looking pale and solemn, Françoise was going to and fro, supplying the soldiers with the things they needed. They had set up a makeshift field-kitchen in a corner of the courtyard and were joking as they waited to eat.

Meanwhile the captain seemed delighted. He had visited the bedrooms and the large main room of the mill overlooking the river. Now he sat chatting to Merlier beside the well.

'You've got a real fortress here,' he said. 'We can certainly hold out until this evening. Those rogues are behind time... They should have been here by now.'

The miller looked grim: he could see his mill going up in flames. But he made no comment, considering that it was pointless to do so. When he eventually spoke, it was merely to say:

'You ought to hide the boat behind the mill-wheel. There's a small space for it there. It may come in useful.'

The captain gave an order. He was a good-looking man of about forty, tall, with a pleasant expression. The sight of Françoise and Dominique seemed to give him pleasure. He now turned his attention towards them, as if he had forgotten the impending fight. His eyes kept following Françoise and it was plain that he found her attractive. Then he turned to Dominique and said sharply:

'So you're not in the army, young man?'

'I'm not French,' Dominique replied.

This explanation did not seem to meet with the captain's full approval. He gave a wink and half-smiled: Françoise was more agreeable company than a gun-barrel. Seeing his grin, the young man added:

'I'm not French but I can put a bullet into a man at five hundred yards... Take a look at my gun over there, behind you.'

'You may find some use for it,' the captain replied simply.

Françoise came up to Dominique, trembling slightly, and held out her hands to him, as if seeking his protection, whereupon, without paying any attention to the people around them, he reached out and gripped them tightly. The captain gave another smile but said nothing. He remained sitting with his sword between his legs, gazing into the distance, seemingly occupied with his own thoughts.

It was now already ten o'clock and beginning to be very hot and sultry. Nothing was stirring. In the courtyard the soldiers had started eating. Not a sound came from the village, where the inhabitants had all barricaded their house doors and windows. In the street, a solitary dog stood howling. From the neighbouring woods and meadows, overcome by the heat, an endless distant murmur came wafting in on the stifling air. A cuckoo called to its mate. Then once more deep silence reigned.

Suddenly, in the drowsy air, a shot rang out. The captain sprang to his feet, the soldiers dropped their half-empty bowls and in a few seconds everyone was at his post and the mill was manned on every floor. Meanwhile the captain had run out on to the road but was unable to see anything; it stretched out, white and deserted in both directions. A second shot rang out and still there was nothing to see, not even a shadow. The captain swung round and looked up towards Gagny. He was at last rewarded by the sight of a little puff of smoke drifting up, like gossamer, between a couple of trees. The wood itself was still dark and quiet.

'The scoundrels have taken to the forest,' he muttered to himself. 'They must know we're here.'

The shooting continued more heavily between the French soldiers posted round the mill and the Prussians concealed in the wood. The bullets kept whistling over the Morelle but without causing any casualties to either side. The firing became sporadic; soldiers were shooting from behind every bush but still there was nothing to be seen except little puffs of smoke drifting lazily in the air. This went on for a couple of hours. The captain was humming nonchalantly to himself. Françoise and Dominique had remained in the courtyard and were standing on tiptoe peering over a low wall. In particular they were watching a little soldier who had been stationed on the bank of the Morelle. Lying on his stomach behind the hulk of an old boat, he would take a quick look, fire and then crawl into a trench a little further back to reload. His movements were so precise and quick and looked so comical that they found themselves smiling as they watched. He must have caught a glimpse of the head of one of the enemy because he jumped to his feet and took aim; but before he could pull the trigger, he uttered a cry, spun round and dropped back into the trench where for a brief moment his legs jerked convulsively like those of a chicken whose head has been chopped off. He had been struck by a bullet full in the chest. It was the first casualty. Instinctively, Françoise reached out and nervously gripped Dominique's hand.

'Don't stand there,' called the captain, 'they're shooting this way.'

And indeed at that moment a sharp crack came from the direction of the old elm and a piece of branch came twirling down. However, in their anxiety to see what was happening, the couple were unable to tear themselves away. Suddenly, at the edge of the forest, a Prussian soldier appeared from behind a tree, as though from the wings of a stage, flailing the air with his arms as he fell on his back. And then once again nothing stirred; the two dead men seemed to be lying asleep in the bright sunshine and the landscape still slumbered on, deserted. Even the crackle of gunfire had ceased. Only the Morelle went babbling gently on.

Old Merlier looked at the captain in surprise, as though enquiring if it was all over.

'Here comes the big push,' the latter said in a low voice. 'Look out and keep out of the way.'

Before he had finished speaking, there was a terrifying burst of gunfire. The old elm seemed on the point of toppling over as a shower of leaves swirled down into the courtyard: the Prussians had aimed too high. Dominique dragged Françoise away, almost carrying her in his arms, while Merlier followed, shouting:

'Go down to the small cellar, it's got very thick walls.'

But they did not heed him and went instead into the main room where a dozen soldiers were waiting silently, peering through the gaps in the closed shutters. The captain had remained alone in the courtyard, crouching down behind the low wall while the bursts of firing continued unabated. The soldiers whom he had posted outside were giving ground very slowly but as the enemy forced them from their cover, they crawled back one by one into the mill: their orders were to gain time and not expose themselves, so that the Prussians should not discover the size of the force opposing them. Another hour went by and when a sergeant came in and announced that there were only two or three men left outside, the officer pulled out his watch and muttered:

'Half-past two... Well, we must hang on for four hours longer.'

He ordered the main gate of the courtyard to be closed and everything was made ready for a determined resistance. As the Prussians were on the opposite bank of the Morelle, there was no immediate danger of attack. In fact, there was a bridge about a mile away but they were no doubt ignorant of its existence and it was hardly likely that they would attempt to ford the river. So the captain merely ordered a careful watch to be kept on the road: the Prussians' main effort would come from the woods across the river.

Once more the firing had died down. In the bright sunshine the mill seemed dead. The shutters were all closed and not a sound came from inside. However, the Prussians were gradually beginning to show themselves at the edge of the Gagny woods, poking their heads out and growing bolder. In the mill, as a number of soldiers were taking aim, the captain shouted:

'No, don't fire yet. Wait till they're closer.'

The Prussians were moving forward very cautiously, keeping a wary eye on the mill. This silent, gloomy, ivy-covered building made them uneasy. However, they still kept coming on. When there were about fifty of them in the meadow opposite, the officer shouted one word:

'Fire!'

There was an earsplitting volley of gunfire, followed by isolated shots. Françoise started trembling and involuntarily put her hands to her ears. Dominique was standing watching behind the soldiers and when the smoke had partly cleared he could see three Prussians lying on their backs in the middle of the meadow. The others quickly flung themselves behind the willows and poplars. The siege began.

For more than an hour the old mill was riddled by a hail of bullets. When they hit stonework, they were flattened and fell back into the water, but they buried themselves in the woodwork with a dull thud. Now and again a creaking sound showed that the mill-wheel had been hit. The soldiers inside the mill were husbanding their ammunition and firing only when they had a target. The captain kept consulting his watch and as a bullet came through one of the shutters and lodged itself in the ceiling, he muttered:

'Four o'clock. We'll never be able to hold out.'

And indeed, under the extremely heavy fire, the old mill was gradually being shot to pieces. One of the shutters fell off into the water and had to be replaced by a mattress. Old Merlier kept continually exposing himself to see what damage was being inflicted on his mill-wheel, whose creaks and groans were going straight to his heart. The poor old wheel was finished; it could never be repaired again now. Dominique had begged Françoise to take shelter but she insisted on staying with him and had sat down behind a large oak cupboard for protection. But then a bullet struck the cupboard with a resounding thud and Dominique placed himself in front of her. Although he had not yet fired a shot, he was holding his gun in his hand; he could not get to the window because the space was completely occupied by soldiers. At every shot, the floor quivered.

'Look out! Look out!' the captain yelled suddenly.

He had just glimpsed a dark mass of Prussian soldiers debouching from the woods. They immediately opened up heavy and sustained fire: it was as if a whirlwind had struck the mill. Another shutter fell off and bullets came shooting through the gaping hole. Two soldiers tumbled to the floor. One of them did not move; he was bundled into a corner out of the way. The other one was writhing in agony and begging someone to put him out of his misery; nobody paid any attention to him, for the hail of bullets was still continuing and everyone was trying to take cover and find a loophole to return the fire. A third soldier was wounded; he did not say anything but slipped down beside a table, with wild, staring eyes. Shocked and horrified at the sight of these dead men, Françoise had automatically pushed her chair away and sat down on the floor where she felt she would be safer. Meanwhile they had brought along every mattress in the house and succeeded in half-blocking the window again. The room was becoming littered with wreckage, broken weapons and shattered pieces of furniture.

'Five o'clock,' said the captain. 'Hang on, men. They'll be trying to get across the river.'

At that moment, Françoise uttered a cry. A ricocheting bullet had just grazed her forehead and a few drops of blood were trickling down her face. Dominique looked across at her; then, walking over to the window, he fired his first shot and kept on firing. He loaded and fired, loaded and fired, paying not the slightest attention to what was taking place around him, although now and again he would glance over towards Françoise. He was not firing hurriedly, however; he was taking very deliberate aim. The Prussians were now creeping along through the poplars in an attempt to cross the Morelle, as the captain had predicted; but as soon as one of them ventured into the open, he would fall to the ground with a bullet from Dominique's gun in his skull. The captain was amazed at the young man's prowess and complimented him on it, saying that he would be delighted to have many more marksmen like him in his company. Dominique did not hear him. A bullet grazed his shoulder; another one scratched his arm. He still went on firing.

Two more French soldiers were dead. The mattresses had been cut into shreds and were no longer of any use to block the windows. It seemed as if one final burst of gunfire would enable the Prussians to capture the mill. The position was no longer tenable. However, the captain kept saying:

'Hold on... Just half an hour more.'

Now he was counting the minutes; having promised his superiors to hold the enemy up until evening, he was not prepared to give one inch of territory before the time when he had decided to withdraw. He had still retained his affability, continually reassuring Françoise with a smile. He had picked up one of his dead soldiers' rifles and was firing himself.

Only four French soldiers were left in the room. The Prussians were massing on the opposite bank of the Morelle and it was plain that they were on the point of crossing the river. A few more minutes went by. The captain was still doggedly refusing to order the retreat when the sergeant ran in shouting:

'They're coming up the road! They're going to take us in the rear!'

The Prussians must have discovered the bridge. The captain pulled out his watch.

'Just five minutes more,' he said. 'They'll take at least five minutes to get here.'

And at six o'clock precisely he finally gave the order for his men to withdraw through a little door opening on to a side lane. There they jumped into a ditch and made off in the direction of the forest of Sauval. As he was leaving the captain saluted old Merlier very politely, offered his apologies and even added:

'Keep them in play. We'll be back.'

Meanwhile Dominique was left all alone in the room. Oblivious to everything, he still kept firing, with no idea of what had happened. All he knew was that he must defend Françoise; he had not noticed the departure of the French soldiers, so he kept on aiming and reloading, bringing down his man every time he fired. Suddenly there was a loud noise: the Prussians had forced their way into the courtyard from the rear. He fired his last shot and then they were on him; smoke was still coming from the barrel of his gun.

Four men seized hold of him and he was surrounded by others, all shouting in their harsh, ugly language. They nearly slit his throat on the spot; Françoise leapt forward, begging them to spare him, but at that moment an officer came in and ordered them to hand their prisoner over. After exchanging a few words in German with his men, he turned towards Dominique and said roughly, in very good French:

'You'll be shot in two hours' time.'

3

It had been laid down by the German general staff that any Frenchman not in the regular armed forces who was caught bearing arms would be shot. Even the civilian militia were not recognized as belligerents. By making such a terrible example of the peasants defending their homes, the Germans wanted to prevent the mass uprising that they feared.

The commanding officer, a tall gaunt man of about fifty, started briefly to interrogate Dominique. Although he spoke excellent French, his rigid, uncompromising manner was completely Prussian.

'Are you French?'

'No, I'm Belgian.'

'Why were you bearing arms? This war doesn't concern you.'

Dominique made no reply. At that moment, the officer caught sight of Françoise who was standing listening, pale as a ghost; her white forehead was streaked with blood from her graze. He looked from one to the other of the young couple, apparently realizing the situation, and then merely added:

'You don't deny that you were shooting?'

'I was shooting as long as I could,' Dominique replied quietly.

This confession was pointless for he was blackened with gunpowder, covered in sweat and stained with drops of blood from the wound on his shoulder.

'Very well,' the officer said. 'You'll be shot in two hours' time.'

Françoise did not cry out but clasped her hands and raised them in a silent despairing gesture which the officer did not fail to notice. Two soldiers led Dominique away into an adjoining room where he was to be held under close guard. The girl's legs collapsed under her and she fell into a chair, too overcome by emotion to shed any tears. Meanwhile the officer kept watching her closely and finally spoke to her.

'Is that your brother?' he enquired.

She shook her head. He remained as unsmiling and unbending as ever. After a pause, he asked:

'Has he been living in the district long?'

She nodded.

'Then he must know the woods round here very well?'

This time she spoke, looking at him with some surprise:
'Yes, sir.'

He said no more and, turning on his heels, he asked to see the
mayor of the village. Françoise stood up. Some of the colour had
now returned to her cheeks, for she thought she had understood
the drift of the officer's questions and her hopes were reviving.
She ran to fetch her father herself.

As soon as the firing had stopped, old Merlier had hurried
down to the wooden gallery to examine his mill-wheel. While
he adored his daughter and felt a strong affection for his future
son-in-law, his mill-wheel also had a large claim on his heart.
Now that his two children, as he called them, had come through
the fighting relatively unscathed, his thoughts had turned to the
other object of his affections. It had certainly suffered a great
deal of damage. He leaned over the large wooden structure and
studied its wounds with a woebegone expression. Five of the
blades had been shot to pieces and the main framework was
riddled with bullets. He poked his finger into the bullet holes to
discover how deep they were; he was thinking of possible ways
of mending all this damage. When Françoise came down to fetch
him, he was already plugging some of the holes with bits of
wood and moss.

'They want to see you, Father.'

And at last her tears welled up as she told her father what she
had just heard. Old Merlier shook his head: you couldn't shoot
people like that; he'd have to see. And he went back into the mill
as unperturbed and taciturn as ever. When the Prussian officer
asked for victuals for his men, he replied that the inhabitants of
Rocreuse were not in the habit of being bullied and that you
wouldn't get far with them by threatening violence. He would
undertake to take care of everything but only on condition that he
was left to do things his own way. At first the officer seemed
annoyed at his calm manner but then, impressed by the old man's
plain speaking, he agreed. He even called him back with a further
query:

'What's the name of those woods over there?'
'The Sauval woods.'
'How far do they extend?'
The miller gave him a blank look.
'I don't know,' he replied and walked away.

An hour later, all the food and money requested by the officer had appeared in the mill courtyard. Night was now falling and Françoise was anxiously watching the soldiers' movements. She did not move far away from the room in which Dominique was being held. At about seven o'clock, her heart started pounding as she saw the officer go in to speak to his prisoner and for the next quarter of an hour she could hear the sound of raised voices. At one moment, the officer came to the doorway and gave an order in German which she did not understand; but when she saw twelve men carrying rifles line up in the courtyard, she was seized by a violent trembling, so violent that she felt she might die. This was the end: they were going to execute him. The twelve men stood there for ten minutes and Dominique's voice could be heard still vigorously refusing to give any information. Finally the officer came out again and, slamming the door violently behind him, said:

'Very well, you can think it over... You've got till tomorrow morning.'

And he motioned to the twelve men to dismiss. Françoise was in a terrible state of shock but old Merlier had merely continued calmly smoking his pipe and watching the firing squad with curiosity. Now he came over and, taking his daughter's arm, said in his gentle fatherly way:

'Now calm down, my darling. You must try to sleep. Tomorrow there's another day and we shall see what happens.'

He led her away to her room, locking the door behind him as he left her. In his view, women were rather useless creatures. If there was anything important to do, they'd be sure to make a mess of it... However, Françoise did not go to bed but stayed sitting on it for a long time, listening to the noises in the house. The Prussian soldiers camping in the courtyard were laughing and singing; they must have gone on eating and drinking until eleven o'clock, for the din seemed endless. In the mill itself, she could hear the occasional heavy tramp of feet; no doubt sentries were being relieved. But what interested her most were the sounds coming from the room immediately underneath her own, which was the room in which Dominique was being held. Several times she lay down and put her ear to the floor. Dominique must have been walking to and fro from the wall to the window, for she could hear the regular sound of his steps.

Then there was silence; he must have sat down. Meanwhile, all the various other noises were dying down too and eventually the whole house settled down to rest. When everything seemed quiet, she opened her window as gently as possible and leaned out.

Outside, the night was warm and still. The courtyard was lit only by a sliver of moon which was on the point of sinking behind the Sauval woods. The long dark shadows of the trees were cutting the meadows into strips while in the moonlight the grass looked like a carpet of soft green velvet. But Françoise did not linger to enjoy the charm of the mysterious night landscape. She was examining the area immediately around the mill to discover where the Germans had posted their sentries; their shadows could clearly be seen stretching out along the Morelle. In front of the mill, there was only one, on the far bank of the river beside a willow whose branches were dipping into the water. Françoise could see him plainly: a tall young man standing quite still and looking up at the sky, like a pensive shepherd.

Having carefully inspected the surrounding countryside, Françoise went back and sat down on her bed, where she remained for a whole hour, lost in thought. Then she listened again: everything was deathly still. She went back to the window and again looked. She must have been concerned that one of the moon's horns had still not completely disappeared behind the trees, for she went back to her vigil. At last the time she was waiting for seemed to have come: the night was pitch black; she could no longer see the sentry opposite and the countryside stretched out all around like a pool of ink. She listened for a second and then decided to act. Running down beside her window was a ladder consisting of iron bars fixed into the wall. This ladder led up from the mill-wheel to the loft; it had formerly been used by the millers to inspect certain pieces of machinery and later on, when the machinery had long since been changed, it had become overgrown by ivy which covered the whole of this side of the mill.

Boldly, Françoise clambered out over the window sill, caught hold of one of the rungs and hung suspended in space. She then began to climb down, greatly hindered by her petticoats. Suddenly a piece of stone came loose and fell with a loud splash into the Morelle. She stopped, frozen with fright; then, realizing that the constant rush of water over the mill-race made it impossible for any sound she might make to be heard in the distance, she continued climbing down more confidently, feeling for the rungs under the ivy with her feet. When she was level with the room in which Dominique was held, she stopped; the window of this lower room was not exactly below her bedroom window and when she reached out sideways from the ladder, her hand could feel only the wall. This unexpected snag almost dashed her hopes: would she have to climb back to her room, leaving her scheme uncompleted? Her arms were tiring and the gentle murmur of the Morelle directly below her was starting to make her feel dizzy. Quickly she began to pull off tiny pieces of plaster from the wall and fling them against Dominique's window. There was no response: perhaps he was asleep? She prised off more pieces, scraping the skin off her fingers in doing so. And her grip was starting to weaken. She was on the point of falling backwards off the ladder when Dominique gently opened his window.

'It's me,' she whispered. 'Catch hold of me, darling, I'm falling off.'

Never before had she spoken to him so endearingly.* He leaned out of the window, caught hold of her and dragged her into the room. Once there, she burst into hysterical tears, doing her best to fight back her sobs so that the guards should not hear. Finally, with a supreme effort, she regained her composure.

'What about the guards?' she enquired.

Still bewildered at her unexpected appearance, Dominique merely pointed towards the door. From the other side, there came the sound of snoring; overcome by fatigue, the guard had lain down to sleep on the floor, reasoning that by blocking the doorway he would ensure that his prisoner would not be able to go far away.

'You must get away,' she said urgently. 'I've come here because I want you to escape and to say goodbye to you.'

He did not seem to be listening but merely kept saying:

'It's you, it's you... My goodness, how you scared me! You might have killed yourself!'

He caught hold of her hands and kissed them.

'Oh Françoise, I do love you so... You're brave and kind. The only thing I was afraid of was dying before seeing you for the last time... But now you've come they can shoot me. Just a quarter of an hour together and then I'll be ready.'

He had gradually drawn her into his arms and her head was
resting on his shoulder. Danger had brought them closer together
and clasped in each other's arms they could think only of their
love.

'Françoise darling,' said Dominique fondly, 'it's St Louis's day
today, our wedding-day, the day we've been looking forward to
for so long. You see, nothing has been able to keep us apart,
because here we are together, alone, just as we'd planned. That's
right, isn't it? It's our wedding morning.'

'Yes,' she replied, 'yes, it's our wedding morning.'

Trembling, they exchanged a kiss . . . But all at once, Françoise
broke free as the dreadful reality of their situation suddenly came
back to her.

'You must escape,' she gasped. 'You must get away, there's
not a moment to lose.'

And as he reached out in the dark to take her in his arms once
more, she said with the same tenderness she had shown on first
seeing him:

'Oh my dearest, please, you must listen to me . . . If you die I
shan't be able to go on living either. In an hour's time it'll be
light. I want you to go at once.'

She rapidly outlined her plan. The ladder went down to the
mill-wheel; once there, he could scramble over the blades into the
boat moored beside it and then easily reach the far bank of the
river and make his escape.

'But they must have posted sentries,' he objected.

'Only one, right opposite the mill, by the first willow.'

'But supposing he sees me and gives the alarm?'

Françoise shuddered and pressed into his hand a knife which
she had brought down with her. Neither said a word.

'But how about your father and you?' Dominique said after a
pause. 'You see, I can't run away. When the Prussians find I'm
not here, they'll shoot you on the spot . . . You don't know what
they're like, they were offering to let me go free if I agreed to
show them the way through the Sauval woods. Once they
discover I'm gone, they're capable of anything.'

Françoise refused to waste time arguing. To all his protests she
merely replied:

'You've got to escape for my sake . . . If you really love me,
Dominique, you won't wait a second longer.'

She promised to climb back into her room. Nobody would know that she had helped him. Again she flung herself into his arms and held him tight, kissing him passionately to convince him; but before agreeing he asked her one last question:

'Do you swear that your father knows what you're doing and wants me to try and escape?'

'It was my father who sent me,' replied Françoise resolutely.

This was not the truth; but at that moment she had only one thought in her mind; she wanted desperately for him to be safe, for she could not bear the realization that the coming dawn would be the signal for his execution. Once he was far away, all sorts of disasters might fall on her head but she was prepared to accept them gladly as long as her lover survived. In her single-minded devotion, she wanted one thing above all else: he must not die.

'All right,' said Dominique, 'I'll do what you say.'

Nothing further was said. Dominique went over to open the window again, but a sudden noise halted them in their tracks. The door had rattled and they thought it was being opened. Had a patrol heard them talking? They stood clasped in each other's arms, petrified with fear. Once again the door shook; but it did not open. They both gave a sigh of relief; it was the soldier lying across the doorway who had turned over. Complete silence ensued; and then the snoring began once more.

Dominique insisted that Françoise should first climb up to her bedroom. He took her in his arms and silently they bade each other farewell. He helped her to grasp the ladder and then caught hold of it himself, but refused to go down a single rung before he was sure that she was safe. When Françoise had clambered back into her bedroom, she whispered softly down to him:

'Goodbye for now, darling. I love you!'

She stayed looking out of her window trying to follow Dominique's movements. It was still pitch dark. She looked for the sentry but could not see him; there was only the willow gleaming pale in the shadows. For a second or two she could hear the rustling sound of Dominique's body against the ivy. Then she heard the mill-wheel creak and a slight splash which told her that he had found the boat. A moment later she was even able to pick out the dark shape of the boat against the grey surface of the Morelle. Once more an agonizing fear gripped her by the throat Every second she imagined that she could hear the sentry giving

the alarm and any little random sound seemed in the dark to
be the noise of soldiers running, of weapons clattering against
each other, of rifles being cocked. However, the seconds ticked
by and the solemn silence of the countryside remained unbroken. Dominique must surely be approaching the opposite
bank now but Françoise could no longer see anything at all.
Not a sound was to be heard. Then, suddenly, there was a
trampling of feet, a hoarse cry and the thud of a body falling to
the ground, followed by an even deeper silence. And then, as
though sensing the hand of Death passing close by as she peered
out into the gloom, Françoise felt a sudden icy shudder run
through her whole body.

4

As dawn was breaking, the mill suddenly reverberated with
loud shouting. Old Merlier came up to unlock Françoise's door
and she went down into the courtyard, very pale but composed.
When she arrived there, however, she was unable to suppress a
shudder when she saw the dead body of a Prussian soldier lying
next to the well on an outspread greatcoat...

Other soldiers were gathered round the corpse, gesticulating
and shouting angrily. Some of them were shaking their fists in
the direction of the village. Meanwhile the commanding officer
had summoned old Merlier as mayor of the commune.

'Take a look at that,' he said in a voice trembling with rage.
'One of my men has been found murdered by the side of the
river. We must bring the murderer to book and punish him in
such a way that no one else will be tempted to follow his
example. I shall rely on your full co-operation.'

'Anything you like,' the miller said, as phlegmatic as ever. 'But
it's not going to be easy.'

The officer bent down and pulled aside part of the coat hiding
the dead man's face. He had received a horrible wound: he had
been stabbed in the throat and the weapon, a black-handled
kitchen knife, was still protruding from it.

'Look at that knife,' the officer said to old Merlier. 'It may help
our investigations.'

The old man gave a start but immediately recovered himself
and without a flicker of emotion replied:

'Everybody round here has got a knife like that. Perhaps your man was tired of having to fight and decided to put an end to himself... That sort of thing does happen.'

'Hold your tongue!' the officer shouted in a fury. 'I don't know what's stopping me from burning the whole village down.'

Fortunately he was too angry to notice the change in the expression on Françoise's face. She had had to sit down on the stone bench beside the well. In spite of herself, she found it impossible to take her eyes off the corpse lying on the ground almost at her feet. He was a tall, handsome young man, looking somewhat like Dominique, with fair hair and blue eyes, and this resemblance had suddenly sickened her. She was thinking that perhaps the dead boy had left a sweetheart behind in Germany who would weep bitter tears on learning of his death. And it was her knife sticking in the dead man's throat. She had killed him.

Meanwhile the officer was still talking of the dire penalties that he would inflict on Rocreuse when some Prussian soldiers came running up. They had just discovered Dominique's escape. Turmoil ensued. The officer rushed up to the room, saw the open window, realized what had happened and came back fuming with rage.

Old Merlier was extremely put out by Dominique's escape.

'The idiot!' he muttered. 'He's ruining everything.'

When Françoise heard this comment, she felt a stab of fear. However, her father had no suspicion that she was involved. He shook his head and said to her in an undertone:

'Well, we really are in the soup now!'

'It was that scoundrel!' the officer shouted. 'It was that scoundrel and he'll have reached the woods by now... Well, he's got to be caught or else the whole village will pay the penalty!'

He turned to the miller:

'Look here, you must know where he's hiding?'

Old Merlier chuckled to himself as he waved a hand towards the wide expanse of wooded hillside.

'How on earth can you set about finding a man in there?' he said.

'Oh, there must be hideouts that you know about. I'll give you ten men and you can act as guide.'

'All right. But it'll take a week to beat through all the woods in the district.'

The studied calmness of the old man's replies further infuriated the officer. He realized, in fact, how ridiculous such an operation would be. At that moment he caught sight of Françoise sitting pale and trembling on the bench. Struck by the girl's anxious attitude, he stood looking closely from one to the other for a moment without speaking. Then he asked roughly:

'Isn't that man your daughter's lover?'

Old Merlier went pale with anger and for a second seemed as if he would fling himself at the officer's throat. He drew himself stiffly up and made no reply. Françoise put her head between her hands.

'Yes, that's the answer,' the officer went on. 'You or your daughter helped him to escape. You're his accomplices... Now, for the last time, will you hand him over?'

The miller made no reply. He had turned away and was gazing into the distance with an air of indifference, as if the officer were not addressing him. For the Prussian, this was the last straw.

'Very well,' he snarled, 'we'll shoot you on the spot.'

And once again, he called out the firing squad. Old Merlier remained as phlegmatic as ever. He gave a slight shrug of his shoulders: all this fuss seemed rather tasteless. No doubt he found it difficult to believe that it was so easy to have anyone shot like that. Then, when the firing squad had lined up, he said gravely:

'So you really mean it? All right then, if you absolutely must have someone, it might as well be me.'

But at this moment, Françoise jumped wildly to her feet and said breathlessly:

'Please sir, I beg you, please don't do anything to my father. Shoot me instead, I was the one who helped Dominique escape. It's all my fault.'

'Keep quiet, girl!' her father exclaimed. 'Why are you lying like that? She spent the night locked up in her bedroom. I give you my word, sir, she's not telling the truth.'

'No, I'm not lying,' the girl went on passionately. 'I climbed out of the window and talked him into escaping. That's the truth, the real truth!'

The old man went as white as a sheet. He could see in her eyes that she was telling the truth and he was appalled. Oh, those silly children who acted only as their hearts dictated! What a mess they made of everything!

'She's mad,' he burst out angrily, 'you mustn't listen to her. She's just making up stupid stories... Come on, let's get it over with!'

She still tried to protest. Flinging herself on her knees, she clasped her hands begging for mercy from the officer who stood calmly watching this touching conflict between father and daughter.

'So that's how it is!' he said eventually. 'Well, I shall hold your father because the other man's got away. Try and get him back for me and your father can go free.'

For a moment she stared at him wide-eyed, appalled at his dreadful proposal.

'But that's horrible,' she whispered. 'Where can I possibly find Dominique now? He's gone and I've no idea where he is.'

'Well, it's your choice. Him or your father.'

'Oh God, how can I choose? Even if I knew where Dominique was, I shouldn't be able to choose!... You're cutting my heart in two... I'd sooner die myself, straightaway. Oh please, please kill me!'

The sight of her tears and her despair finally exhausted the officer's patience.

'That's enough!' he exclaimed sharply. 'I'm prepared to be lenient, I'll give you two hours. If your sweetheart isn't here by then, your father will pay the penalty for him instead!'

He ordered old Merlier to be taken away and shut up in the same room as Dominique had been held in. The old man asked for some tobacco and started to smoke. His stolid face showed no sign of emotion. But once he was alone, as he smoked, two large tears welled up into his eyes and trickled slowly down his cheeks: how his poor darling daughter must be suffering!

Françoise had remained behind in the middle of the courtyard. Soldiers were coming and going, laughing and making remarks, jokes that she could not understand. She stood watching the doorway through which her father had just been taken away and slowly put her hand to her forehead as if her skull were splitting open.

The officer turned on his heels, saying once more:

'You've got two hours. Try and make good use of them!'

She had two hours! The words went buzzing round her head. Without thinking, she left the courtyard and walked away straight ahead. Where should she go? She was making no attempt to decide what to do because she realized how pointless it would be. All the same, she would have liked to see Dominique. They could have come to some agreement and perhaps found some way out of their dilemma. Still dazed and bewildered, she walked down to the bank of the Morelle, crossed over below the weir on some large stepping-stones and automatically made her way towards the first willow in the corner of the meadow. When she reached it, she bent down and saw a pool of blood. Her face went pale: so that was where it had happened. She followed Dominique's footsteps in the trampled grass. He must have been running, for they were spaced wide apart, cutting diagonally across the field. Then she lost track of him; but in the next meadow she thought she had picked it up again. The tracks led to the edge of the forest and here all trace of steps was obliterated. Nevertheless, Françoise plunged into the wood: she felt relieved at being alone. She sat down for a while but then, realizing that the minutes were ticking by, she leapt to her feet. How long was it since she had left the mill? Five minutes? Half an hour? She had lost all sense of time. Perhaps Dominique had gone to ground in a thicket she knew, where they had eaten hazel nuts together one afternoon. She went to the thicket and peered into it. A solitary blackbird flew away, singing its soft, wistful call. Then the thought occurred to her that he might have hidden in a cleft in a rock where he would sometimes lie in wait when out shooting; but the cleft was empty. What was the point of looking for him? She felt sure that she wouldn't find him, yet she was slowly becoming more and more anxious to do so. She started walking faster. Suddenly, the thought came to her that he must have clambered up a tree, so she began to look upwards and call out his name every fifteen or twenty steps, to tell him that she was near. Her call was answered by a cuckoo. A breeze rustling in the branches made her think that he was climbing down from a tree. On one occasion she even imagined that she saw him and she stopped and caught her breath, almost tempted to run away. What would she say to him? Was she going to fetch him back so that he'd be shot? No, she'd not mention anything like that, she'd warn him to go away at once and not stay in the neighbourhood. Then the thought of her father waiting for her return caused her a sudden pang of distress; she collapsed in tears on the grass, crying out loud:

'Oh God, oh God, what am I doing here?'

She was mad to have come. And seized with panic, she set off at a run to find her way out of the forest. Three times she took the wrong track but just as she was beginning to think that she would never succeed in getting back to the mill, she came out into the meadow opposite Rocreuse. As soon as she saw the village, she halted: was she going to go back alone?

She was still standing there when she heard a voice calling softly: 'Françoise! Françoise!'

She saw Dominique's head peeping out of a ditch. Merciful heavens! She'd found him! Did God wish him to die? She stifled a cry and slipped down into the ditch beside him.

'Were you looking for me?' he asked.

'Yes,' she replied. Her head was spinning and she hardly knew what she was saying.

'What's been happening?'

She looked down and said hesitantly:

'Nothing very much, I was just anxious and wanted to try and see you.'

He was reassured and went on to explain that he hadn't wanted to go too far away as he was afraid for their sakes: those Prussian blackguards were capable of taking their revenge on women and old men. Anyway, all was well and he added with a laugh:

'We'll just have to put off our wedding for a week, that's all!'

Then, as she still looked upset, he became serious:

'What's the matter? You're hiding something from me!'

'No, I promise I'm not, it's just that I'm out of breath from running.'

He kissed her and said it was not wise for them to go on talking any longer. He was about to make his way back along the ditch into the forest when she stopped him. She was trembling.

'Look, it might be just as well to stay here. There's nobody searching for you so there's no danger.'

'You're hiding something from me, Françoise,' he said again.

Once more she swore that she was not hiding anything. Her only reason was that she preferred to know that he was close at hand; and she mumbled a few other explanations which seemed so strange that by now he himself would not have agreed to go away. In any case, he firmly believed that the French would soon be back: he'd seen troops in the direction of Sauval.

'Oh, I do hope they hurry up and get here as soon as possible,' she murmured eagerly.

At that moment, the clock in the Rocreuse church tower struck eleven; the chimes came clearly and distinctly over the meadows. Panic-stricken, she sprang to her feet: she had left the mill two hours ago.

'I tell you what,' she said quickly, 'if we need you, I'll go up to my bedroom and wave a handkerchief out of the window.'

And she ran off while a very anxious Dominique lay down at the edge of the ditch to keep watch on the mill. As she came into Rocreuse, Françoise met old Bontemps, a tramp who knew every inch of the district like the palm of his hand. He wished her good morning. He had just seen the miller surrounded by Prussian soldiers, he said. And he went on his way mumbling incoherently and making many signs of the cross.

'The two hours are up,' said the officer when Françoise appeared.

Old Merlier was sitting on the bench next to the well, still smoking his pipe. Once again, the girl fell on her knees in tears appealing for mercy for her father. She was playing for time, for her hopes of seeing the French return were rising. She thought that she could almost hear the tramp of their boots as she knelt moaning at the officer's feet. If only they could arrive and liberate them in time!

'Please, just one hour more, only an hour. Surely you can give us one hour longer!'

The officer was unmoved. He ordered two men to seize hold of her and take her away so that they could proceed with the execution undisturbed. Françoise was in a torment: she couldn't let her father be murdered like this; no, she'd sooner die with Dominique. And then, just as she was about to run up to her room, Dominique himself came into the courtyard.

The officer and his men gave a roar of triumph; but Dominique himself walked over to Françoise as if there was nobody else present and said to her, quietly and a trifle sternly:

'That was wrong of you, Françoise. Why didn't you take me back with you? I've only just learnt from old Bontemps what's been happening... Anyway, here I am!'

5

It was three o'clock in the afternoon. Large black clouds had gradually been massing until they had covered the whole sky, the tail-end of a local storm. The livid sky and ragged copper-coloured clouds had turned the valley, so cheerful in the sunshine, into a gloomy, sinister-looking death-trap. The Prussian officer had been content merely to shut Dominique up again in a room without giving any indication of how he was going to treat him. Ever since midday, Françoise had been in an agony of distress. Despite her father's attempts to persuade her, she had refused to leave the courtyard. She was waiting for the French to return. But the hours were slipping by, night was approaching and her sufferings were increased by the thought that any time gained would be unlikely to change the dreaded outcome.

However, at about three o'clock, the Prussians started making preparations to leave. As on the previous day, the officer had been closeted for some time with Dominique. Françoise realized that her sweetheart's fate was being decided. She clasped her hands and prayed. Her father was sitting beside her still wearing the phlegmatic, dogged expression of an old peasant who never tries to struggle against the inevitable.

'Oh dear God, dear God!' Françoise said brokenly. 'They're going to kill him!'

The miller put his arm round her and lifted her on to his knee like a child.

At that moment the officer came out, followed by Dominique escorted by two soldiers.

'Never!' Dominique was shouting. 'I'd sooner die!'

'Think carefully, young man,' the officer said. 'If you won't help us, someone else will. I'm making you a generous offer. If you show us the way to Montredon through the woods, I'll let you go. There must be paths you know.'

Dominique said nothing.

'So you still refuse?'

'Shoot me and be done with it,' Dominique replied.

From where she was sitting, Françoise was appealing to him with clasped hands. She had only one thought in her mind: she was urging him to be a coward. But old Merlier caught hold of her hands so that the Prussians would not see the distraught girl's gesture.

'He's right,' he said softly. 'It's better to die.'

The firing squad was lined up. The officer was watching for a sign of weakness from Dominique, still hoping to persuade him. Silence fell; in the distance, violent claps of thunder were heard. The whole countryside was sweltering in the sultry heat. Then, suddenly, the silence was broken by a shout:

'The French are here!'

And so they were. On the Sauval road, the red line of trousers could be seen at the edge of the wood. In the mill, pandemonium broke loose as the Prussians scuttled to and fro, although no shots had yet been fired.

'It's the French!' cried Françoise, clapping her hands.

She went berserk. Springing up from her father's lap, she stood laughing and waving her arms about in the air. At last they'd come and they'd come in time because Dominique was still standing there alive!

She was deafened by a burst of gunfire, like a shattering thunder-clap. She spun round. Muttering: 'Well, at least we'll settle this matter first,' the officer had himself pushed Dominique up against the wall of a shed and given the order to fire. When Françoise looked round, Dominique was lying on the ground with a dozen bullets through his chest. She was completely dazed; no tears came to her eyes as with a glazed expression she went over and sat down on the ground beside the shed, a few feet away from the body. She looked at it, making an occasional vague, childish gesture with her hand. The Prussians had taken old Merlier hostage.

It was a splendid fight. The Prussian officer had swiftly ordered his men to battle stations, realizing that should they try to retreat they would quickly be smashed. They might as well sell their lives as dearly as possible. It was now the turn of the Prussians to be defending the mill and of the French to do the attacking. Firing began with earsplitting violence and persisted for a good half hour. Then there was a dull explosion and a cannon ball broke off a main branch of the ancient elm. The French had brought up their artillery and a gun battery, set up directly above the ditch in which Dominique had been hiding, now commanded the whole length of the main street of Rocreuse. The outcome would not be long delayed.

Poor old mill! Cannon balls were smashing their way through it; half of its roof was shot off; two of its walls collapsed. But the most distressing sight was the damage inflicted on the side overlooking the Morelle. Torn from its shattered walls, the ivy was hanging down in shreds; the river was carrying away vast quantities of wreckage and through a breach in the wall Françoise's bedroom could be seen, her bed still with its white curtains carefully drawn. The old mill-wheel received two direct hits in quick succession: it groaned in its death throes, its blades were carried off by the current and its frame collapsed. The cheerful old mill was giving up the ghost...

Then the French launched their attack. There was a fierce hand-to-hand struggle. Under the rust-coloured sky, the death trap of Rocreuse was filling up with dead bodies. The tall isolated trees and the screens of poplars cast grim dark shadows over the broad meadows. To left and right, the woods were like the walls of an arena enclosing the fighters while the gurgling springs and streams and water-courses filled the panic-stricken landscape with the sound of their sobbing.

Still crouching down beside Dominique's body, Françoise had not moved out of the shadow of the shed. Old Merlier had been killed on the spot by a stray bullet. Then, after the Prussians had all been wiped out and the mill was in flames, the first person to come into the courtyard was the French captain. This was his only successful engagement since the beginning of the campaign and, bursting with pride, with his head held high, he came prancing in, every inch the dashing and debonair young officer. Seeing Françoise crouching, crazed with grief, between the dead bodies of her sweetheart and her father amidst the smoking ruins of her beloved mill, he gallantly waved his sword towards her, shouting gleefully:

'We've won! We've won!'

CAPTAIN BURLE

IT was nine o'clock and the inhabitants of Vauchamp had just gone to bed, leaving the little town in silence and darkness in the icy November rain. In the Rue des Récollets, one of the narrowest and most deserted in the St Jean district, just one lighted window remained on the third floor of an old house whose broken gutters were disgorging torrents of water. Madame Burle was still awake and sitting beside her meagre fire of vine-stumps while her grandson Charles was doing his homework in the dim light of a lamp.

The flat which she rented for one hundred and twenty francs a year consisted of four enormous rooms, quite impossible to heat in winter. Madame Burle slept in the largest of them; her son, the regimental paymaster Captain Charles Burle, occupied the bedroom overlooking the street next to the dining-room; and young Charles slept in an iron bedstead tucked away at the far end of the immense disused drawing-room with its peeling wallpaper. The few sticks of furniture belonging to the captain and his mother, a solid mahogany Empire suite, dented and battered by many moves from one garrison town to another, were barely visible in the dim light which fell like a fine haze from the lofty ceiling. The cold, hard, red-painted floor-tiles were freezing to the feet, for there were only a few odd squares of carpet in front of the chairs in this icy room swept by piercing draughts from the warped doors and window-frames.

Madame Burle sat sunk in her yellow velvet armchair beside the fireplace, her face cradled in her hands, looking at the final wisps of smoke from a vine-root with the vacant stare of an old woman living in the past. She would spend whole days sitting like this, a tall, long-faced figure whose thin lips never smiled. As the widow of a colonel who had died just as he was about to be made a general, and the mother of a captain, whom she had accompanied even throughout his campaigns, she had become imbued with ideas of duty, honour and patriotism which had turned her into an unbending old lady, as it were shrivelled up by the harshness of strict military discipline. She rarely complained. When her son had been widowed after five years of marriage, she had undertaken her grandson's upbringing as a matter of course, like a sergeant sternly drilling his recruits. She ruled the child with a rod of iron, never tolerating the slightest caprice or unruly behaviour, making him work well into the night and staying up herself until midnight to see that his homework was completed. Under this harsh regime, Charles, who was a delicate, gentle, little boy, was growing up pale and wan; he had fine eyes but they always seemed unnaturally bright and large.

One single thought was always turning over in Madame Burle's mind during her long periods of silent meditation: her son had let her down. She was obsessed by this idea and she would continually go back in her mind over her life, from the time of his birth, when she had seen him as a future hero who would reach the highest rank, in a blaze of glory, to the present narrow garrison life filled with the same dull, never-ending routine, his decline into the post of a regimental paymaster captain, from which he would never escape and in which he was becoming inert and apathetic. And yet there had been a time, at the beginning, when she had been proud of him: for a while she had been able to think that her dream was coming true. Burle had come straight out of the crack cavalry school of Saint-Cyr to distinguish himself by his gallantry at the battle of Solferino,* capturing a whole enemy battery with a handful of men. He was decorated, his heroism was reported in the papers and he became known as one of the bravest men in the army. Then slowly this hero had put on weight and become submerged in fat—relaxed, contented, stout, and cowardly. By 1870, he had not gone beyond the rank of captain. He was captured in his first skirmish and had returned from Germany an angry man, swearing that they wouldn't catch him fighting again, it was all too stupid. Being incapable of learning any other trade and so obliged to stay in the army, he had managed to obtain a post as regimental paymaster, a niche, he said, where at least they'd let him kick the bucket in peace. On the day this happened, Madame Burle had felt her heart break. Her dream had come to an end. Since then she had gritted her teeth and retreated implacably into her shell.

The wind was gusting down the Rue des Récollets and the windows shuddered under the deluge of rain. The old woman looked up from the dying embers of the vine-stocks to make sure that Charles was not falling asleep over his Latin translation. This little lad of twelve had become her last hope of finally achieving her dogged ambition of making the name of Burle famous. At first she had loathed her grandson with all the hatred she had felt for his mother, a little laceworker, pretty and delicate, whom the captain foolishly married when she had resisted his frantic attempts to make her his mistress. When his mother had died and his father had relapsed into a life of debauchery, Madame Burle had pinned all her hopes on her poor, sickly little grandson whom she was bringing up in such difficult circumstances. She wanted him to be strong, for he was to become the hero which Burle had failed to be, and so, in her cold, harsh way, she anxiously watched over him as he grew up, drumming courage into his head and feeling his limbs to test their strength. Little by little, blinded by her passionate ambition, she had come to believe that here at last was the man of the family. In fact, the child had a dreamy, tender nature and felt a physical horror of army life, but, being a very quiet, obedient boy and terrified of his grandmother, he repeated everything he was told and seemed resigned to becoming a soldier.

Meanwhile Madame Burle had noticed that the translation was not progressing very well. Bemused by the sound of the storm, Charles had dropped off to sleep, pen in hand, with his eyes still fixed on the paper. Her bony finger rapped sharply on the edge of the table and with a start he began feverishly thumbing the pages of his dictionary. Still without a word, the old woman began pulling the vine-stocks together in a vain attempt to rekindle the blaze.

During the period when she had still believed in her son, she had sacrificed all her savings and he had frittered away her meagre income in riotous living, the nature of which she had never dared investigate closely. Even now, he was ransacking the house and letting everything go to rack and ruin: they were on the brink of destitution, the rooms were stripped of furniture and hot meals a rare luxury. She never mentioned such things to him: with her respect for discipline, he still remained the master, the head of the house. Only sometimes she would shudder at the thought that Burle might well, one day, do something foolish that would prevent Charles from getting into the army.

As she stood up to fetch another vine branch from the kitchen, a terrible squall hit the house, rattling the doors, wrenching off a shutter and spilling a torrent of water from the broken gutters down on to the windows. Above the din, she was surprised to hear the doorbell ringing. Who could it be, at such a time and in such weather? Burle never came home before midnight, if indeed he came home at all. She opened up and an officer came in, soaked to the skin and swearing:

'Christ Almighty! What a foul night!'

It was the regimental adjutant Laguitte, a game old soldier who had served under Colonel Burle in the good old days. Born and bred in the barracks, he had risen, far more through courage than through intelligence, to the rank of battalion commander, when, as the result of a wound, a muscle contraction in his thigh had made him unfit for active service and forced him to accept a post as adjutant. He even had a slight limp, though you had to be careful not to tell him so to his face, because he refused to admit the idea.

'It's you, Major Laguitte,' exclaimed Madame Burle in surprise.

'Yes, blast it!' growled Laguitte, 'and I must be a damned fool and damned fond of you to be out in this damned rain... It's not fit weather to send a priest out in!'

He shook himself and his boots spread large puddles of water all over the floor. He looked around.

'I absolutely must see Burle! Is he in bed already, the lazy hound?'

'No, he's not home yet,' the old woman replied in her gruff voice.

Laguitte looked exasperated.

'What? Not come home?' he exclaimed angrily. 'In that case, they were having me on at that café of his, Mélanie's, you know all about it, don't you? I go in and there's this maid who laughs in my face and tells me that the captain's gone off to bed. Damn and blast it, I guessed as much, I was itching to tug her ears!'

He calmed down and walked round the room, looking upset and in two minds as to what to say next. Madame Burle was watching him closely.

'Did you want to speak to him personally?' she asked eventually.

'Yes,' he replied.

'And I can't pass on a message for you?'

'No.'

She did not insist but she still stood watching the adjutant who seemed unable to decide whether to leave or not. Finally, he burst out again:

'Ah well, can't be helped, damn and blast it! Since I'm here, you might as well know the truth, it'll probably be better.'

And he sat down in front of the fireplace and stretched out his muddy boots as if there had been a bright fire blazing there. Madame Burle was just going back to her seat in the armchair when she noticed that, overcome by sleep, Charles's head had dropped on to the open pages of his dictionary. The adjutant's arrival had momentarily aroused him and then, seeing that no one was paying any attention, he had been unable to resist dropping off to sleep again. His grandmother was on her way to give him a rap on his hands, all white and frail in the light of the lamp, when Laguitte stopped her:

'Please don't, let the little fellow sleep. It's not very funny, he doesn't need to hear it.'

The old woman went back to her armchair. Silence fell. They both looked at each other.

'Well, here goes,' said the adjutant at last, emphasizing his remark with a vicious jerk of his chin: 'This time that swine Burle has really done it!'

Madame Burle did not flinch, although her face grew pale as she sat up rigidly in her chair. The adjutant went on:

'I'd been suspecting something all along. I'd made up my mind to tell you about it one day. Burle was spending too much and he had an idiotic look on his face that worried me. But I never thought... Damn and blast it! How stupid can you get to play a dirty trick like that?'

He slapped his knee furiously again and again, speechless with indignation.

'He's been stealing?'

'You can't imagine what it is... Just think... I never used to check, myself! I passed all his accounts through. I merely signed at the bottom of the page. You know what it's like in the mess. Only when the annual inspection was coming up, because of the colonel, who's a bit of a stickler, I used to say: "Watch your figures, old man, it's me who's got to carry the can!" And I didn't worry at all... All the same, for the last month or so, because he'd got such a queer look and people were saying some rather nasty things, I began looking a bit more closely into his accounts and going through his books. Everything seemed perfectly in order to me, nothing wrong at all...'

He broke off, seized by such a burst of rage that he had to let off steam straightaway.

'Damn and blast it! It's not the swindling that annoys me, it's the beastly way he's behaved towards me! He's made a bloody fool of me, Madame Burle, do you realize?... Blast him! Does he think I'm an old idiot?'

'So he's been stealing?' his mother asked again.

'This evening,' the adjutant went on, somewhat more calmly, 'I'd just finished dinner when in comes Gagneux. You know Gagneux, the butcher on the corner of the Place aux Herbes. And there's another damned scoundrel, too, who got the contract and then feeds our men on old cows-meat from God knows where! So I greet him like the dirty dog he is and he proceeds to take the lid off the whole rotten business. And what a business! Apparently Burle only ever gave him payment on account, a real swindle, and such an unholy muddle that it'll be the devil's own job to straighten it out. To cut a long story short, Burle owes him two thousand francs and the butcher is talking of going to spill the beans to the colonel if he doesn't get his money... But the worst thing of all is that that swine Burle, to land me in the soup, used to give me a false receipt every week which he simply signed in Gagneux's name. Fancy playing a trick like that on an old friend like me! Damn and blast the whole bloody thing!'

Laguitte stood up waving his fists in the air and then fell back again in his chair.

'So he's been stealing,' Madame Burle said again. 'It was bound to happen.'

Then, without a word of judgement or condemnation of her son, she added simply:

'We haven't got two thousand francs. We might have thirty francs in the house.'

'I suspected that,' said Laguitte. 'And do you know where all the money goes? It goes to Mélanie, a trollop who's driven Burle crazy... Women! I said before that they'd be the ruination of him! I just don't know what's wrong with that swine. He's only five years younger than me and he still can't keep away from them, the randy old goat!'

There was another silence. Outside the rain was pouring down harder than ever and in the sleeping little town you could hear the crash of slates and chimney pots brought down by the gale.

'Ah well,' said the adjutant, getting to his feet, 'we shan't settle anything by sitting here talking... It was just to warn you. I must be off.'

'What can we do?' asked the old woman in a low voice. 'Is there anyone we can approach?'

'Don't be downhearted, we'll just have to see. If only I had two thousand francs of my own... But I've no money, as you know.'

He stopped short in embarrassment. He was an old bachelor, with no wife or children, and he systematically drank all his pay, and anything left over from his bills for absinthe* and brandy he lost at gambling. With all that, a very honest man, on principle.

'Never mind,' he went on, standing in the doorway, 'I'll still go along and rout out the old rascal at his lady-love's. I'll move heaven and earth... Burle, the son of *the* Burle, condemned for theft! It'd be the end of the world, it can't be possible! I'd sooner blow the whole place up... So don't worry, confound it all! It's even more annoying for me!'

He gripped her hand tightly and disappeared into the shadow of the staircase while she held up the lamp to light his way. When she had put the lamp down on the table, she stood motionless for a moment in the enormous bare and silent room and a flush of tenderness rose to her cheeks as she looked pensively at Charles, still asleep with his face resting on the pages of his dictionary: with his long fair hair and pale complexion he looked like a little girl. But this tenderness which softened her harsh, cold features lasted only a second before her face set once more into its usual air of grim determination. Sharply, she rapped the boy's hand:

'Your translation, Charles!'

The lad woke up with a shiver and with a scared look began hurriedly turning over the pages of his dictionary. At that very moment Laguitte, slamming the street door behind him, was drenched from head to foot with a downpour of rain from the gutter and his swearing could be heard even above the storm. Then the only sound audible against the pounding rain was the gentle scratch of Charles's pen on the paper. Madame Burle had gone back to her seat in front of the fireplace and was sitting as she always sat every evening, as stiff as a ramrod, staring at the dead embers of the fire, lost in her dogged obsession.

2

The Café de Paris, kept by the widow Madame Mélanie
Cartier, stood in the Place du Palais, a large irregular square
planted with dusty oaks. In Vauchamp people would say:
'Coming to Mélanie's?' Here, at the end of the first room, quite a
large one, there was a second room, called the 'sofa-room', which
was very narrow, with imitation leather upholstered sofas
running all round the walls and four marble tables standing in the
corners; and it was here that Mélanie, leaving the front bar-room
in the charge of her maid Phrosyne, would spend her evenings in
the company of a few 'regulars', an inner circle who were known
in the town as the 'sofa-room gentlemen'. It was a hallmark:
thereafter, every mention of their names would evoke smiles in
which condemnation competed with secret envy.

Madame Cartier had been widowed at the age of twenty-five.
Her husband had been a wheelwright who had astounded
Vauchamp by taking over the Café de Paris on the death of an
uncle; and one fine morning he had brought her back from
Montpellier which he visited every six months to lay in his
supply of liqueurs. As part of the equipment of setting up his
business, he had taken a wife, doubtless to his taste, who was
prepossessing and likely to increase the consumption of alcohol.
No one ever discovered where he'd picked her up; and indeed he
didn't actually marry her until after a six months' trial period
behind the bar. As a matter of fact, opinions on Mélanie were
divided; some said she was superb; others described her as bossy.
She was tall, with pronounced features and coarse hair which
came right down to her eyebrows. But nobody denied her ability
to twist men round her little finger. She had fine eyes and she
used them shamelessly to gaze at her 'sofa-room gents' until they
grew pale and amenable. And rumour had it also that she was a
fine figure of a woman: in the Midi, that's the sort of woman they
like . . .

Cartier had died in a strange way. There was talk of a squabble
between the couple and of an abscess brought about by a kick in
the stomach. However that might be, Mélanie found herself very
awkwardly placed, for the café was not doing at all well. The
wheelwright had squandered his uncle's money by drinking his

own absinthe and spending lengthy sessions at his own billiard table. For a while it looked as though she would have to sell up. But she liked the life and for a lady, everything was laid on. She never needed more than a few customers and the front room could remain empty. So all she did was to put white and gold paper on the walls and new imitation leather on the sofas. First of all she entertained a pharmacist in her newly decorated room; there followed a spaghetti manufacturer, a solicitor and a retired magistrate. And by these means the café remained open, although the waiter hardly served twenty drinks a day. The authorities turned a blind eye as long as the proprieties were observed; after all, a lot of respectable people would have been compromised.

In the evening, half a dozen locals, men with modest private means, would still come in for their game of dominoes in the big front room: Cartier was dead and some queer goings-on were taking place in the Café de Paris but they saw nothing and kept to their old habits. As the waiter was proving superfluous, Mélanie got rid of him and now it was Phrosyne who would light the single gas-light in the corner for their game. Occasionally, attracted by the stories they had heard and egging each other on 'to go to Mélanie's', a gang of young men would burst into the bar-room, laughing loudly to hide their embarrassment. They would be greeted with icy dignity; they rarely saw the proprietress or, if she happened to be there, she overwhelmed them with her beauty and her disdain, leaving them completely at a loss for words. She was far too intelligent to forget herself and behave in any way foolishly. While the main room remained in darkness, lit only in the corner where the gentlemen of leisure were performing their ritual game of dominoes, she would serve the sofa-room regulars herself: friendly but discreet, she would occasionally give way to an impulse, if she felt so inclined, to rest her arm on the shoulder of one of them to follow some particularly neat play in their game of *écarté*.

One evening these gentlemen, who had grown to tolerate each other's presence, were disagreeably surprised to discover Captain Burle ensconced on one of the sofas. He had, it seemed, come in that morning, quite by chance, to have a glass of vermouth. Mélanie was alone and they had chatted together. That evening, when he came back, Phrosyne had shown him straightaway into the small back room.

Two days later, Burle was the reigning monarch, without, however, putting the pharmacist, the spaghetti manufacturer, the solicitor or the retired magistrate to flight. The captain, a short, broad man, adored tall women. In the regiment he was nick-named Skirty because of his constant womanizing, a taste he satisfied whenever and however he could and all the more vigorously when there was an extra large morsel to enjoy. Whenever the officers or even the ordinary soldiers saw some great bag of flesh with incredibly opulent charms, a veritable giant balloon of fat, whether she was dressed in fine clothes or in rags, they would exclaim: 'Just the job for Skirty!' Everything was grist to his mill and in the barrack-room of an evening, they all prophesied that it would be the death of him. And so that 'fine figure of a woman' took him completely and irresistibly into her power; he sank without trace into her capacious maw. It took him no longer than a fortnight to be reduced to an amorous stupor, a fat little man drained dry, even though he was still as fat as ever. His tiny eyes lost in his bloated face would follow her everywhere she went, like the eyes of a beaten dog, and the sight of that broad masculine face with its coarse bristly hair held him in a constant ecstasy of delight: he could think of nothing else. For fear that she might stop his rations, as he put it, he was prepared to tolerate the presence of the 'sofa-room gentlemen' and forked out the last farthing of his pay. The situation was summed up by a sergeant: 'Skirty has found his hole and he'll not budge.' A man as good as dead!

It was nearly ten o'clock when Major Laguitte flung open the door of the Café de Paris. Through the doorway, as the door slammed behind him, you could catch a glimpse of the Place du Palais, pitch-dark and like a mud-lake bubbling under the pouring rain. Wet to the skin by now and leaving a trail of water behind him, the adjutant made straight for the bar where Phrosyne was sitting reading a novel. 'So that's the way you make a fool of an officer, you bitch!' he shouted. 'I ought to . . .'

And he swung his arm as though to give her a box on the ears that would have sent her flying. The frightened little maid shrank back while the domino players turned round to look, open-mouthed, unable to understand what it was all about. But the adjutant wasted no time; he pushed open the sofa-room door and went in at the very moment that Mélanie was charitably engaged in offering the captain his grog in tiny spoonfuls, like a pet canary. That evening the only other customers had been the retired magistrate and the pharmacist and they had both left early, in a depressed mood. And as Mélanie needed three hundred francs the following day, she was seizing the opportunity of wheedling them out of the captain.

'Come along luvvy duvvy... Give Mummy your little beaky-weaky... It's good, isn't it, you naughty little boy...'

Flabby and goggle-eyed, the captain, purple in the face, was sucking the spoon in a paroxysm of pleasure.

'Christ Almighty!' bellowed the adjutant standing in the doorway. 'You're getting women to look after you now, are you? They told me you hadn't come and told me to go away and all the time you're here going barmy!'

Burle sat up and pushed the grog away. Mélanie stepped forward, looking annoyed, as if she wanted to protect him with her large frame. But Laguitte looked her squarely in the eyes with that determined expression that is very familiar to women running the risk of getting their face slapped.

'Get out!' he said simply.

She still hesitated for a second but when she could almost hear the slap whistling past her ear, white with rage she went out to join Phrosyne at the bar.

When they were alone at last, Laguitte took up his stance in front of the captain and then, crossing his arms, he bent forward and with all his might yelled:

'You dirty bastard!'

Completely taken aback, the other man was on the point of losing his temper but Laguitte did not give him time.

'Shut up! What a dirty trick to play on a friend... You plastered me with dud receipts which could have landed both of us in gaol. Is that a decent thing to do? How could you play that sort of dirty game when we've known each other for thirty years?'

Burle subsided into his seat and went ghastly pale. He was trembling feverishly all over. Walking round him and banging his fist on the table, the major went on:

'So you've turned into a miserable little petty thief of a clerk, have you? And all for that cow out there, too!... If you'd done it for your mother, that would at least have been something honourable but cooking the accounts and then bringing the proceeds round to this lousy place, that's what makes me sick, for Christ's sake!... Well? What the hell's gone wrong with your head to knock yourself up at your age with a bossy old sow like that? Don't give me any blarney, I saw the pair of you playing your little games a moment ago!'

'You go gambling yourself,' faltered the captain.

'Yes, I do, damn you,' the adjutant replied, even more infuriated by this remark, 'and I'm a damned fool to do it because I'm losing every penny I've got and it's no credit to the French army. But Christ Almighty, if I do gamble, I don't go in for stealing! Kill yourself if you like and let your mother and your little lad starve but at least keep your fingers out of the till and don't land your friends in the shit!'

He stopped. Burle sat staring with an idiotic look on his face. For a second, the only sound to be heard was the clumping of the major's boots.

'And not a bean!' he went on violently. 'Well? Can you see youself with the handcuffs on? Oh, you rotten bastard!'

He calmed down, seized Burle by the wrist and dragged him to his feet.

'Come along! We've got to do something at once, I shan't get a wink of sleep with this on my mind... I've got an idea.'

In the large front bar, Mélanie and her maid were excitedly whispering to each other. When Mélanie saw the two men emerge, she was bold enough to go up to them and say, in her most ingratiating voice: 'What's the matter, captain? Are you off so soon?'

'Yes, he is,' Laguitte replied curtly, 'and I don't expect him ever to set foot in your dirty hole again.'

The little maid caught her mistress by the arm and was unwise enough to mutter the word 'drunk', whereupon the adjutant finally let fly with the slap that he'd been itching to give for some time. The two women ducked and he succeeded only in hitting the back of Phrosyne's neck, flattening her bonnet and breaking her comb. The gentlemen of independent means were indignant.

'Hell, let's go,' said Laguitte, pushing Burle out on to the pavement. 'If I stay, I'll bash the lot of them in there.'

As they crossed the square the water came up to their ankles. The wind drove the rain streaming down their faces. As they walked along, the captain said nothing when the adjutant started once more to tell him off, even more angrily than before, for his 'fart-arsing about'. 'Lovely weather for a walk, wasn't it? If he hadn't been so stupid, they'd both be snug in bed instead of paddling about like this.' He went on to talk about Gagneux. A complete and utter rogue whose rotten meat had given the whole regiment the squitters three times already. His contract expired next week. The devil if they'd accept his tender for the next one!

'That's my pigeon, I can choose who I like,' grunted the adjutant. 'I'd sooner lose my right arm than let that poisoner get another penny out of us!'

He swore profusely as he slipped up to his knees in a gutter and then said:

'I'm going to see him... You wait outside while I go up... I want to find out if he's really got the guts to go and see the colonel tomorrow, as he was threatening to do... A butcher, for Christ's sake! Fancy getting involved with a butcher! God, you're certainly not proud. That's one thing I'll never forgive you for.'

They had reached the Place aux Herbes. Gagneux's house was in darkness but Laguitte knocked vigorously on the door and it was eventually opened. Left alone in the dark, Captain Burle did not even think of seeking shelter but stood motionless in the pouring rain at the corner of the market square. His head was buzzing and he felt quite incapable of thought. He did not feel bored, for he had lost all sense of time. With its windows and doors all closed, the house seemed dead; he just stood looking at it. When the adjutant emerged an hour later, it seemed to Burle as if he had only just gone in.

Laguitte looked sombre and said nothing. The captain did not dare ask any questions. For a brief moment they looked for each other, dimly, in the gloom. Then they set off once again through the dark streets that were like some river-bed in spate. They groped their way along side by side, in silence. Absorbed in his thoughts, Laguitte had even stopped cursing. However, when they were once again crossing the Place du Palais, seeing that the Café de Paris was still lit up, he tapped Burle on the shoulder and said:

'If you ever go back to that hole again... '

'Don't worry,' the captain replied, not letting him finish his sentence. And he held out his hand. But Laguitte went on:

'No, I'll take you as far as your house, so that I can at least be sure you won't go back there again tonight.'

They walked on. As they went down the Rue des Récollets, they both slackened their pace. Then, having reached his door, the captain took his keys out of his pocket and at last decided to speak:

'Well?' he asked.

'Well,' replied the adjutant gruffly, 'I'm as big a bastard as you... I've played a shit's trick... God blast your eyes! Our men are going to have to eat rotten meat for another three months.'

And he explained that Gagneux, as well as being a disgusting little man, was a crafty bugger who had gradually led him on to make a deal: he wouldn't go and see the colonel, he'd even forget about the two thousand francs and give Laguitte properly signed receipts in exchange for the false ones; but in return he insisted that his tender would be accepted for the next allocation of supplies of meat to the regiment. It was a bargain.

'So you see,' Laguitte went on, 'just think what a packet he must be making in order to be able to let us off those two thousand francs!'

Choking with emotion, Burle gripped his old friend's hands, unable to do more than stammer a few confused words of thanks and moved to tears at the thought that the adjutant had just perpetrated such a dishonest action purely in order to save him.

'It's the first time I've ever done a thing like that,' grunted the adjutant, 'but it was the only way... Damn and blast it! Fancy not having two thousand francs tucked away in one's drawer! It's enough to put you off gambling for good... Well, it's my bad luck! I'm a pretty poor sort of chap... Anyway, just listen to me: don't do it again, because I certainly won't, for Christ's sake!'

The captain gave him a hug and when he had gone in, the adjutant stood for a moment by the door to make sure he had gone to bed. Then, as it was striking midnight and the rain was still pelting down, he made his way laboriously home through the streets now plunged in darkness, sick at heart at the thought of what he had done to his men. He stopped and said out loud in a changed voice, full of affection and pity:

'Poor buggers! Think of all the old cow they'll be eating for the sake of two thousand francs!'

3

The regiment was stupefied. Skirty had broken off with
Mélanie. By the end of the week, there was proof positive: the
captain was no longer setting foot in the Café de Paris; it was
being said that the pharmacist had slipped into his place, almost
before it was cold, to the great chagrin of the former magistrate.
And, even more incredibly, Captain Burle was now cloistered in
the Rue des Récollets. He was definitely settling down, to the
point of spending all his evenings at his own fireside, going over
Charles's lessons with him. His mother, who had never breathed
a word to him about his unsavoury dealings with Gagneux, sat in
her armchair as before, looking as strict and stern as ever; but in
her eyes you could read the belief that he was cured.

One evening, a fortnight later, Laguitte decided to invite
himself to dinner. He felt some embarrassment at the thought of
seeing Burle again, not, indeed, on his own account but on the
captain's, fearing that it might bring back painful memories.
However, since the captain was a reformed character, he made up
his mind to call on him and have a spot of dinner together.

When Laguitte arrived, the captain was in his room and it was
Madame Burle who let him in. After announcing that he had
come to take pot-luck, he enquired in a whisper:

'Well?'

'Everything's all right,' replied the old lady.

'Nothing fishy?'

'Absolutely nothing... In bed by nine o'clock, not a single late
night, and he seems very cheerful.'

'Well I'm damned! That's wonderful!' exclaimed the adjutant.
'I knew he needed a good shake-up. His heart's still in the right
place, the old devil!'

When Burle appeared, he gave him a hearty handshake and
before sitting down to dinner, they stayed chatting genially in
front of the fire, singing the praises of domesticity. The captain
declared that he wouldn't change his home for a king's ransom;
when he'd taken off his braces, put on his slippers and stretched
out in his armchair, he wouldn't call the king his cousin, he said.
The adjutant agreed as he eyed him closely. It was certainly true
that his change of heart had not made him any thinner; in fact, he
seemed to have swollen as, with goggle-eyes and puffy lips, he

sat half asleep slumped in his chair, saying again and again:

'There's nothing like family life! Family life's the thing for me!'

'That's splendid,' said the adjutant, worried at seeing him looking so completely exhausted, 'but don't overdo it, will you?... Take some exercise, go to a café now and again.'

'What would I be doing in a café... I've got everything I want here. No, I'm staying at home.'

Charles was tidying away his books when Laguitte was surprised to see a maid come in to lay the table.

'You've taken someone on?' he said.

'We had to,' Madame Burle replied with a sigh. 'My legs aren't much good these days and everything was getting neglected... Luckily old Cabrol let me have his daughter. You must know Cabrol, the old man who sweeps up the market? He couldn't think what to do with Rose. I'm teaching her some cooking.'

The maid left the room.

'How old is she?' enquired the adjutant.

'Just seventeen. She's stupid and dirty but I only give her ten francs a month and she doesn't eat anything but soup.'

When Rose came back with a pile of plates, Laguitte, who was not much interested in girls, followed her with his eyes, surprised at her ugliness. She was short, very swarthy, and slightly humpbacked, with a face like a monkey's, the nose squashed flat, a broad slit of a mouth and narrow, glassy, greenish coloured eyes. She was broad in the beam, long-armed and looked very strong.

'Heavens above! What a phizog,' said Laguitte with a grin when the maid had left the room again in search of salt and pepper.

'Ah well,' sighed Burle unconcernedly, 'she's very obliging, she does everything she's asked. After all, it's all you need to do the washing-up.'

They had a very pleasant meal. There was some beef broth and mutton stew. Charles was encouraged to talk about his life at school. To show what a good boy he was, Madame Burle asked him several times: 'You do want to be a soldier, don't you, Charles?' And a smile came to her pale lips when the lad replied with the cowed obedience of a trained dog: 'Yes, grandmamma.' Burle had put his elbows on the table and was munching gently, absorbed in his own thoughts. There was a cosy atmosphere round the table, lit by a single lamp which left the corners of the immense room half in darkness. It was an air of comfortable lethargy, the friendly informality of people who are not very well-off, who don't bother to change plates for every course, and who feel a thrill of surprise when a bowl of whipped whites of egg and cream custard appears on the table, as a treat, for pudding.

Rose, whose heavy-heeled tread was making the table rock as she walked round the room, had not once opened her mouth while she was serving but now, standing behind Burle, she said in a hoarse voice:

'Would you like cheese, sir?'

Burle gave a start: 'What's that? Oh, cheese, yes, hold the plate tightly.'

He cut himself a piece of Gruyère while the girl stood watching him through her narrow eyes. Laguitte was laughing to himself. He had been amused by Rose ever since the meal began. Lowering his voice, he whispered in Burle's ear:

'I think she's wonderful, you know. Fancy having a nose and a mouth like that . . . Why don't you send her round to the colonel one day, so that he can see her. It'll cheer him up!'

He beamed at her ugly face in an avuncular fashion and, wanting to be able to look more closely at her, he said:

'And how about me, my girl? I'd like some cheese too.'

She came over with the plate and, sticking his knife into the cheese, he so far forgot his manners as to laugh as he looked at her, when he discovered that one of her nostrils was larger than the other. Rose stolidly allowed herself to be stared at, waiting until the gentleman had stopped laughing.

She cleared the table and disappeared. While the adjutant and Madame Burle continued to chat, the captain dropped off to sleep at once beside the fire. Charles had gone back to his homework. Peace hovered over the room, the peace of a bourgeois family gathered together in good fellowship in the same room. At nine o'clock Burle woke up, yawned and announced that he was going to bed; he was sorry but he just couldn't keep his eyes open. When Laguitte left half an hour later, Madame Burle was unable to find Rose to light his way to the door: she must have already gone to her room; she was like a hen, that girl, she could sleep like a log for twelve hours at a stretch.

'Don't bother to disturb anyone,' the adjutant said on the landing, 'my legs aren't much better than yours but if I hold on to the banisters, I shan't break anything… Well, I'm a very happy man. All your troubles are over now. I've been watching Burle and I promise you he's not up to any mischief… Damn it all, it really was time for him to give up chasing skirts. It would have led to trouble.'

The adjutant went on his way delighted at having seen a house of such thoroughly nice people; and they were all living on top of each other, there was no chance of any hanky-panky there!

The thing that really pleased him in this sudden conversion was that he no longer had to check Burle's accounts: there was nothing more boring than all that paperwork. Now that Burle was settling down, all he had to do was smoke his pipe and countersign everything, without a second thought. Even so, he did keep half an eye on the books, but he found the receipts all in order, the totals all balancing correctly; no irregularity at all. After a month, he merely leafed through the receipts and checked the totals, as, indeed, he always had done. But that morning, without any suspicion and purely because he happened to be lighting his pipe at the time, his eyes lingered over an addition and he noticed a mistake of thirteen francs; the total had been increased by thirteen francs to make the account balance; there had been no mistake in the actual figures because he compared them with the receipts. This struck him as rather suspicious. He did not mention the matter to Burle but promised himself to keep a check on the additions. The following week, another mistake: nineteen francs short. He was so worried by this that he sent for all the ledgers, shut himself up in his office and spent one horrible morning checking everything, every sum, cursing and sweating, his mind reeling with figures. In each total, there were a few francs short: it was a paltry theft, ten francs here, eight francs there, eleven francs, and, in the most recent accounts, the figure had even dropped to three or four francs, while in one case Burle had stolen only one and a half francs. So for the last two months, Burle had been nibbling away at the cash in the till. By comparing dates, the adjutant was able to ascertain that the famous 'lesson' he had received had kept him straight for barely a week. This was the last straw. He exploded:

'Christ All-bloody-mighty!' he bellowed, alone in his office, banging the ledgers with his fist, 'That's an even dirtier trick!…

At least Gagneux's false receipts showed some guts... and now he's sunk to the level of a cook trying to make a few sous on the sly with a saucepanful of stew... Cooking the totals, for Christ's sake!... Buggering about with one franc fifty!... God Almighty! You might at least show some pride, you bastard! Make off with the whole till and blue it on some actress!'

It was the shabby meanness of all these thefts that made him so angry. In addition, he was furious at having been taken in yet again by those false totals, such an obvious and stupid way of cheating. He stood up and paced up and down his room for a whole hour, beside himself with rage, not knowing what to do and talking to himself out loud.

'One thing's for sure, everybody knows what he's like. I must do something... Even if I ticked him off good and proper every morning, he'd still stick a couple of francs in his pocket every afternoon... But what's he spending it on, for Christ's sake? He's stopped going out at night, he's in bed by nine o'clock every evening and everything looks so fair, square, and above board at home... Has the bastard got some other nasty habit we haven't yet discovered?'

He sat down at his desk and totted up the amounts that were missing. They came to five hundred and forty-five francs. Where could they find that money? The annual audit was coming round shortly; it only needed that old fuss-pot of a colonel to take it into his head to check a total for the whole thing to be discovered. This time, Burle was sunk.

This thought made him feel calmer. He stopped swearing but a chill came over him as the stiff, despairing image of Madame Burle crossed his mind. At the same time, his heart was so full on his own account that he could hardly breathe.

'Come on,' he muttered to himself, 'the first thing to do is to see exactly how things stand with that bugger. There'll still be time to do something afterwards.'

He went round to Burle's office. From across the road he caught a glimpse of a skirt disappearing through a half-open door. Thinking that here was the key to the mystery, he crept quietly up to the door and listened. He at once recognized Mélanie's high-pitched voice, so characteristic of big women. She was complaining about the 'sofa-room gentlemen' and mentioned an I.O.U. that she couldn't see how she was going to pay; the bailiffs were in and everything was going to be sold up. Then, as the captain scarcely bothered to reply, saying that he hadn't a penny, she finally burst into tears and called him 'Mummy's little darling'. But, despite every endearment, she was obviously unable to get round him because all that Burle would say, in a firm, unsympathetic voice, was: 'Out of the question. Out of the question.' After an hour, she swept out in a fury. Astonished at the turn things were taking, the adjutant waited for a second before going into the room where the captain was sitting alone. He found him quite calm and, resisting the temptation to call him a double-dyed bastard, Laguitte kept his own counsel, anxious to discover the truth first.

There was nothing sinister to be seen in the office. A solid round leather cushion lay on the cane seat of the armchair placed in front of the dark wood table and in a corner stood the cash box, firmly shut. Summer was coming on and the song of a canary floated through the open window. Everything was spick and span and the cardboard boxes were giving off their reassuring smell of old documents.

'Wasn't it that bitch Mélanie that I saw going out as I came in?' enquired Laguitte.

Burle shrugged his shoulders and replied quietly:

'Yes, it was. She was after me again trying to squeeze a couple of hundred francs out of me... She won't get ten, she won't even get ten sous!'

'Won't she?' the other man replied, trying to sound him. 'I heard that you'd started seeing her again.'

'Me? Good God no! I've had enough of cows like that.'

Laguitte took his leave, completely mystified. Where on earth were those five hundred and forty-five francs going? Could the old reprobate have taken to drink or gambling now that he'd given up women? He made up his mind to take Burle by surprise that very evening, so as to be able to question his mother as well and perhaps manage to worm the truth out of him. That afternoon, his leg was hurting atrociously; he had been having a lot of trouble recently and had had to resign himself to taking to a stick to avoid limping too obviously. It irked him dreadfully and he would say, with a mixture of sorrow and anger, that he now really was a disabled soldier. Nevertheless, that evening he made the effort and, hauling himself out of his armchair, he dragged himself to the Rue des Récollets, leaning heavily on his stick under cover of darkness. It was striking nine as he arrived. The street door was ajar and he made his way up. He was on the third floor landing, taking a breather, when he was surprised to hear voices from the floor above. He thought he could recognize Burle's voice and so, out of curiosity, he went on upstairs. On the left, at the end of the corridor, he could see a ray of light coming from a doorway, but his boots creaked, the door was shut and he found himself in complete darkness.

'It's idiotic,' he thought to himself. 'It must be the cook going to bed.'

All the same, approaching as quietly as he could, he put his ear to the door. He could hear two voices and his jaw dropped: it was that bastard Burle and that hideous monster Rose.

'You promised me three francs,' she was saying. 'Let me have them.'

'I'll give you them tomorrow, my little darling,' the captain replied beseechingly. 'I couldn't manage it today. You know I always keep my promises.'

'No, give me my three francs now or else I'll send you packing downstairs.'

She must have got undressed already and been sitting on her trestle bed because it creaked every time she moved. The captain could be heard shifting from one foot to another like a cat on hot bricks. He went up to the bed:

'Do be a kind girl. Make room for me.'

'Leave me alone!' exclaimed Rose in her grating voice. 'I'll scream, I'll tell the old girl downstairs everything... Just hand over the three francs!'

She was insisting on her three francs with the stubbornness of a mule.

Burle lost his temper; then he wept; and finally he took a pot of jam out of his pocket, stolen from his mother's larder. Rose seized hold of it and, without bothering about bread, immediately started digging into it with the handle of a fork which was lying on top of her chest-of-drawers. It was good jam but when the captain thought he had succeeded in placating her, she pushed him away again as stubbornly as ever.

'You can stuff your jam. I want three francs!'

At this last demand, speechless with rage, the adjutant lifted his stick, ready to split open the door. Christ Almighty! What a bitch! And think of a captain in the French army standing for such a thing! He forgot all about Burle's nasty tricks, he could have strangled that horrible little skivvy for her behaviour. Fancy trying to bargain with an ugly mug like that! It was she who ought to be paying the captain. But he restrained himself, to hear what was going to happen.

'You're making me miserable,' the captain was saying, 'and when I've been so nice to you... I've given you a dress and some earrings and then a little watch... You don't even use my presents.'

'So what? Just to spoil them?... My Dad looks after all my things for me.'

'And what about all the money you've got out of me?'

'Dad's investing it for me.'

There was silence. Rose was thinking.

'Look, if you swear that you'll let me have six francs tomorrow night, I'll agree... So kneel down and swear you'll bring me six francs. No, you must get down on your knees.'

A shudder ran through the adjutant and he moved away from the door to lean against the wall. His legs were giving way under him and in the pitch-dark staircase he was brandishing his stick like a sabre. Good God Almighty! Now he could understand why that bastard Burle was staying home all the time and going to bed at nine o'clock! So that was his wonderful change of heart, by Christ! And with a revolting little trollop that the most depraved of troopers wouldn't have touched with a barge-pole!

'For God's sake,' said the adjutant out loud, 'why didn't he stick to Mélanie?'

What was to be done now? Go in and give the pair of them a taste of his stick? That was his first thought; then he took pity on the old lady downstairs. The best thing was to leave them to their rutting. You'd never get Burle to behave decently. When a man sank as low as that, the only thing to do was to throw a spadeful of mud over him and get rid of him like the rotting carcass of some poisonous beast. And even if you shoved his nose in his own shit, he'd only start again the next day and end up stealing a few sous to buy sticks of barley sugar for lice-ridden little beggar-girls. Christ Almighty! And it was money belonging to the

French army! And what about the honour of the flag? And the respectable name of Burle that would end up in the gutter! Christ Almighty! It mustn't end like that!

For a moment the adjutant half relented. If only he had those five hundred and forty-five francs! But he hadn't got a brass farthing. Yesterday evening, after getting drunk like any sub-altern, he'd lost an enormous sum at cards. He deserved to have to limp! He ought to have been killed!

So he left the loathsome couple to their antics and went downstairs to ring at Madame Burle's door. After a good five minutes, the old lady herself came to open it.

'I'm sorry,' she said. 'I thought that sleepy-head Rose was still here... I must go and give her a shake in bed.'

The adjutant stopped her.

'What about Burle?' he asked.

'Oh, he's been snoring away ever since nine o'clock. Would you like me to go and knock on his door?'

'No, please don't do that... All I wanted is a little evening chat with you.'

In the dining-room Charles was sitting in his usual place at the table and had just finished his Latin translation. But he had a terrified look on his face and his hands were trembling. Before sending him off to bed, his grandmother would read him accounts of famous battles, in order to stimulate his sense of pride in family heroism. That evening, the story of the *Avenger*, a ship full of dead and wounded which went to the bottom in the midst of the ocean, had left the little boy in a dreadful state of nerves, his head whirling with horrible nightmare visions.

Madame Burle asked Laguitte to let her finish reading the story. Then, as the last sailor shouted: 'Long live the Republic!', she solemnly shut the book. Charles was as white as a sheet.

'You heard that, didn't you?' the old lady said. 'It's the duty of every French soldier to die for his country.'

'Yes, Grandma.'

He kissed her on the forehead and went off to bed, trembling with fear, in the vast room where the slightest creak in the woodwork brought him out in a cold sweat.

The adjutant had been listening earnestly. Yes, by God, honour was honour and he must never let that scoundrel Burle bring dishonour on that poor old woman and the young lad.

Since the youngster had such a liking for military life, he must be able to get into Saint-Cyr, holding his head high. But the adjutant was still trying to dismiss from his mind a dreadful thought which had been troubling him ever since the mention of those six francs upstairs when Madame Burle picked up the lamp to show him out. As they walked past the captain's bedroom, she was surprised to see the key in the door, something she had never seen before.

'Come in,' she said, 'it's bad for him to sleep so much, it makes him lethargic.'

And before he could stop her, she pushed open the door and stood rooted to the spot when she saw that the room was empty. Laguitte had gone very red and he looked so foolish that all at once dozens of little details fell into place in her mind and she realized the truth.

'You knew about it, you knew all about it,' she stammered. 'Why didn't you warn me? Heavens above, in my own house, with his son sleeping in the next room...and with that scullery maid, that hideous-looking scullery maid!....And he's been stealing again, I can feel it in my bones!'

She stood there, white-faced and rigid. Then she added harshly:

'I wish he were dead!'

Laguitte took hold of her two hands and clasped them tightly for a second in his own. Then he quickly took his leave, for he had a lump in his throat and he would have burst into tears. Christ Almighty! This time his mind really was made up!

4

The audit was due to take place at the end of the month. The adjutant still had ten days to act. The very next day he limped his way to the Café de Paris, where he ordered a beer. Mélanie had gone very pale and Phrosyne took him his beer very reluctantly, fully expecting to have her face slapped. But the adjutant seemed very relaxed; he asked for a chair to rest his leg on and then drank his beer like any honest thirsty citizen. He had been sitting there an hour when he saw two brother officers crossing the square, the battalion commander Morandot and Captain Doucet.

'Come and have a drink,' he called out to them when they were in earshot.

The officers could hardly refuse. When the little barmaid had served them, Morandot asked:

'So you come here now, do you?'

Captain Doucet gave a knowing wink.

'Have you become one of the "sofa-room gents"?'

Laguitte merely laughed. Then they started pulling his leg about Mélanie, whereupon he gave a good-natured shrug of his shoulders; she was a fine figure of a woman, when all was said and done, and though people were very ready to make jokes about her, those who were prepared to run her down would still have been quite glad of a nibble. Then he turned towards the bar and, making his voice as affable as possible, he called out:

'Three more beers please, Madame Mélanie!'

Mélanie was so surprised that she stood up and fetched the beers herself. When she came to the table, the major engaged her in conversation, even going so far as to give her a gentle tap or two on her hand which was resting on the back of one of the chairs. At this, Mélanie herself, used to getting both kicks and ha'pence, began to flirt with the major, imagining that she had attracted the fancy of the old cripple, as she used to call him privately when talking with Phrosyne. Doucet and Morandot were exchanging glances. Well! Well! Damned if their old adjutant wasn't following in Skirty's footsteps! The regiment would certainly enjoy that!

Meanwhile Laguitte had been keeping one eye on the Place du Palais through the open door and now he suddenly exclaimed:

'I say, there's Burle!'

'Yes, this is the time he goes by,' said Mélanie, also coming to look. 'He comes this way every afternoon when he leaves the office.'

Despite his bad leg, the adjutant had jumped to his feet and, pushing his way through the chairs, he shouted:

'Hullo, Burle! Come and have a beer!'

The captain was quite taken aback and wondered how Laguitte came to be at Mélanie's with Doucet and Morandot. However, he automatically came over and stood, still hesitating, in the doorway.

The adjutant ordered a beer and then, turning round, he said:

'What on earth's the matter?. . . . Come in and sit down. Do you think anybody's going to eat you?'

When the captain had come in and sat down, there was a moment of embarrassment. As she brought the glass of beer, Mélanie's hands were trembling slightly, for she was in constant fear that there would be a row which would lead to the closing of her establishment. She now felt worried by the adjutant's amiability and was just trying to slip away when Laguitte invited her to have a drink with the gentlemen; and, acting as if he owned the place, he had already ordered a glass of anisette. Mélanie found herself forced to sit down between him and the captain. The adjutant kept saying, in a bullying tone:

'I insist that these ladies be shown respect!... For heaven's sake, let's behave like gentlemen! We'll drink Mélanie's health!'

Burle was looking at his glass with an embarrassed smile on his face. Shocked at the toast, the two other officers were trying to stand up and leave. Fortunately, the room was empty, with only the usual group of players having their customary game of dominoes who kept looking meaningly at each other each time they heard an oath; so scandalized were they at seeing so many people in the room that they were thinking of taking their game to the Café de la Gare if the military were going to invade their private domain. The only other occupants were a whole swarm of buzzing flies, attracted by the filth of the tables which Phrosyne nowadays bothered to wash only on Saturdays; she herself had gone back to her novel which she was reading sprawled out behind the bar.

'Well? Aren't you going to drink Madame Mélanie's health?' snapped the adjutant to Burle. 'You might at least show some manners!'

And as Doucet and Morandot once more stood up to leave:

'Wait a second, for God's sake! I'm coming with you. The trouble is that that brute there has never known how to behave!'

The two officers stood there, amazed at the adjutant's sudden outburst. Mélanie, trying to smooth matters down, laid a restraining hand on the two men's arms and gave a soothing laugh.

'No, leave me alone! Why wouldn't he drink your health? I'm not going to allow you to be insulted, do you understand?... I'm fed up to the teeth with this pig!'

At this insult, Burle went white to the teeth and, standing up, said to Morandot:

'What's the matter with him? He's invited me here to create a row... Is he drunk?'

'Damn and blast your eyes!' bellowed Laguitte.

And, rising to his feet on his trembling legs, he leant over and gave the captain a resounding slap across the face. Mélanie barely had time to duck to avoid receiving some of it on her own ear. There was a dreadful commotion. Phrosyne started to scream as if it was she who had been hit. The terrified domino players took refuge behind their table, imagining that all these soldiers were about to draw their sabres and hack each other to pieces. Meanwhile Morandot and Doucet had caught hold of the captain by his arms to prevent him from hurling himself on the adjutant and were leading him gently towards the door. Once outside, they succeeded in calming him down a little by putting all the blame on to Laguitte. The colonel would pass judgement, because they would go and see him to tell him all about the affair that very evening, since they had been witnesses. When they had persuaded Burle to leave, they went back into the café where Laguitte, in a very emotional state and close to tears, was pretending to be calm as he finished off his beer.

'Look here, Laguitte,' Major Morandot said, 'this is a very bad business. The captain isn't of equal rank with you and you know very well that it's impossible for him to be granted permission to fight you.'

'We'll see about that!' retorted the adjutant.

'But what did he do to you? He wasn't even talking to you... Two old comrades like you, it's absurd!'

Laguitte made a vague gesture.

'Never mind! He was getting on my nerves.'

That was all he would say and no one was ever any the wiser. All the same, it caused a tremendous stir. The general opinion in the regiment was that Mélanie, furious at having been dropped by the captain, had succeeded in getting her claws in Laguitte and by retailing horrific stories about Burle had persuaded the adjutant to slap the captain's face. Who would ever have credited it, of that hardened old sinner Laguitte, after all the dreadful things he used to say about women. Well, it'd been his turn to be curbed. Despite the general revulsion against Mélanie, this adventure set her up as a woman to be reckoned with, a woman to be both feared and desired, and henceforth her establishment was to flourish greatly.

The following day, the colonel sent for the adjutant and the captain. He gave them both a sharp dressing down, accusing them of bringing the army into disrepute in a notorious place. What did they intend to do about it now, since he could not possibly authorize them to fight? This was the question which had kept the whole regiment on tenterhooks ever since the previous day. An apology seemed to be excluded because of the slap in the face; however, since Laguitte could hardly stand because of his bad leg, it was felt that a reconciliation might be brought about if the colonel insisted.

'Well now,' the colonel went on, 'are you both prepared to let me act as arbitrator?'

'Excuse me, colonel,' the adjutant interposed, 'I wish to resign my commission.... Here's my resignation. I think that settles everything. Will you please fix the day for the duel?'

Burle looked at him in surprise. For his part, the colonel felt that he should make some observations of his own:

'That's a very serious decision you're making, Laguitte... You've only two years to go before retirement.'

The adjutant broke in again:

'That's my concern,' he said gruffly.

'Well, yes, certainly... Very well then, I'll forward your resignation and as soon as it's approved, I'll fix the day for the duel.'

The outcome of this interview stunned the regiment. What on earth had got into their crazy adjutant to make him want to risk getting his throat cut by his old comrade Burle? Mélanie's name was again mentioned and her being such a fine figure of a woman; all the officers had by now become obsessed by her and intrigued by the thought that she must be a really hot bit of stuff to make those two tough old campaigners lose their heads in that way. The battalion commander, Major Morandot, happening to meet Laguitte, made no secret of his concern. Assuming he wasn't killed, what was he going to live on? He had no private means and he'd have a job to afford anything better than dry bread on the pension he'd get from his decoration and his half-pay. While Morandot was speaking, Laguitte said not a word but stared vacantly into space, completely oblivious to anything apart from his own dogged obsessions. Then, when the other man tried to discover the reasons for his hatred of Burle, he merely repeated his former phrase, accompanied by the same vague gesture:

'He was getting on my nerves. Never mind!'

Every morning, in the barrack-room and in the mess, the first question was: 'Well, has his resignation come through yet?' Everyone was awaiting the duel and above all discussing its probable outcome. Most people thought that Laguitte would be run through in a couple of seconds because it was absurd to want to fight at his age, with a gammy leg that wouldn't even allow him to lunge. A few people, however, shook their heads knowingly: true, Laguitte had never been a genius; indeed, for the last twenty years his name had been a password for stupidity; but in the old days, he was known as the best swordsman in the regiment; and, brought up in the military school, he had risen from the ranks to become a battalion commander through his extreme bravery and complete disregard of danger. Burle, on the other hand, was a very ordinary swordsman and had the reputation of being a coward. Anyway, they'd all have to wait and see. And excitement grew as that confounded resignation was an interminable time coming through.

The man who was most worried and upset was certainly the adjutant: a week had already passed and the general audit was due to start the day after tomorrow. There was still no news. He was appalled by the thought that he might have slapped his old friend's face and sent in his resignation for nothing, without holding back the scandal for a single minute. If he were to be killed, however, at least he would be spared the aggravation of knowing about it; and if he killed Burle, as he was relying on doing, they would hush the matter up at once: he would have saved the honour of the army and the youngster would get into Saint-Cyr. But those miserable pen-pushers at the Ministry would have to get a move on, blast their eyes! The adjutant was on tenterhooks: he could be seen lurking around the post-office, looking out for each delivery, questioning the colonel's duty orderly, in order to find out what was happening. He spent sleepless nights and took to his stick, no longer caring what people might think when they saw him limping heavily.

On the day before the audit, Laguitte was making his way yet again to the colonel when he was dismayed to see Madame Burle who was taking Charles to school. He had not seen her since his last visit and she, for her part, had shut herself up in her flat in the Rue des Récollets. Almost in a state of collapse, he moved over to leave the whole pavement free for her and the boy. Neither of them greeted the other, which made the little boy open his eyes wide in astonishment. Stiff as a ramrod, Madame Burle brushed coldly past without the quiver of an eyelid. And when she had gone by, he looked after her with eyes full of bewilderment.

'For Christ's sake,' he grunted, forcing back his tears, 'don't tell me I'm becoming a woman!'

As he was going in to see the colonel, a captain in the office said:

'Well, that's it! Your papers have come through.'

'Ah!' he murmured, white as a sheet.

He could still see in his mind's eye that stiff and implacable old lady walking away holding her grandson's hand. Good God! To think that he had been awaiting the arrival of those papers so anxiously for the last week and now they had come he felt all upset and excited!

The duel took place next morning behind a low wall in the barrack yard. It was a bright sunny day, with a nip in the air. Laguitte had almost to be carried to the spot. One of his seconds gave him his arm while he supported himself on his stick with the other. Burle, whose yellow unhealthy-looking face was bloated with fat, was walking as if in a dream, like someone benumbed by a night of debauchery. Not a word was exchanged. Everyone wanted to put an end to the proceedings with all possible speed.

Captain Doucet, who was one of the seconds, engaged the swords, stood back and said:

'Go ahead, gentlemen!'

Burle attacked at once, in order to put Laguitte to the test and see what he might expect. For the last few days he had been living in a nightmare world of absurdity, unable to understand what was happening. He did, indeed, suspect something but he rejected this suspicion with a shudder for he could see death at the end of it and refused to believe that a friend could play such a macabre joke on him in order to settle such a matter. Moreover, Laguitte's leg gave him a certain confidence. He would prick him in the shoulder and there the matter would end.

For nearly two minutes the swords clinked and scraped together, steel against steel. Then the captain disengaged and attempted to lunge; but the adjutant, his wrist suddenly discovering its strength of earlier days, made a fierce parry 'in quinte' and, had the captain tried to counter, he would have been pierced through and through. Hastily, he broke off, ghastly pale as he felt himself at the mercy of this man who, for this once, had let him off. He was, at last, beginning to understand: this was an execution.

However, planted firmly on his bad legs, Laguitte, solid as a rock, was biding his time. The two opponents were staring at each other. Into Burle's baffled gaze there came an imploring look, a plea for mercy: he knew that he was about to die and, like a naughty child, he was promising never to do it again. But in the adjutant's eyes there was no spark of pity; honour was at stake and he must stifle any feeling of compassion that might be prompted by his own good nature.

'Let's finish if off!' he muttered to himself.

This time it was he who attacked. There was a flash of steel as his sword darted from right to left and back again and then like a streak of lightning planted itself straight in the captain's chest. He fell like a log, without a sound.

Laguitte let go of his sword and looked down at that poor bastard Burle lying flat on his back with his potbelly up in the air. He kept repeating, in an angry, broken voice:

'Christ Almighty! Christ Almighty!'

They led him away. Both his legs were affected and his seconds had to support him on both sides, for he was unable even to use his stick.

Two months later, the former adjutant was limping painfully in the sun along a deserted street in Vauchamp when he again met Madame Burle and young Charles. They were both dressed in deep mourning. He tried to avoid them but he had difficulty in walking and they were coming straight towards him, not altering their pace in the slightest. Charles still had his gentle, scared, girlish expression. Madame Burle, unbending as ever, was looking harsher and more gaunt. As Laguitte stepped sideways into a carriage gateway, leaving the whole street clear for them, she suddenly stopped in front of him and held out her hand. He hesitated, then finally put out his own and shook it, but he was trembling so much that he made the old lady's arm shake. They looked each other in the eyes without a word.

'Charles,' said his grandmother at last, 'shake hands with Major Laguitte.'

The child obeyed, without understanding. The major had gone as white as a sheet. He could hardly bring himself to touch the little boy's frail fingers. Then, realizing that he ought to say something, the only thing he could think of was:

'You're still hoping to send him to Saint-Cyr?'

'Certainly, when he's old enough.'

Next week, Charles was carried off by typhoid. One evening, pursuing her policy of making him tough, his grandmother had once more read him the heroic story of the *Avenger*. That night, he became delirious. In fact, he had died of fright.

THE WAY PEOPLE DIE

I

THE Comte de Verteuil was fifty-five years old. He came from one of the most illustrious of French families and was a man of great wealth. Disapproving of the government of the day, he had made the best use of his talents that he could. He had contributed learned articles to periodicals, which had resulted in his being elected to the Academy of Moral and Political Sciences.* He had launched into various enterprises, devoting himself in turn to agriculture, stockbreeding and the fine arts. For a short while he had even sat in Parliament where he had distinguished himself by his violence in the opposition.

The Comtesse Mathilde de Verteuil was forty-six years old. Her golden hair and fair complexion, which age seemed merely to have made more ethereal, gave her the reputation of still being the most adorable of the many adorable, beautiful, fair-haired women of Paris. Earlier, she had been a trifle thin; in her lovely maturity, her shoulders were as round and lustrous as ripe fruit. She had never been more beautiful. When she went into a drawing-room, the silken glow of her flesh and her gleaming golden hair made her seem like a star in its ascendant; she was the envy of women half her age.

The de Verteuils' marriage was of the sort never to arouse the slightest comment. It had been arranged as most marriages were in their circles. People even said that for at least six years they had got along very well together. They had a son, Roger, now a lieutenant, and a daughter, Blanche, whom they had married off a year ago to Monsieur de Bussac, a senior legal officer in the Conseil d'État.* They had joined the Establishment through their children. For years now they had gone their own separate ways, while still remaining good friends, albeit selfish ones. They consulted each other, behaved punctiliously towards each other in public and afterwards retired to their own quarters where they entertained their own personal friends as each saw fit.

However, one night Mathilde came back from a ball at about two o'clock in the morning. Her maid helped her to undress and, as she was leaving the room, she said:

'The master was not feeling very well this evening, ma'am.'

The countess, already half asleep, lazily turned her head and murmured:

'Is that so?'

She stretched herself out in the bed and added:

'Wake me up at ten tomorrow, I'm expecting my milliner.'

Next day, when the count did not come down for lunch, the countess, after first enquiring after him, decided to go upstairs to see him herself. She found him looking pale but as scrupulously polite as ever. Three doctors had already called, held a whispered consultation and left prescriptions; they would call again that evening. The sick man was being attended by two manservants who were bustling about in solemn silence, their steps discreetly muffled by the thick rugs. The very large cold bedroom seemed half-asleep but impeccably tidy, with not one piece of furniture out of place. This was illness with decorum and decency, fastidious and ready to receive visitors.

'Aren't you feeling well, my dear?' enquired the countess as she came in.

The count made an effort to smile.

'A little out of sorts,' he replied. 'All I need is rest. Thank you for troubling to come and see me.'

Two days went by. The room was still decorous; everything was in its place; medicine bottles disappeared into cupboards without leaving any trace on the furniture. The servants did not even allow boredom to show on their cleanshaven faces. However, the count knew that his life was in danger. He had insisted that the doctors tell him the truth and he was letting them have their way, without a murmur of complaint. In the main, he lay there with his eyes closed or else stared straight ahead as though communing with his loneliness.

The countess had been telling her friends that her husband was indisposed. She had made no change in her habits; she was eating, sleeping and going about her business in accordance with her normal routine. Every morning and evening she came up person-ally to ask her husband how he was.

'Well, are you feeling better, my dear?'

'I am indeed, much better, thank you, my dear Mathilde.'

'If you wished, I could stay with you.'

'No, there's no necessity. Julien and François can manage. There's no need for you to tire yourself.'

They understood each other. They had lived separate lives and they wanted to die separate deaths. The count was enjoying that bitter pleasure of the egoist who wishes to depart alone, without seeing around his bed the tedious spectacle of people pretending to mourn. Both for his own sake and for that of the countess, he wanted to make the unpleasantness of their final conversations as brief as possible. His last wish was to disappear with decorum, like a well-bred man who hopes not to disturb or offend anyone.

However, one evening he could barely breathe and he knew that he would not last the night. So when the countess came upstairs that evening to pay him her customary visit, he said to her, managing to produce a final smile:

'Don't go out. . . I'm not feeling very well.'

He was anxious to protect her from what society might be tempted to say. For her part, she was expecting to receive such a warning from him. She settled herself in a chair in his bedroom. The doctors were now in constant attendance on the dying man. The two servants were still performing their final duties with the same quiet attentiveness. The children Roger and Blanche had been sent for and were standing at the bedside with their mother. Other relatives were in an adjacent room. The night passed in solemn expectation. In the morning the sacraments were brought and the count took communion in front of everyone; he was giving his final support to religion. His ceremonial duties were concluded; he was free to die.

But he was in no hurry and seemed to be calling on new forces in order to avoid dying noisily or in disorder. Only his breathing filled the vast sombre room with a rasping sound like that of a clock whose mechanism is not functioning properly. He was gentlemanly in his leavetaking. And when he had embraced his wife and children, he gently pushed them away and fell back facing the wall. He died alone.

Then one of the doctors leant over, closed his eyes and said in a low voice: 'It's all over.'

The silence was broken by sighs and sobs. The countess, Roger and Blanche had fallen on their knees and were weeping into their clasped hands; their faces could not be seen. Then her two children led their mother away; as she reached the door, she stopped and, as though to emphasize the depth of her grief, her body was shaken by one final sob. And now the dead man became merely a part of the solemn ceremonial of his funeral.

The doctors departed; their shoulders were bowed and they looked vaguely sorry. A parish priest had been asked to watch over the body. The two servants stayed with the priest and sat in their chairs, stiff and straight-backed; this was how they had expected their duties to end. One of them caught sight of a spoon lying on a piece of furniture; he stood up and quickly slipped it into his pocket so that nothing might disturb the impeccable tidiness of the room.

Downstairs in the large drawing-room, hammering could be heard; it was the tapestry-hangers turning the room into a mortuary chapel. It took a whole day to embalm the corpse; the embalmer worked behind closed doors, alone with his assistants. When the count was carried down the following morning and exposed to view, he was wearing evening-dress and had all the freshness of youth.

From nine o'clock onwards on the morning of the funeral, the house was filled with the hum of voices. The son and son-in-law of the deceased greeted the throng of callers in a ground-floor drawing-room; they bowed, maintaining the polite silence of people who are in a state of grief. All the dignitaries who were coming to pay their last respects belonged to the aristocracy, the army and the judiciary: there were even senators and members of the Academy.

Finally, at ten o'clock, the funeral procession set off for the church. The hearse was that provided for first-class funerals, with plumes and silver-fringed hangings. The pall-bearers were a French Marshal, a duke who was an old friend of the deceased, a former Minister, and an Academician. Roger de Verteuil and Monsieur de Bussac led the mourners. Behind came the funeral procession, a slow-moving tide of black-gloved people wearing black neckties, all persons of consequence who found difficulty in breathing in the cloud of dust raised as they shuffled along like a flock of sheep.

The neighbourhood had been alerted and every window was crammed with spectators; people were lining the streets, raising their hats and shaking their heads as they watched the hearse pass on its triumphal way. The traffic was halted by the interminable line of mourning carriages, largely empty; omnibuses and cabs were forming long queues at every crossroads and you could hear the cabbies swearing and cracking their whips. Meanwhile the countess had stayed at home and shut herself up in her rooms; she had announced that she was too grief-stricken to appear. She was lying dreamily on a sofa, playing idly with a tassel of her belt and watching the ceiling with a great feeling of relief.

The church service lasted almost two hours. The clergy were all on parade; ever since the early morning, there had been nothing but priests everywhere, rushing round in surplices, issuing orders, mopping their brows and noisily blowing their noses. A catafalque stood in the centre of the black-draped nave, blazing with candles. The mourners finally found their places, with the ladies on the left and the gentlemen on the right; and the organ boomed out its lament, the deep-voiced cantors rumbled, the choir-boys wailed in shrill sorrow while long green flames darted from the torch-holders, adding their funereal pallor to the pomp and circumstance of the ceremony.

'Isn't Fauré supposed to be going to sing?' a deputy enquired of his neighbour.

'Yes, I believe so,' replied the neighbour, a former Préfet, meanwhile smiling at the ladies across the aisle.

And as the singer's voice soared, setting the whole nave ringing, he added in a low voice, swaying his head in delight: 'What a technique, eh? What resonance!'

All those present were enraptured. The ladies sat with vacant smiles on their lips, thinking of their evenings at the Opera. What a wonderful voice Fauré had! A friend of the deceased even said:

'He's never sung better! What a pity old Verteuil can't hear him, he liked his voice so much!'

The cantors walked round the catafalque in their black copes. The priests, a good twenty in number, added to the elaborate ceremonial, waving their hands about, repeating Latin phrases and brandishing holy water sprinklers. And finally the congregation themselves filed past the coffin, handing the sprinklers from one to the other. Then it was time for everyone to leave, after shaking hands with the family. As they gathered outside, they were dazzled by the light.

It was a lovely June day and threads of gossamer were floating in the warm air. At this stage in the proceedings, in the little square in front of the church, there was much bustling to and fro and the procession took a long time to re-form. Those who did not wish to go further now made themselves scarce. At the end of a street, a couple of hundred yards away, you could already see the plumes on the hearse waving in the air, then vanishing while the square was still jammed with carriages. Carriage doors were slamming and horses trotting briskly over the paving sets. However, everyone eventually rejoined the procession and it moved off in the direction of the cemetery.

People were settling themselves comfortably in their carriages; you could almost imagine, in this springlike air, that you were making your way slowly towards the Bois de Boulogne. As the hearse was now out of sight, the burial quickly went out of people's minds and everyone started chatting; the ladies discussed the summer season while the men talked business.

'Are you going to Dieppe again this year, my dear?'

'Perhaps. But it won't be before August. . . We're going down to our estate on the Loire on Saturday.'

'And then, my dear fellow, he discovered the letter and there was a duel, oh, quite a gentlemanly affair, nothing more than a scratch, I dined with him in the club that evening. He even took five hundred francs off me.'

'There's a meeting of shareholders the day after tomorrow, isn't there? They want me to join the board but I'm so frantically busy that I don't know whether I'll be able to.'

The funeral procession had just entered an avenue where the trees were casting cool shadows and the birds were twittering gaily in the sunlit foliage. All at once, unthinkingly, one of the ladies, leaning out of her carriage window, blurted out:

'Oh, isn't it absolutely delightful here!'

At that very moment the procession turned into the Montparnasse cemetery.* Everyone fell silent and the only sound was that of the wheels grating on the gravel. They had to go a long way, for the Verteuil family tomb was at the far end, on the left. It was a tall, white marble building, rather like a chapel, richly decorated with statues. They placed the coffin in front of the chapel door and the speeches began.

There were four of them. The former Minister went over the political career of the deceased, whom he depicted as a modest genius who would have saved France had he not disdained intrigue. This speaker was followed by a friend who spoke of the private virtues of the man whom they were gathered to mourn. Then an unknown gentleman made a speech on behalf of a company of which the count had been honorary chairman. Finally a drab little man expressed the sorrow felt by the *Académie des sciences morales et politiques.*

Meanwhile the mourners had started looking at the neighbouring graves and reading the inscriptions on the marble slabs. Those who were making some effort to listen were able to catch only a few words here and there. One tight-mouthed old man, having succeeded in hearing these words: '...the qualities of feeling, the generosity and kindness of his noble heart...' jerked his chin and muttered: 'Oh yes, I knew him very well, he was an utter scoundrel!'

The last farewells rose into the air and vanished. After the priests had blessed the body, everyone left and in this remote corner of the cemetery, the only people left were the gravediggers who now lowered the coffin. The ropes made a quiet scraping sound and the oak coffin creaked. The Comte de Verteuil had come home to his ancestors.

Meanwhile, on her sofa, the countess had not stirred. She was still playing with the tassel of her belt and looking up at the ceiling, lost in her thoughts; and gradually a rosy flush coloured the cheeks of this most adorable of fair-haired Parisian beauties.

II

Madame Guérard was a widow. Her husband, whom she had lost eight years ago, had been a judge. She belonged to the upper ranks of the middle classes and owned property worth two million francs. She had three children, three sons, each of whom had inherited half a million francs on the death of their father. However, these scions of this stern, cold and straitlaced family had sprouted wildly. Where they had picked up their desires and vices, God alone knew; but the fact was that in a very few years they had squandered every sou of their five hundred thousand francs. Charles, the eldest, had developed a passion for engineering and had dissipated vast sums on extraordinary mechanical inventions. The downfall of the second son, Georges, had been brought about by women, while the third son, Maurice, had been swindled by a friend over a venture to set up a theatre. By now, all three were dependent on their mother who, while prepared to offer them board and lodging, was prudent enough not to let the keys of any cupboard out of her sight.

All four of them lived in an immense flat in the Rue de Turenne, in the Marais* district of Paris. Madame Guérard was sixty-eight and with advancing age had developed a number of little quirks. She insisted that her house should be as quiet and tidy as a convent. She was extremely mean, keeping check on every lump of sugar, locking away with her own hands any bottle that had been opened and issuing linen and crockery as the particular occasion required. Her sons were doubtless fond of her and despite their selfishness and their age—they were all in their thirties—their mother's word was law. All the same, whenever she saw herself alone, surrounded by these three great hulking sons of hers, she felt something of an inner panic; she was always afraid that they might ask her for money which she would not feel able to refuse. Because of this, she had been careful to put her money into real estate: she owned three houses in Paris and some building sites in Vincennes. These properties caused her a great deal of trouble; but she was happy because they gave her a good excuse for not handing out large sums of money at any one time.

Charles, Georges and Maurice would indeed have eaten their mother out of house and home if they had been given the chance. They were solidly encamped and squabbled over every morsel, each meanwhile accusing the other of greed. Their mother's death would make them rich once more; they knew this and their knowledge served them as a pretext to sit tight and do nothing. Although the subject was never mentioned, they were constantly preoccupied with the question of how the estate would be divided up; if they could not come to some agreement, they would have to sell up, which is always a disastrous operation. And they thought of these matters without any evil in their minds but merely because you have to think of everything. They were cheerful, good-tempered and moderately honest; and, like everyone else, they wanted their mother to live as long as possible. She didn't bother them. They were merely biding their time.

One evening, on leaving table, Madame Guérard felt unwell. Her sons insisted that she lie down and when she assured them that she was feeling better and that it was only a sick headache, they left her with her maid. But the next day the old lady's condition worsened and the family doctor was sufficiently worried to ask for a second opinion. Madame Guérard was seriously ill. And so for a week, high drama was played out in the dying woman's bedroom.

As soon as she found herself bedridden, her first concern had been to have every key in the house brought to her bedside, and she had hidden them under her pillow. She had every intention of continuing to rule the household from her bed and to protect the cupboards from being stripped bare. Many conflicting feelings were struggling in her mind and she was so torn by doubt that it was only after much hesitation that she was able to decide what to do. As her three sons stood there in her bedroom, she would eye them uncertainly; she was seeking inspiration.

One day, she felt that she could trust Georges; so, beckoning to him, she whispered:

'Look, here's the key to the larder, go and get some sugar out. Be careful to lock it up again properly and bring the key back to me.'

Another day, she felt suspicious of Georges and kept a close watch on him as soon as he showed signs of moving, as if scared of seeing him slip the knick-knacks on the mantelshelf into his pocket. She called to Charles and this time handed him a key, whispering:

'My maid will go with you, keep your eye on her while she gets the sheets out and then lock the cupboard up yourself.'

On her death-bed she was tormented by one thought: she would no longer be in charge of the household expenditure. She recalled her children's fecklessness, she knew that they were lazy, greedy, crackbrained and grasping. She had long since ceased to have any regard for them. They had realized none of her dreams, they offended all her ideas of thrift and austerity. Her affection alone survived and forgave. In her pleading eyes, you could see her begging them to wait until she was no longer there before clearing out the drawers and sharing out the estate. Any attempt to divide it up before her eyes would have been torture for her avaricious spirit, now so close to extinction.

However, Charles, Georges and Maurice were being very kind to her. They arranged for one of them to be always near at hand and they showed honest affection in all they did for her. Yet in spite of themselves they brought into the sickroom the unconcern of the outer world, the aroma of their cigars, their interest in the news of the town. And in her selfishness, the sick woman suffered at not being at the centre of her children's lives, now that she was dying. Then, as she grew weaker, her suspicions led to an ever-increasing embarrassment between the young men and herself. Even had they not been thinking of the considerable fortune that they were due to inherit, she would have encouraged them to do so by the way in which she was defending it to her very last gasp. She kept watching them so narrowly and with such obvious fear in her eyes that they had to look away. Then she started thinking that they were waiting for signs that her death-throes had begun; as indeed they were, for their thoughts were being constantly drawn back to this idea by the mute questioning look in her eyes. It was she herself who was lending fuel to their cupidity. When she saw one of them lost in thought, she would call out to him, white in the face:

'Come over here, close to me... What are you thinking about?'

'Nothing, Mother.'

But he had given a start. She would slowly shake her head and say:

'I'm causing you a lot of bother, my sons. Never mind, don't worry, I shan't be here much longer!'

They would gather round her, promising that they loved her and would help her to get well. She would give a stubborn jerk of her head and reply: 'No!' She became more and more distrustful. Her death-throes were atrocious, poisoned by thoughts of money.

Her illness had lasted three weeks. There had already been consultations with five doctors, the best in Paris. Madame Guérard's maid was helping her sons to look after her and, despite all efforts, a certain untidiness had crept into the house. Hope had now been abandoned, for the doctors had confirmed that the sick woman might die at any moment.

Then one morning, when her sons thought that she was asleep, they were quietly discussing among themselves, by the window, a problem that had arisen. It was July 15th. Madame Guérard had been accustomed to collect the rents in person. They were embarrassed because they could not see how they could collect these rents themselves. The concierge had already asked for instructions but their mother was so weak that they could not consider discussing business matters with her. On the other hand, should the worst happen, they would need the money from the rents in order to meet certain personal expenses.

'Well now,' whispered Georges, 'if you like I'll go and call on the tenants... They'll understand the situation and pay me.'

But the other two did not seem to relish the idea. They too had become suspicious.

'We could come with you,' said Charles. 'All three of us have some expenses to settle up.'

'That's all right. I'll hand the money over to you.... Surely you don't imagine that I'm capable of making off with it?'

'No, but it would be better for us all to go together. It would look more businesslike.'

And they looked at each other with eyes already glinting with anger and resentment at the thought that the division of the estate was looming up and each of them wanted to make sure he got the lion's share. All of a sudden, Charles put into words a thought that was already in the others' minds.

'Look here, the best thing to do will be to sell up... If we're already starting to quarrel now, we'll soon be at each other's throats.'

At this moment they heard a death-rattle and turning their heads they saw their mother, pale as a sheet and trembling all over, who had frantically lifted herself half up in bed. She had heard what they were saying and, stretching out her emaciated arms, she called out several times in a horrified voice: 'Children, children...' and then fell back convulsed on to her pillow. She died with the dreadful thought that her children were robbing her.

The three sons fell, terrified, on to their knees at the dead woman's bedside, kissing her hands and sobbing as they closed her eyes. For a brief moment they had returned to childhood and realized that they were orphans. But the horrible circumstances of her death stayed in their minds and filled them with a feeling of remorse and hatred. The body was laid out by the maid and they sent for a nun to keep watch over it. Meanwhile the three sons were kept busy notifying the death, ordering the letters announcing it and making the arrangements for the funeral. At night, they took it in turns to keep watch with the nun. In the room, with the curtains drawn, the dead woman lay stretched out in the middle of the bed with her hands clasped and a silver crucifix lying on her chest. A candle was burning beside her and a sprig of palm was standing in a vessel of holy water. The chill shudder of dawn brought the vigil to an end; the nun asked for a glass of hot milk because she was not feeling very well.

An hour before the funeral procession was due to set off, the staircase was thronged with people. The carriage entrance was hung with black draperies fringed with silver and the coffin lay there as though at the end of a chapel, surrounded by candles and covered with wreaths and bunches of flowers. Each caller took a sprinkler and sprinkled the corpse with holy water. At eleven o'clock, the procession set off with the three sons leading the mourners. Behind them came judges, some leading industrialists, a solemn collection of representatives of the middle classes, walking with measured tread as they cast furtive glances at the passers-by who stopped to watch. Twelve carriages brought up the rear of the procession. They were remarked upon and counted as they passed through the quarter.

Meanwhile, the onlookers were sympathizing with Charles, Georges and Maurice as they walked behind the coffin in their dark coats and black gloves, with their cheeks red with tears and their heads reverently cast down. Indeed, the general verdict was unanimous: they were burying their mother in style. It was a first-class hearse and people calculated that it would cost them several thousand francs. One old lawyer said with a sly grin:

'If Madame Guérard had been paying for the funeral herself, she'd have had six carriages less.'

The church porch was draped in black, there was organ music and the absolution was given by the vicar of the parish. Then, after filing past the coffin, the mourners came up to the three sons standing in line ready to shake hands with those who were unable to proceed to the cemetery. For ten minutes, biting their lips and holding back their tears, they stood with arms outstretched, shaking hands with people they did not even recognize.

They were greatly relieved when the church had emptied and they found themselves once more walking slowly behind the coffin.

The Guérard family vault was in the Père-Lachaise cemetery.* Many mourners remained on foot while others got into the carriages. The funeral procession crossed the Place de la Bastille and went along the Rue de la Roquette. Passers-by looked up and raised their hats, while workmen of the district watched the rich funeral go by as they munched their sausages sandwiched between huge chunks of bread.

The procession turned right as it entered the cemetery and halted in front of the tomb: a small monument in the shape of a Gothic chapel on which were written the words 'The Guérard Family', cut in black letters on the pediment. The open-work cast-iron gate stood wide open, allowing a glimpse of an altar-table inside, on which candles were burning. All around were similar tombs in rows like the streets of a town; they reminded you of the shop-fronts of furniture-dealers, with wardrobes, chests-of-drawers and secretaires, all recently finished, arranged for display in symmetrical groups. The mourners' attention wandered as they examined the architecture of the tombs and tried to find a little shade under the trees of a nearby avenue. One of the ladies had gone over to admire a magnificent bush of sweet-scented roses growing on one of the graves.

In the meantime the coffin had been lowered. A priest was saying the final prayers as the gravediggers in their blue jackets stood waiting a few yards away. The three sons were shaken by sobs, with their eyes fixed on the gaping vault from which the flagstone had been lifted; it was in this cool shade that they too would one day rest. As the gravediggers approached, their friends led them away.

And two days later in the office of their mother's solicitor, they were going at each other hammer and tongs, teeth clenched and not a tear to be seen, like sworn enemies determined not to relinquish one single penny. It would have been not in their own interest not to rush into selling their various properties; but they flung unpleasant truths in each other's faces: Charles would squander every penny on his madcap inventions; Georges was certainly being fleeced by some tart; Maurice was surely involved in some wild speculation which would swallow up all their capital. The solicitor vainly tried to persuade them to reach an amicable agreement. When they parted they were threatening to issue writs against each other.

Their dead mother was coming back to life inside them, in all her miserliness and terror of being robbed. Once death has been poisoned by money, nothing but anger can result and the living will fight over the coffins of their dead.

III

At the age of twenty, Monsieur Rousseau had married Adèle Lemercier, an orphan of eighteen. On their wedding day, the pair of them possessed as their sole worldly wealth a total of seventy francs. In the beginning they sold notepaper and sticks of sealing wax in the carriage entrance of a house. Next they rented a shop no bigger than a pocket-handkerchief and spent the following ten years in this miserable hole gradually working up their business. Now they had a stationer's shop in the Rue de Clichy* which was worth a good fifty thousand francs.

Adèle was not very robust; she had always had a slight cough. The shop was airless and she was perpetually stuck behind the counter. Neither of these things was good for her. They had consulted a doctor who had advised rest and a nice walk when the weather was suitable. But such prescriptions are impossible to follow if you want to put together a little capital and enjoy it in peace. Adèle said that she would rest and start taking her walks as soon as they had sold up and retired to the country.

However, Monsieur Rousseau was worried to see his wife looking so pale and with such a hectic flush in her cheeks. But he had his shop to attend to and could not be forever on the look-out to prevent her from behaving unwisely. For weeks on end he was unable to find the time to discuss her health with her. Then, if he happened to hear her little dry cough, he would get angry and make her put on her shawl and come for a walk with him up the Champs-Elysées. But she would come back tired and coughing worse than ever; Monsieur Rousseau would once more become absorbed in all his problems and his wife's condition would again be forgotten until a new crisis arose. Business is like that: you die in harness without ever having had time to look after yourself.

One day Monsieur Rousseau took the doctor aside and asked him bluntly if his wife's life was in danger. The doctor began by saying that you must trust to nature and that he had seen many people more ill than Adèle who had pulled through. On being pressed, he admitted that Monsieur Rousseau's wife had tuberculosis and was indeed in an advanced stage of the disease. Rousseau went pale. He loved his wife for the help she had given him in setting up their business together, long before they could look forward to eating white bread every day. In Adèle he had found not only a wife but an associate whose energy and intelligence he greatly appreciated. Were he to lose her, it would be his business as well as his love that would suffer. However, he must be brave; he could not afford to shut down his shop in order to give way to his sorrow. So he kept his feelings to himself and tried not to perturb Adèle by appearing with eyes red with tears. He continued his daily round. After a month, if he happened to think of these sad matters, he had managed to persuade himself that doctors are often wrong. His wife did not seem to be more ill. And he reached the stage of watching her slowly die before his eyes without feeling too much grief himself; preoccupied with his business, he was expecting a disaster but kept putting it off to some unknown future date.

Sometimes Adèle would say:

'You'll see how well I'll be once we've retired to the country! My goodness, we've only got eight years to wait. They'll soon pass.'

And it never once occurred to Monsieur Rousseau that they could in fact retire at once, with more modest savings. For one thing, Adèle wouldn't like it; when you've set yourself a figure, you have to stick to it.

Meanwhile Madame Rousseau had already had to take to her bed a couple of times, but had been able to get up and return to her place behind the counter. The neighbours said: 'There's a little woman who's not long for this world.' They were not mistaken. At the very moment that stocktaking was due to start, she had to take to her bed for the third time. The doctor came in the morning, chatted with her and casually signed a prescription. But Monsieur Rousseau was warned and knew that the end was near. However, his stocktaking kept him downstairs in the shop and all he could do was to take five minutes off now and then. He accompanied the doctor upstairs and then came down with him. He would go back for a second time before lunch and get to bed at eleven o'clock, tucked away in a cubby-hole where he had had a trestle bed set up. The sick woman was being tended by their maid Françoise. She was a dreadful girl from the Auvergne;* she had large clumsy hands and her cleanliness and manners left much to be desired. She treated the dying woman with scant ceremony, brought her her medicines with surly looks and made a fearful clatter as she swept out of the room, leaving it in a deplorable state of untidiness: filthy medicine bottles were left lying about on the chest-of-drawers, wash-basins were never cleaned, dusters were left hanging on the backs of chairs and the floor was so cluttered up that you hardly knew where to put your feet. Despite all this, Madame Rousseau remained uncomplaining and merely knocked on the wall when the maid failed to reply to her call. Françoise had other things to do besides looking after her; she had to keep the shop clean, cook meals for the master and his assistants, not to mention going shopping and other unscheduled tasks. So Madame couldn't expect her to be constantly at her beck and call. She'd look after her when she could spare the time.

In any case, even from her bed, Adèle maintained her interest in the business; she kept herself informed as to the sales and every evening she would ask her husband how things were going. She was worried about the stocktaking. As soon as her husband was able to slip away and come upstairs, her only concern was to discover the probable size of the profits. She was distressed to hear that it had been a rather poor year, fourteen hundred francs less than the previous year. Even when she was prostrate with fever, she was still able to remember last week's orders; she worked out the amounts and, in fact, was still running the business. And if he forgot the time, it was she who sent him back downstairs to his job. Staying up with her wouldn't help her to get better and it was bad for business. She felt sure that the assistants were sitting looking out of the window and she would add:

'Do go down and don't forget to get in lots of registers because the school year is beginning soon and we might run out of them.'

For a long time she deluded herself as to the true state of her health. She kept on hoping that she would be out of bed next day and take up her usual place behind the counter again. She even made plans: if she could go out soon, they'd go and spend Sunday in Saint-Cloud.* She had never felt like seeing trees so much in her life! Then suddenly one morning she became very serious.

During the night, as she had lain awake all alone with her eyes open, she had realized that she was going to die. She said nothing until that evening but lay looking up at the ceiling, thinking. In the evening, she asked her husband not to go away and speaking quietly, in a matter-of-fact voice, as if showing him a bill, she said:

'Tomorrow I want you to go and fetch a solicitor. There's one quite close by, in the Rue Saint-Lazare.'

'What for?' exclaimed Monsieur Rousseau. 'There's no need to do that yet, that's for sure!'

But she went on in her calm, reasonable way:

'Perhaps not. But it will stop me worrying if I know that our affairs are in order. When we got married, we agreed to have a joint estate. That was when neither of us had two pennies to rub together. But now we do have a little money, I don't want any family to come along and take it away from you... My sister Agatha isn't so nice that I want to leave her anything. I'd sooner take it with me.'

And she insisted that her husband should go along next day and fetch a solicitor. When he came, she questioned him closely, anxious to make absolutely sure that the will could not be contested. When the will had been signed and the solicitor had left, she stretched out in her bed and said quietly:

'Now I'll die happy... I'd certainly earned the right to retire to the country and I admit that I'm sorry about missing that. But at least you'll be able to go... You must promise to retire to the place we'd decided on, you know, the place where your mother was born, near Melun.* That thought would make me happy.'

Monsieur Rousseau burst into tears. She consoled him and gave him some good advice. If he got tired of living alone, he ought to get married again; but he shouldn't choose too young a woman, because girls who marry widowers do it for their money. And she mentioned the name of an acquaintance of theirs whom she would be glad for him to marry.

That very night her death-throes began. They were frightful; she was suffocating and pleading for air. Françoise had dropped off to sleep in her chair. The only thing that Monsieur Rousseau could do as he stood beside the dying woman's bed was to hold her hand tightly, tell her that he was with her and would not leave her. In the morning she suddenly became very calm. She was very pale and breathing gently with closed eyes. Her husband thought that it would be safe for him to go downstairs with Françoise to open up the shop. When he came back upstairs he found his wife still looking very pale and lying in exactly the same position; but her eyes were open. She was dead.

Monsieur Rousseau had been expecting her to die for so long that he did not shed any tears but merely felt suddenly quite exhausted. He went downstairs again, watched Françoise put up the shutters once more and then wrote out in his own hand the words: 'Closed on account of death' on a piece of paper which he stuck on the centre shutter with four pieces of sealing wax. Upstairs the whole morning was spent cleaning and tidying up the room. Françoise passed a cloth over the floor, removed the medicine bottles and put a lighted candle and a cup of holy water beside the dead woman. Adèle's sister Agatha would be coming and she had a viper-like tongue. The maid did not want to give her the chance of calling her a slut. Monsieur Rousseau had sent one of his assistants to complete the necessary formalities. He himself went off to the church where he spent a long time discussing the charges for the funeral. He could see no reason why he should be rooked merely because he had been bereaved. He had been very fond of his wife and he felt sure that if she could still see him, she would be pleased that he was haggling with the priests and undertakers. However, he wanted a proper funeral; after all, there were the neighbours to consider. In the end, he reached an agreement to pay the church one hundred and sixty francs and the undertakers three hundred. He calculated that with all the extras, he would not get away under five hundred francs.

When Monsieur Rousseau went home he found his sister-in-law Agatha comfortably installed beside the dead woman. Agatha was a tall, gaunt woman with red eyes and thin bluish lips. He and his wife had not been on speaking terms with her for the last two years and had stopped seeing her. She stood up politely and embraced her brother-in-law. Death puts an end to all our disagreements. And now Monsieur Rousseau, who had been unable to shed a tear all that morning, suddenly burst into sobs as he saw his poor wife lying there stiff and pale, more pinched than ever and her cheeks so fallen-in that he could hardly recognize her. Agatha remained dry-eyed. She had ensconced herself in the best armchair and was running a calculating eye round the room as though drawing up a careful inventory of all the furniture. She had not yet raised the question of claims on the estate but it was plain that she was very much concerned and must be wondering if there was a will.

On the morning of the funeral, when it came to placing the body into the coffin, it was discovered that the undertakers had made a mistake and had sent one that was too short. They had to go and fetch another. Meanwhile the hearse stood waiting in front of the shop and the neighbours were all agog. This caused Monsieur Rousseau further distress. If only the delay might bring her back to life! But at last they carried poor Madame Rousseau downstairs and the coffin was displayed for a brief ten minutes in the entrance, which was draped in black. About a hundred people were waiting in the street, local tradesmen, other tenants of the house, friends of the family and a few workmen wearing their short tunics. The funeral procession set out, led by Monsieur Rousseau as chief mourner.

As it passed by, the women of the neighbourhood hurriedly crossed themselves and whispered: 'It's the stationer's wife, isn't it? The little woman with such a sallow complexion who was all skin and bones? Ah well, she'll be better off where she's going. But isn't life sad! Them with all their money and slaving away at their business so as to be able to enjoy their old age. Well, how will she be enjoying it now?' And they thought Monsieur Rousseau looked most distinguished as he walked along bareheaded behind the hearse, all by himself, with his sparse hair blowing in the wind.

In church the priests made short work of the funeral service, which lasted only forty minutes. Agatha had sat down in the front row and seemed to be counting the candles. No doubt she was thinking that her brother-in-law could have been less ostentatious; after all, if there was no will and she inherited half her sister's estate, she would have to pay her share of the funeral expenses. The priests said a final prayer, the holy water sprinkler was passed from hand to hand and they left the church. Almost everybody slipped away. The carriages drove up and a handful of ladies climbed into them. Behind the hearse there were now only Monsieur Rousseau, still bareheaded, and about thirty others, friends who did not dare to go away. The hearse was draped in a simple black cloth adorned with a white fringe. The passers-by raised their hats and walked quickly on.

As Monsieur Rousseau had no family vault, he had merely taken a five-year concession in the Montmartre cemetery,* promising himself to exhume his wife later on and install her in her permanent resting-place when he had bought a grant in perpetuity.

The hearse stopped at the end of an avenue and the coffin was carried through the low gravestones to a hole dug in the soft earth. The mourners shifted from one foot to the other in silence. The priest mumbled a few words and left. All around there stretched tiny gardens enclosed in iron railings, graves planted with wallflowers and evergreens; the white tombstones seemed quite new and cheerful amidst all this greenery. Monsieur Rousseau was greatly attracted by one of the stones, a slim column topped by a symbolic urn. That morning a stone-mason had called and pestered him with suggestions for tombstones. He reflected that once he had bought his lease in perpetuity, he would have a similar column erected with the same sort of pretty vase placed over his wife's grave.

But now Agatha led him away, and when they had got back to the shop she at last decided to raise the question of claims on the estate. When she learned that there was a will, she shot to her feet and flounced out of the room, slamming the door behind her. That was the last time she'd set foot in that pigsty! And Monsieur Rousseau still felt a lump in his throat from time to time, but the thing which really made him feel fidgety and upset was the thought that the shop was shut on a weekday.

IV

It had been a hard January. No work and not a bite to eat in the house or a lump of coal for a fire. The Morisseaus were destitute and starving. She was a washerwoman and her husband a bricklayer. They lived in the Rue Cardinet, in the Batignolles* district of Paris, in a gloomy old house that stank to high heaven. Their room on the fifth floor was so dilapidated that the rain came through the holes in the ceiling. But they would not have complained if only their son Charlie did not need proper food if he was to grow up into a man.

He was a sickly child who fell ill on the slightest provocation. When he had been fit to go to school and had worked hard, trying to learn everything at once, he would come home ill; yet he was such a bright boy, a little ugly duckling, too good-natured by half and very articulate for his age. On the days when they hadn't had even a crust of bread to give him, his parents would cry like children, the more so because little children were dying like flies in every part of the house because it was so insalubrious.

The streets were iced up and so Charlie's father at last managed to find a job. He hacked the ice out of the gutters with a pick and in this way managed to bring home two francs in the evening. Until building work picked up again, this would at least manage to keep the wolf from the door.

But one day when he came home, he found Charlie in bed. His mother did not know what was the matter with him. She had sent him over to his aunt's in Courcelles; she was an old-clothes dealer and might be able to find a warmer jacket for him than his linen smock, in which he was shivering with cold. His aunt had only some old men's overcoats which were too large and the little lad had come back trembling and looking as fuddled as if he had been drinking. Now his face was all red as it lay on the pillow and he was gabbling nonsense: he thought he was playing marbles, and he was singing snatches of songs.

His mother had hung a tattered piece of shawl up at the window to close off a broken pane; there were only two window-panes left uncovered at the top through which you could see the livid grey sky. The wardrobe was empty; they were so poverty-stricken that all the bed-linen had had to go to the pawnbroker's. One evening, they had been forced to sell a table and two of their chairs. Charlie had been sleeping on the floor but ever since he had become ill they had given him their own bed and even that was not very comfortable, for they had had to remove the wool from the mattress and sell it to a second-hand dealer, handful by handful, half a pound at a time, for four or five sous. Now it was the turn of the father and mother to sleep on the floor on a straw palliasse not fit for a dog.

Meanwhile the pair of them were watching Charlie twisting and turning in bed. What was the matter with the kid, ranting and raving like that? Perhaps he'd been bitten by some animal or someone had given him something bad to drink? Madame

Bonnet, one of their neighbours, had come in and, sticking her face down close to the little boy's, she had announced that he'd caught a chill. She knew all about it, she'd lost her husband in exactly the same way.

His mother wept as she held Charlie in her arms. His father rushed out to fetch a doctor and brought him back with him. He was a very tall, stern-looking man who listened to the child's back and tapped his chest without uttering a word. Then Madame Bonnet had to go back to her room to fetch a pencil and paper for him to write his prescription. When he had left the room, still without saying a word, the mother, choking with sobs, asked him:

'What is it, doctor?'

'Pleurisy,' he answered curtly, not bothering to explain further. Then he asked:

'Have you got your name down for relief?'

'No, doctor. We weren't too badly off last summer. It's this winter that's done for us.'

'That's a pity.'

And he promised to call back. Madame Bonnet lent them four francs for the chemist. With Monsieur Morisseau's two francs they bought two pounds of beef, some coal and some candles. The first night everything went well. They kept the fire in and the sick boy, perhaps drowsy from the warmth, had stopped talking out loud. His little hands were burning but his parents felt relieved when they saw him sink into a feverish slumber. Next day they were horrified to see the doctor shaking his head at the bedside with a look on his face that seemed to suggest that there was no hope.

For the next five days there was no change in the boy's condition. Charlie lay on his pillow in a sleep of exhaustion. Destitution lurked more threateningly than ever in every corner of the room, like the wind which forced its way in through the holes in the roof and the window. On the second evening they sold his mother's last chemise, on the third they had to pull more handfuls of wool from the sick boy's mattress to pay the chemist. After that, there was nothing else to do; there was nothing left to sell.

Morisseau still had his two francs a day breaking ice; but they didn't go very far. As the extreme cold might be the death of his son, he was hoping for a thaw, while at the same time dreading it.

Each morning when he went off to work he was pleased to see the streets all white and then, when he thought of his little boy, he prayed for a ray of sun, a touch of spring warmth to clear the snow away. If only they had had their name down for parish relief, they would have had the doctor and the medicine for nothing. Charlie's mother had gone to the local municipal council's office but they told her that there were too many calls on their funds at the moment, she'd have to wait. Despite this, she managed to get some bread coupons and one kind lady gave her five francs. After that, they were once more completely destitute.

On the fifth day, Morisseau came back home with his two francs for the last time. The thaw had started and he was laid off. That was the end: the stove remained unlit, there was nothing to eat and they could no longer take the prescriptions down to the chemist. The father and mother sat shivering with cold in the room whose walls were dripping with moisture, watching their young son gasping for breath. Madame Bonnet had stopped calling on them because she was a sensitive woman and it made her too sad. The people living in the house hurried past the door. Occasionally, the mother would burst into tears and fling herself on the bed, clasping her son in her arms as though to bring him relief and make him well. The father stood for hours staring blankly out of the window, lifting up the old shawl to watch the large drops of melting snow make black spots on the street below. Perhaps the thaw was helping Charlie to recover.

One morning the doctor announced that he would not be calling again. There was no hope for the child.

'It's this damp weather that has done it,' he said.

Morisseau shook his fist at the sky. So any weather at all would do in poor wretches like them? It'd been freezing and that was bad for you; now it was thawing and that was even worse! If his wife would agree, he'd heap a bagful of coal on the stove and put an end to all three of them at one go. That would do the trick, the sooner the better…

However, the mother had gone to the town hall again and this time they had promised to send relief. So they waited. What a dreadful day! A dismal chill invaded the room from above and in one corner the rain was coming through and they had to put a bucket to collect the drips. They had had nothing to eat since the previous day and the boy had had only a cup of tea to drink which had been brought up by the concierge. The father, quite distraught, was sitting at the table holding his throbbing head in his hands. At every footstep the mother kept rushing to the door, thinking that at last the promised help had arrived. It struck six; there was no sign of anything. Slowly dusk descended, full of slush, and as sinister as the pangs of death.

Suddenly, in the threatening darkness, Charlie cried out in a broken voice:

'Mummy! Mummy!'

His mother rushed to the bed. She felt a gasp of breath on her cheek, then silence; she could dimly make out the child's head, thrown stiffly back on to the pillow. She gave a wild, pitiful cry:

'Bring the light, quickly! Charlie dear, say something to me!'

There were no candles left. In her haste to strike the matches, she broke them in her fingers. Then, with trembling hands, she felt her son's face.

'Dear God, he's dead!.... Morisseau, he's dead!'

His father lifted his head, unable to see in the darkness.

'Well, what about it? So he's dead... He's better off like that.'

Hearing the mother's sobs, Madame Bonnet decided to make her appearance, carrying a lamp. Then, as the two women were laying the child's body straight, there came a knock on the door: it was the promised aid: ten francs and some bread and meat coupons. Morisseau gave a hollow laugh and said that the relief committee always missed the boat. What a poor little corpse it was, lying there all thin and as light as a feather! A sparrow killed by the frost and brought in out of the street could hardly have looked much smaller than that tiny heap of skin and bone on the mattress.

However, Madame Bonnet had now once again assumed her helpful rôle. She was explaining that it wouldn't bring Charlie back to life to have starving people around him. She offered to go and fetch bread and meat and added that she would bring some candles as well. They let her do as she wanted. When she came back she laid the table and served piping hot sausages which the ravenous Morisseaus set on like hungry wolves, beside their dead boy whose pale little face could just be seen in the shadow. The stove was roaring away; it was very cosy. Now and again big tears welled up in the mother's eyes and overflowed in big drops on to her piece of bread. Wouldn't Charlie have been warm! How he'd have loved the sausage!

Madame Bonnet insisted on keeping watch over the body. At about one o'clock, after Morisseau had finally dropped off to sleep with his head resting on the end of the bed, the two women made some coffee. Another neighbour, an eighteen-year-old dressmaker, was invited in and in return for the hospitality brought along a little brandy left in the bottom of a bottle. The three sat sipping their coffee, telling each other whispered tales of weird sorts of deaths; gradually their voices grew louder and their gossip widened its scope to include the house, the neighbourhood, a crime that had been committed in the Rue Nollet.* Now and again, the mother stood up and would go over to look at Charlie, as though making sure he hadn't moved.

Since they had not notified the death that evening, they had to keep the little boy for the whole of the next day; and as they had only one room, they lived with Charlie, ate with him and slept with him. Occasionally they forgot all about him; then, when they suddenly remembered, their loss came back to them all over again.

Finally, on the second day, the coffin was delivered, no bigger than a toy-box, made of four roughly-planed wooden planks; it had been provided free by the municipality on the grounds of certified poverty. And now, it was off to church at the double! Following Charlie were his father with two of his pals whom he had met on the way, then his mother with Madame Bonnet and their other neighbour, the little dressmaker. Everybody was floundering in mud up to their calves. It was not raining but the fog was so thick that it was soaking their clothes. At the church the priest made short work of the funeral service and then off they dashed again over the slippery, wet paving stones.

The cemetery was miles away, beyond the fortifications. They went down the Avenue de Saint-Ouen, beyond the gates of the city limits, and finally they arrived. The cemetery was a vast enclosed space, a waste land shut in by white walls. It was full of weeds and dug up into mounds of earth while in the background there stretched out a row of gaunt trees whose branches made black smudges against the sky.

The funeral procession struggled forward slowly over the sodden soil. It had started to rain and they had to wait for the old priest to decide to venture out of the shelter of his chapel. Charlie was going to his last rest in the bottom of a paupers' grave. The field was scattered with crosses blown down by the wind and wreaths rotted by the rain, a field full of mourning and poverty, ravaged and trampled over, overflowing with the heaped-up corpses of the cold and hungry poor from the working-class suburbs of Paris.

Now it was all over. The soil slid down on to Charlie lying at the bottom of his little hole and his parents went off without even being able to kneel down beside his grave in the slimy mud that came up to their ankles. Outside the cemetery, as the rain had stopped, Morisseau, who still had three francs left over from the charity board's relief, invited his two pals and the two neighbours to a drink in a wineshop. They sat down at the table and drank a couple of litres of wine and ate a piece of Brie. Then his pals offered another round of the same. When the company got back to Paris, they were very merry.

V

Jean-Louis Lacour was seventy years old. He had been born and had grown old in La Courtelle, a tiny hamlet of a hundred and fifty souls, tucked away in the wilds amongst the wolves. In the course of his whole life he had been to Angers,* less than forty miles away, on one occasion only; and at that time he had been too young to remember anything about it. He had had three children, two sons, Antoine and Joseph, and a daughter Catherine. She had married, her husband had died and she had gone back to live with her father, together with her twelve-year-old son Jacquinet. The family lived on a small farm which was just large enough to provide them with food and the bare necessities of clothing. They could not be described as belonging to the poor of the district but they had to work hard. They had to earn their bread with a mattock and their glass of wine had come from the sweat of their brow.

La Courtelle lies hidden at the end of a valley, shut in on all sides by woods. The parish was too poor to have a church; Mass was said by the priest from neighbouring Cormiers and, as it involved a five-mile journey, he came only once a fortnight. The houses, a score of ramshackle old cottages, stretched higgledy-piggledly along the one main street. Hens pecked about in the dung in front of the houses and the sight of a stranger passing through along the road was so extraordinary that all the women would crane their necks while the children basking in the sun would run off, screaming like scared animals.

Jean-Louis had never had a day's illness in his life. He was tall and as gnarled as an oak. The sun had baked his skin until it had the colour and toughness and stillness of a tree. With advancing years, he had lost his tongue. He now never spoke, considering such an activity pointless. He kept his gaze fixed on the ground and his body was permanently bent in an attitude of work.

Last year he had been even more energetic than his sons, reserving all the heaviest tasks for himself, working away in silence in his field which seemed to know him and be in awe of him. But one day, two months ago, he had fallen down and for two hours had lain like a felled tree over a furrow. The following day, he had gone off to work again and then, all of a sudden, his arms had given way and the earth refused to obey him. His sons had shaken their heads and his daughter had wanted him to stay at home. But he had put his foot down and so they had sent Jacquinet along to keep him company and give a shout if his grandfather were to fall over.

'What are you doing here, young lazybones?' said Jean-Louis to the lad, who was hanging about him all the time. 'When I was your age, I was earning my keep.'

'I'm looking after you, Grandpa,' replied the boy.

This remark brought Jean-Louis up with a start. He said no more. That evening when he came home, he went to bed and stayed there. Next day, when his sons and daughter went off to the fields, they came in to look at their father, since they had not heard him stirring. They found the sick man lying stretched out in bed with his eyes open. He seemed to be thinking. His skin was so tanned and leathery that they could not see the colour of his face.

'Well, Dad, feeling out of sorts?'

He grunted and shook his head.

'All right, if you're not coming with us, we'll be off and leave you here.'

He made a sign for them to go off without him. The harvest had begun and every hand was needed. If they missed a morning's work, there might even be a storm which would blow the sheaves away. Even Jacquinet went along with his uncles and mother. Old Lacour was left behind alone. When they returned home that evening, they found him still in the same position, lying flat on his back with his eyes open and still seeming to be thinking.

'Well, Dad, feeling any better?'

No, he was not feeling any better. He gave a grunt and shook his head. What could be done for him, then? Catherine had the idea of heating some wine up with herbs. But it was too strong and nearly killed him. Joseph said they'd see about it next day and they all went to bed.

Next day, before going off on their harvesting, the sons and daughter gathered round his bed for a minute or two. The old man was definitely ill. Never before had he remained lying on his back like this. Perhaps they'd better send for the doctor after all? The trouble was that it would mean going to Rougemont, twelve miles there and twelve miles back; that made a good twenty-four miles in all. You'd be losing a whole day's work. The old man, who was listening to his children, started to become agitated and seemed to be annoyed. He didn't need a doctor. It cost too much.

'You don't want us to?' Antoine asked. 'All right, so can we go off to work, then?'

Of course they could go off to work! What good could they do if they stayed? The soil needed looking after more than he did. When he kicked the bucket, that only concerned God and him, but if the harvest were lost, everyone would suffer. And so three days went by with the children going off every morning to the fields and Jean-Louis lying quite still, all alone, taking a drink from a jug when he got thirsty. He was like an old horse falling down in exhaustion and being left to die in a corner. He had been working for sixty years and now he could take his leave, because he would merely be taking up space and getting in his children's way. Would you hesitate to cut a tree down when its branches started falling off? Even his children were not feeling any great emotion. Working on the land had made them used to such things and they lived too close to it to feel any resentment if it wanted to take him from them. A brief look in the morning and a brief look at night was all they could afford. If their father recovered after all, it would prove that he was tough. If he died, it would mean that Death had taken up his abode in his body and everyone knows that when that happens, nothing can turn him out, whether it be medicine or signs of the cross. Of course, you would care for a sick cow, because saving a cow means saving at least four hundred francs.

Every evening Jean-Louis looked questioningly at his children for news of the harvest. When he heard them calculating the number of sheaves and discussing the fine weather that was helping them to bring in the harvest, his eyes gave a flicker of approval. They again considered the possibility of sending for a doctor but decided that it really was too far. Jacquinet would never be able to go that distance and the men could not spare the time. The only thing the old man wanted was for the game-keeper, an old crony of his, to come and see him. Old Nicholas was older than Jean-Louis because he had had his seventy-fifth birthday at Candlemas. But he was as upright as a poplar. He came and sat down beside his old friend, shaking his head. Jean-Louis had been unable to speak since that morning and he lay looking at him through his pale blue eyes. Old Nicholas, himself a man of few words, merely sat watching him too, unable to find anything to say. So the two old men stayed face to face for a good hour without uttering a word but glad to see each other, doubtless going over in their minds events from the far distant past. It was that evening that, when they came home, the children found old Lacour dead, stretched out stiffly in his bed, his eyes staring at the ceiling.

Yes, the old man had died without stirring a limb and his last breath had left his body to become one with all the other breaths of Mother Nature. Like animals which hide away to die uncomplainingly, he hadn't disturbed the neighbours, he had carried out his last duty all by himself, perhaps apologetically because he was giving his children the trouble of disposing of his body.

'Father's dead,' said Antoine to the others; and the others, Joseph, Catherine and even Jacquinet, repeated:

'Father's dead.'

No one was surprised. Jacquinet peered inquisitively, Catherine pulled out her handkerchief, the two men walked around in solemn silence, pale underneath their tan. Their old man had hung on pretty well, say what you would, he was still pretty tough! And the children felt consoled and proud at the thought of how tough the family was. That night, they watched over their father's body till ten o'clock and then they all fell asleep; Jean-Louis was once more left on his own, with his staring eyes. At first light, Joseph went off to Cormiers to warn the priest. But there were still some sheaves to be got in, so Antoine and Catherine went out to the fields, leaving Jacquinet to look after the corpse.

The little boy became bored at having to stay with his grandfather, so every now and again he would go out into the street to throw stones at the sparrows and watch a pedlar busily displaying his silk scarves to two of the neighbours; then, remembering the old man, he would rush back indoors to make sure that he hadn't moved, but soon slipped out again to watch a couple of dogs fighting. Since he had left the door open, the hens came in and walked undisturbed round the bed, vigorously pecking the mud floor. A scarlet cockerel stood on tiptoe, craning his neck and peering upwards with his fiery red eyes wide open in astonishment at seeing a body lying stretched out so inexplicably on the bed. It was a cautious and sagacious cock who knew that the old man was not accustomed to stay in bed once the sun was up. Finally, he gave his loud clarion crow; perhaps he had understood and was singing his own funeral song for the dead man, while the hens took their departure one by one, clucking and pecking at the earth.

The parish priest of Cormiers let it be known that he could not come over until about four o'clock. Meanwhile, ever since morning, the wheelwright could be heard sawing wood and hammering nails. Those who did not already know said: 'Ah, Jean-Louis must have died', because the villagers were familiar with such sounds. Antoine and Catherine had come back from the fields; the harvest was over. They could not say that they were disappointed; they had not seen such good corn for years. The whole family now waited patiently for the priest, keeping themselves occupied in order to distract their thoughts: Catherine put the soup on while Joseph fetched water from the well. They sent Jacquinet to find out if the grave had been dug in the cemetery. It was not until five o'clock that the priest finally arrived in a gig, with a youngster who acted as his altar-boy. He stopped in front of the Lacours' door, jumped down and took his stole and surplice out of a paper bag. While he was putting them on, he said:

'Hurry up, I've got to be back by seven.'

However, nobody hurried. They had to go and ask two friendly neighbours to carry the bier. The same bier and the same black cloth, worm-eaten, worn and faded, had both been used for the last fifty years. The old man was lifted up and placed by his children in the coffin that had been brought round by the wheelwright. It was made of such thick wood that it looked like an old kneading trough. Just as they were about to set off, Jacquinet dashed up with the news that the hole was not yet quite dug but that they could come along all the same.

The priest led the procession, reading in a loud voice out of a book in Latin. Next came the little altar-boy carrying an old copper holy water holder with a holy water sprinkler in it. It was not until they were halfway through the village that another lad came out of the barn in which Mass was said every fortnight and went ahead of the procession carrying a large cross fastened to the end of a stick. Then came the body on a bier carried by two peasants and, finally, the family. Gradually the whole village joined the procession and a crowd of ragged little urchins, bareheaded and barefooted, brought up the rear.

The cemetery lies at the other end of La Courtelle, so that the two peasants twice had to put down the bier on the way in order briefly to get back their breath and spit on their hands, while the procession came to a halt. Then off they went again; you could hear the tramp of wooden clogs on the hard earth. When they reached the cemetery, the hole was not, in fact, quite ready. The gravedigger could be seen still working at the bottom of the pit, bending down and then reappearing at regular intervals with spadefuls of earth.

How peaceful the cemetery was as it slumbered in the bright sun! It was surrounded by a hedge where warblers nested and every September the boys of the village would come along and pick blackberries. It was like a garden planted in open country, with everything growing at random. At the far end, there were enormous currant bushes and in one corner a pear tree, grown to the size of an oak. Down the middle ran an avenue of limes, a cool walk in the heat of summer, and the old men of the village would come to smoke their pipes in its shade. The uncultivated empty piece of land was covered in tall weeds; superb thistles and other wild flowers spread out in colourful display and clouds of white butterflies were swarming and swooping. The sun was blazing, grasshoppers were chirping and bright golden flies were buzzing in the shimmering heat. In the silence, quivering with life, you could detect the final joyous paean of the dead, the rich sap of the earth burgeoning in the red blood of the poppies.

They had placed the coffin down beside the hole, while the gravedigger went on throwing up his spadefuls of earth. The boy carrying the cross had quickly stuck it into the earth at the dead man's feet and at his head the priest stood reciting Latin from his book. The villagers' main interest was in the grave-digger. They stood in a circle round the hole watching the movement of his spade. And when they looked up, the priest had vanished with the two lads and the only people left were the waiting family.

At last the hole was ready.

'Come on, that's deep enough!' shouted one of the peasants who had been carrying the bier.

And everybody lent a hand in lowering the coffin. Yes, old Lacour would be comfortable in that hole! He knew all about the earth and the earth knew all about him. They'd get on well together. Fifty years ago when he had struck the first blow of his mattock into it, the earth had made this final appointment with him, for the pair of them. Their love affair had been bound to end like this; the soil would take and hold him tight. And what a peaceful place to rest in! He would hear only the light-footed birds hopping in the grass; no one else would tread on him and he would remain in his corner undisturbed for years, because not two people died each year in La Courtelle and the young could grow old in their turn and die without disturbing his old bones. It was a peaceful, sunny death, a sleep without end in the calm of the countryside.

His children came up to the grave. Catherine, Antoine and Joseph each took a handful of earth and cast it on to the old man. Jacquinet had been collecting poppies and he threw them on at the same time. Then the family made its way home, the animals returned from the fields, the sun sank beneath the horizon and the warm night sent the drowsy villagers to sleep.

COQUEVILLE ON THE SPREE

COQUEVILLE is a little village snuggling down in a rocky inlet five miles from Grandport. A fine broad sandy beach stretches out at the foot of the ramshackle old cottages stuck halfway up the cliff-face like shells left high and dry by the tide. When you climb to the left, up on to the heights of Grandport, you can see the yellow expanse of beach very plainly to the west, looking like a tide of gold dust flowing out of the gaping slit in the rock; and if you have good eyes, you can even make out the tumbledown cottages standing out, rust-coloured against the stone, with the bluish smoke from their chimneys drifting upwards to the crest of the enormous ridge blocking the horizon.

It's an out-of-the-way hole. Coqueville has never succeeded in bringing its population up to the two hundred mark. The gorge running down to the sea, on the edge of which the village is situated, is so steep and winding that it is almost impassable for horses and carts. This prevents communication and isolates the village so that it seems miles away from any of the neighbouring hamlets. As a result, the inhabitants' only communication with Grandport was by water. They were almost all fishermen living from the sea and had to transport their catch there by boat every day. They had a contract with a large firm of wholesalers, Dufeu's, which bought their fish in bulk. Old Dufeu had been dead for some years but the business had been carried on by his widow; she had merely taken on an assistant, a tall fair-headed young fellow called Mouchel, whose job was to visit the villages along the coast and strike bargains with the villagers. This Monsieur Mouchel was the only link between Coqueville and the civilized world.

Coqueville deserves to have an historian. It seems certain that in the Dark Ages the village was founded by the Mahés, a family which found its way there, settled down and proliferated at the foot of the cliff. At first, the Mahés must have flourished by intermarriage, since for centuries you find nothing but Mahés. Then, under Louis XIII,* there appeared a Floche. No one really knows where he came from. He married a Mahé and from that moment onwards a strange phenomenon occurred: the Floches prospered and were so prolific that they ended up by engulfing the Mahés, whose numbers decreased while their wealth passed into the newcomers' hands. Doubtless the Floches had brought new blood, a sturdier constitution and a temperament more suited to face the strong winds and rough seas of their profession. However that might be, the Floches were by now the bosses of Coqueville.

You will have realized that this shift in numbers and wealth had not taken place without terrible strife. The Mahés and the Floches hated each other like poison; centuries of loathing seethed between them. Despite their decline, the Mahés were proud, as befitted a former conqueror. After all, they were the founders and ancestors. They would speak with scorn of the first of the Floches, a beggar and a tramp whom they had taken into their bosoms out of pity, and they expressed eternal regret at having given him one of their daughters. If you were to believe them, this Floche had produced nothing but a breed of lewd rogues who spent their nights in copulation and their days in pursuit of heiresses. There was no insult too foul to heap on the powerful tribe of Floches, with the bitter fury of ruined and decimated aristocrats against the arrogant and prolific middle classes who had dispossessed them of their mansions and their wealth that were theirs by right of inheritance. Needless to say, success had turned the Floches, on their part, into an arrogant lot. They were sitting pretty and could afford to sneer. They made fun of the ancient race of Mahé and swore to turn them out of the village if they didn't knuckle under. For them, the Mahés were down-and-outs who, instead of wrapping themselves proudly in their tattered finery, would be better employed mending it. Thus Coqueville found itself the prey of two warring clans; about one hundred and thirty of its inhabitants determined to take over the other fifty, for no other reason than that they were stronger. Struggles between mighty empires tell the same story.

Amongst the recent squabbles which had been tearing Coqueville apart, we may mention the famous feud between Fouasse and Tupain and the spectacular brawls between the Rouget couple. It must be explained that in the old days everyone was given a nickname, which later on became a surname, because it was difficult to disentangle all the cross-breedings of Mahé and Floche. Rouget had certainly once had an ancestor who had flaming red hair; as for Fouasse and Tupain, no one knew the reason for their names, since in the course of the years many nicknames had lost any rational explanation. Well, old Françoise, a sprightly old girl of eighty, still alive, had married a Mahé and produced Fouasse; then, after being widowed, had remarried a Floche and given birth to Tupain. Hence the mutual antagonism of the two brothers, a hatred kept alive by the fact that questions of inheritance were involved. As for the Rougets, they fought like cat and dog because Rouget accused his wife Marie of carrying on with a dark-haired Floche, the tall and sturdy Brisemotte.* Rouget had already flung himself a couple of times on the latter, knife in hand, screaming that he would have his guts for garters. He was an excitable little man, always flying into rages.

But Coqueville's major concern at the moment was neither Rouget's rages nor Tupain's and Fouasse's squabbles. There was a wild rumour going round that a Mahé, Delphin, a whipper-snapper of twenty, had the audacity to be in love with Margot, the beautiful daughter of La Queue, the wealthiest of the Floches and mayor of the village. This La Queue was a very considerable person indeed. He was called La Queue because under Louis-Philippe, his father, obstinately clinging to fashions prevalent in his youth, had been the last man in the village to tie his hair in a pigtail.* Now La Queue owned *Zephyr*, one of Coqueville's two large fishing boats and by far the best, a fine seaworthy vessel, newly built. The other cutter was the *Whale*, a rotten old tub owned by Rouget and manned by Delphin and Fouasse, while La Queue sailed with a crew consisting of Tupain and Brisemotte. The latter were always making sarcastic comments about the *Whale*, describing it as an old tub which, one fine day, would disintegrate like a handful of mud. So when La Queue heard that this good-for-nothing young Delphin, the *Whale*'s cabin-boy, was daring to make sheep's eyes at his daughter, he gave her a couple of well-directed slaps in the face as a warning that she would never become a Mahé. Margot was furious and responded by loudly proclaiming that she would pass on the same treatment to Delphin if he ever had the nerve to start prowling around her. It was maddening to have your ears boxed because of a young man whom you'd never really bothered to look at properly. Although only sixteen, Margot was as strong as a man and already as lovely as any lady; she had the reputation of being high and mighty, a young madam who had no time for sweethearts. So you can well understand how those two slaps, Delphin's audacity and Margot's anger had kept every tongue wagging in Coqueville.

However, there were people who said that Margot was not as angry as all that at seeing Delphin hanging around her. This Delphin was a small young fellow with a face tanned by the sea and a mop of blond curls that hung down over his eyes and neck. And, despite his slender build, he was very strong and quite capable of tackling someone three times his size. Rumour had it that he would sometimes go off and spend the night in Grandport. This gave him a reputation with the girls of being something of a wolf, and when talking together they would accuse him of 'living it up', a vague phrase which suggested all kinds of secret pleasures. Whenever she mentioned his name, Margot seemed to become rather too excited, while when he looked at her through his tiny bright eyes, he would give a sly grin and show not the slightest concern whether she was angry or scornful. He would walk past her front door, slip into the bushes and stay watching her for hours, as lithe and patient as a cat stalking a tom-tit; and when she suddenly discovered him right behind her, so close at times that she would detect his presence by the warmth of his breath, he did not take himself off but would put on such a gentle, wistful look that she was left speechless with surprise and remembered to be annoyed only after he had gone. There is no doubt that, had her father seen her, she would have collected another box on the ears. Things could certainly not go on like this for ever; but although she kept swearing that one day she would give Delphin the promised box on the ears, she never in fact took advantage of any opportunity of doing so when he was there. This made people say that she'd do better not to keep on talking so much about it, since the truth was that she still had given no sign of keeping her word.

All the same, nobody ever imagined that she would ever marry Delphin. It seemed merely a case of a passing fancy by a flirtatious young girl. As for marriage between the most poverty-stricken of the Mahés, who would find it hard to contribute even half a dozen shirts to the matrimonial estate, and the mayor's daughter, the richest heiress among the Floches, the whole idea would be monstrous. Unkind people hinted that she might none the less quite possibly get together with him but that she would certainly never marry him. A rich girl can enjoy herself as she pleases but when she has her head screwed on straight, she doesn't do anything silly. Anyway, the whole of Coqueville was taking a passionate interest in the matter and was curious to see the outcome. Would Delphin end up getting his ears boxed? Or would Margot get a kiss on her cheek in some remote corner of the cliffs? They'd have to wait and see. Some people supported the box on the ears, others the kiss on the cheek. Coqueville was all agog.

In the whole village there were only two people who did not belong either to the Mahé or the Floche camps: the priest and the gamekeeper. The latter, a tall lean man whose real name no one knew but whom everyone called the Emperor*, doubtless because he had served under Charles X, in fact exercised no serious supervision whatsoever over the game of the district, which consisted of nothing but bare rock and deserted heathland. He had got the job because a *sous-préfet** had taken him under his wing and had created on his behalf this sinecure where he was free to squander his very modest salary undisturbed. As for Father Radiguet, he was one of those simple-minded priests whose bishops are anxious to get rid of by tucking them away in some God-forsaken hole where they can stay out of mischief. Radiguet was a decent sort of man who had reverted to his peasant origins and spent his time working in his exiguous little garden hewn out of the rock-face, and smoking his pipe as he watched his lettuces grow. His only weakness was a love of food, although he was hardly in a position to show a discriminating palate, since he was forced to make do with a diet of mackerel and cider, of which he sometimes drank more than he could hold. All the same, he was a good shepherd to his flock and they would come along, at infrequent intervals, to hear him say Mass, purely to oblige him.

However, after managing to remain neutral for a long time, the priest and the gamekeeper had been forced to take sides. Conservative at heart, the Emperor had opted for the Mahés while the priest had become a Flochite. This had given rise to complications. As the Emperor had absolutely nothing to do all day long and was tired of counting the boats leaving Grandport harbour, he had taken it into his head to act as the village policeman. As a

Mahé supporter, he favoured Fouasse against Tupain, tried to catch Brisemotte and Rouget's wife red-handed and, above all, turned a blind eye when he saw Delphin slipping into Margot's back-yard. The trouble was that these goings-on led to violent disagreement between him and his direct superior, the mayor La Queue. While being sufficiently respectful of discipline to listen to the mayor's rebukes, the gamekeeper would then go away and do as he thought fit, thereby causing complete chaos in Coqueville's public administration. You could never go near the glorified shed that served as Coqueville's town hall without being deafened by the sound of some flaming row or other between the two. Father Radiguet, on the other hand, having joined the triumphant clan of the Floches, who showered him with gifts of superb mackerel, secretly encouraged Rouget's wife to stand up to her husband and threatened Margot with all the torments of hell if she ever let Delphin lay as much as a finger on her. In a word, anarchy reigned supreme, with the army in revolt against the civil authority and religion conniving at the frolics of the wealthier members of his flock, so that, in this dead-and-alive little hole looking out upon the infinite expanse of the sky and the vast sweep of the ocean, you had a whole community of fully one hundred and eighty souls at daggers drawn with each other.

In the midst of all this turmoil, Delphin alone never lost his good spirits; young and in love as he was, he did not give a damn for anything or anybody, as long as Margot would one day be his. He may well have been planning to snare her like a rabbit, but being a sensible lad despite his wild ways, he was going to see to it that the priest should tie the knot that would ensure that they would live happily ever after.

One evening as he was lying in wait for her in a lane, Margot finally took a swing at him and then blushed purple in confusion when, instead of waiting for the blow to land, Delphin caught hold of her hand and feverishly covered it in kisses.

She was trembling as he whispered to her:

'I love you. Will you love me?'

'Never!' she cried in a shocked voice.

He gave a shrug of his shoulders and said quietly, with a tender look in his eyes:

'Please don't say that... We'll get on very well together, the pair of us. You'll see just how nice it is.'

2

That Sunday, the weather was dreadful, one of those sudden September storms which blow up with terrible force on the rocky coast round Grandport. As dusk was falling, Coqueville caught a glimpse of a vessel in distress being driven before the wind. But the light was failing and there was no question of going to her rescue. Since the previous day, *Zephyr* and the *Whale* had been tied up in the tiny natural harbour to the left of the beach, between the two granite sea-walls. Neither La Queue nor Rouget were going to risk venturing out. Unfortunately, Madame Dufeu's representative, Monsieur Mouchel, had taken the trouble to come over personally on Saturday to offer a bonus if they made a real effort: catches were poor and the Central Market was complaining. So when they went to bed on Sunday with the rain still pelting down, the fishermen of Coqueville were bad-tempered and full of grumbles. It was always the same old story: when the demand was good, the fish just weren't there. And they all discussed the ship that had been seen passing during the gale and which by now was no doubt lying at the bottom of the ocean.

Next day the sky was still black and the sea running high, booming and thundering and reluctant to calm down, even though the wind was blowing less strongly. It then dropped completely and though the waves were still rearing and tossing furiously, both boats went out that afternoon. *Zephyr* returned at about four o'clock, having caught nothing. While Tupain and Brisemotte were tying up in the little harbour, La Queue stood on the beach, shaking his fist angrily at the sea. And Monsieur Mouchel was expecting something from them! Margot was there with half Coqueville, watching the heavy swell of the dying storm and sharing her father's resentment against the sea and the sky.

'Where's the *Whale*?' someone asked.

'Over there, behind the point,' replied La Queue. 'If that old tub gets back safe and sound today, it'll be lucky.'

His voice was full of scorn. He went on to suggest that it was quite understandable for the Mahés to risk their lives like that; when you haven't got two pennies to rub together, you don't have much choice. As for him, he'd sooner let Monsieur Mouchel go begging.

Meanwhile Margot was scrutinizing the rocky point behind which the *Whale* was hidden. Finally she asked her father:

'Did they catch anything?'

'Them!' he exclaimed. 'Not a thing!'

Noticing that the Emperor was grinning, he calmed down and added more quietly:

'I don't know if they've caught anything but as they never do...'

'Perhaps they have caught something today after all,' said the Emperor teasingly. 'It has been known to happen.'

La Queue was about to make a heated retort when Father Radiguet arrived and succeeded in soothing him. From the flat top of the church, Radiguet had just caught a glimpse of the *Whale* which seemed to be in pursuit of some large fish. This news created great excitement among the villagers gathered on the beach, with the Mahé supporters hoping for a miraculous catch and the Floches very keen for the boat to come back empty-handed. Margot was craning her neck and looking out to sea.

'There they are!' she exclaimed briefly.

And in fact a black speck could be seen beyond the point.

Everyone looked. It looked like a cork bobbing up and down on the sea. The Emperor could not even see the black speck: you had to be from Coqueville to recognize the *Whale* and its crew at that distance.

'Yes,' Margot went on, for she had the best eyes of anyone in the village, 'Fouasse and Rouget are rowing and the boy's standing in the bow.'

She called Delphin 'the boy' to avoid mentioning him by name. Now they were able to follow the course of the boat and try to understand its strange manoeuvres. As the priest had said, it seemed to be pursuing a fish which kept swimming away to escape. It was an extraordinary sight. The Emperor thought that their net had probably been carried away but La Queue exclaimed that they were just being lazy and footling about. They wouldn't be catching seals, that was for sure! The Floches all found this an hilarious remark while the Mahés felt annoyed and pointed out that anyway Rouget had guts and was risking his life while certain other people stuck to dry land at the slightest puff of wind. Once again, Father Radiguet had to intervene because fists were being clenched.

'What on earth are they up to!' exclaimed Margot suddenly. 'They've gone again!'

They all stopped glowering at each other and everyone scanned the horizon. Once more the *Whale* was hidden behind the point. This time, even La Queue was becoming uneasy. Since he was unable to explain to himself what they were doing, and fearing that Rouget might really be making a good catch, he was beside himself with rage. No one left the beach even though there was nothing particular to see. They stayed there for two hours, still waiting for the boat which kept appearing and then vanishing. In the end it disappeared altogether. La Queue declared it must have gone to the bottom and in his anger he even found himself wishing in his heart of hearts that this might be true; and as Rouget's wife happened to be present with Brisemotte, he looked at them with a conspiratorial grin and gave Tupain a friendly tap on the shoulder to console him for the loss of his half-brother Fouasse. But he stopped laughing when he saw his daughter Margot on tiptoe peering silently into the distance.

'What do you think you're doing here?' he said gruffly. 'Off you go back home. . . And have a care, Margot!'

She made no move but suddenly called out:

'Look, there they are!'

There was a cry of surprise. With her sharp eyes, Margot swore that she couldn't see a soul on board. No Rouget, no Fouasse, nobody! The *Whale* was running before the wind as though abandoned, changing tack every minute as it bobbed lazily up and down. Fortunately a breeze had sprung up from the west which was driving the boat landwards, in an oddly capricious way, so that it yawed first to port and then to starboard. The whole of Coqueville was by now assembled on the beach. Everybody was calling out to everyone else and there was not a woman or a girl left at home to prepare the supper. It could only be some sort of disaster, something inexplicable and so mysterious that they all felt quite at a loss. Rouget's wife thought quickly and decided that she ought to burst into tears. The most Tupain could do was to look miserable. All the Mahés were looking distressed while the Floches were trying hard to show some decorum. Margot had sat down on the beach as if her legs had suddenly collapsed.

'What on earth are you doing there?' exclaimed La Queue, seeing her at his feet.

'I'm tired,' she said simply.

And she turned her head to look out to sea, holding her face in her hands and peering through the tips of her fingers at the *Whale* bobbing up and down even more lazily, like a cheerful boat that has had too much to drink.

Theories were now flying thick and fast. Perhaps the three men had fallen into the sea? But for all three to do that at once seemed very odd. La Queue was trying to persuade people that the *Whale* had split open like a rotten egg. But as she was still afloat, the others merely shrugged their shoulders. Then he remembered that he was mayor and began to talk about various formalities, as if the men were really drowned.

'What's the point of talking like that!' exclaimed the Emperor. 'How could people die as stupidly as that? If they'd fallen in, Delphin would have been here by now!'

They all had to agree; Delphin could swim like a fish. But in that case, where on earth could the three men be? Everyone was shouting. 'I'm telling you it is!' 'And I'm telling you it isn't!' 'Stupid!' 'Stupid yourself!' And they were getting to the stage of exchanging blows, so that Father Radiguet was forced to make an appeal for the cessation of hostilities while the Emperor hurriedly tried to restore order. Meanwhile the boat continued to bob lazily up and down under everyone's eyes. It was as though she was dancing and laughing at them all and as she drifted in on the tide, she seemed to be greeting the approaching land with a series of slow, rhythmical curtsies. She was a crazy boat, that was for sure!

Margot was still hiding her face and peering through her hands. A rowing-boat had just put out from the harbour to go to meet the *Whale*: losing patience, Brisemotte seemed anxious to put an end to Marie Rouget's uncertainty. Now Coqueville's whole attention was focused on the rowing-boat. They started shouting: Could he see anything? The *Whale* kept coming on, still looking mysterious and saucy. At last they saw him catch hold of one of the mooring ropes and stand up to look into the boat. Then suddenly he burst into fits of laughter. They were all mystified. What could he see that was so funny?

'Hi there! What's up?' they shouted excitedly. His only reply was to go on laughing even more loudly, making signs that they were soon going to find out. Then he tied the *Whale* to his own boat and towed her in. And the inhabitants of Coqueville were stunned at the extraordinary sight that met their eyes. The three men, Rouget, Fouasse and Delphin, were lying flat on their backs, fast asleep, blissfully snoring and dead drunk. In the middle, there lay a small cask that had been stoved in, a cask that had been full when they had picked it up. They had been drinking from it and it must have been good stuff, because they had drunk it all except for a litre or so that had spilled out into the boat and become mixed with seawater.

'Oh, what a pig!' cried Rouget's wife and stopped snivelling.

'Well, that's a fine catch, I must say,' said La Queue, putting on a dignified air.

'Hang on!' said the Emperor. 'People catch what they can and after all, they did catch a barrel at least, which is more than those who didn't catch anything.'

Piqued by this remark, the mayor said no more. But Coqueville's other inhabitants were commenting excitedly. Now they could understand! When boats get drunk, they prance about, just like human beings, and that boat had certainly had a bellyful! The tipsy old so-and-so! She'd been zigzagging about just like a drunk who couldn't find his way home. And some were laughing at it and some were annoyed, for the Mahés found it funny and the Floches thought it disgusting. They all gathered round the *Whale*, peering open-eyed at the three happy fellows snoring away with smiles all over their faces, completely oblivious to the crowd bending over them. Neither the insults nor the laughter could greatly disturb them. Rouget was unable to hear his wife accusing him of drinking the lot. Fouasse did not feel the sly kicks in his ribs being given him by his brother Tupain. As for Delphin, he looked charming, with his fair hair, pink cheeks and air of rapturous delight. Margot had stood up and was silently contemplating the young man with a hard look in her eyes.

'Better get them to bed!' a voice cried.

But at that very moment, Delphin started to open his eyes and, still with his blissfully happy expression, began to look around at the crowd of people watching him. At once, everybody started questioning him, so excitedly that he felt quite bewildered, especially as he was still as drunk as a lord.

'Well, what's all the fuss?' he stammered. 'It's a little cask. There wasn't any fish, so we caught a little barrel.'

That was all he would say. Each time he said it, he added simply:

'It was jolly good.'

'But what was in it?' they asked him crossly.

'Oh, I don't know. It was jolly good.'

By now the whole of Coqueville was bursting with curiosity. They all stuck their noses into the boat and sniffed hard. There was unanimous agreement that it was a liqueur of some sort but nobody could guess what liqueur. The Emperor, who flattered himself that he had drunk everything that a man can drink, said that he was going to see. Solemnly he took in the hollow of his hand a little of the liquid floating in the bottom of the boat. The crowd fell suddenly silent and waited expectantly. However, after taking a sip, the Emperor shook his head uncertainly, as if still in doubt. He tasted it twice again, with a surprised and worried look on his face, more and more embarrassed. Eventually he was forced to admit:

'I don't know... It's queer. I expect I'd be able to say if it wasn't for the seawater. But my word, it really is very queer.'

People looked at each other in amazement that even the Emperor didn't dare to pass a definite judgement on what it was. Coqueville eyed the little cask with respect.

'It was jolly good,' said Delphin once again. He seemed to be laughing up his sleeve.

Then, with a broad grin and a wave of his hand, he added:

'If you want some, there's still some left... I saw lots of little barrels... little... little barrels...'

He kept on humming the words like a refrain from some lullaby, looking fondly at Margot, whom he had only just caught sight of. She lifted her hand angrily but he did not blink an eyelid and waited for the slap with a tender look in his eyes.

Intrigued by the thought of this mysterious, delicious drink, Father Radiguet also dipped his finger into the bottom of the boat and sucked it. Like the Emperor, he too shook his head uncertainly: no, he couldn't place it, it was most surprising. One thing only they all agreed on: the cask must have come from the vessel in distress which they had noticed on Sunday and which must have been wrecked. English ships often carried cargoes of liqueurs and fine wines of that sort to Grandport.

The light was slowly fading and the villagers at last started to make their way home in the dark. Only La Queue stayed behind,

sunk in thought, turning over in his mind an idea that he wanted
to keep to himself. He stopped and listened for the last time to
Delphin who was being carried away, still gently singing:

'Little barrels . . . little barrels . . . if you want some, there are
still some left!'

3

That night the weather changed completely. When Coqueville
woke up next day, the sun was shining brightly, the sea was as
calm as a mill-pond, spread out like a piece of green satin. And it
was warm, a golden autumnal warmth.

La Queue was first out of bed in the village, his mind still in
confusion from last night's dreams. He stood for a long time
looking out to sea, to left and right. Finally, he said irritably that he
supposed that they'd better keep Monsieur Mouchel satisfied and
immediately set out with Tupain and Brisemotte, threatening
Margot that he would tickle her ribs if she didn't watch her step. As
Zephyr was leaving harbour and he saw the *Whale* riding heavily up
and down at her moorings, he cheered up somewhat and shouted:

'Well, anyway there'll be nothing doing from them today . . .
Blow out the candle, lads, that drowsy lot are all in bed!'

As soon as he was out at sea, La Queue set his nets, after which
he went to look at his pots, that is his long wicker lobster pots, in
which you can occasionally catch red mullet as well. But despite
the calm sea, his search went unrewarded; all the pots were empty
except the last one in which, as if to rub salt into the wound, they
found one tiny mackerel which he angrily flung back into the sea.
That was the way it went: sometimes weeks would pass and the
fish would give Coqueville a miss; and it always happened when
Monsieur Mouchel was keen to buy. When La Queue pulled his
nets up an hour later, the only thing he had caught was a bunch of
seaweed. He clenched his fists and swore; it was all the more
irritating because the Atlantic was unbelievably calm and was
lying lazily stretched out, drowsing under a blue sky like a sheet
of burnished silver, on which *Zephyr* slid slowly and gently along
on an even keel. La Queue decided that he would make for
harbour after he had dropped his nets once more. He would
return and have another look in the afternoon; and he threatened
God and all his saints in outrageously blasphemous terms.

Meanwhile Rouget, Fouasse and Delphin were still sound asleep and did not rouse themselves until lunch-time. They could not remember anything except that they were vaguely aware of having enjoyed an amazing treat such as they had never known before. That afternoon, when they were down at the harbour, the Emperor tried to question the three of them, now that they had regained full use of their faculties. Perhaps it was something like a sort of brandy mixed with liquorice juice? Or could it be better described as a kind of sweet rum, with a burnt flavour? First they said yes, then they said no. The Emperor half suspected it might be ratafia* but he couldn't swear to it. Rouget and his crew were too exhausted to go fishing, especially as they knew that La Queue had gone out unsuccessfully that morning; so they were thinking of waiting until the following day before going to look at their pots. They sat with parched throats slumped on blocks of stone, gazing at the incoming tide and barely able to keep awake. Then suddenly Delphin sat up, sprang on to the block of stone and, looking far out to sea, shouted:

'Look over there, guv'nor!'

'What is it?' asked Rouget, stretching himself.

'A barrel.'

Their eyes lit up as the other two sprang to their feet and scanned the horizon.

'Where is it, lad? Where is the barrel?' asked Rouget excitedly.

'See that black dot over there, on the left?'

The others could not see anything. Then Rouget uttered an oath:

'Christ Almighty!'

He had just caught sight of the barrel, no bigger than a lentil, against the pale sea, caught in the slanting rays of the setting sun. He ran down to the *Whale* with Delphin and Fouasse sprinting after him like startled rabbits, scattering showers of pebbles as they ran.

As the *Whale* was clearing the harbour mouth, the news of the sighting of the barrel spread like wildfire and the women and children rushed down to the beach. People were shouting:

'A barrel, a barrel!'

'Can you see it? The current's carrying it towards Grandport!'

'Hurry up! That's it, on the left. A barrel!'

And Coqueville streamed down on to the beach, with the children turning cartwheels and the women holding up their skirts with both hands so as to scramble down more quickly. Very soon the whole village was assembled on the beach, just as the evening before.

Margot appeared briefly and then ran back home as fast as she could to warn her father, who was discussing a summons with the Emperor. In the end La Queue came out livid with rage and said to the gamekeeper:

'Stop bothering me! Rouget must've sent you along to waste my time. Well, he's not going to get that one, you'll see!'

When he saw the crew of the *Whale* already three hundred yards off shore rowing madly towards the black dot bobbing up and down in the distance, he became even more enraged.

'No, they're not going to get it! Over my dead body!'

And now Coqueville saw a splendid sight, a wild race between *Zephyr* and the *Whale*. When the crew of the latter saw the other boat leaving harbour, realizing the danger they redoubled their efforts. Although they had a start of some four hundred yards, it was still an even contest, because *Zephyr* was far lighter and faster. Excitement on the beach was rising to fever pitch. The Mahés and the Floches had instinctively formed into two groups and were following the changing fortunes of the race with passionate interest, each cheering its own boat on. At first the *Whale* held on to its lead but once *Zephyr* was properly under way, she could be seen to be steadily overhauling the other boat. The *Whale* put in a final spurt and for a few minutes managed to hold her advantage, only to be again overhauled as *Zephyr* came up on her at tremendous speed. From that moment onwards, it became apparent that the two boats would reach the barrel roughly together. Victory would depend on circumstances and the slightest error of judgement would determine the issue.

'The *Whale*, the *Whale*!' the Mahés were yelling.

The words froze on their lips. Just as the *Whale* was almost touching the barrel, *Zephyr* boldly slipped in between and pushed the barrel away to the portside, where La Queue harpooned it with a boathook.

'*Zephyr*! *Zephyr*!' howled the Floches.

And as the Emperor muttered something about 'foul play' under his breath, a few rough words were exchanged. Margot was clapping her hands. Father Radiguet, who had come down to the beach holding his breviary, uttered a profound remark which suddenly dowsed everyone's excitement and filled them all with alarm.

'Perhaps they're going to drink the lot, too,' he muttered sadly.

Out at sea a violent squabble had arisen between the *Whale* and *Zephyr*. Rouget was accusing La Queue of being a thief while the latter replied by calling Rouget a ne'er-do-well. The two men even picked up their oars to knock each other on the head and the race showed signs of turning into a naval battle. As it was, shaking their fists at each other, they promised to settle the matter ashore, threatening to slit each other's throats as soon as they were on land.

'What a shyster,' grunted Rouget. 'You know, that cask was bigger than the one yesterday... It's yellow, too. It must be something special.'

Then, in a resigned voice:

'Let's go and look at the pots. Perhaps there'll be some lobsters.'

And the *Whale* moved ponderously away to the point on the left.

On board *Zephyr*, La Queue had been obliged to speak sharply to Tupain and Brisemotte on the subject of the barrel, for the boathook had loosened one of the hoops and a red liquid was oozing out; the two young men took some of it on the tip of their finger and licked: it was delicious. Surely there wouldn't be any harm in trying just a glass of it? But La Queue put his foot down; he stowed the barrel away and said that the first person to try and have another lick would hear from him. Once ashore, they'd see.

'Shall we go and have a look at the pots, then?' asked Tupain sulkily.

'Yes, in a minute,' replied La Queue. 'There's no hurry.'

He too had been casting fond glances at the cask and in a sudden fit of listlessness, he felt tempted to return to harbour straightaway to see what its contents tasted like. He was bored with fish.

'All right,' he said after a pause. 'Let's get back, it's getting late. We'll look at the pots tomorrow.'

But just as he was giving up any idea of fishing, he caught sight of another barrel to starboard, a very tiny cask which was floating upright and spinning like a top. That was the end of any thoughts of fishing nets or lobster pots; they weren't mentioned again. *Zephyr* set off in pursuit of the cask which he picked up quite easily this time.

Meanwhile the *Whale* was engaged in a similar venture. When Rouget had already pulled up five completely empty lobster pots,

Delphin, still on the lookout, shouted that he could see something. But it didn't look like a barrel, it was too long.

'It's a piece of wood,' said Fouasse.

Rouget let his sixth lobster pot slide back into the sea without bothering to pull it completely out of the water.

'Let's go and have a look all the same,' he said.

As they approached, it seemed to them like a plank, a crate or a tree-trunk. Then they gave a cry of joy. It was a real barrel but a very queer one, a sort they had never seen before. It looked like a tube bulging in the middle with both ends closed by a layer of plaster.

'Isn't it strange!' exclaimed Rouget delightedly. 'I want the Emperor to taste this one... Come on, you two, let's get back!'

They agreed not to broach the barrel straightaway and the *Whale* returned to harbour just as *Zephyr* was tying up. The villagers were all still waiting expectantly on the beach. Cheers greeted this unhoped-for catch of three barrels. The young boys flung their caps into the air while the women scurried off to fetch some glasses. They immediately decided to sample the drinks on the spot. Any flotsam and jetsam belonged to the whole community, there was no disputing that! However, they gathered in two groups, the Mahés with Rouget, while the Floches formed a circle round La Queue.

'The first glass is for the Emperor!' cried Rouget. 'Tell us what it is!'

The liqueur was a lovely golden yellow. The gamekeeper raised his glass, looked at it, sniffed it and decided to take a sip.

'It's from Holland,' he announced after a long pause.

He offered no further information, and the Mahés all drank with due deference. It was slightly viscous and they were surprised by the flowery taste. The women thought it was very good; the men would have preferred a little less sugar. However, in the end, after a third or fourth glass, it did seem quite strong. The more they drank, the better they liked it. The men were becoming merry and the women felt a bit funny.

Meanwhile, despite his recent exchange of words with the mayor, the Emperor was now hanging round the Floche group. The larger barrel contained a dark red liqueur, while the tiny cask held a liquid as clear as a mountain stream; and it was this last that was the deadliest of them, really peppery and strong enough to take the skin off the roof of your mouth. None of the Floches was able to place either the red or the clear one. Yet some of them were fairly expert and were annoyed not to know the name of the liqueurs that they were drinking with such enjoyment.

'Here you are, Emperor, see what you think of this,' La Queue called out at last, making the first move.

The Emperor, who had been hoping for such an invitation, once again assumed his role as taster-in-chief. Having tried the red one, he said:

'There's some orange in it.'

For the clear one, he merely said:

'That's a real beauty!'

That was all they could get out of him, because all he did was to keep nodding his head with a knowing look and a pleased expression on his face, like a man who has just done a good job.

Father Radiguet alone seemed unconvinced. He wanted to put a name to them and since, according to him, he had the names on the tip of his tongue, in order to complete his information he kept emptying one glass after another, repeating as he did so:

'Now, wait a second, I know what it is... I'll be able to tell you in a minute.'

Meanwhile, everyone was becoming merry, the Mahés as well as the Floches. The latter were laughing particularly loudly because they were mixing their drinks and this made them all the merrier. Both groups were, however, keeping strictly to themselves and not offering any drinks to the other, although they were casting friendly glances at one another; but they were ashamed to admit openly that they would like to try the other group's drink, which was surely better than their own. Despite their rivalry, the two brothers Tupain and Fouasse spent the whole evening in close proximity to one another without once showing signs of wanting to square up to each other. It was noticed, too, that Rouget and his wife were drinking out of the same glass. As for Margot, she was serving drinks to the Floches and as she kept filling the glasses too full, the surplus spilt on to her fingers which she was continually licking, so that, although obeying her father's orders not to drink, she had become tipsy, like the girls during the grape-harvest. It was not unbecoming; on the contrary, she was looking all pink and her eyes were sparkling like candles.

The sun was setting; the evening was soft and springlike. Coqueville had demolished the contents of all three barrels and no one was thinking of going home to supper; they were too comfortable on the beach. When it was quite dark, Margot, sitting some distance away from the others, felt someone breathing down the back of her neck: it was Delphin, very merry, crawling on all fours and prowling round her like a wolf. She stifled a cry in order not to draw her father's attention, for he would certainly have booted his behind.

'Do go away, stupid!' she muttered, half laughing and half annoyed, 'You'll get caught!'

4

Next day, when Coqueville awoke, the sun was already high in the heavens. It was an even warmer day and the sea lay stretched out sleepily under a cloudless sky. It was one of those lazy sorts of day when it's wonderful not to have to do anything. It was Wednesday and until lunchtime Coqueville recovered from its indulgence of the previous evening. Then everyone went down to the beach to take a look.

Fish, Madame Dufeu, Monsieur Mouchel and everything connected with them were forgotten. La Queue didn't even mention going to look at their lobster pots. At about three o'clock they sighted some barrels, four of them, bobbing up and down in front of the village. *Zephyr* and the *Whale* set off in pursuit but as there was enough for all, they didn't squabble and each boat took its share.

At six o'clock, after exploring the bay, Rouget and La Queue came back with three barrels each. And once more, they went on the spree. The women had brought tables down to the beach to make things more comfortable. They even fetched benches and set up two open-air cafés, just like those in Grandport. The Mahés sat on the left, the Floches on the right, separated from each other by a mound of sand. However, that evening the Emperor kept going from one group to the other, carrying round glassfuls of each liqueur, so that everybody could taste the contents of each of the six barrels. By about nine o'clock, everyone was much merrier than on the previous evening. And next morning, no one in Coqueville could ever remember how they had managed to get to bed.

On Thursday, *Zephyr* and the *Whale* picked up only two

barrels; that is, two barrels each: but they were enormous. On Friday, the catch was superb, and beyond their wildest dreams: seven barrels, three for Rouget and four for La Queue. And now for Coqueville there began the Golden Age. Nobody did a stroke of work. The fishermen slept off the effects of the night before and did not wake till noon. Then they would go down for a stroll along the beach and look longingly out to sea. Their only concern was which liqueur would come in on the tide. They would sit there for hours, gazing out to sea, and a cry of joy would go up as soon as a barrel hove into view. From the top of the rock, the women and children would wave their arms about wildly at the sight of the tiniest clump of seaweed bobbing up and down in the waves. *Zephyr* and the *Whale* held themselves in readiness to leave at a moment's notice. They sailed out and scoured the bay, fishing for barrels in the same way that people fish for tunny, spurning the carefree mackerel which disported themselves in the sun and the soles floating idly at the surface. Coqueville followed their expeditions from the beach, chuckling with delight. Then, when evening came, they drank their catch.

What really attracted Coqueville's fancy was that the barrels were never-ending. Whenever there seemed to be none left, still they came. The lost ship must have had a wonderful cargo on board and Coqueville, which had become cheerfully selfish, joked about the wrecked vessel: it must have been a proper liqueur cellar, large enough to make every fish in the Atlantic tipsy! What is more, they never caught two identical barrels, for they were of every size, shape and colour, and in every barrel there was a different liqueur, so that the Emperor was in a permanent haze. He had drunk everything that was going and now he was all at sea! La Queue declared that he had never seen such a cargo in his whole life. Father Radiguet expressed the view that it must have been ordered by some native king wanting to set up a cellar. As a matter of fact, Coqueville was so drowsy and fuddled by drinking so many unknown liqueurs that it had given up any attempt to understand.

The ladies preferred the cordials: moka, cacao, peppermint and vanilla. One evening, Marie Rouget drank so much anisette that she was ill. Margot and the other girls went for curaçao, bénédictine, trappistine and chartreuse. The blackcurrant syrup was reserved for the children. The men, of course, enjoyed it most when they had picked up brandies, rums and Holland gins, the sort of stuff that stings the palate. And then there were the surprise items. A cask of resinated raki from Chios threw Coqueville into a state of complete bewilderment; they thought that they'd come across a barrel of turpentine; all the same, they drank it up, because it's a shame to waste anything; but they talked about it long afterwards. Arak from Batavia, caraway seed schnapps from Sweden, tuica calugaresca from Romania and Serbian slivovitz★ also threw Coqueville's ideas on what you can pour down your throat into utter confusion. Basically, they betrayed a weakness for kümmel and kirsch, the sort of spirits that are as clear as crystal and powerful enough to fell an ox. How was it possible for such wonderful drinks to have been invented? Up till now, Coqueville had had experience of only the rawest of spirits; and not everyone had known them. And so their imagination began to run riot and they felt like going down on their knees to worship such an inexhaustible variety of intoxicating liquor. Fancy being able to get drunk every day on something new that you didn't even know the name of! It was like a fairy story, a shower of nectar, a fountain spurting with every sort of extraordinary liquid, distillations scented with the fruits and flowers of the whole of creation!

And so on Friday evening, there were seven barrels set up on the beach and the whole of Coqueville was there as well; indeed, the villagers were there all the time for, thanks to the mild weather, they were all living on the beach. Never had they known such a gorgeous week in September. They had been on the spree since Monday and there was no reason for it not to last for ever if divine Providence continued its supply of barrels. Father Radiguet saw the hand of God in all this. All business was suspended; why toil and sweat when pleasure was handed to you, in a bottle, while you slept? They had all become members of the leisured classes, people who were in a position to drink expensive liqueurs without having to worry who was footing the bill. With their hands in their pockets, the inhabitants of Coqueville lounged about in the sun awaiting their evening treat. As a matter of fact, they were never sober; kümmel, kirsch and ratafia were the links in an unbroken chain of jollification; in the space of seven days, Coqueville was being inflamed by gin, made sentimental by curaçao and hilarious by brandy. And they were as innocent and as ignorant as babes in arms, drinking everything the good Lord provided with the simple faith of true believers.

It was on Friday that the Mahés and the Floches started fraternizing. Everyone was very merry that evening. The barriers between them had already begun to crumble the previous day, when some of the tipsiest among them had kicked away the mound of sand separating the two groups. There was only one further step needed. The Floches were busily emptying their four barrels while the Mahés were similarly engaged in finishing off their three small casks, which happened to contain liqueurs of the same colours as the French flag, red, white, and blue. The Floches were very envious of the blue one because a blue liqueur seemed to them something quite out of the ordinary. Now that he was never sober, La Queue had become extremely genial and he suddenly went across unsteadily, with a glass in his hand, realizing that as mayor, it was up to him to make the first move.

'Look, Rouget,' he said, stumbling somewhat over his words, 'would you care to have a drink with me?'

'I don't mind if I do,' replied Rouget, swaying with emotion.

And they fell on each other's necks. At this touching sight, everyone burst into tears and the Mahés and the Floches embraced each other after being at daggers drawn for three centuries. Father Radiguet, greatly stirred, again spoke of the hand of God. They drank each other's health in the three liqueurs, red, white and blue.

'*Vive la France!*' the Emperor cried.

The blue one was no good at all, the white one just passable; but the red one was terrific. After that, they set about the Floches' barrels. Then they started dancing. As there was no band, some of the young men obliged by whistling and clapping their hands. This set the girls going. It was a proper binge. The seven barrels were all placed in one long line and everyone could choose the one he liked best. Those who had had enough lay down on the sand and had a nap; when they woke up, they started again. The dancers gradually spread out until there was dancing all over the beach. This open-air hop went on till midnight. The sea lapped gently and the stars shone brightly in the calm of the fathomless depths of the heavens. It was like some primitive tribe, in the infancy of the world, peacefully cradled in the joyous intoxication of their first barrel of brandy.

However, Coqueville still went home when it was time to go to bed. When there was nothing left to drink, the Mahés and the

Floches, supporting and carrying each other as best they could, eventually made their way back to their houses. On Saturday, the celebration went on until nearly two o'clock in the morning. During the day, they had caught six barrels, two of which were enormous. Fouasse and Tupain nearly came to blows and Tupain, who became aggressive when drunk, threatened to do his brother in. But everyone was disgusted at such an exhibition, the Floches as well as the Mahés. Was it sensible to go on squabbling like that when the whole village was overflowing with brotherly love? So they forced the two brothers to drink each other's health, which they reluctantly did. The Emperor promised himself to keep an eye on them. The Rouget couple were not very happy either. When Marie had been drinking anisette, she allowed Brisemotte to take liberties that were not to her husband's liking, all the more so as drink had made him also amorously inclined. Father Radiguet had tried to pour oil on troubled waters by preaching the forgiveness of sins, but everyone was apprehensive at the possibility of an outburst.

'Ah well,' said La Queue, 'things will sort themselves out. If there's a good catch tomorrow, you'll see... Your very good health!'

However, La Queue himself was not entirely guiltless. He was still keeping a sharp eye on Delphin and trying to kick his backside every time he saw him sidling up to Margot. The Emperor indignantly pointed out that there was no sense in trying to prevent two young folk from having fun but La Queue still swore that he'd see his daughter dead rather than let Delphin have her. Anyway, Margot didn't want him.

'That's right, isn't it?' he shouted. 'You're too proud ever to marry a tramp, aren't you?'

'No, I never would, papa!' Margot invariably replied.

On Saturday, Margot drank a good deal of a very sweet liqueur. You can't imagine how sweet it was. As Margot was quite unsuspecting, she soon found herself sitting on the ground beside the barrel. She was laughing happily to herself: it was heavenly, she could see stars and hear dance tunes singing in her ears. Then it was that Delphin slid up to her under the cover of the barrel and took her hand.

'Will you, Margot?' he asked her.

'It's papa who doesn't want me to,' she replied, still smiling.

'Oh, that doesn't matter,' retorted the boy. 'Old people never do, you know... As long as you want to...'

And he boldly planted a kiss on her neck. She squirmed with pleasure and little shivers ran down her back.

'Stop it, you're tickling...'

But she made no mention of giving him a slap. For one thing, she couldn't have done it, because her hands had gone all weak, while for another, she was finding those little kisses on her neck rather nice. It was like the liqueur which was filling her with a delicious feeling of languor. After a while, she twisted her head and stretched out her chin, like a cat.

'Look,' she said in a voice that trembled, 'I'm itching just there, under my ear... Oh, that's wonderful...'

They had both forgotten La Queue. Fortunately the Emperor was on the alert. He drew Father Radiguet's attention to them.

'Look over there, Father. They'd better get married.'

'Morality would certainly suggest so,' observed the priest sententiously.

And he promised to see what he could do about arranging it next day: he would personally have a word with La Queue. Meanwhile La Queue himself had drunk so much that the Emperor and the priest had to carry him home. On the way, they tried to make him see reason with regard to Delphin and his daughter; but all they could get out of him was grunts. Delphin followed behind them, taking Margot home under the bright starry sky.

Next day, *Zephyr* and the *Whale* had already picked up seven barrels by four o'clock. At six o'clock they caught two more. That made nine in all. And so Coqueville celebrated the Sabbath day. It was the seventh day of inebriation and it was a celebration to end all celebrations, a beano such as no one had ever seen before nor would ever see again. Mention this to anyone from Lower Normandy and they'll chuckle and say:

'Ah yes, what a binge they had in Coqueville!'

5

Meanwhile, even as early as Tuesday, Monsieur Mouchel had expressed surprise at seeing neither Rouget nor La Queue. What the devil were they up to? The sea was calm, they should have made a splendid catch. Perhaps they were waiting in the hope of getting a big haul of lobsters and sole which they could bring over all together. So he decided to be patient and see what happened on Wednesday.

But on Wednesday, Monsieur Mouchel got cross. It must be remembered that Dufeu's widow was an awkward customer; it did not take long for her to become abusive. So although he was a fine, upstanding young fellow, well-built, with a mop of fair hair, she made him quake in his shoes, despite his secret dreams of one day making her his wife; he was thus always careful to show her every attention while reserving the right to bring her to heel with a good slap round the face if he ever became the boss. Well, that Wednesday morning, the widow raged and swore, complaining that no fish was being delivered and putting the blame on him for gadding about with the local girls instead of concentrating on whiting and mackerel, of which there should have been a plentiful supply. Thus provoked, Monsieur Mouchel declared that it was Coqueville's fault for not having kept their word. For a brief moment, Madame Dufeu's surprise at the news of such strange behaviour made her forget her anger. What on earth was Coqueville thinking of? They'd never done that sort of thing before. But she hastened to add that she didn't give a damn about Coqueville, that it was Monsieur Mouchel's responsibility and if he kept on being taken in by the fishermen, she'd have to decide what measures to take. This remark made the young man very uneasy and he consigned Rouget and La Queue to the bottomless pit. But perhaps they'd come next day.

Next day was Thursday and still neither of them put in an appearance. In the late afternoon, a despairing Monsieur Mouchel climbed up to the rock to the left of Grandport, where he had a view of Coqueville in the distance, together with its yellow strip of beach. He stayed looking for a long time. It seemed peaceful enough under the sun. Wisps of smoke were coming out of the chimneys: no doubt wives were getting the supper ready. Monsieur Mouchel saw that Coqueville was still there and that it hadn't been crushed by a fall of rock. He was more mystified than ever. Just as he was about to go down, he thought he could see two dark spots in the bay, the *Whale* and *Zephyr*. He went back and reassured the widow: Coqueville was out fishing.

Night came and went; it was Friday and still no trace of Coqueville. Monsieur Mouchel climbed a dozen times up to the rock. He was beginning to lose his nerve; Madame Dufeu was treating him abominably and he could think of no possible explanation to give her. Coqueville was still there, lazily basking in the sun like a lizard. But this time Monsieur Mouchel could not see any smoke. The village seemed dead. Had they all crawled into their holes and given up the ghost? Certainly, the beach seemed to be swarming with people but that could well be heaps of seaweed brought in by the tide.

On Saturday, still nobody appeared. The widow had stopped shouting and was sitting there tight-lipped and with eyes set hard. Monsieur Mouchel spent two hours up on his rock. He was becoming curious and beginning to feel that he must discover for himself why the village seemed so deserted.

Finally, the sight of those tumbledown old cottages blissfully drowsing in the sun irritated him so much that he resolved to leave very early on Monday, so as to be there by nine o'clock in the morning.

Getting to Coqueville was no easy matter. Monsieur Mouchel decided to go by land, so that he could descend on the village unawares. He drove in a horse and cart as far as Robigneux, where he left them in a barn, since it would have been foolhardy to risk driving down the gullies. He set off at a steady pace for Coqueville, a distance of more than four miles over the roughest of tracks. The road, in fact, runs through a wild and picturesque landscape, twisting and turning as it descends between two enormous sloping walls of rock, so narrow in parts that three men could not walk abreast. Further on, it ran along a sheer drop, until the gorge suddenly opened out to give views over the immense blue horizon and the sea. But Monsieur Mouchel was in no mood to admire the landscape and he swore as the boulders rolled away under his feet. It was all Coqueville's fault and he promised to show them the rough edge of his tongue when he arrived. He was now nearly there and as he came round the last bend in the rock he caught sight of the twenty or so houses which comprised the village, huddled together against the cliff-face.

It was just striking nine. The sky was blue and it was so warm that you could have thought it was June. The air was clear and there was a golden glow and a cool salty smell of sea. Monsieur Mouchel set off down the only street of the village, which he had often visited, and as he had to pass Rouget's house, he went in. The house was empty. Then, he had a brief look into Tupain's, Fouasse's and Brisemotte's cottages. Not a soul to be seen; the doors were all open but the rooms were empty. What could it mean? A cold shiver began to run down his spine. Then he thought of the local authorities: the Emperor would certainly be able to give him information. But the Emperor's house was as empty as all the rest; so even the gamekeeper wasn't there! By now, the silence of the deserted village filled him with terror. He hurried on to the mayor's house where another surprise awaited him. The inside of the house was in a frightful mess: beds left unmade for the last three days, dirty crockery lying about all over the place, chairs tipped up as if there had been a fight. Now completely unnerved and with thoughts of some dreadful cataclysm running through his mind, Monsieur Mouchel made for the church, determined to leave no stone unturned; but the priest was no more visible than the mayor. Religion had vanished together with any civil authority.

Coqueville had been abandoned and left with not a breath of life, not even a dog or a cat. And not even poultry, for the hens had left as well. Absolutely nothing at all: empty and silent, Coqueville lay plunged in slumber beneath the vast blue sky.

Heavens above! It wasn't surprising if Coqueville wasn't supplying any fish! Coqueville had moved out, Coqueville was dead! The police must be informed. Monsieur Mouchel was deeply moved by this mysterious disaster; but then, thinking that he might as well go down as far as the beach, he uttered a sudden cry. There, flat out on the sand, lay the entire population. He thought at first that there must have been a general massacre, but the sound of heavy snoring quickly disabused him. On Sunday night, Coqueville had celebrated until such a late hour that its inhabitants had been quite incapable of going home to bed. So they had slept on the beach, in the place where they had toppled over around the nine barrels of liqueur, now completely empty.

Yes, the whole of Coqueville lay there plunged in sleep; and I mean by that the women and children and old men, as well as the working men. There was not one still on his feet. Some were lying face down, some on their backs; others lay curled up. As you make your bed, so you must lie on it. And so the whole lot were scattered all over the beach where their drunkenness had landed them, like a handful of leaves blown at random by the wind. Some of the men had tipped over with their heads hanging down while some of the women were showing their backsides. It was all free and easy, a dormitory in the open air, good honest folk and not a trace of embarrassment, because embarrassment is the enemy of enjoyment. There happened to be a new moon and so, thinking that they had blown out their candles, the inhabitants of Coqueville had let themselves go. Day had come and the sun was shining brightly, straight into the sleepers' eyes; but not one eye blinked. They were all sleeping like logs and beaming all over their faces with that wonderful innocence of the drunk. The hens, too, must have come down early to peck at the barrels, because they too were lying on the sand, dead drunk. There were even five cats and three dogs, flat on their backs with their paws in the air, tipsy from licking the sugary dregs left in the glasses.

Monsieur Mouchel picked his way through the sleepers for a while, taking care not to disturb anyone. He realized what had happened because they had picked up some casks from the wrecked English vessel in Grandport. His anger had completely evaporated. What a touching sight it was! Coqueville was reconciled and the Mahés were lying down with the Floches . . . When the last glass had been drained, the worst enemies had fallen into each other's arms: Tupain and Fouasse were snoring away hand in hand, like brothers who henceforth would find it impossible to quarrel over legacies. As for the Rougets, they offered an even more charming picture: Marie lay sleeping between Rouget and Brisemotte, as though saying that from now on they would live happily like that, for ever afterwards . . .

But there was one group that provided a particularly touching family scene: Delphin and Margot were lying with their arms round each other's necks, cheek to cheek, with their lips still open in a kiss, while the Emperor was lying crosswise at their feet, keeping guard over them; La Queue was sound asleep and snoring away like any happy father who had found a husband for his daughter; and Father Radiguet, who had toppled over like all the rest, was holding his arms outspread as though blessing them. In sleep, Margot was still holding up her pretty little face like the muzzle of a lovesick cat who enjoys being tickled under its chin.

So the spree ended in a wedding. And later on, Monsieur Mouchel himself married the widow and tanned her hide as he had promised.

Mention all this to anyone from Lower Normandy and they'll chuckle and say:

'Ah yes, what a binge they had in Coqueville!'

A FLASH IN THE PAN

ONCE a month during the fruit season, a swarthy little girl with a mop of black hair would appear in the house of Monsieur Rostand, a solicitor in Aix-en-Provence, with a basket of apricots or peaches so enormous that she had difficulty in carrying it. As soon as it became known that she was waiting in the large downstairs hall, the whole family would come down to see her.

'Ah, it's you, Naïs,' the solicitor would say. 'You've brought us some fruit. You're a good girl. . . And how's your father?'

'Very well, thank you, monsieur,' the little girl would reply with a flash of white teeth.

Then Madame Rostand would take Naïs Micoulin into the kitchen and question her about the olives, the almonds and the vines. The most important thing was to discover whether there had been any rain on the stretch of coast at L'Estaque, where the Rostands had their property, La Blancarde, which was farmed by their tenant Micoulin. There were only a few dozen almond and olive trees but the question of rain was still the most urgent, for this part of the country was chronically prone to drought.

'There've been a few drops,' Naïs would say. 'The grapes could do with some more.'

Then, having delivered her news, she would be offered a hunk of bread and some leftovers of meat before going back to L'Estaque in the cart of a butcher who came over to Aix once a fortnight. Often she would bring shellfish, a spiny lobster, or a nice fish, for old Micoulin was keener on fishing than on ploughing. Whenever she came during the school holidays, Frédéric, Rostand's son, would run down to the kitchen and tell her when the family would be coming to stay at La Blancarde and remind her to get all the fishing tackle ready. He was on friendly terms with her because he used to play with her when he was quite young; but since the age of twelve, she had started calling him 'Monsieur Frédéric' as a mark of respect. Indeed, every time old Micoulin heard her speak too familiarly to the son of his landlord, he would give her a sound box on the ears. But that did not prevent the children from remaining good friends.

'And you won't forget to mend the nets?' the schoolboy would say.

'Don't worry, Monsieur Frédéric,' Naïs replied, 'We'll have everything ready for you.'

Monsieur Rostand was an extremely wealthy man. He had bought a superb townhouse, the Hôtel de Coiron, in the Rue du Collège, very cheaply. Built in the late seventeenth century, it had no fewer than twelve windows at the front and enough rooms to house a whole community; as the household comprised only five people, including two old servants, it seemed lost in such spacious quarters. The solicitor occupied only the first floor. After advertising the ground floor and second floor for ten years without finding any tenants, he had finally decided to close up those rooms, leaving two-thirds of the house to be taken over by spiders. The gloomy empty house echoed like a cathedral at the slightest sound in the vast entrance hall; it had a monumental staircase and could easily have held a whole modern house. Immediately after buying the house, Monsieur Rostand had erected a partition to divide the principal drawing-room, some forty feet long and twenty-five feet wide and lit by six large windows; one half of the room he took as his own office while the other half was for his clerks. There were four further rooms on the first floor, the smallest of which measured nearly twenty-three feet by sixteen. Madame Rostand, Frédéric and the two old maidservants had rooms with ceilings as high as most chapels. The solicitor had been forced reluctantly to convert a former boudoir into a kitchen in order to provide a more convenient service, because previously, when the ground floor kitchen had been in use, all the food arrived completely cold after being carried through the damp and icy-cold hall and up the staircase. But the worst feature of these ridiculously large quarters was the totally inadequate furniture. Monsieur Rostand's immense study contained only a sadly inelegant Empire settee and eight matching armchairs in green Utrecht velvet scattered sparsely round the room, while tiny occasional tables of the same period stood in the middle, looking like dolls' furniture; on the mantelshelf there was a frightful modern marble clock standing between two vases, while the floor covering consisted of shiny garish red tiles. The bedrooms were even more sparsely furnished. Everywhere you could sense the scornful indifference of the southern Frenchman, however wealthy, for any comfort or luxury, in this sun-blessed country where everybody lives as much as possible out of doors. The Rostands were certainly quite unaware of the desolation and gloom of these vast, deathly cold rooms which had all the sadness of ruins, compounded by the poverty and sparseness of the furniture.

The solicitor was, however, an extremely astute man. He had inherited from his father one of the largest practices in Aix and with an energy rare in a land where people are generally bone-idle, he had succeeded in building it up still further. Small in stature, always on the go, with a ferrety face, he devoted himself wholeheartedly to the advancement of his practice; his pursuit of wealth was, indeed, so singleminded that he did not even take time off to read a newspaper during his rare moments of relaxation at his club. His wife on the other hand had the reputation of being one of the most distinguished and intelligent women of Aix. She had been born a de Villebonne and this had left her with an aura of considerable prestige, despite having married beneath her station. But she was so straitlaced and practised her religious duties with such stubborn, narrow-minded and methodical routine that she had become, as it were, quite dried up.

So Frédéric was growing up between an inordinately busy father and an excessively puritanical mother. During his school years, he had been a dunce of the first water, going in terror of his mother but with such an unconquerable distaste for work that he would sometimes sit for hours over his books without reading a line, thinking of other things, while his parents, watching him, imagined that he was hard at work. Exasperated by his laziness, they finally packed him off to boarding school where, delighted at having escaped his parents' watchful eye, he still managed to work no harder. So, becoming alarmed at the signs of his incipient emancipation, they took him away from the school in order to be able to have him once again under their observation. In this way he completed his two final years of education, so closely guarded that he was forced to work; his mother would inspect his exercise books and compel him to go over his lessons, standing over him all the time like a policeman. Thanks to this careful supervision, Frédéric failed his school-leaving examination only twice.

The Law Faculty of Aix has an excellent reputation and young Frédéric naturally applied to join it. As the former seat of a High Court, there is no shortage of barristers, solicitors and lawyers of all sorts engaged in the administration of justice; but law is still studied, even by those who have no intention of ever practising it. Frédéric merely continued to live in the same way as he had at school, giving the impression of working hard whilst doing as little as possible. Most reluctantly, Madame Rostand had had to allow her son greater freedom. He could now go out whenever he wanted and was expected to be present only at mealtimes; he had to be in by nine o'clock every night except on those days when he was allowed to go to the theatre. He now embarked on the life of the provincial student which is both very monotonous and full of temptations, unless spent wholeheartedly working.

One has to know Aix-en-Provence personally, with its quiet streets, so quiet that grass grows over them, and its general drowsy atmosphere, in order to realize the emptiness of the life of a student there. The ones who work can kill time in studying; but those who are not interested in following their courses have only two resources against boredom: going to cafés, where they play cards for money, or going to certain other establishments where they do worse things. As young Rostand turned into an enthusiastic gambler, he spent most of his evenings playing cards, but he ended them elsewhere. With the lustfulness of a schoolboy finally set free, he flung himself into the only sort of debauchery that the town had to offer, since Aix lacked the emancipated girls that you meet everywhere in the Latin Quarter of Paris. When his evenings proved too short, he turned them into nights by stealing a house-key. In such pursuits he passed his years of law school quite agreeably.

Frédéric had also now come to the realization that he must show himself to be an obedient son. Gradually he acquired the imperturbable hypocrisy of all children bullied by their parents. His mother could now proclaim herself fully satisfied: he accompanied her to Mass, behaved impeccably at all times and told her enormous lies without blinking an eyelid and with a note of such sincerity in his voice that she accepted them. So skilful did he become that he was never at a loss, always able to find an excuse and supporting his case by extraordinary stories carefully elaborated in advance. He used to pay his gambling debts by borrowing from his cousins and had a whole complicated system of bookkeeping. Once, after an unexpected win, he even managed to fulfil his dream of spending a week in Paris by arranging an alleged invitation from a friend who owned an estate near the Durance.*

Moreover Frédéric was a handsome young man, tall, with regular features and a thick black beard. His vices made him attractive, especially to women. Those people who knew of his pranks would give a wry smile but since he had the decency to conceal this shady side of his character, you had to be grateful to him for not advertising his riotous style of living, unlike some less mannerly students who were the talk of the town.

Frédéric was now rising twenty-one and would soon be taking his law finals. His father was still young and unwilling to hand over his practice straightaway; he talked of getting his son into the public prosecutor's office, for he had friends in Paris whom he could persuade to have him made a deputy public prosecutor. The young man did not say no; he never opposed his parents openly; but his lips curled in a slight smile which suggested his firm intention of continuing the life of idleness which was so much to his liking. He knew that his father was rich; he was the only son; why should he give himself the slightest trouble? Meanwhile, he strolled down the Cours Mirabeau* smoking cigars, went to gay house-parties in neighbouring country-houses and patronized houses of ill fame, daily and in secret. All this did not prevent him from being at his mother's beck and call or showing her every solicitude. When he felt completely fagged out and extremely liverish from some particularly violent excesses, he would come back to his parents' vast, freezing house in the Rue du Collège and enjoy a delicious rest cure. The boredom of the empty and forbidding high-ceilinged rooms was cool and tranquillizing. Here, while pretending to his mother that he was staying home to keep her company, he would recuperate until such time as, having recovered his appetite and his health, he would start plotting some new escapade. In a word, the nicest young man you could ever want to meet, as long as you didn't interfere with his pleasures.

Meanwhile, Naïs used to come to the Rostand house with fruit and vegetables every year and every year she had grown up a little more. She was exactly the same age as Frédéric, perhaps three months older. So each time, Madame Rostand would say to her:

'How grown up you're getting, Naïs!'

Naïs would smile and show her dazzling white teeth. More often than not, Frédéric was not at home. But one day, during his last year at university, just as he was going out, he met Naïs in the hall, holding her basket. He stopped in his tracks in surprise. He could no longer recognize the lanky boyish-looking girl whom he had seen only the summer before at La Blancarde. She was in every way superb: her nut-brown face beneath her thick crop of black hair, the full curves of her figure, her broad shoulders, her magnificent arms, her bare wrists. In the space of a year she had shot up like a young sapling.

'It's you!' he stammered.

'Yes, Monsieur Frédéric,' she said looking him straight in the face with her large, brown, smouldering eyes. 'I've brought you some sea-urchins. When are you coming to La Blancarde? Shall we get the nets ready?'

Still staring at her, he said softly, apparently not having heard what she had said:

'Naïs, you look wonderful! What have you got there?'

The compliment made her laugh. Then, as he playfully took hold of her hands, just as he used to do when they were playmates, her face became serious and, suddenly reverting to the same familiar form of speech of those days, she said in a low, rather hoarse voice:

'Not now, Frédéric! Your mother's coming.'

2

A fortnight later, the Rostand family were on their way to La Blancarde. The solicitor had to wait until the courts were in recess and in any case the month of September was the pleasantest to spend by the sea, for the heat was dying down and the nights were becoming deliciously cool.

La Blancarde was not in L'Estaque itself, which is a small town situated close to the outermost suburbs of Marseilles, at the far end of a bay completely enclosed by rocks. The property stood beyond the town, perched on top of a cliff. Set in a clump of tall pines, the yellow front could be seen from all around the bay. It was one of those heavy, square, old buildings with irregular windows which people call châteaux in Provence. In front of the house was a broad terrace beyond which the ground fell sheer to a tiny pebbly beach. Behind, there was a large area of poor land where the only plants that could be persuaded to grow were a few vines, olives and almond trees. Also, one of the disadvantages and dangers of La Blancarde was that the sea was constantly battering the foot of the cliff and that underground springs filtered through the mixture of clay and rock, softening it, so that every so often enormous masses of earth would break away and fall with a terrifying noise into the water. The property was slowly being eroded and some of the pines had already been engulfed by the sea.

The Micoulins had farmed the property as tenants for forty years. In accordance with local custom, they did the cultivation and shared the crops with the owner. The crops were poor and they would have starved had they not been able to do a little fishing in the summer; between ploughing and sowing, there was time to set a few nets. The family consisted of old Micoulin himself, a tough and rough old man with a swarthy, deeply-lined face who struck terror in his household; the mother, a tall woman broken down by long hours of working the land in the pitiless sun; a son who was serving on board the *Arrogante*; and Naïs who had been sent out to work in a tile-factory by her father, despite all the work she had to do in the home. The farmer's house, a tumbledown old cottage clinging to the cliff-face, rarely heard the cheerful sound of a laugh or a song. Micoulin was a taciturn old ogre, endlessly brooding over the vicissitudes of his life. The two women showed him the respect born of fear that wives and daughters owe to the head of the family in southern France. Almost the only sound that ever disturbed the peace and quiet of the house was the furious voice of the mother standing with arms akimbo bawling Naïs's name as soon as she had attempted to make herself scarce. The girl would hear her a good half mile off and have to come back, livid with suppressed anger.

In L'Estaque they called her 'the lovely Naïs'; but she was not a very happy girl. When she was already sixteen, her father, on the slightest pretext, would hit her in the face hard enough to make her nose bleed; and even now that she was turned twenty, she would have bruised shoulders for weeks on end as a result of her father's brutal treatment. He was not an unkind man but merely using his royal prerogative to enforce the strictest obedience, maintaining his legitimate right, inherited from the Roman *paterfamilias*, of life or death over his family. One day when, during a thrashing, Naïs had dared to lift a hand to defend herself, he had almost killed her. After such punishment Naïs was left inwardly boiling with rage: she would sit on the ground in some dark corner, dry-eyed, brooding over the indignity she had suffered. In her sombre fury she would stay like this in silence for hours on end, turning over in her mind plans of vengeance that she would never put into effect. It was her own father's blood in her that was angrily rebelling, in the blind urge always to be on top. She would look scornfully at her cowed old mother trembling with fear as she humiliated herself before her father. She would often say: 'If I had a husband like that, I'd kill him!'

Naïs had even come to prefer being thrashed because at least it gave her a shaking-up; at other times her life was so narrow and restricted that she was consumed with boredom. Her father forbade her to go down to L'Estaque and kept her constantly busy on jobs up at La Blancarde; and even when there was nothing to do, he wanted to keep his eye on her. So she used to look forward impatiently to the month of September, for as soon as the owners moved in, Micoulin was obliged to relax his strict supervision, for Naïs used to run errands for Madame Rostand and was able to make up for the sort of life she led during the rest of the year.

One morning, old Micoulin had realized that this grown-up daughter of his could bring a couple of francs a day into the family. So he released her and packed her off to work in a tile-factory. Although the work was very hard, Naïs was delighted. She would set off in the morning for the other side of L'Estaque and stay there until evening, toiling away in the sun, turning over tiles so that they dried. It was a manual labourer's job and her hands became all rough; but she no longer felt her father on her back all the time; she could enjoy herself in the company of young men without constraint. And in this laborious job, she developed and turned into a beauty. In the hot sun, her face became a deep golden brown and her sturdy neck took on the appearance of a rich collar of amber; her jet-black hair grew thick and long, as though to protect her face from the whiplash of her curls; the constant bending and stretching gave her the strong and supple body of a young athlete; and indeed, when she straightened up amidst the red clay tiles spread out on the beaten earth, she looked like some antique Amazon, a terracotta statue suddenly brought into vigorous life by the flaming rays of the sun. When Micoulin saw that his daughter was becoming such a beauty, his beady little eyes started watching her like a hawk. She was too cheerful: he couldn't believe that it was natural for a girl to be so happy. And he promised himself to strangle any sweethearts whom he caught prowling round her skirts. However, although Naïs could have had dozens of sweethearts, she discouraged them and made fun of all the young men she met. Her only good friend was a hunchback who worked in the same tile-factory as herself, a little man who went by the name of Toine. He had been sent as a foundling from Aix and had been adopted by L'Estaque. This little Punch-like figure had a charming laugh and Naïs tolerated him because he was so gentle. She could twist him round her little finger and would often bully him to vent her bad temper after her father had given her a thrashing. In any case, Toine was of no importance; everybody made fun of him. Micoulin once said that he had no objection to his daughter's little hunchback; he knew her too well, she was too proud.

That year when Madame Rostand had moved into La Blancarde, she asked her tenant if he would lend her Naïs as one of her own maids was ill. It so happened that the tile-factory had laid off its workers at the time; moreover Micoulin, however harsh he might be towards his own family, was more forthcoming when it came to his landlord and would have given his consent even had the request for his daughter's services inconvenienced him. Monsieur Rostand had had to go to Paris to deal with some pressing business and Frédéric and his mother were left alone. During the first few days the young man had usually felt the need to take plenty of exercise; the fresh air would tempt him to go fishing with Micoulin, helping him to set or pull up his nets; or else he would go for long walks through the gorges that run down to L'Estaque. Then, after his initial burst of enthusiasm, he would lie day after day drowsing in the shade of the pine trees on the edge of the terrace, watching the monotonous blue sea and eventually growing bored. Generally a fortnight at La Blancarde was all he could stand. After that he would think up some excuse to slip away every morning into Marseilles.

The day after the owners had arrived, Micoulin called up to Frédéric's bedroom as soon as the sun was up. He was on his way to haul up his pots, those long wicker baskets with a narrow aperture used to catch fish that feed on the bottom. But the young man turned a deaf ear to the invitation; he did not seem tempted by the idea of going fishing. When he got up he settled himself under the pine trees, flat on his back, gazing up at the sky. His mother was surprised not to see him go off on one of his long excursions, from which he would return ravenous.

'Aren't you going out?' she asked him.

'No, mother,' he replied. 'As Papa's not here I'll stay and keep you company.'

Micoulin heard this reply and muttered in his dialect:

'Ah well, Monsieur Frédéric will soon be nipping off to Marseilles.'

However, Frédéric did not go into Marseilles. The week went by and still he lay flat on his back changing position only when the sun caught up with him. As a pretext, he took a book with him but he hardly glanced at it; more often than not, it lay unread on the baked earth among the dry pine needles. The young man did not even look at the sea; he kept his eye on the house, seemingly interested in the housework being performed by the maids as they kept coming and going all the time across the terrace; and when it was Naïs who went by, a glint of desire lit up in the young master's eye. Then Naïs would walk more slowly, swaying her hips as she did so without once looking in his direction.

This little game lasted for several days. In his mother's presence, Frédéric would treat Naïs almost rudely if she was serving clumsily; and when he rebuked her, the girl coyly lowered her eyes, almost as if enjoying his irritation.

One day at lunch, Naïs broke a salad bowl. Frédéric flared up:

'What a stupid girl!' he exclaimed. 'What on earth does she think she's up to?'

And he stood up in a rage, saying that his trousers were completely ruined. In fact, a drop of oil had fallen on to his knee; but he made a tremendous fuss:

'What are you staring at?' he shouted. 'Don't just stand there! Bring me a napkin and some water.'

Naïs dipped the corner of a table napkin into a cup of water and knelt down in front of Frédéric to rub out the stain.

'Don't bother,' Madame Rostand was saying. 'There's no need.'

But the girl kept hold of her master's leg and continued to rub it vigorously with her splendid strong arms. He still kept on scolding her.

'I've never seen such carelessness,' he said roughly. 'She couldn't have broken the salad bowl nearer to me if she'd tried . . . Our china wouldn't last long in Aix if she was serving us there!'

His harsh reaction was so disproportionate to the fault that when Naïs had left the room, Madame Rostand felt compelled to expostulate and calm him down:

'What have you got against the poor girl? Anyone would think that you can't stand her. Please try to treat her more politely. Remember that you used to play together as children and she's not like an ordinary servant.'

'Well, she just gets on my nerves, that's all,' replied Frédéric, making sure that he sounded very fierce.

That evening, after dark, Naïs and Frédéric met at the end of the terrace where they could not be seen. They had not yet exchanged a single word alone. Nobody in the house could hear them. In the warm, still air a scent of resin drifted down from the pine trees. In a gentle whisper, falling back into the same familiar way of speaking they had used as children, she asked:

'Why did you lose your temper with me like that, Frédéric? You were horrible.'

His reply was to take hold of her hands, draw her towards him and kiss her full on the lips. She did not protest and then went away, leaving him behind; he sat down on the parapet because he did not want his mother to see him in such a state of excitement. Ten minutes later, Naïs was serving at table with her usual air of rather aloof composure.

Frédéric and Naïs had made no arrangement to see each other again but one night they met at the edge of the terrace under an olive tree, at the top of the cliff; during the meal they had several times looked at each other with burning insistence. It was a warm night and Frédéric had remained standing at his window, smoking cigarettes as he peered into the darkness. At about one o'clock he saw a dim shape slipping along the terrace. He climbed down to a shed roof and then, with the help of some long poles lying in a corner, he clambered down on to the terrace, taking care not to risk waking his mother. Once on the ground he walked over to the old olive tree, certain that Naïs was waiting for him.

'Is that you?' he asked in a low voice.

'Yes,' she replied simply.

He sat down beside her in the short grass and put his arm round her waist. She rested her head on his shoulder. For a moment they did not speak. The old olive tree with its gnarled trunk sheltered them under its leafy roof. In front of them the sea stretched out black and still under the stars. At the end of the bay Marseilles lay hidden in a haze; only the Planier lighthouse on the left kept shining out every minute, its yellow beam piercing the night and then vanishing; and there seemed something gentle and tender in this light that continually disappeared on the horizon only suddenly to return.

'Is your father away, then?' asked Frédéric.

'I climbed out of the window,' she replied in her deep voice.

They did not speak of their love; it had deep roots in their childhood and now they could remember playing together when desire was already stirring in their childish games. Lovingly they began to stroke each other; nothing seemed more natural. They could not put their feelings into words: all they wanted was to make love. He found her lovely and exciting with her country tan and earthy smell; she felt the pride of a girl so often thrashed who was becoming the mistress of her young master. She gave herself to him. When the couple climbed back into their rooms the same way as they had come, day was beginning to break.

3

It was a wonderful month. There was not a drop of rain and the blue satin of the sky was not speckled by a single cloud. The sun rose pink and glassy and set in a golden haze. Yet it was never too hot, for the sea breeze rose and died away with the sun; then followed the nights, deliciously cool and fragrant with the scent of herbs which, warmed during the day, perfumed the darkness.

The countryside round L'Estaque is superb. Broad promontories of rock project on each side of the bay while the offshore islands seem to block the horizon, turning the sea into a vast lagoon, intensely blue in colour when the weather is fine. In the distance, at the foot of the mountains, lies Marseilles with its houses rising in tiers on the foothills; in clear weather you can see from L'Estaque the grey jetty of La Joliette* with the delicate mastwork of the ships in the harbour; further back can be seen the house fronts set in clumps of trees, and the dazzling white chapel of Notre Dame de la Garde on a height towering up to the sky. And from Marseilles the whole coast curves round, cut by wide inlets before it reaches L'Estaque and fringed with factories which now and then belch forth long plumes of smoke. When the sun is at its zenith, the sea, looking almost black, seems to be slumbering between the two white rocky promontories, set off with warmer tints of brown and yellow. It is like some vast painting, a glimpse of a corner of the Orient rising up in the blinding, shimmering light.

But L'Estaque does not have only this outlook over the sea. The village is backed by mountains and crossed by roads which vanish into the midst of a jumble of fallen rocks. The Marseilles-Lyons railway line runs among the massive rocks, bridging ravines and suddenly penetrating into the rock itself, to emerge nearly three miles further on through the Nerthe tunnel, the longest in France. Nothing can rival these wild and majestic gorges which snake through the hills, the narrow tracks at the foot of precipitous chasms whose arid slopes are planted with pine trees, the walls of rock tinged with shades of rust and blood. Sometimes these gorges open out and you can see a tiny olive grove in the hollow of a valley or an isolated house hiding behind its painted front and closed shutters. Then there are the tracks full of brambles, impenetrable thickets, tumbled boulders, dried up torrents, every imaginable feature to surprise you as you walk through the scrub. And on top, above the black line of pines, the endless silken ribbon of the delicate blue sky.

There is also the narrow strip of coast hemmed in between rock and sea, the red earth where the tile-factories, the main industry of the region, have excavated immense holes to extract clay. The soil is broken up and full of gullies, sparsely planted with a few stunted trees which seem as if their source of life has dried up under a searing gust of passion. Walking along the tracks you could imagine that you are on a layer of plaster in which you sink up to your ankles and the slightest breath of wind sends up clouds of dust which settle on the hedgerows. Little grey lizards lie drowsing at the foot of walls as hot as ovens while flights of chirping grasshoppers, crackling like sparks, flee from the furnace of scorched grass. In the heavy, motionless, slumbering noonday air the only sign of life is the monotonous chant of the cicadas.

For a whole month this countryside of fire and flame was the scene of the young couple's love. It was as if the torrid sky had set fire to their blood. For the first week they were content to meet at night under the same olive tree on the edge of the cliff. Their ecstasy was beyond words; and as the cool night calmed their frenzied lovemaking, they would sometimes lie with their faces and their burning hands turned towards the passing breeze which refreshed them like a mountain stream. Below them at the bottom of the cliff, the sea murmured its delight. The pungent smell of seaweed intoxicated them with desire. Then, as they lay in each other's arms, tired and contented, they would look across the water towards Marseilles glowing in the night and the red lights at the entrance to the harbour reflected blood-red in the sea; the flickering gaslights marking the long sinuous line of the suburbs to right and left; in the middle, over the town, other lights sparkled and glittered while the gardens on Bonaparte Hill showed up as two twinkling lines which sloped up and curved over the skyline. All these lights on the far side of the sleeping bay seemed to be illuminating some dream town that would vanish with the dawn. And the vast bowl of the sky above the dark confused shapes on the horizon cast a spell over them, making them stir uneasily and clasp each other more tightly. The stars overhead flooded them with their radiance; in Provence, on such clear nights as these, the constellations seem like living fire. Trembling at the spectacle of these vast spaces, they would lower their eyes and look only at the single star of the Planier lighthouse, watching its friendly beam affectionately as they once more sought each other's lips.

But one night they found themselves being watched by the round face of the full moon on the horizon. A trail of fire shone over the sea as if the golden scales of a giant fish, some deepwater eel, were gliding in endless rings over the surface and a yellow half-light dimmed the lights of Marseilles as it bathed the hills and inlets of the bay. As the moon rose higher, the light grew brighter and the shadows sharper. This silent witness of their lovemaking embarrassed them. They became afraid that they might be caught if they stayed too close to La Blancarde and next time they met they climbed over a piece of broken-down wall and went in search of all the other hiding-places which the countryside offered. First they took refuge in a disused tile-factory: the ruined shed had a cellar underneath in which the mouths of two kilns were still gaping open; but this hole in the ground depressed them, for they preferred to feel the open sky above them. So they explored the red clay quarries and discovered delightful little nooks only a few yards square where the only sound to be heard was the barking of the dogs guarding the homesteads. They went even further afield, straying along the rocky coast going towards Niolon; they also followed the narrow tracks at the bottom of the gorges, looking for caves and remote gullies. For a whole fortnight their nights of love were full of playful adventure. The moon had gone and it was dark once more; but La Blancarde now seemed to have become too small to hold their love, they needed the whole length and breadth of the land to consummate it.

One night as they were walking along a path above L'Estaque, making for the gorge of the Nerthe, they thought they heard a muffled footstep following them behind a small spinney of pine trees beside the path. They stopped and listened uneasily.

'Can you hear that sound?' Frédéric asked.

'Yes, it must be a stray dog,' said Naïs in a low voice.

They went on; but at the next bend in the path, when the spinney came to an end, they plainly saw a black figure slip behind some rocks. It was certainly a human being but of an odd shape, like a hunchback. Naïs gave a slight exclamation.

'Stay here,' she said quickly.

She ran off in search of the shadowy figure. Soon Frédéric heard a rapid whispering. Then she came back, a trifle pale but calm.

'What was it?' he asked.

'Nothing,' she replied.

Then, after a moment's hesitation, she went on:

'If you hear footsteps, don't be scared. It's Toine. You know, the hunchback. He wants to keep guard over us.'

In fact, Frédéric had sometimes felt that they were being followed by a shadowy figure providing a sort of protection around them. Naïs had several times tried to chase Toine away;

but the poor creature was asking only to be her watchdog: he wouldn't show himself, he wouldn't make a sound, why not let him do what he wanted? Ever since then, had the lovers listened during their passionate embraces in ruined tile-factories, in the middle of disused quarries or in the depths of remote gorges, they would have detected nearby the sound of stifled sobs. It was their watchdog Toine, crying with his face buried in his hands.

And not only did they want their nights to themselves; they were growing bolder and prepared to take advantage of every opportunity. Often if they met in a corridor or in one of the rooms of La Blancarde, they would exchange a long kiss. Even at meal times when she was serving and he had asked for some bread or a table napkin, he would manage to squeeze her fingers. The straitlaced Madame Rostand noticed nothing and still kept accusing her son of being too strict towards his former playmate. One day she nearly caught them but, hearing the rustle of her dress, the girl quickly knelt down and started dusting off her young master's shoes with her handkerchief.

They enjoyed a thousand and one other little pleasures. After dinner, in the cool of the evening, Madame Rostand often felt like a walk; she would take her son's arm and they would go down to L'Estaque, with Naïs carrying her shawl, just in case. The three of them would walk down to watch the return of the sardine fishermen. Out at sea, lamps were bobbing up and down and soon they could pick out the black shapes of the boats as they slowly rowed in with a muffled creaking of oars. On the days when the catch had been plentiful, there were shouts of joy as the women ran up with their baskets and the three-man crew of each boat began to empty the nets which had been piled up under the thwarts. The nets looked like a sort of broad dark ribbon spangled with silver; the sardines caught in the mesh by the gills were still threshing about, glinting like metal strips before dropping into the baskets like a shower of silver coins in the pale light of the lamps. Madame Rostand would often remain looking at a boat, fascinated by the spectacle; she would let go of her son's arm and stay talking to the fishermen while Frédéric, standing beside Naïs outside the circle of light, would squeeze her wrists with all his might.

Meanwhile, as usual, old Micoulin remained as silent as a dogged, wily animal, whether he was going off to do some fishing or coming to do some digging. But recently, beneath this same sly air, there was an uneasy look in his beady grey eyes. Without saying a word he would keep casting sidelong glances at his daughter. She seemed changed and there was something about her that he could sense but not explain. One day when she dared to stand up to him, he struck her so hard that he split her lip and that evening Frédéric, noticing as he kissed her that her lip was swollen, sharply questioned her.

'Oh, it's nothing, just a slap my father gave me,' she answered.

Her voice was grim; but when Frédéric showed annoyance and said he would do something about it, she replied:

'No, let him be, I can deal with it. . . Don't worry, it won't last for ever!'

She never referred to her father's harsh treatment of her but on the days when he had been hitting her, she clung to her lover more passionately than ever, as though taking revenge on the old man.

For the last three weeks, Naïs had been slipping out almost every night. At first she had been extremely cautious but with increasing confidence she had grown more reckless. When she realized that her father suspected something, she again became cautious and on two successive nights failed to turn up as arranged. Her mother had been telling her that her husband had been unable to sleep at night: instead, he would get up and wander around the house. But on the third day, Frédéric's beseeching look made her throw caution to the winds. She came down to the terrace at about eleven o'clock, promising herself not to stay more than an hour; she was hoping that her father would be so sound asleep in the early part of the night that he would not hear her.

Frédéric was waiting for her under the olive trees. Without mentioning her fears, she refused to go further afield: she felt too tired, she said, which happened to be true since, unlike Frédéric, she could not sleep during the day. They lay down in their usual spot above the sea, facing the lights of Marseilles. The Planier lighthouse was casting its friendly beam and as she lay watching it, Naïs fell asleep on Frederic's shoulder. He did not move and gradually, overcome by fatigue, his own eyes closed. Clasped in each other's arms, his breath mingled with hers.

Not a sound could be heard but the chirping of the green grasshoppers. The sea was sleeping, like the lovers. Then a dark shape came out of the shadows and approached. It was Micoulin who had been awakened by the creaking of a window and had found Naïs's bedroom empty. He armed himself with a hatchet, just in case, and left the house. When he saw a black patch under the olive tree, he gripped the handle of the hatchet more firmly. But the two young people did not move and he was able to come right up to them, bend down and look at their faces. As he recognized the young master, a stifled cry escaped him. But he could not kill him like that: the blood would spurt out on to the ground and give him away. The price was too high.

He straightened up; two deep creases furrowed the corners of his mouth while his leathery old face was set in grim determination and suppressed fury. But a peasant can't kill his master openly because even when dead and buried, the master is still the stronger. So, shaking his head, old Micoulin crept stealthily away, leaving the two lovers to sleep on.

When Naïs came in shortly before dawn, very anxious at having been out so long, she found the window just as she had left it. At breakfast, as Micoulin looked at her chewing her piece of dry bread, he showed no sign of emotion. She felt reassured: her father did not know anything.

4

'Aren't you interested in going fishing these days, Monsieur Frédéric?' old Micoulin asked one evening.

Madame Rostand was sitting on the terrace in the shade of the pine trees embroidering a handkerchief while her son was reclining nearby, idly tossing pebbles.

'No, not really,' the young man replied. 'I'm getting lazy.'

'You're missing a lot,' the farmer went on. 'Yesterday our pots were full of fish. You can catch anything you like at the moment... It'd give you something to do. Why not come out with me tomorrow morning?'

He seemed so friendly that Frédéric, thinking of Naïs and not wanting to offend him, finally agreed.

'All right, I'll come... But I warn you, you'll have to wake me up. At five in the morning I'm still sleeping like a log.'

Madame Rostand had stopped her embroidering and was looking a trifle uneasy.

'And above all, mind you take care,' she said. 'I'm always scared when you're out in a boat.'

Next morning, when old Micoulin called up to Frédéric, his window remained firmly shut, so the farmer said to his daughter, in a voice in which she failed to detect the sarcasm:

'You go up, Naïs... Perhaps he'll hear you.'

So it was Naïs who woke Frédéric up. Still half asleep, he tried to pull her into his warm bed but, quickly returning his kiss, she slipped out of his reach. Ten minutes later the young man appeared, dressed in a grey linen suit. Old Micoulin was sitting on the parapet of the terrace, waiting patiently.

'It's quite cool already,' he said. 'You'd better bring a scarf.'

Naïs went upstairs to fetch one. Then the two men went off down the steep steps leading to the sea while Naïs stood looking after them. When they reached the bottom, old Micoulin glanced up at Naïs and again two deep furrows creased the corners of his mouth.

The mistral, that terrible wind from the north-east, had been blowing for the last five days. The previous evening it had died down but at sunrise it had started to blow again, although not very strongly at first. At this early hour, the angry sea, whipped up by the gusty wind, was a deep mottled blue and under the slanting rays of the rising sun, the crest of each wave was tipped with fire. The sky was practically white, like a piece of crystal. In the far distance, Marseilles could be seen so clearly that you might have counted the windows of the houses, while the rocks round the bay were all gleaming in a most delicate shade of pink.

'It's going to be rough coming back,' observed Frédéric.

'Could be,' grunted Micoulin laconically.

He was rowing in silence and did not turn round. The young man looked for a moment at his bent back, his thoughts turning to Naïs; all he could see was the nape of the old man's weather-beaten neck and the two red lobes of his ears, pierced with gold rings. Then he leant sideways and looked with interest down into the sea which was racing past their boat. The water was becoming ruffled and the only things he could see were long wisps of seaweed floating on the surface, barely visible, like some drowned woman's hair. He felt sad and even a trifle frightened.

'I say, Micoulin,' he said after a long pause. 'The wind seems to be getting up. Let's be careful. You know I swim like a lead soldier.'

'All right, I know that,' replied Micoulin in his flat voice.

And he kept on steadily rowing. The boat was beginning to bob up and down and the little fire-tipped tops of the waves had turned into crests of foam blown up into spray by the gusts of wind. Frédéric did not want to show that he was scared; but he did not feel at all easy in his mind and would have given a good deal to be closer to the shore. Becoming impatient he called out:

'Where the devil have you put your pots today?... Have we got to go to Algiers?'

But old Micoulin replied in the same phlegmatic way:

'We're nearly there, we're nearly there.'

He suddenly let go of his oars, stood up and looked towards the shore for his two landmarks; he then had to row on for another five minutes before he reached the centre of the cork buoys marking the position of his pots. Then, before starting to haul them up, he looked back for a few seconds towards La Blancarde; Frédéric followed his gaze and could clearly see a patch of white underneath the pines. It was Naïs' pale dress; she was still leaning over the parapet of the terrace.

'How many pots have you got?' asked Frédéric.

'Thirty-five. We mustn't be too long.'

Micoulin caught hold of the nearest float and heaved up the first basket. The sea was very deep indeed here and there seemed to be no end to the rope. Finally the pot surfaced, together with the large stone which held it on the bottom; and as soon as it was out of the water, three fish started flapping about like birds in a cage. It was like the sound of wings beating. There was nothing in the second pot but in the third there was a spiny lobster violently flipping its tail, a fish not caught very often. Seeing this, Frédéric became quite excited and forgot his fears; he leaned over the side of the boat, his heart beating fast as he waited for the next pot to appear. Each time he heard the sound of wings beating, he experienced the same feeling as a sportsman who has just bagged a bird. Meanwhile all the thirty-five pots were hoisted up one by one, streaming with water, into the boat. There were at least fifteen pounds of fish, a splendid haul for the Bay of Marseilles which for various reasons, chiefly through using nets with too fine a mesh, had been considerably depleted in recent years.

'That's that,' said Micoulin. 'Now let's get back.'

He carefully stowed his pots in the stern. But Frédéric again became rather anxious when he saw that the old man was preparing to hoist the sail and asked whether it wouldn't be wiser to row back, in view of the weather. Micoulin merely shrugged: he knew what he was doing. And before finally hoisting the sail, he cast a glance once more towards La Blancarde. Naïs was still there, in her white dress.

Then, with the suddenness of a clap of thunder, the disaster occurred. Later on, when trying to explain to himself what had happened, Frédéric remembered that the boat had been caught in a violent squall of wind and immediately capsized. And he could recall nothing else, only a sensation of extreme cold and an overwhelming feeling of terror. He owed his life to a miracle: he had been thrown on to the large sail which held him up. Seeing the accident, some fishermen came to the rescue of him and of old Micoulin, who was already striking out for the shore.

Madame Rostand was still asleep and they did not tell her of her son's narrow escape. Dripping with water, Frédéric and Micoulin were met at the foot of the terrace by Naïs who had witnessed the dramatic incident from afar.

'Just my luck,' the old man was shouting. 'We'd picked up our pots and were just starting back... You can't win!'

Naïs was as pale as a sheet; she glared at her father.

'Yes, that's right,' she said, in a low voice. 'You can't win... but if you yaw with the wind behind you know what happens...'

Micoulin flared up.

'Come on, you idle good-for-nothing! What do you think you're doing? Can't you see that Monsieur Frédéric is shivering? Give him a hand quickly!'

A day in bed was all that Frédéric needed to recover. He told his mother that he'd had a sick headache. Next day he found a very grim-faced Naïs. She turned a deaf ear to any suggestion of meeting but when they happened to run across each other in the hall one evening, she spontaneously hugged him and gave him a passionate kiss. She never confided her suspicions to Frédéric but from then on she kept guard over him. Then, after a week, she began to have doubts. Her father was following his normal routine and even seemed gentler than usual, for he struck her less often.

One of the Rostands' outings every year was to go and have a bouillabaisse on the beach in a rocky cove. Afterwards, as there were partridges in the hills, the men of the party would go off on a shoot. This year Madame Rostand decided to take Naïs along to help serve the meal and she refused to listen to the objections of her father whose displeasure was plainly shown in the deep furrows of his brutal-looking face.

They left early. The weather was perfect, neither too hot nor too cold. The deep blue sea stretched out as smooth as a mirror beneath the golden rays of the sun; where there were currents, the blue was ruffled and took on metallic purple tints, whilst where it was still, the blue was paler, milky and transparent, like a piece of shot-silk stretching far out to the glassy horizon. The boat glided gently through the water, as calm as a mill-pond.

They landed on a narrow beach at the mouth of a gorge and picked a spot on a patch of sunburnt turf to serve as a picnic table.

The preparation of the bouillabaisse was quite a ceremony. First, Micoulin went off by himself to haul up his pots, which he had set the day before. By the time he returned, Naïs had already gathered enough thyme, wild lavender and dry twigs to make a good big fire. Today it was the old man's job to make the bouillabaisse, that traditional fish-soup of Provence the recipe for which is passed from father to son amongst the fishermen along the coast. His was an awesome bouillabaisse, extremely peppery and giving off an overpowering smell of crushed garlic. The Rostands watched its preparation with amused interest.

'Well, Micoulin,' said Madame Rostand, condescending to make a joke for once in honour of the occasion, 'is it going to be up to last year's?'

Micoulin seemed in the best of spirits. First he cleaned the fish in seawater while Naïs took a big pan out of the boat. The actual cooking took hardly any time at all: the fish was put into the pan and covered in water, with onions, olive oil—half a glassful—garlic, a handful of pepper and a tomato; then the pan was put on the fire, a blazing fire on which you could have roasted a whole sheep. The fishermen say that the secret of making a bouillabaisse lies in the heat; the pan must be completely hidden in the flames. Meanwhile the farmer was solemnly cutting slices of bread into a salad bowl. After half an hour he poured the liquid on to the bread and served the fish separately.

'Well, that's it,' said Micoulin. 'Remember that it's got to be eaten piping hot.'

And the bouillabaisse was eaten to the accompaniment of the customary witticisms.

'I say, Micoulin, how much gunpowder did you put into it?'

'It's first-rate but you need a cast-iron throat.'

He sat quietly eating, gulping down a slice of bread in each mouthful. He also showed how flattered he felt at lunching with his landlords by sitting slightly to one side.

After lunch, everyone rested until the sun had lost a little of its heat. Meanwhile the dazzling red-spattered rocks were mottled by the deep shadows of the dark, bushy, evergreen oaks and the pinewoods marched up the slopes of the gorge in regular columns like an army of tiny soldiers. The air was hot and heavy with silence.

Madame Rostand had brought along her everlasting piece of embroidery which never left her hands. Naïs was sitting beside her watching with apparent interest the movement of her needles. But she was keeping a close watch on her father. He was stretched out on the ground a few yards away, having a snooze. Frédéric was asleep, too, a little further away, his face hidden under the turned-down brim of his straw-hat.

At about four o'clock, they woke up. Micoulin swore that he knew of a covey of partridges at the far end of the gorge. He'd seen them again only three days ago. Hearing this, Frédéric allowed himself to be tempted and they both picked up their guns.

'Now please take great care,' called Madame Rostand. 'If your foot slips, you can easily shoot yourself.'

'Yes, it does happen,' said Micoulin placidly.

They went off and disappeared behind some rocks. Naïs suddenly stood up and followed them at a distance, murmuring: 'I'll go and see as well.'

Instead of keeping to the path, when she reached the end of the gorge she took to the bushes and went quickly along to the left, taking care not to set any boulders rolling. At last she caught sight of Frédéric standing at a bend in the track on the other side of the gorge. They had probably already flushed the partridges because he moved on quickly, bending forward with his gun at the ready. Her father was not in sight; but then suddenly she saw him close by, on the same slope as herself; he was crouching down and seemed to be waiting for something. Twice he put his gun to his shoulder. If the partridges were to fly between him and Frédéric, the two might easily hit each other as they fired. Slipping from bush to bush, Naïs finally reached a position directly behind the old man and stood there, anxiously waiting.

Minutes went by. Opposite them, Frédéric had vanished in a dip in the ground. Then he came into sight again and stood for an instant, not moving. Once again, still crouching down, Micoulin took careful aim at the young man. But Naïs leaped forward and kicked up the barrel of the gun which went off with a loud report that reverberated round the gorge.

The old man sprang to his feet and when he saw Naïs, he seized his gun by the barrel as if to brain her with the butt. White as a sheet, the girl stood her ground, her eyes flaming with fury. He did not dare to hit her but merely muttered in dialect:

'Don't worry, I'll get him yet!'

When Micoulin had fired, the partridges had flown off and Frédéric had brought down a brace of them. The Rostands made their way back to La Blancarde. Their tenant was pulling on the oars, still with the same calm, dogged look on his brutal face.

5

September had come to an end. After a violent storm, the air had become much cooler, with heavy night dews. The days were drawing in and Naïs was firmly refusing to meet Frédéric at night on the excuse that she was too tired and that they would catch cold lying on the rain-soaked ground. But as she came over to the house at about six o'clock every morning and Madame Rostand rarely stirred until some three hours later, she would go up to the young man's room and stay there for a while, listening all the time for the slightest sound through the door, which she always left open.

This was the period of their love when she showed her greatest tenderness. She would hold Frédéric close, slipping her hand round his neck to bring his face near to hers and look at him passionately with her eyes full of tears. She always had the feeling that she would never see him again. Then she would quickly cover his face with kisses as if promising that she would be able to defend him.

'What's wrong with Naïs?' Madame Rostand kept asking. 'She looks different every day.'

And indeed she was losing weight, her cheeks were becoming hollow and her eyes no longer sparkled. There were long periods when she would sit saying nothing and then she would suddenly start up like someone waking from a dream.

'If you're not feeling well, girl,' Madame Rostand kept telling her, 'you must look after yourself.'

'Oh no, ma'am, I'm very well and very happy. I've never been so happy.'

One morning as they were checking the linen, she ventured to ask:

'Will you be staying on late at La Blancarde this year?'

'Until the end of October,' replied Madame Rostand.

And Naïs stood for a moment with a faraway look in her eyes and then, without realizing that she was speaking out loud, she exclaimed:

'Still three more weeks!'

A constant struggle was taking place inside her. She longed to keep Frédéric close to her all the time but felt continually tempted to cry out: 'Go away!' She was going to lose him; from their very first meeting she had told herself that their season of love would never return. One evening, when she was feeling particularly depressed, she asked herself whether she should not let Frédéric be killed by her father, so that he would never go with any other woman; but the thought of Frédéric, with his soft white skin and genteel ways, so much more like a little lady than herself, lying dead, was unbearable. No, she would save him without his knowing anything about it; he would quickly forget her but she would be happy in the knowledge that he was alive. In the morning she would often say to him:

'Don't go out, don't go in a boat, the weather's treacherous!'

At other times she would advise him to go away from La Blancarde.

'You must be bored, you won't love me any more. Go and spend a few days in town.'

He was bewildered at these changes in her mood, and he was finding his little country girl less lovely now that her face was becoming thin and drawn and he was beginning to be satiated by the violence of their lovemaking. He was hankering after the eau-de-Cologne and face powder of the tarts of Aix and Marseilles.

Her father's words kept ringing in her ears: 'I'll get him yet! I'll get him yet!' She would wake up in the night dreaming that shots were being fired. Her nerves were all on edge and she would cry out if a stone slipped from under her feet. Whenever he was out of her sight, she felt worried about 'Monsieur Frédéric'. And the most terrible thing of all was that from morning till night she could hear Micoulin doggedly muttering to himself: 'I'll get him yet!' He had made no further reference to Frédéric nor said a word nor made the slightest movement. But for Naïs, the old man's eyes, his every gesture, his whole demeanour told her that he would kill his young master at the first opportunity, when there was no risk of being brought to justice. And afterwards it would be Naïs's turn. In the meantime, he kicked her about like some animal that had misbehaved.

'Is your father still as horrible as ever?' Frédéric asked her one day, as he lay smoking a cigarette in bed while she bustled to and fro tidying his room.

'Yes,' she answered. 'He's going out of his mind.'

And she showed him her legs, black and blue with bruises. Then she muttered under her breath the words that she often used:

'It won't go on for ever.'

During the first few days of October, she seemed more depressed than ever. She was absent-minded and her lips kept moving as if she was talking to herself. On several occasions Frédéric saw her standing at the top of the cliff apparently looking at the pine trees around her and trying to measure the depth to the bottom. A few days later he came upon her picking figs with the hunchback Toine in a remote corner of the property. Toine used to come and help Micoulin when there was too much to do on the farm. He was standing under the fig tree with Naïs perched on a big branch making fun of him by shouting to him to open his mouth and then throwing figs at him which squashed all over his face. The poor creature was opening his mouth and closing his eyes in an ecstasy of delight with an expression of sheer bliss on his big moon-face. Frédéric could hardly feel jealous, of course, but he could not resist the temptation of pulling her leg.

'Toine would give his right arm for us,' she replied sharply. 'You mustn't be unkind to him, we might need him.'

The hunchback continued to come every day to La Blancarde. He was working on top of the cliff, digging out a trench to carry water to one end of the property where they were trying to establish a vegetable garden. Sometimes Naïs would go and watch him and there would be a lively conversation between the two. He dawdled so much over his work that in the end Micoulin called him a lazy good-for-nothing and hacked him on the shins, as he did his daughter.

There had been two days of rain. Frédéric was due to return to Aix the following week and had agreed to go out on one last fishing expedition with Micoulin before leaving. Seeing Naïs turn as white as a sheet, he smiled and added that this time he wouldn't choose a day when the mistral was blowing. So, realizing that he was leaving so soon, the girl agreed to have one more meeting with him at night; they met on the terrace at about one o'clock. The rain had washed the soil and a pervasive odour of cool greenery hung in the air. When this dried-up countryside is thoroughly soaked, the colours and scents take on an extraordinary intensity: the red earth bleeds, the pine trees glitter like emeralds and the white rocks gleam like freshly laundered linen. But at night the lovers could smell only the overpowering scent of thyme and lavender.

Force of habit led them towards the olive trees and Frédéric was just about to make for the one under which they had first made love when Naïs, as if suddenly remembering something, dragged him away from the edge saying in a trembling voice:

'No, not there!'

'What's the matter?' he enquired.

At first, she had difficulty in finding words; then she said that after the heavy rains they had had yesterday, the cliff was not safe. She added:

'Last year there was a landslide quite close to here.'

They sat down further away under another olive tree. Naïs seemed uneasy as they lay in each other's arms. All at once she burst into tears but refused to say what had upset her. Then she became silent and cold and when Frédéric teased her about the way she now seemed bored with him, she flung herself wildly into his arms and said in a whisper:

'You mustn't say that sort of thing, I love you too much. But I'm not very well, you know. And then, this is the end for us, you'll be going away... Oh God, it's the end!'

He vainly tried to comfort her: he'd be coming back sometimes and they'd have another two months to look forward to next autumn; but she kept shaking her head; she could feel that this was the end. Finally they lapsed into an embarrassed silence and lay looking at the sea with Marseilles twinkling in the distance and the solitary Planier lighthouse now seeming to be shining sadly, all alone; gradually this vast panorama filled them with melancholy. When he left her at about three o'clock, he could feel her shivering, icy-cold, as he again took her into his arms and kissed her on the lips.

That night Frédéric could not sleep. He read until dawn and then, restless from lack of sleep, when day broke he went over to his window. At that very moment old Micoulin was on his way to row out and inspect his lobster pots. As he was passing along the terrace, he looked up:

'Well, Monsieur Frédéric, not coming out with me this morning?' he asked.

'No, not today, Micoulin,' Frédéric called back. 'I've slept too badly. Let's go tomorrow.'

The farmer trudged off; he had to go down and fetch his boat at the foot of the cliff, right under the olive tree where he had caught his daughter and Frédéric together. When he had vanished from sight, Frédéric turned his gaze and was amazed to see Toine already at work: the hunchback was near the olive tree using his mattock to repair the trench that had been damaged by the heavy rains. The air was cool and it was pleasant standing at the window. The young man went back into his room to roll himself a cigarette; but as he was making his way to the window again, he heard a terrible noise, like a clap of thunder. He rushed to the window.

It was a landslide. All he could see was Toine jumping clear in a cloud of red dust, waving his mattock. At the edge of the precipice the olive tree was slipping down out of sight and dramatically plunging into the sea. A column of foam spouted upwards. At the same time a dreadful cry rent the air. And then Frédéric saw Naïs who had dashed to the side and, bracing herself on her arms, was leaning far out over the parapet to discover what had happened down below. She hung there suspended with her wrists as if cemented to the stonework. But she must have sensed that someone was watching her, for she turned her head and, seeing Frédéric, shouted:

'My father! My father!'

An hour later they found the horribly mutilated body of old Micoulin under the pile of boulders. Toine was feverishly explaining how he had nearly been carried away and everybody agreed that a trench should not have been dug there because of the danger of percolating water. Old Madame Micoulin wept bitterly; Naïs followed her father's coffin to the churchyard dry-eyed; her lids were red but she had not been able to shed a single tear.

The day after the disaster Madame Rostand insisted on returning to Aix. Frédéric was very glad to go, too, now that his lovemaking had been disturbed by the tragedy; anyway, country girls were definitely not a patch on local tarts. He began to lead his old life again. Touched by his filial devotion at La Blancarde, his mother now allowed him greater freedom, so he spent a pleasant winter. He arranged for some charming ladies of the town to come and visit him from Marseilles, putting them up in a room that he had rented in the suburbs. He spent nights away from home and did not return to the cold family mansion in the Rue du Collège unless his presence seemed absolutely indispensable; he had hopes that his life would flow on in this delightful manner for ever.

At Eastertime, Monsieur Rostand had to go to La Blancarde. Frédéric found an excuse not to go with him. When the solicitor returned, he said at lunch:

'Naïs is getting married.'

'Not really!' Frédéric exclaimed, unable to believe his ears.

'And you'll never guess who to,' Monsieur Rostand continued. 'She gave me all sorts of good reasons for it.'

Naïs was marrying the hunchback Toine. In this way, there would be no change at La Blancarde: Toine would be kept on as the tenant; he had been looking after the property ever since old Micoulin's death.

The young man listened with an embarrassed smile. And then he too agreed that it was an arrangement that suited everyone.

'Naïs has begun to look quite old and ugly,' went on Monsieur Rostand. 'I didn't recognize her. It's extraordinary how quickly they go to seed, these girls living by the sea. She used to be very good-looking, young Naïs.'

'I suppose so. Just a flash in the pan,' said Frédéric, and calmly finished off his cutlet.

DEAD MEN TELL NO TALES

I DIED on a Saturday morning at six a.m., after an illness lasting three days. My poor wife was rummaging in a trunk for some bed-linen. When she stood up and saw me stretched out, all stiff, with my eyes open, not breathing, she rushed over to my bedside, thinking that I had fainted. She felt my hands and bent over to look into my face. Then, horrorstruck, she burst into tears and stammered distractedly:

'Dear God! Dear God! he's dead!'

I could hear everything but the sounds were muffled and seemed to be coming from a great distance. My left eye was still capable of perceiving a vague gleam, a milky sort of light in which objects were melting into one another; but my right eye was completely paralysed. My whole being was in a sort of syncope, as if I had been struck by lightning. I was reduced to a state of complete inertia; not one muscle of my body would obey me. And in this state of numbness, all that remained was an ability to think, sluggishly but still with complete clarity.

My poor Marguerite had fallen on her knees beside my bed and she was sobbing in a heart-rending voice:

'Dear God! He's dead! He's dead!'

Could this strange state of torpor be death? This complete physical impotence which still left my intelligence capable of functioning? Was it my soul still lingering on inside my skull before it took flight for ever? I had been subject to fits since earliest childhood and had almost succumbed to bouts of fever on two occasions, when still quite young. After that, those around me had become used to my chronic bad health; and when I had had to take to my bed in our room in the furnished hotel in the Rue Dauphine* the day after our arrival in Paris, I myself had dissuaded Marguerite from sending for a doctor. I thought all I needed was a little rest; I was merely tired out after the journey. Nevertheless, I was in a dreadfully agitated state of mind. We had come up from our home in the country at extremely short notice, almost penniless, with barely enough money to see us through to my first month's salary in the government office job to which I had just been appointed. And now I had died from this unexpected attack of fever.

Could this really be death? I'd always imagined that it would be so much darker, so much quieter than this. Even as a lad I had been afraid of dying. Being a sickly child, people would stroke my hand with pity in their eyes. I always had the feeling that I would not live long, that I was going to an early grave. And the idea of being buried filled me with a dread that I could never come to terms with, despite the fact that it never left me, night or day; and as I grew up, this idea became an obsession. Sometimes, after thinking about it for days, I would imagine that I had succeeded in conquering my fear. All right, you'll die and that will be the end of you, everyone has to die some day, there could be nothing more normal and proper. I would almost manage to be cheerful about it: I could look death in the face without flinching! And then, quite suddenly, an icy shiver would run down my spine and I would become sick with fear, as if some giant hand were holding me suspended over a precipice. My terror at the thought of being buried would flood back and all my fine reasoning would be swept away. How often would I wake up in the night with a sudden start, not knowing what unseen spirit had chilled me with its icy breath; and I would clasp my hands and stammer: 'Oh God, oh God, we all have to die!' My chest would contract with fear and the inevitability of death seemed all the more horrible in the confusion of my sudden awakening. And I was so unnerved that I hardly dared to go to sleep again, for sleep was so akin to death. Suppose I were to go to sleep for ever, close my eyes and never open them again?

I don't know if others suffer in this way but my life has been wrecked by such fears. Death has always stood between me and everything I loved. I can recall my happiest moments with Marguerite, the first few months of our marriage when she would be sleeping beside me and I would be thinking of her and making plans for our future; and my feeling of joy would constantly be destroyed by the presentiment that we must inevitably be torn apart; so all my hopes were poisoned and I would be thrown into a deep depression. What was the point of our present happiness if we were fated to be separated? My morbid imagination gloated over the idea of bereavement: which of us would go first? And the thought of either alternative filled my eyes with tears as the picture of our broken lives unrolled before me. Even during the happiest periods of my life such

thoughts would overcome me and no one could understand my
sudden fits of sadness. When some good luck came my way,
people were amazed to see me looking so gloomy; it was because
the thought of my utter extinction had suddenly crossed my
mind. The terrible question: 'What's the use?' kept ringing in my
ears like a death-knell. But the greatest torment of all is to have to
keep all such thoughts to yourself, as a shameful secret, a sickness
that you can never admit to anyone. Often a husband and wife
lying in bed, side by side, must feel the same cold shiver of horror
run through them; yet neither of them will say a word, because
you don't talk about death any more than you utter certain
obscene expressions. You're so afraid of death that you dare not
mention it; you keep it hidden in the same way as you hide your
genitals.

All these thoughts were running through my mind as
Marguerite continued desperately sobbing. I felt sorry not to be
able to comfort her by telling her that I was in no pain. If death
was merely this bodily weakness, then I had indeed been wrong
to be in such dread of it. I had a smug feeling of well-being and
restfulness that cancelled all my worries. Above all, my memory
had become extremely active; my whole life was passing rapidly
before my eyes like a spectacle from which I felt completely
divorced. It was an odd and amusing experience, as though some
distant voice was telling the story of my life.

I was pursued by the memory of a tiny patch of countryside
near Guérande, on the road to Piriac. The road makes a bend and
a little pinewood sweeps down a rocky slope. I was seven at the
time. I used to go there with my father to a little, half-ruined
house to eat pancakes with Marguerite's parents, who were even
then barely managing to scrape a living working in the local salt-
marshes. Then I recalled my boarding-school at Nantes and its
dreary old walls where I grew up longing for the broad horizons
of Guérande with its salt-marshes stretching as far as the eye
could see at the foot of the town and the immense ocean spread
out under the sky. Now there came a black hole in my memories;
my father died and I got a job as a clerk in the hospital. My
monotonous life had begun; the only bright spots were my
Sunday visits to the old house on the Piriac road. But there things
were going from bad to worse, for the salt-marshes were in dire
straits and the whole region was being reduced to abject poverty.

Marguerite was still only a child. She was fond of me because I pushed her round in a wheelbarrow. But later on, when I asked her to marry me, I realized from her terrified look that she thought me hideously ugly. Her parents gave their consent straightaway, to get her off their hands. She was a dutiful daughter and didn't protest. Once she had grown used to the idea of becoming my wife, she no longer seemed quite so unhappy. I remember that on our wedding day, it was raining cats and dogs in Guérande and when we went home she had to strip down to her petticoat because her dress was wet through.

And that was all the youth I ever had. We lived in Guérande for a while and then one day I came home and found her crying her heart out. She was bored and wanted to move. After six months of pinching and scraping and working overtime, I managed to save enough and when a former friend of the family succeeded in finding a job for me, I had taken her with me to Paris, so that the poor girl would be less miserable. In the train she was laughing all the time. When night came, as the third class seats were so hard, I took her on to my knees so that she could sleep more comfortably.

But all that belonged to the past; and now I had just died and my wife was kneeling, sobbing, on the tiled floor beside the narrow bed of our lodging-house room. The white spot that I could see with my left eye was growing dimmer but I could still remember the room perfectly. The chest-of-drawers was on the left, the fireplace on the right and on the mantelshelf above there stood a clock which was not working because it had lost its pendulum; its hands pointed to six minutes past ten. The window looked out on to the Rue Dauphine. All the traffic of Paris seemed to be going through that deep, gloomy street, making a din that set the window-panes rattling.

We knew not a soul in Paris. As we had left in a hurry, I was not expected to report for work until the following Monday. Ever since I had been forced to take to my bed, I had had the feeling of being imprisoned in this room where we had landed up, bewildered, after our journey, having spent some fifteen hours in the train, and stunned by the bustle in the streets. My wife had looked after me, kind and cheerful as always, but I could sense how worried she was. Every so often, she would go over to the window and glance down into the street; and she would come back looking very pale, scared by the size of Paris where she knew not one brick or stone and which was creating such a deafening roar. And what was she going to do should I never wake up? What would become of her, all alone in this immense metropolis, completely ignorant, and without anyone to support her?

Marguerite had caught hold of one of my hands dangling limply beside the bed and she was kissing it as she repeated:

'Oh Olivier, do say something! Oh God, he's dead, he's dead!'

So death didn't mean complete annihilation, for I could hear her and I was capable of reasoning. It had only been this thought of annihilation that had terrified me ever since I was a child. I could not imagine the total destruction of my whole being, my complete extinction; and it would be for all eternity, century upon century without ever coming to life again! Sometimes when I saw in my newspaper a mention of a date in the next century, a shudder would run through me, for by that time I should certainly not be still alive and that year in a future that I should never see, when I should no longer exist, filled me with terror. Didn't the world exist only for me and wouldn't it collapse when I abandoned it? It had always been my hope to be able to meditate on life once I was dead; but no doubt my present state wasn't death and I should surely be waking up soon. Yes, in a few minutes, I should lean forward and take Marguerite in my arms and dry her tears. What a joyful reunion that would be! And how much more dearly we should love each other then! I'd rest for a couple of days and then start work. A new life would begin for us both, a happier, richer life. But there was no need to hurry; later on would do, for the moment I was too exhausted. Marguerite was wrong to be so sad merely because I didn't feel strong enough at the moment to turn my head on the pillow and smile up at her. In a very short while, when she next said: 'He's dead! Oh God, he's dead!' I'd kiss her and say to her very, very softly, so as not to scare her: 'No, my darling, I was just asleep, you can see, I'm alive and I love you.'

2

Hearing Marguerite's cries, someone pushed open the door and a voice exclaimed:

'What's the matter? . . . Has he had another attack?'

I recognized the voice. It was Madame Gabin, an old woman who lived next door on the same landing. When we had arrived, she had sympathized with our predicament and had been very obliging. She had also immediately told us all about herself. Last winter, a hard-hearted landlord had sold up all her furniture, since when she had been living in the hotel with her daughter Adèle, a little girl of ten. They both earned a living by cutting out lampshades, which brought them in two francs a day at most.

'Heavens above, is he dead?' she asked, lowering her voice.

I realized that she was coming over to look at me. Then she touched me and said in a pitying voice:

'Oh, you poor girl, you poor girl!'

By now Marguerite was exhausted and sobbing like a child. Madame Gabin helped her to her feet and sat her down in a rickety armchair beside the fireplace, trying to comfort her.

'Come on now, you mustn't take on like that. Just because your husband has passed on, there's no point in thinking it's the end of the world. Of course, when I lost my hubby, I felt just like you, I couldn't swallow a mouthful for three whole days . . . But that didn't do any good, quite the reverse, it made me feel much worse. Come on now, be sensible, for goodness' sake!'

Marguerite gradually calmed down; she was rapidly becoming exhausted, although every now and then she was shaken by sobs. Meanwhile the gruff old woman was firmly taking charge.

'Now don't you worry, dear,' she kept saying. 'My little Dédé has just gone off to hand in our work and neighbours must stand by each other, mustn't they? . . . Well, I can see you haven't finished unpacking yet, but there is some linen in the chest-of-drawers, isn't there?'

I heard her opening the chest-of-drawers. She must have taken out a towel that she spread over the bedside table. Next she struck a match, which made me think that she was lighting one of the tallow candles from the mantelshelf, since we hadn't any wax tapers. I was able to follow her every movement about the room and realize everything she was doing.

'Oh, the poor gentleman!' she murmured. 'What a good thing it was that I heard you cry out, my dear.'

Then suddenly the vague gleam of light that I could still see with my left eye disappeared. Madame Gabin had just closed my eyes. I hadn't felt her fingers touching my eyelids. When I realized what had happened, a slow chill started creeping over my body.

The door now opened again and her little ten-year-old daughter Dédé came in, piping in her shrill voice:

'Mummy, Mummy! Oh, I knew you were here. Here's the money. We got three francs twenty for our lampshades. I took them twenty dozen!'

'Sh, sh! Don't make a noise,' her mother said, vainly trying to keep her quiet.

As the little girl still kept on talking, her mother must have pointed to the bed, for she stopped abruptly and I could sense that she was retreating uneasily towards the door.

'Is the gentleman asleep?' she asked in a low voice.

'Yes. Now go away and play,' her mother replied.

But the child stayed where she was. She must have been staring at me with a scared look on her face, half realizing what had happened. Suddenly she was seized with a sort of panic and ran out of the room, knocking over a chair.

'Oh Mummy, he's dead!'

Silence fell. Marguerite was sitting exhausted in the armchair; she had stopped crying. Madame Gabin continued to prowl round the room. She was muttering between her teeth:

'You can't keep anything from children these days. Look at her. As God's my witness, I'm bringing her up properly! Whenever she runs an errand or I send her to deliver our lampshades, I work out how long it'll take, to make sure she doesn't go gallivanting about. But it's no use, she knows everything, she saw straightaway what had happened, yet she's only ever seen one dead person, her uncle François, and she wasn't quite four at the time... What can you do, children aren't children any more.'

She broke off and changed the subject:

'I say, dear, we mustn't forget, there are a lot of formalities, we've got to notify the Town Hall and make arrangements for the funeral. You're in no fit state to see to all that and I don't want to leave you on your own. What do you say to letting me go and see if Monsieur Simoneau is at home?'

Marguerite made no reply. I felt as if I was witnessing all this from a great distance. Occasionally, it seemed to me that I was floating round in the room like a flickering flame while a stranger, a shapeless mass, was lying inert on the bed. All the same, I should have preferred her not to agree to asking Monsieur Simoneau to help. I'd caught sight of him three or four times during my short illness. He occupied a neighbouring room and had been very obliging. Madame Gabin had told us that he was merely passing through Paris, having come to collect some outstanding debts on behalf of his father, recently deceased after leaving Paris to go and live in the country. Simoneau was a tall, strapping young fellow, very good-looking. I had taken an instant dislike to him, perhaps because he was so healthy. On the previous day, he had once again come in and I had felt unhappy to see him sitting close to Marguerite. She looked so pretty and fresh beside him! And he had looked at her very attentively when she smiled at him and said how kind he was to come and ask after me!

'Here's Monsieur Simoneau,' announced Madame Gabin in a hushed voice as she returned.

He pushed the door gently open and as soon as she caught sight of him, Marguerite burst into tears again. The presence of this man, the only friend she had in Paris, had awakened her grief. He made no attempt to comfort her. I could not see him but in the darkness which surrounded me I could picture his face and clearly imagine him looking perturbed and unhappy to see this poor young woman in such despair. And yet she must have looked most appealing with her fair hair all dishevelled, her pale face and her dear little feverish, childlike hands!

'I'll be very glad to do anything you require,' Monsieur Simoneau said gently. 'I'll take care of everything if you like.'

She could only stammer a few words of thanks in reply. But Madame Gabin went out with the young man and I heard her mention the word 'money' as she passed close by my bed. Funerals cost a lot of money and she was afraid that the poor young woman was penniless; anyway, they could enquire from her. Simoneau cut the old woman short: he didn't want Marguerite to be bothered; he would go to the Town Hall and he would see to the arrangements for the funeral.

When silence again fell, I wondered to myself how much longer this nightmare would last. I must be alive because I could understand the slightest things that were taking place around me. I was also beginning to realize exactly the sort of state I was in: it must be a sort of catalepsy, of which I had heard. Even as a child, at the time of my worst nervous troubles, I had suffered similar attacks, lasting several hours. It was obviously one of these that had reduced me to this state of complete immobility, similar to death, which was misleading everyone round me. But my heart would start beating properly again, my blood would start circulating and my muscles would relax. I should wake up and comfort Marguerite. So, with these arguments running through my mind, I urged myself to be patient.

Hours went by. Madame Gabin had fetched her lunch but Marguerite was refusing to eat anything. Through the open window there came the noise from the Rue Dauphine below. A little clink of the copper candlestick against the marble top of the bedside table suggested to me that they were replacing the old candle. At last Simoneau returned.

'Well?' the old woman asked him in a low voice.

'Everything's arranged,' he replied. 'The funeral will set off from here at eleven o'clock tomorrow morning. You needn't worry about anything and don't talk about all this in front of that poor girl.'

Madame Gabin now pointed out that the doctor still had not come to certify death.

Simoneau went over and sat down beside Marguerite, trying at first to comfort her, but he soon fell silent. 'The funeral will set off from here at eleven o'clock tomorrow morning.' These words were ringing in my ears like a death-knell. And there would be the doctor to certify death, in Madame Gabin's words! Surely he would see straightaway that I was merely unconscious? I started waiting for his arrival with frantic impatience.

Meanwhile the day dragged on. To avoid wasting her time, Madame Gabin had fetched her lampshades and had even asked if Dédé could join her, saying that she didn't like leaving children too long on their own.

'Come on in,' she whispered to the little girl as she ushered her into the room. 'And remember, you must behave yourself and not look over there or else there'll be trouble.'

She was forbidding her daughter to look at me; it seemed the right thing to do. However, Dédé must certainly have been looking furtively in my direction now and again, because I heard her mother slapping her arm and saying crossly:

'If you don't get on with your work, I'll send you out of the room and tonight that gentleman will come along when you're in bed and pull your feet!'

Both mother and daughter had sat down at our table and I could distinctly hear the sound of their scissors cutting out the lampshades; no doubt this was quite a difficult and complicated operation, for they were not getting on very fast. To fight back my growing anxiety, I started counting the lampshades one by one.

The only sound to be heard in the room was the click of scissors. Overcome by fatigue, Marguerite must have dozed off. Twice Simoneau got to his feet and I was tortured by the thought that he was taking advantage of the fact that Marguerite was asleep to press his lips on her hair and kiss it. I didn't know him but I was sure that he loved my wife. Then suddenly little Dédé laughed. It was the last straw.

'What are you laughing at, you silly girl?' her mother asked her. 'I'll send you out on to the landing if you're not careful. Well, what are you laughing at?'

The little girl stammered that she hadn't been laughing but coughing. But I imagined that she must have seen Simoneau bending over Marguerite and that she found that funny.

The lamp had already been lit; there was a knock at the door. 'That'll be the doctor,' the old woman said.

It was indeed the doctor. He did not even bother to apologize for being so late. No doubt he had had to climb many flights of stairs in the course of the day. The light was very dim. He asked:

'Is this where the body is?'

'Yes, doctor,' replied Simoneau.

Marguerite stood up, trembling. Madame Gabin had sent Dédé out on to the landing, because a child has no business seeing that sort of thing, and she was trying to lead my wife over to the window to spare her the painful spectacle.

Meanwhile, the doctor had quickly made his way towards the bed. I had the feeling that he was tired, impatient and in no mood to linger. Did he take hold of my hand? Did he place his own hand on my heart? I can't say one way or the other; but it seemed to me that he had, quite unconcernedly, been content merely to bend over me.

'Shall I bring the lamp over so that you can see better?' Simoneau offered obligingly.

'No, there's no need,' the doctor replied calmly.

No need? This man, who was holding my life in his hands, thought there was no need to make a thorough examination! And yet I wasn't dead!

'At what time did he die?' he went on.

'At six o'clock this morning,' replied Simoneau.

A furious protest surged up inside me, despite the terrible weight that was holding me down. Oh the horror of not being able to say a word or stir a single limb!

The doctor added:

'This sultry weather is dreadful. There's nothing so exhausting as this early spring weather.'

And he moved away from the bed and, with him, all my chances of survival. Shouts and sobs and abuse were struggling convulsively for utterance, stifled for lack of breath. Ah, that miserable doctor, so blinkered in his professional routine that he had become nothing more than a robot who took people's deaths as a mere formality! What a complete idiot the man must be! All his pretended medical science was a sham, since he couldn't distinguish between a dead man and a live one. And now he was leaving me and going away!

'Good night, doctor,' Simoneau said.

There was silence. The doctor must have been bowing to Marguerite who had come back into the room, while Madame Gabin was closing the window. Then he left and I heard his footsteps going downstairs.

So this was the end. I was doomed: my last hope was vanishing with those footsteps. If I didn't wake up before eleven o'clock tomorrow, I'd be buried alive. And this thought was so terrifying that I lost consciousness of everything around me: it was a swoon as deep as death itself. The last sound I heard was the click of Madame Gabin's and Dédé's scissors. The funeral vigil was beginning. Nobody spoke. Marguerite had refused to go and sleep in her neighbour's room and was reclining in the armchair, pale and beautiful, with her closed lids still wet with tears, while Simoneau sat opposite her, silently watching her in the darkness.

3

I cannot begin to describe all that I went through the following morning. It was an anguish that has remained with me like some appalling dream during which I experienced such confused and peculiar feelings that it would be difficult for me to detail them here. And what made my suffering even more intense was that I was still hoping against hope that I would suddenly wake up. But as the time for the funeral approached, my feeling of dread grew more and more oppressive.

It was not until the following morning that I once again became aware of the people and objects surrounding me. As I was dozing, the clatter of a window-catch aroused me. It was Madame Gabin letting in some fresh air. It must have been about seven o'clock, for I could hear the cries of street traders, the high-pitched voice of a little girl selling chickweed and a hoarse voice offering carrots for sale. At first this noisy awakening of the Paris streets helped to calm me: it seemed impossible that they would be putting me underground amidst all this activity; and I remembered something else which further reassured me: I re-called that I had seen a similar case to mine when I had been employed in the hospital in Guérande. Like me, a man had remained asleep for twenty-eight hours, a sleep so deep, in fact, that the doctors were hesitating whether they should not declare him dead; and then he had sat up and been able to get out of bed straightaway. I myself had already been sleeping for twenty-five hours. If I woke up at about ten o'clock, there would still be time.

I tried to work out who was in the room and what they were doing. Young Dédé must have been playing on the landing, because the door was open and I could hear a child laughing outside. Simoneau had no doubt left: I could detect no sign of his presence. Only Madame Gabin could be heard shuffling round in her slippers. Finally someone spoke:

'Now dear,' the old woman said, 'you're to drink up while it's still hot, it'll do you good.'

She was addressing Marguerite and the gentle drip of a filter on the mantelpiece told me that she was making coffee.

'I must say that I needed that,' she went on. 'Staying up all night's bad for you at my time of life. And it's so sad in the night, in a place where something dreadful's happened. . . Now do have some coffee, dear, just a drop.'

And she forced Marguerite to take a cup.

'You see? It's warm, it cheers you up. You need to get your strength back for what you've got to go through today. Now if you were really sensible, you'd go to my room and wait there.'

'No, I want to stay here,' Marguerite replied firmly.

This was the first time I had heard her voice since the previous day and I was deeply moved. It was quite changed, broken with emotion. Oh my darling Marguerite, I could feel her close beside me, offering me my last consolation, I knew that her eyes never left my face, and that she was crying broken-heartedly.

But the minutes were ticking by and I heard a sound at the door which I could not at first understand. It was as if a piece of furniture was bumping against the wall of the narrow staircase. Then, when I heard Marguerite starting to cry again, I realized what was happening: they were bringing up my coffin.

'You're too early,' said Madame Gabin, crossly. 'Put it down behind the bed.'

What was the time, then? Possibly nine o'clock. So the coffin had already arrived. I could see it dimly through my blurred eyes, a brand-new coffin made of roughly planed boards. Oh God! Was this the end? Was I going to be carried out in this wooden box which they'd put down at the head of my bed?

But one final and pleasant surprise was still in store for me: despite her grief, Marguerite insisted on getting me ready herself for my last journey. With the help of the old woman, she dressed me with all the tenderness of a wife and sister and as she slipped each garment over my body, I could feel her again holding me in her arms. Overcome by emotion, she kept stopping, hugging me tightly and bathing my face in tears. How I longed to return her caresses and cry out: 'I'm alive!' but I continued to lie there, an inert mass of flesh.

'I shouldn't do that, it's a waste,' the old woman kept saying.

'No, I want to dress him in his best,' Marguerite replied brokenly.

I realized that she was dressing me as if for our wedding. I had kept those clothes, intending to wear them only on very special occasions. Now she sank back exhausted into the armchair.

Suddenly I heard Simoneau's voice. No doubt he had just come into the room.

'They're downstairs,' he said quietly.

'About time too,' replied Madame Gabin, lowering her voice as well. 'Tell them to come up, we mustn't linger.'

'I'm afraid of the effect on his poor wife.'

The old woman seemed to be thinking. Then she said:

'Look, Monsieur Simoneau, you make her go into my room. She mustn't stay here. It'll be a kindness to her... Meanwhile, we can get everything done here in a jiffy.'

Her words went straight to my heart and you can imagine the agonies I went through during the ensuing struggle. Simoneau went up to Marguerite and begged her not to stay in the room.

'For pity's sake,' he said imploringly, 'please come with me, there's no point in exposing yourself to unnecessary suffering.'

'No, I won't,' my wife kept saying. 'I'm going to stay here until the end. Don't forget that he's all I've got in the world and when he's gone, I shall be all alone.'

While this was happening, Madame Gabin was standing beside the bed, muttering to the young man:

'Go and pick her up and take her away in your arms.'

Was Simoneau going to do as she suggested and carry her off like that? All of a sudden she cried out. I made a frantic effort to get to my feet but all my strength had deserted me. So I lay there, so paralysed that I couldn't even open my eye-lids to see what was taking place under my very nose. The struggle continued as my wife clung to the furniture, crying:

'Let me go, Monsieur, oh please let me go, I want to stay here!'

He must have been holding her tightly, for she started whimpering like a child. He carried her off protesting and as her sobs died away, I could see the two of them in my mind's eye; strong and powerful as he was, he was lifting her off the ground and holding her close against his chest, while she had her arms round his neck, sobbing in a heartrending fashion but eventually giving up the struggle and letting him take her away where he wanted.

'Heavens above! That wasn't easy,' murmured Madame Gabin. 'Well, now we've cleared the stage, let's get on with the job.'

In my jealous rage, Simoneau's action in carrying her off in this way seemed like a criminal abduction. I hadn't been able to see Marguerite since the day before, but I had been able to hear her and now I couldn't even do that. She'd been taken away from me even before I was under the ground. And he was alone with her behind the partition, consoling her, perhaps even kissing her.

The door opened again and there was the sound of heavy footsteps in the room.

'Let's be quick before she comes back,' Madame Gabin was saying.

She was addressing some unknown persons whose only reply was to grunt.

'I'm not a relative, you know, just a neighbour. There's nothing in it for me... I'm seeing to all this out of sheer kindness of heart. And it's not a cheerful job, either. I spent the night in this room and it wasn't all that warm at about four o'clock in the morning, I can tell you. Well, I've always been stupid, I'm too kind to people.'

At this point they pulled the coffin into the room. I realized what was happening and that I was doomed because I was not going to be able to wake up. My mind became confused; a black fog was swirling round inside my head. I was so overcome by exhaustion that it was almost a relief to realize that there was no further hope for me.

'They haven't been mean with their wood,' remarked one undertaker in a hoarse voice. 'It's too long.'

'Ah well, he'll be more comfortable,' replied another voice jokingly.

I wasn't a heavy man, which pleased them, since there were three flights of stairs to go down. Just as they were catching hold of my shoulders and feet, Madame Gabin suddenly exclaimed, crossly:

'You naughty little girl! You're always poking your nose in where you shouldn't! I'll teach you to peep round the corner!'

It was Dédé pushing her untidy mop of hair round the door to have a look at the man being put into his wooden box. There was the sound of two loud slaps, followed by a burst of tears; and when her mother came back into the room, she talked about her daughter while the men were putting me into the coffin:

'She's ten years old and she's not a bad little girl but she's far too nosey. I don't spank her a lot but she's got to learn to do as she's told.'

'Oh, all little girls are like that, you know,' said one of the men. 'When there's a dead person in the house, they always keep hanging around.'

I was lying comfortably stretched out and but for my left arm, which was pressing against one of the sides, I could have imagined myself still on the bed. As they had pointed out, I fitted in very nicely, because I was so short.

'Wait a second!' exclaimed Madame Gabin. 'I promised his wife to put a pillow under his head.'

But the undertakers were in a hurry and pushed the pillow under very roughly. One of them was swearing as he looked for his hammer. They had left it downstairs and had to go down to fetch it. The lid was placed on and all of a sudden my whole body was jarred as the first nail was driven in with two blows of the hammer. So this really was the end; my life was finished... And quickly the nails were driven home with sharp, repeated blows of the hammer; they worked skilfully and unconcernedly, like men nailing the lid on a box of fruit. Henceforth, every sound reaching me was muffled and long drawn-out, with a strange echo, as if the deal coffin had turned into a big sounding-box. The last words I heard in the bedroom in the Rue Dauphine were spoken by Madame Gabin:

'Go down gently and be careful of the second-floor banister, it's loose.'

They were carrying me away. I felt as though I was being tossed in a stormy sea; but from this moment onwards, my memories are very vague. However, I do recall that my only concern, a sort of instinctive and quite absurd one, was to try to memorize the route to the cemetery. I didn't know a single Paris street or the exact location of the principal cemeteries that I had occasionally heard mentioned, but this didn't prevent me from concentrating all my remaining thoughts on working out whether we were turning left or right. The hearse was bumping me about over the paving stones. All around there was the rumble of traffic and the sound of footsteps of passers-by which created a confused murmur, magnified by the sounding-board effect of the coffin. At first, I was able to follow the route fairly clearly. Then we stopped and I was moved; I realized that we had reached the church. But as soon as the hearse set off again, I lost all sense of direction. A peal of bells informed me that we were passing close to a church, while a gentler, more continuous rumble made me think that we were going along beside an esplanade. I felt like a condemned man being led to execution, awaiting the final blow which never came.

We stopped again and I was lifted out of the hearse. And now everything happened very quickly. The sounds had all ceased and I could sense that I was in a deserted spot, under some trees and the sweep of the sky. No doubt there were some mourners, people from the hotel, Simoneau and a few others, because I could hear whispering. There was some chanting and a priest mumbled some Latin. Then, for a couple of minutes, there was nothing to be heard but the sound of footsteps. Suddenly, I felt myself sinking and ropes were vibrating against the sides of the coffin like a bow playing on a cracked double-bass. This was the end. A staggering blow, like the bursting of a shell, exploded just to the left of my head; a second blow exploded at my feet; a third, even stronger, struck over my stomach. This last one was so loud that I thought it had split the coffin in two. And then I lost consciousness.

4

How long I remained in that state I find it impossible to say. For a person completely unconscious, a second is the same as eternity. I no longer existed. Then, gradually, a confused feeling of being alive revived. I was still in a sort of sleep but I had started dreaming; against the impenetrable darkness blocking my future, a nightmare was taking shape. It was a weird figment of my imagination and one which had often tormented me in the past when, with my horrible propensity for inventing dire catastrophes, I would lie awake, open-eyed, savouring the masochistic pleasure of dreaming up disasters.

Thus I would imagine that my wife was expecting me somewhere, I think in Guérande, and that I was on my way by train. Just as the train was going through a tunnel, there was a frightful rumbling sound, like a clap of thunder: it was a double landslide. The train was completely undamaged and every compartment intact; but the roof of the tunnel had collapsed at both ends and so we found ourselves trapped in the middle of a mountain, immured by the rockfall. We were condemned to a horrible, lingering death, with no hope of help, for it would take a month to unblock the tunnel, using powerful equipment and extreme care. We were imprisoned in a sort of cellar without any exit. The death of every passenger was merely a matter of time.

As I have said, my imagination was frequently exercised by such horrible situations. I would think up all sorts of variants. I peopled my drama with a full cast of men, women and children, a hundred or so, and this crowd of people gave me scope for an endless variety of episodes. There was a certain amount of food on the train but this supply was quickly exhausted and without quite resorting to cannibalism, the starving passengers fought like tigers over the few remaining scraps of bread. An old man, at his last gasp, was brutally punched and driven away, a mother fought like a tigress to hold on to a few mouthfuls of food for her child. In my own compartment, two young newly-weds had given up hope and lay motionless and dying in each other's arms. The track itself was clear and passengers were able to climb down and prowl along the train like wild beasts in search of their prey. Class distinctions had vanished; one very rich man, a senior government official it was whispered, was crying on a work-man's shoulder and addressing him like a brother. The lights had soon failed and the furnace of the locomotive had finally gone out. As we moved from carriage to carriage, we groped our way along the wheels to avoid bumping into each other until we reached the engine, which we could recognize from its cold piston-rod and its bulging sides, a slumbering, impotent giant lying motionless in the darkness. You could imagine no more frightening spectacle than this train totally immured under-ground like someone buried alive, with all its passengers dying one by one.

I used to revel in every tiny horrible detail. The darkness was pierced by screams and suddenly a man, whom I hadn't seen and hadn't realized was sitting beside me, slumped down against my shoulder. But it was the cold and lack of air which was really affecting me now. Never had I felt so cold; a mantle of snow seemed to be settling on my shoulders, my head was reeling in the clammy air and at the same time I felt that I was being stifled as the roof of rock seemed to be collapsing and pressing down on to my chest. The whole mass of the mountain was crushing me. But a cry of relief rang out. For some time we had been imagining that we could hear dull thuds in the distance and hopes were beginning to rise that they had started to dig us out. But now relief was at hand from another quarter; one of our number had just discovered an air-shaft in the tunnel and we all ran over to look at it. A blue patch could be seen at the top, no larger than a blob of sealing wax; but this tiny patch of blue filled us with joy. We stood craning out necks endeavouring to snatch a breath of fresh air. We could clearly distinguish some black dots frantically working; they must surely be workmen setting up a winch to haul us to safety. A cry burst from our throats. We were saved! We were saved! Everyone was shouting and waving their arms towards this tiny blue patch.

It was the sound of these shouts which woke me up. Where was I? Was I still in the tunnel? I was lying stretched out and I could feel my body enclosed between walls on both sides. I tried to sit up but my head struck violently against some hard object. I must be surrounded by rock on all sides. And the blue patch had disappeared; the sky was no longer visible, even in the distance. I was still suffocating and my teeth were chattering as a shiver ran through my whole body.

Suddenly everything came back to me. My hair bristled with horror and an icy tremor shook me from head to foot as the dreadful truth flooded into my brain. Had I finally been freed from the paralysis that had held me stiff and corpselike in its grip for so long? Yes, I could move and I ran my trembling hands along the sides of the coffin. There remained one final test: I opened my mouth and tried to speak, instinctively calling Marguerite's name. But my call turned into a scream and my voice echoed round the coffin in a terrifying, earsplitting shriek. Oh dear God! Could it be true? I could move and I could call out that I was alive; but there was no one to hear me, I was entombed under the ground...

I made one final effort to control myself and gather my wits about me. Wasn't there some way of escape? I started to relive my dream; my brain was still reeling and in my imagination the airshaft and the patch of blue sky were mingling with the reality of the hole in which I was suffocating. With wild, staring eyes I probed the darkness. Perhaps I might be able to see a slit, a hole, a sliver of light? But in the gloom all around me, I could see only a stream of twinkling lights and specks of red which spread out and vanished, leaving a black, bottomless abyss. Then my brain cleared and I thrust the stupid nightmare from my mind. If I was to save myself, I should need all my wits.

First of all, my greatest danger seemed to be the ever-increasing stuffiness which was threatening to suffocate me. No doubt I had been able to do without air for so long because my physical functions had been paralysed; but now that my heart had started beating and my lungs were breathing again, if I didn't free myself as quickly as possible, I should be asphyxiated. I was also suffering from the cold and I was afraid of becoming numb and dying, like people who topple over into a snowdrift and never climb out.

While I kept on reminding myself that I must remain quite calm, I could feel waves of panic sweeping over me. So in an effort to pull myself together, I tried to recall everything I knew about methods of burial. I must have been buried in a five-year concession and that effectively put paid to one of my hopes; for I had noticed that as each hole was filled up in the paupers' graves, the end of the most recent coffin was left exposed. Had that been the case, I should only have needed to break through one plank to escape, whereas if I was in a hole that had been filled up to the top, there was a tremendous weight of earth above me and this would prove a formidable obstacle. Hadn't I read somewhere that in Paris graves were dug out to a depth of six feet? How could I get through such an enormous thickness of earth? Even should I be able to split the lid of my coffin open, wouldn't the earth come pouring in like fine sand and fill my nose and mouth so that I would die a second, horrible death, drowned in slime?

However, I carefully explored the space all around me. The coffin was a large one and I had no difficulty in moving my arms. As far as I could discover, there were no gaps in the lid and though the left and right sides of the coffin were only roughly planed, they were tough and solid. I bent my arm back across my chest and felt beyond my head. There, in the end plank, I discovered a knot that gave a little when I pressed against it. So I laboriously rocked it until at last it fell out. Then, inserting my finger, I felt the earth beyond; it was a thick, wet clay. But that got me no further. I even regretted having removed the knot, as the slime might be able to seep though the hole. I decided to try another experiment and tapped all round the coffin to see if there might perhaps be a hollow space on one side or the other. But the sound was the same wherever I tapped. However, when I gently knocked the end of the coffin, the sound seemed to me to be higher pitched; but this could have been caused by the shape or method of construction.

Then, with my arms held above my chest, I began gently pushing with my fists. The lid did not move an inch. Next I tried bracing myself on my back and feet and pushing with my knees. There was not even a creak. Finally, exerting my full strength and using every muscle in my body, I pushed until my bones cracked and then lashed out until I was bruised all over. It was then that I lost my head.

Until now I'd been determined to remain clear-headed and control the bursts of impotent rage which threatened to sweep over me like the fumes in a drunkard's head. Above all, I had been resisting the temptation to shout because I realized that if I started shouting, I should be lost. And now, all at once, I began shouting and screaming. I had reached the limits of my endurance; scream upon scream burst from my lips until I could scream no more. I was calling for help in a voice that I could not recognize as my own, becoming more hysterical with every shout I uttered. I was screaming that I didn't want to die, while at the same time I was scratching at the boards with my nails and writhing convulsively like a trapped wolf.

I don't know how long this outburst of hysteria lasted but I can still feel those hard, unyielding wooden planks which I was vainly trying to force my way through and still hear my screams and sobs reverberating inside them. A last flicker of reason was urging me to control myself but I was powerless to do so.

In the end I lapsed into a state of nervous exhaustion. Barely conscious, I lay painfully waiting to die. The coffin was as solid as a rock: I should never manage to break it open; and the certainty of this left me completely sapped of energy and of the courage to make any further attempt. And now another ordeal was added to the cold and lack of air: the pangs of hunger which soon became unbearable. Through the knot-hole, I tried to gather a few pinches of earth which I then swallowed: they merely increased my sufferings. I took hold of my arm in my clenched teeth and sucked at my skin, tempted to bite into my flesh and drink my blood, but I could not quite bring myself to do it.

By now, I was longing to die. Till then I had always had a horror at the thought of annihilation and now I had reached the stage of hoping for it, even praying for it. To be completely wiped out! And it would be impossible for it to be too complete. How childish I'd been to be afraid of that sleep without dreams, that black stillness that would last for ever! Death would be a happy release, because it would, in one fell swoop, obliterate all consciousness for all eternity. To be able to become like a stone, a handful of dust, simply to cease to be!

Yet my groping hands were still continuing automatically to feel around the inside of my coffin. Suddenly, something pricked my left thumb and the slight pain roused me from my torpor. What could it be? I felt again and realized that it was a nail which the undertakers had hammered in askew without noticing, and which had missed the edge of the coffin. It was a very long nail with a very sharp point. The head of the nail was in the lid but I could feel that it was loose. Now I had only one thought in my mind: I must get that nail. Holding my right hand above my waist, I began to rock the nail to and fro. It was no easy task, for the nail was not very loose. I had to change hands frequently, because my other hand was awkwardly placed and quickly became tired. While I was working desperately at the nail, a plan was taking shape in my head whereby it could prove to be my salvation. I must get it out, at all costs. But could I do it in the short time left to me? I was weak from hunger and forced to stop, because my head was reeling and my hands had lost their strength. My mind was in a whirl. I had already sucked up the drops of blood oozing from my pricked thumb, now I bit hard into my arm and drank my blood... Spurred on by the pain and invigorated by the taste of this warm, salty wine moistening my lips, I set to work again with both hands. At last I managed to free the nail and pull it inside the coffin.

It was at this moment that I realized that I was going to succeed. My plan was simple. I jabbed the point of the nail into the lid of the coffin and dragged it in a straight line as far as I could; and I kept on moving the nail backwards and forwards to score as deep a groove as possible. My hands became stiff and sore but with the force of despair I kept doggedly on. When I judged that the groove was deep enough, I turned over on to my front and bracing myself on elbows and knees, I pushed up with my back. I heard the lid creak but it refused to split. The groove was obviously not deep enough, so I turned on to my back and started scraping away with the nail once more. It was laborious work. After a while I turned over again and made another attempt; and this time the lid split from top to bottom...

Well, I was not yet safe but hope was beginning to stir. I stopped pushing and lay completely still for fear that the soil might slide down and bury me. I planned to use the lid as a sort of shield whilst I tried to hollow out a shaft in the earth. Unfortunately this proved difficult in the extreme, for the heavy lumps of clay kept slipping down and pressing on the lid, making it impossible for me to move it. I would never reach the surface, for these lumps were already weighing down so strongly on my back that my face was being thrust against the bottom of the coffin. Just as I was beginning to panic, I thought, as I stretched out, preparatory to bracing myself, that I could feel the end of the coffin giving way under my pressure. I kicked hard against it with my heels, thinking there might be a hollow space there, where they were in the process of digging a grave.

Suddenly I felt that my feet were free. My intuition had proved correct: an open grave had recently been dug out there and all that I now had to do was to break through a narrow bank of earth. I slid out into the open. Thank God! I was saved!

For a moment I lay on my back looking up at the sky. It was night time and the stars were shining in the dark, velvety, blue sky. The wind was rising, bringing warm gusts of spring air and a scent of trees. Thank God! I was saved, I could breathe, I was warm and I was weeping tears of joy. I clasped my hands together and in a broken voice offered a prayer of thanks to heaven. How wonderful it was to be alive!

5

My first thought was to make my way to the caretaker of the cemetery and get him to arrange for me to be taken home. But on second thoughts, still confused in my mind, I hesitated. Wouldn't everybody be frightened when they saw me? And why be in such a hurry, now that everything was going to be all right? Apart from the small wound in my left arm where I had bitten myself, there was nothing wrong with me and indeed the slight fever brought on by this wound was stimulating me and giving me an unexpected feeling of energy. I would certainly be able to walk without help.

So I decided to take my time, for my mind was still in something of a muddle. In the grave next to mine, I had noticed the gravediggers' spades and the thought came to me that I ought to make good the damage I had done and fill up the hole in such a way that nobody would notice my resurrection. At the time I had no clear idea in mind, I merely felt that it was pointless to publicize what had happened; in fact, I felt rather ashamed of being still alive when everyone thought I was dead. It took me less than half an hour to cover up all traces of my escape.

I jumped out of the grave. What a wonderful night it was! The cemetery was plunged in silence and the dark trees were casting still shadows on the white gravestones. As I was trying to find my sense of direction,* I saw that one half of the sky was glowing as if on fire. That must be Paris and I set off in that direction, keeping in the shadow of the overhanging branches of an avenue of trees. But I had barely gone fifty yards before I was forced to stop and sit down, out of breath, on a stone bench. Only then did I examine myself closely: I was completely dressed, even down to my shoes; the only thing missing was a hat. How I blessed Marguerite's sense of piety in having me properly clothed! And the sudden memory of Marguerite brought me to my feet: I wanted to see her.

At the end of the avenue, my way was blocked by a wall. I clambered up on to a gravestone and, hanging from the coping, I let myself drop on the far side. I fell heavily. Picking myself up, I followed for a few minutes a wide, deserted street that ran beside the cemetery. I had not the slightest idea where I was but I kept saying to myself determinedly that I would find my way back into Paris and then certainly be able to get to the Rue Dauphine. Some people went by but, seized by a sudden feeling of distrust, I didn't speak to them; I didn't feel that I wanted to confide in anyone at the moment. I realize now that I was already suffering from a high fever and becoming delirious. In the end, just as I was coming out into a main street, I was overcome by dizziness and fell heavily on the pavement.

Here there is a gap in my life. I remained unconscious for three weeks. When I finally came to, I was lying in a strange bedroom. I was being looked after by a man who merely told me that he had picked me up one morning in the Boulevard Montparnasse and taken me back to his house. He was a retired doctor. When I thanked him, he replied briefly that my case had intrigued him and he had wanted to observe me. Moreover, during the first few weeks of my convalescence, he would not allow me to ask any questions. Nor, later on, did he ask me any. I stayed in bed for another week; my mind was still unclear and I did not even try to go back over all that had happened, for I found it both tiring and saddening. I felt afraid and in no mood to talk. I'd go and see how things were once I was fit enough to leave the house. Perhaps, during my delirium, I might have blurted out a name but the doctor never referred to anything that I might have said. He was as discreet as he was kind.

Meanwhile, summer had come and one morning in June I received permission, at last, to go for a short walk. It was a superb day, with a cheerful sun making the old streets of Paris look young again. I went slowly along, asking the way to the Rue Dauphine from passers-by at every street-crossing. At last, I reached my goal but I had difficulty in recognizing the furnished hotel in which we had stayed. I was like a scared child. If I showed myself to Marguerite too unexpectedly, I was afraid she would be overcome by shock. Perhaps the best thing would be to warn old Madame Gabin first of all? But I didn't like the idea of anyone coming between Marguerite and me... I couldn't make up my mind; deep down inside me, I felt a great emptiness as if, long ago, I had sacrificed myself.

The house looked golden in the sunshine. I had recognized it by its cheap restaurant on the ground floor from which you could have meals sent up to your room. I looked up to the third floor, at the end window on the left. It was wide open. Suddenly a young woman, with her hair undone and her shift slipping off her shoulder, came to the window and rested her elbows on the sill to look out; she was immediately followed by a young man who bent over and kissed the back of her neck. It was not Marguerite. I felt no surprise; it seemed to me as if it was all part of a dream, like so many other things that I was about to experience.

For a second, I stood hesitating in the street, thinking I might go up and question this happy young couple of lovers who were still laughing and enjoying the sun. Eventually, I decided to go into the little ground-floor restaurant. I felt sure that, with my hollow cheeks and the beard which had grown during my illness, no one would recognize me. Just as I was taking my seat at a table, who should appear but Madame Gabin herself, holding a small cup to fetch herself some coffee. She planted herself in front of the counter and started exchanging the morning's gossip with the owner's wife. I pricked up my ears.

'Well, has that poor little woman on the third floor made up her mind at last?' the woman enquired.

'What could she do?' replied Madame Gabin. 'It was the best thing for her. Monsieur Simoneau has been such a good friend... He'd just completed his business, he was coming into a lot of money and he was offering to take her back with him to his home town, where she'd be able to live with one of his aunts who needs a companion.'

The woman behind the bar gave a little laugh. I was hiding my face behind a newspaper; I had gone very pale and my hands were trembling.

'I imagine that it'll end in their getting married,' Madame Gabin went on. 'But I can assure you I haven't seen any hanky-panky... The poor dear was heartbroken over her husband and he behaved like a proper gentleman. Anyway, they left yesterday. Once she's out of mourning, they'll please themselves what they do, won't they?'

At that moment, the door leading from the hall into the restaurant swung open and Dédé came in.

'Aren't you going to come, Mummy? I've been waiting for you. Do hurry up!'

'I'm coming in a minute. Don't bother me!' her mother replied.

The girl stayed listening to the two women, like the precocious little Paris brat she was.

'And after all, the husband wasn't a patch on Monsieur Simoneau,' said Madame Gabin, following her train of thought. 'I didn't think much of that little whipper-snapper. Always complaining... And as poor as a church mouse. No, really, a husband like that can't be much fun for a woman with some blood in her veins... And Monsieur Simoneau is rich and as strong as an ox.'

'Oh yes,' Dédé broke in, 'I saw him having a wash one day. You should have seen his hairy arms!'

'Now just you run along!' the old woman shouted, giving her a push. 'You're always sticking your nose in where it's not wanted.'

Then she concluded:

'So I reckon that the husband did the right thing in dying. It's a wonderful stroke of luck.'

When I found myself in the street once again, my legs could barely support me. I walked slowly away; and yet I wasn't too unhappy. I even smiled when I looked at my shadow cast by the sun: I really was weedy. It had been a queer notion of mine to marry Marguerite... And I remembered how much she'd disliked Guérande, how impatient she'd become and tired of her boring life. She had shown herself a good wife; but I had never been a proper lover for her. It was a brother she was mourning, not a husband. Why should I disturb her life again? A dead man can't be jealous... When I raised my eyes, I saw that I was standing in front of the Luxembourg gardens. I went in and sat down in the sun. I slipped into a gentle daydream. I felt full of tenderness towards Marguerite now. I could see her living in the provinces like a lady, in her little country town, very happy and loved by everyone. People would make a fuss of her. She would grow into a beauty and have three sons and two daughters... No, I'd done the right thing in dying and I'd certainly not be stupid or cruel enough to come back to life.

Since that time, I've travelled a great deal and lived in many different places. I'm a very ordinary man who's worked and fed like everyone else. I'm no longer afraid of dying, but death doesn't seem to want anything to do with me, now that I can see no point in living. I'm afraid he's forgotten me.

SHELLFISH FOR MONSIEUR CHABRE

MONSIEUR CHABRE had one great sorrow: he was childless. He had married a Mademoiselle Estelle Catinot (of the firm of Desvignes and Catinot). She was tall, beautiful and blonde, only eighteen years of age; but for the last four years he had been anxiously waiting, with growing dismay and wounded pride at the failure of his efforts.

Monsieur Chabre was a retired corn-merchant and a very wealthy man. Despite having lived continently, as befitted a solid middle-class business man bent on becoming a millionaire, he walked with the heavy tread of an old man, although he was only forty-five. His face, prematurely lined with financial cares, was as dull as ditchwater. And he was in despair, for a man who enjoys an investment income of fifty thousand francs a year has the right to feel surprised when he discovers that it is more difficult to become a father than to become rich.

Madame Chabre was twenty-two years old and beautiful. With her peach-like complexion and golden blonde hair curling in ringlets over her neck, she was quite adorable. Her blue-green eyes were like slumbering pools hiding depths difficult to plumb. When her husband complained of their childlessness, she would arch her supple body, emphasizing the curves of her hips and bosom, and her wry half-smile plainly said: 'Is it any fault of mine?' It must be added that in her circle of friends and acquaintances, Madame Chabre was acknowledged as a young woman of perfect breeding, adequately pious and incapable of giving rise to the slightest breath of scandal, brought up, indeed, in the soundest of middle-class principles by a strict mother. Only the nostrils of her little white nose would give an occasional nervous twitch which might have given some cause for concern to anyone but a retired corn-merchant.

Meanwhile the family doctor, Dr Guiraud, a large, shrewd, smiling man, had already been called in for a number of private consultations with Monsieur Chabre. He had explained to him how backward science was: you can't plant a child as you'd plant an oak, dear me no! However, not wishing to leave anyone entirely without hope, he had promised to give thought to the case. So, one July morning he called on Monsieur Chabre and said:

'You ought to go on a holiday to the sea and do some bathing. It's an excellent thing. And above all, eat shellfish, lots of shellfish. Nothing but shellfish.'

Monsieur Chabre's hopes rose.

'Shellfish, doctor?' he asked eagerly. 'Do you think that shellfish . . .?'

'Yes, I do indeed! There's strong evidence of the success of that treatment. So you must understand, every day you eat oysters, mussels, clams, sea-urchins, not forgetting crayfish and lobsters!'

Then, just as he was standing in the doorway ready to leave, he added casually:

'Don't bury yourself in some out-of-the-way place. Madame Chabre is young and needs entertainment . . . Go to Trouville, it's full of ozone.'

Three days later, the couple were on their way. However, the ex-corn-merchant had thought it pointless to go to Trouville, where he'd have to spend money hand-over-fist. You can eat shellfish anywhere, indeed, in an out-of-the-way resort the shellfish would be more plentiful and far cheaper. As for entertainment, there's always too much of that. After all, they weren't travelling for pleasure.

A friend had recommended the tiny resort of Pouliguen, close to Saint Nazaire, a new town with its modern, dead-straight streets still full of building sites. They visited the harbour and loitered round the streets where the shops hesitated between being tiny, gloomy village stores and large luxury grocers. At Pouliguen there was not one single house left unlet. The little timber and plaster houses, looking like garish fairground shacks, which stretched round the bay, had all been invaded by the English and rich Nantes tradesmen. Estelle pulled a wry face when she saw the queer structures in which middle-class architects had given free rein to their imagination.

The travellers were advised to spend the night in Guérande. It was a Sunday. When they arrived just before noon, even Monsieur Chabre, although not naturally a poetic person, was at first struck with admiration by this little jewel of a medieval town, so well-preserved with its ramparts and deep gateways with battlements. Estelle looked at the drowsy little town, surrounded by its esplanades shaded by tall trees, and its charm brought a gleam into the dreamy pools of her eyes. Their carriage drove in through one of the gateways and clattered at a trot over the cobblestones of the narrow streets. The Chabres had not exchanged a word.

'What a dump!' the ex-corn-merchant muttered finally. 'The villages round Paris are far better built.'

Their carriage halted in front of the Hôtel du Commerce, in the centre of the town, next to the church, and as they were getting out, Mass was just ending. While her husband was seeing to their luggage, Estelle was intrigued to see the congregation coming out of church, many of whom were dressed in quaint costumes. Some of the men were wearing white smocks and baggy breeches; these were those who lived and worked in the vast, desolate salt-marshes which stretch between Guérande and Le Croisic. Then there were the share-croppers, a completely different species, who wore short woollen jackets and round broad-brimmed hats. But Estelle was particularly excited by the ornate costume worn by one girl. Her headdress fitted tightly round the temples and rose up to a point. Over her red bodice with wide-cuffed sleeves, she had a silk front brocaded with brightly coloured flowers. Her triple, tight-pleated, blue woollen skirt was held by a belt embroidered in gold and silver, while a long orange-coloured apron hung down, revealing her red woollen stockings and dainty yellow slippers.

'How can they allow that sort of thing!' exclaimed Monsieur Chabre. 'You only see that kind of circus get-up in Brittany.'

Estelle made no reply. A tall young man, about twenty years of age, was coming out of church, giving his arm to an old lady . . . He had a very pale complexion and honey-coloured hair; he looked very self-possessed and was something of a giant, with broad shoulders and muscular arms, despite his youth. Yet he had a delicate, gentle expression which, combined with his pink complexion and smooth skin, gave him a girlish appearance. As Estelle was staring at him, struck by his good looks, he turned his head and his eyes rested on her for a second. Then he blushed to the roots of his hair.

'Well there's someone at least who looks human. He'll make a fine cavalry officer,' said Monsieur Chabre.

'That's Monsieur Hector Plougastel with his mother,' said the hotel maid, hearing this remark. 'He's such a kind, well-behaved boy.'

While the Chabres were taking lunch, a lively argument arose at their table d'hôte. The registrar of mortgages, who took his meals at the Hôtel du Commerce, was speaking approvingly of Guérande's patriarchal way of life and particularly of the high moral standards of the young people. He claimed that it was their religious upbringing which was responsible for their good behaviour. However, a commercial traveller, who had arrived that morning with a stock of false jewellery, recounted with a grin how he'd seen young men and girls kissing behind the hedgerows as he was driving along the road. He would have liked to see what the lads of the town would have done if given the chance to meet a few attractive friendly ladies. And he went on to poke fun at religion, priests and nuns until the outraged registrar of mortgages flung down his napkin and stamped out of the room. The Chabres had gone on eating without saying a word, with the husband furious at the sort of conversation you have to listen to at a table d'hôte while his wife sat with a placid smile on her face as if she didn't understand a word of what they were talking about.

The Chabres spent the afternoon visiting Guérande. The church of St Aubin was deliciously cool and as they walked slowly around inside, they looked up at the arched vaulting supported on slender columns which shot upwards like stone rockets, stopping to admire the strange carved capitals depicting torturers sawing their victims in two and roasting them on grills, using large bellows to fan the flames. Then they strolled round the five or six main streets of Guérande and Monsieur Chabre was confirmed in his view: it was nothing but a dump, with no trade to speak of, just one more of those antiquated medieval towns so many of which had already been knocked down. The streets were deserted, with their rows of gabled houses piled up side by side like so many tired old women. The pointed roofs, the slate-covered pepper-pots and corner turrets and the weather-worn sculptures made some of the quiet back streets of the town seem like museums drowsing in the sun. At the sight of all the leadlighted windows, a dreamy look came into Estelle's eyes; since her marriage she had taken to reading novels and she was thinking of Walter Scott.

But when the Chabres went outside the town and walked all

round it, they found themselves nodding their heads apprecia-
tively. They had to admit that it really was charming. The granite
walls which completely encircled the town had weathered to a
rich honey colour and were as intact as when they had been built,
though ivy and honeysuckle now draped the battlements. Shrubs
had grown on the towers flanking the ramparts and their brightly
coloured flowers, golden gorse and flaming gilly-flower, glowed
under the clear blue sky. Grassy walks under shady age-old oaks
extended all around the town. They picked their way carefully, as
though stepping on a carpet, as they walked along beside the
former moat, partly filled in and further on turning into weed-
covered stagnant pools in whose mysteriously glinting surface
were mirrored the white trunks of birch trees growing close up to
the walls amongst the wispy green undergrowth. Rays of light
shone through the trees lighting up hidden nooks and crannies,
the deep-set posterns where the peace of centuries was disturbed
only by the sudden leaps of frightened frogs.

'There are ten towers, I've just been counting them,' exclaimed
Monsieur Chabre when they had come round to their starting
point.

He had been particularly struck by the four gateways with their
long narrow entrances through which only one carriage could
pass at a time. Wasn't it quite absurd to keep yourself shut in like
that in the nineteenth century? If he'd been in charge he'd have
knocked down the fortress-like gateways, with their useless
loopholes and such thick walls that you could have built a couple
of six-storey dwellings on their sites.

'Not to mention all the building materials you'd get from
demolishing the ramparts,' he added.

They were standing in the Mall, a spacious raised esplanade
which curved in a quarter-circle from the eastern to the southern
gateways. Estelle was gazing pensively over the striking
panorama which spread out for miles beyond the roofs of the
suburbs. First of all there came a dense, dark green belt of gnarled
shrubs and pine trees leaning sideways from the force of the
winds coming in from the ocean. Then followed the immense
plain of desolate salt-marshes, flat and bare, with their square
patches of seawater gleaming like mirrors beside the little heaps
of salt which shone white against the grey expanse of sand.
Further on, at the skyline, she could make out the deep blue of

the Atlantic on which three tiny sails looked like white swallows.

'There's the young man we saw this morning,' said Monsieur Chabre suddenly. 'Doesn't he remind you of Lavière's son? If he had a humpback, he'd look exactly like him.'

Estelle turned slowly round but Hector, standing at the edge of the Mall and equally absorbed in watching the sea on the distant horizon, did not seem to notice that he was being observed. The young woman started walking slowly on again. She was using her long sunshade as a walking stick but she had barely taken a dozen steps before its bow came loose. The Chabres heard a voice behind them.

'Excuse me, madame...'

Hector had retrieved the bow.

'Thank you very much indeed,' said Estelle with her quiet smile.

He really was a nice, well-mannered young man. Monsieur Chabre took to him at once and explained to him the problem facing them of finding a suitable resort, and even asked for Hector's advice.

Hector was very shy.

'I don't think you'll find the sort of place you're looking for either at Le Croisic or Le Batz,' he said, pointing to the church spires of these two little towns on the horizon. 'I think your best plan would be to go to Piriac.'

He gave them some details: Piriac was about seven miles away; he had an uncle living on the outskirts. Finally, in reply to questions by Monsieur Chabre, he said that there were plenty of shellfish to be found there.

The young woman was poking the point of her sunshade into the short turf. The young man kept his eyes averted as though embarrassed to look her in the face.

'Guérande is an extremely pretty place,' she said finally in her soft voice.

'Oh yes, extremely,' stammered Hector, suddenly devouring her with his eyes.

2

One morning, three days after settling in at Piriac, Monsieur Chabre was standing on the platform at the end of the seawall protecting the tiny harbour, stolidly keeping watch over Estelle who was bathing. At the moment she was floating on her back. The sun was already very hot and, decorously dressed in black frock-coat and felt hat, he was warding off its rays by means of a sunshade with a green lining. He looked every inch the holiday visitor.

'Is the water warm?' he enquired, feigning interest in his wife's bathing.

'Lovely!' she replied, turning on to her front.

Monsieur Chabre was terrified of the water and never ventured into it. He would explain that his doctors had explicitly forbidden him to bathe in the sea. When a wave so much as came towards his shoes on the beach, he would start back in alarm as if he were being faced by some vicious animal baring its teeth. In any case, seawater would have disturbed his decorum; he looked on it as dirty and disgusting.

'So it really is warm?' he enquired again, his head swimming from the heat. He felt both drowsy and uncomfortable standing at the end of the seawall.

Estelle did not bother to reply: she was busy swimming a dog-paddle. In the water, she was as fearless as a boy and would swim for hours, to the dismay of her husband who felt it incumbent on him to wait at the water's edge. At Piriac Estelle had found the sort of bathing she liked; she despised gently shelving beaches where you have to walk a long way out before the water comes up to your waist. She would go to the end of the seawall wrapped in her flannel bathrobe, slip it off and take a header without a second thought. She used to say that she needed fifteen feet of water to avoid striking her head on the rocky bottom. Her skirtless one-piece bathing costume clung to her tall figure and the long blue belt tied round her waist emphasized the graceful curve of her firm, full hips. Moving through the clear water, with her hair caught up in a rubber bathing cap from which a few strands of blonde curls were escaping, she looked like some sleek agile dolphin with a disconcertingly pink woman's face.

Monsieur Chabre had been standing in the sweltering hot sun for a good quarter of an hour. He had already consulted his watch three times. Finally he risked a timid comment:

'You've been in a long time, my dear. Oughtn't you to come out? You'll get tired, bathing so long.'

'But I've only just gone in,' the young woman replied. 'I'm as warm as toast.'

Then, turning on her back again, she added:

'If you're bored, you needn't stay. I don't need you.'

He objected with a shake of his head, pointing out how quickly a danger could arise; Estelle smiled at the thought; her husband would be a fat lot of good if she were suddenly attacked by cramp. But at this moment her attention was drawn to the other side of the seawall, towards the bay that lay to the left of the village.

'Good gracious!' she exclaimed. 'What's happening over there? I'm going to have a look.'

And she swam off with a long, powerful breast-stroke.

'Estelle, come back!' shouted Monsieur Chabre. 'You know I can't bear it when you take risks!'

But Estelle was not listening and he had to possess himself in patience. Standing on tiptoe to watch the white speck of his wife's straw hat, he merely transferred his sunshade to the other hand; he was finding the stifling heat more and more unbearable.

'What on earth has she seen?' he muttered to himself. 'Oh, it's that thing floating over there... A bit of rubbish, I expect. A bunch of seaweed, perhaps? Or a barrel. No, it can't be, it's moving.'

Then he suddenly recognized what it was:

'It's a man swimming!'

However, after a few strokes, Estelle had also recognized perfectly well that it was a man. She therefore stopped swimming straight towards him, since that seemed hardly the proper thing. But she mischievously decided not to swim back to the seawall and continued to make for the open sea, pleased to be able to show how bold she was. She pursued her course, pretending not to notice the other swimmer, who was now gradually coming up towards her, as if being carried by the current. Thus, when she turned round to swim back to the seawall, their paths crossed, apparently quite fortuitously.

'I hope you are well, madame?' the young man enquired politely.

'Oh, it's you!' Estelle exclaimed brightly.

And she added with a smile:

'What a small world it is, isn't it?'

It was young Hector de Plougastel. He was still very shy, very well built and looked very pink in the water. For a moment they swam without speaking, maintaining a decent distance between each other. In order to converse, they had to raise their voices. However, Estelle felt that she ought to be polite.

'We're very grateful to you for having told us about Piriac. . . My husband is delighted with it.'

'Isn't that your husband standing by himself on the seawall?' asked Hector.

'Yes,' she replied.

Silence fell again. They were watching her husband who looked like a tiny black insect above the sea. Very intrigued, Monsieur Chabre was craning his neck even more and wondering who the man was whose acquaintance his wife had just made in the middle of the sea. There was no doubt about it, his wife was definitely chatting with him. It must be one of their Paris friends. But running his mind over the list of their friends, he could not think of one bold enough to swim so far out. And so he waited, aimlessly twirling his sunshade round in his hand.

'Yes,' Hector was explaining to the attractive Madame Chabre, 'I've come over to spend a few days in my uncle's château which you can see over there, halfway up the hill. So for my daily swim, I set off from that piece of land jutting out opposite the terrace and swim to the seawall and back. Just over a mile in all. It's wonderful exercise. . . But you're a very daring swimmer, I don't think I've ever met such a daring lady swimmer.'

'Oh I've been splashing about in the water ever since I was a little girl,' said Estelle. 'Water doesn't have any secrets for me, we're old friends.'

To avoid having to talk so loudly, they were gradually drawing closer to each other. On this beautiful warm morning, the sea was like one vast piece of watered silk, drowsing in the sun. Parts were as smooth as satin, separated by narrow bands of shimmering water, stretching out into the distance, currents looking like creases in a cloth. Once they were closer to each other, their conversation took a more intimate turn.

'What a superb day!' And Hector began to point out several landmarks along the coast. That village over there, less than a mile away, was Port aux Loups; opposite was the Morbihan, with its white cliffs standing out sharply as in some watercolour; and finally, in the other direction, towards the open sea, the island of Dumet could be seen as a grey speck set in the blue sea.

Each time Hector pointed, Estelle stopped swimming for a second, charmed to see these distant sights from sea-level against the infinite backdrop of the limpid sky. When she looked towards the sun, her eyes were dazzled and the sea seemed as though transformed into a boundless Sahara, with the blinding sunlight bleaching the immense stretch of sandy beach.

'Isn't it lovely,' she murmured. 'Isn't it really gorgeous!'

She turned over and relaxed, lying back motionless in the water with her arms stretched out sideways. Her gleaming white thighs and arms floated on the surface.

'So you were born in Guérande?' she asked.

'Yes,' he replied. 'I've only been once as far as Nantes.'

In order to talk more comfortably, Hector now also turned over on to his back. He gave details of his upbringing, for which his mother had been responsible: a narrowly devout woman whose values had been the traditional ones of the old aristocracy. He had had a priest as tutor who had taught him more or less what he would have learned in a private school, plus large amounts of catechism and heraldry. He rode, fenced and took a great deal of exercise. And with all this, he seemed as innocent as a babe in arms. He went to Mass every week, never read novels and when he reached his majority, would be marrying a very plain cousin.

'Goodness me! So you're only just twenty,' exclaimed Estelle, casting an astonished glance at this young colossus. Her maternal instincts were aroused; this fine specimen of the Breton race intrigued her. But as they continued floating on their backs, lost in contemplation of the transparent blue sky and quite oblivious of land, they drifted so close together that he slightly knocked against her.

'Oh, I'm sorry,' he said.

And dived and came to the surface five yards away. She burst into laughter and began to swim again.

'You boarded me!' she cried.

He was very red in the face. He swam nearer again, watching her slyly. Under her broad-brimmed straw hat, she seemed to him delightful. He could see nothing but her face and her dimpled chin dipping into the water. A few drops of water dripped from the blonde curls escaping from beneath her bathing cap, and glistened like pearls on the down of her cheeks. He could imagine

nothing more charming than the smile and pretty face of this
young woman swimming ahead of him, gently splashing and
leaving behind her merely a silvery trail.

When he noticed that Estelle realized that she was being
watched and was amused at the odd figure he was certainly
cutting, Hector blushed an even deeper red. He tried to find
something to say:

'Your husband seems to be getting impatient.'

'Oh, I don't think so,' she replied calmly. 'He's used to being
kept waiting when I'm having a swim.'

In fact, Monsieur Chabre was becoming restless. He kept
taking four steps forward, turning round and taking four steps
backward, twirling his sunshade even more vigorously in an
endeavour to cool himself.

It suddenly occurred to Estelle that perhaps her husband hadn't
recognized Hector.

'I'll call out and tell him it's you,' she said.

And as soon as she was in earshot of the seawall, she shouted:

'It's the gentleman we met in Guérande who was so helpful.'

'Oh good!' Monsieur Chabre shouted back. He raised his hat
and said politely:

'Is the water warm?'

'Very pleasant, thank you,' Hector replied.

Their bathe continued under the eye of the husband who could
now hardly complain, even though his feet were excruciatingly
hot from having to stand on the scorching stones. At the end of
the seawall, the water was wonderfully transparent and you could
see the fine sandy bottom some two or three fathoms down,
speckled here and there with pale or dark pebbles amidst waving
tendrils of seaweed rising perpendicularly towards the surface.
Estelle was fascinated by the clearness of the water as she swam
gently along in order not to ruffle the surface, bending her head
forward until the water came up to her nose and watching the
sand and the pebbles stretched out in the mysterious depths
below. She was especially fascinated by the clumps of green
seaweed that seemed almost like living creatures with their
swaying jagged leaves resembling hundreds of crabs' claws, some
of them short and sturdy growing between the rocks and others
long and flexible like snakes. She kept uttering little cries each
time she discovered something new:

'Oh what a big stone! It looks as if it's moving... Oh, there's a tree, a real tree with branches! Oh, there's a fish! It's darting away!'

Then suddenly she exclaimed:

'What on earth is that? It's a wedding bouquet! Do you think there really are wedding bouquets in the sea? Look, wouldn't you say that they're like orange blossoms? Oh, it's so pretty!'

Hector immediately dived and came up with a fistful of whitish seaweed which drooped and faded as soon as it left the water.

'Oh, thank you so much,' said Estelle. 'You shouldn't have bothered... Here you are, keep that for me, will you?' she added, throwing the bunch of seaweed at her husband's feet. For a few moments the young couple continued their swim. The air was filled with spray from their flailing arms and then, suddenly, they relaxed and glided through the water, in a circle of ripples which spread out and died away; and the surging water around them filled them with a private sensual pleasure all their own. Hector was trying to glide along in the wake of Estelle's body as it slid through the water and he could feel the warmth left by the movement of her limbs. All around, the sea had become even calmer and its pale blue had taken on a touch of pink.

'You'll be getting cold, my dear,' urged Monsieur Chabre, who was dripping with sweat himself.

'All right, I'm coming out,' she replied.

And so she did, pulling herself up quickly with the help of a chain hanging down the sloping side of the seawall. Hector must have been watching for her to climb out; but when he raised his head on hearing the spatter of drops she left behind, she was already on the platform and wrapped in her bathing robe. He looked so surprised and disconcerted that she had to smile as she gave a little shiver; and she gave a little shiver because she knew that she was charming when she did so, draped in her bathrobe with her tall figure standing out against the sky.

The young man reluctantly took his leave.

'We hope to see you again,' the husband said.

And while Estelle ran back along the seawall, watching Hector's head disappearing over the water as he swam back across the bay, Monsieur Chabre walked after her with the bunch of seaweed gathered by the young man solemnly held out in order to avoid wetting his frock coat.

3

In Piriac the Chabres had rented the first floor of a large house overlooking the sea. As the village had no decent restaurants, they had had to take on a local woman to cook for them. And a queer sort of cook she was, producing roasts burnt to a cinder and such peculiar-looking sauces that Estelle preferred to stick to bread. But as Monsieur kept pointing out, they hadn't come to enjoy the pleasures of the table. In any case, he hardly touched either the roasts or the sauces for he was stuffing himself, morning, noon and night, on shellfish of every description, with the determination of someone taking medicine. The unfortunate thing was that he loathed these strange, oddly shaped creatures, having been brought up on a typical middle-class diet of insipid hygienic food, and retained his childish predilection for sweet things. The queer flavour and salty fieriness of shellfish burnt his tongue and made him pull a face every time he swallowed them; but in his eagerness to become a father, he would have swallowed the shells themselves.

'Estelle, you're not eating any,' he would exclaim, for he insisted that she should eat as many as he and when Estelle pointed out that Dr Guiraud hadn't mentioned her, Monsieur Chabre replied that, logically, they should both submit to the same treatment. Estelle pursed her lips, let her bright eyes rest for a moment on her husband's pasty paunch and could not repress a slight smile which deepened the dimples on her cheek. She made no comment, for she did not like hurting people's feelings. Having discovered that there was a local oyster bed, she even consented to eat a dozen of them at every meal, not because she, personally, needed oysters; but she adored them.

Life in Piriac was monotonous and soporific. There were only three families of holiday-makers: a wholesale grocer from Nantes, a former lawyer from Guérande, as naive as he was deaf, and a couple from Angers who spent all day waist-deep in the sea, fishing. The restricted company would hardly be described as boisterous. They would greet each other each time they met but made no attempt to further their acquaintance. The greatest excitement was provided by the occasional dogfight on the deserted quayside.

Accustomed to the noise and bustle of Paris, Estelle would have been bored to death had Hector not taken to calling every day. After going for a walk with Monsieur Chabre along the coast, he had become a firm friend of the older man who in an expansive moment had confided to him the purpose of his trip, in the discreetest possible terms, in order not to shock the modest young man's delicate sensibilities. When he mentioned the scientific reason for eating such vast quantities of shellfish, Hector was so amazed that he forgot to blush and looked him up and down without even bothering to conceal his surprise that a man might need to submit to such a diet. Nevertheless, the following morning he presented him with a small basketful of clams which the ex-corn-merchant accepted with obvious gratitude. Since then, being a highly competent all-round fisherman and familiar with every rock in the bay, Hector had never come to the house without bringing some shellfish: superb mussels which he had gathered at low tide; sea-urchins which he cut open and cleaned, pricking his fingers in the process; and limpets which he prised off the rocks with the tip of his knife; in a word, every kind of shellfish, often bearing barbarous names, and which he would never have dreamt of eating himself. No longer having to spend a penny on his diet, Monsieur Chabre was profuse in his thanks.

Hector now had a permanent pretext to come to the Chabres' flat. Every time he arrived carrying his little basket, he would make the same remark when he saw Estelle:

'I'm bringing your husband some shellfish.'

And the couple would exchange a smile with a glint in their half-closed eyes; they found Monsieur Chabre's shellfish rather funny.

Estelle now discovered that Piriac was full of charm. Every day after her bathe, she would go for a walk with Hector; her husband lumbered along, heavy-footed, some distance behind; they often went too fast for him. Hector would point out examples of Piriac's more elegant past, remains of sculpture and delicately worked ornamental doors and windows. By now, what used to be a town had become merely a remote village with its narrow streets blocked by dung heaps and lined with gloomy hovels. But Estelle found the stillness and isolation so charming that she was quite prepared to step over the foul-smelling pools of liquid seeping from the middens, intrigued by every quaint old-

world corner and peering inquisitively at the miserable gim-
crackery lying about the mud floors of the local inhabitants'
poverty-stricken houses. Hector would stop and show her the
superb fig trees in the gardens, with their broad, furry, leathery
leaves overhanging the low fences. They went into the narrowest
little streets and leaned over the brinks of the wells to look at their
smiling faces mirrored in the clear shining water below, while
behind them Monsieur Chabre was busy digesting his shellfish in
the shade of the green-lined sunshade which never left his grasp.

One of Estelle's great joys was to see the groups of pigs and geese
roaming freely round the village. At first she had been terribly
frightened of the pigs because the unpredictable movements of their
fat sturdy bodies supported on such puny little feet made her
continually apprehensive of being knocked into and tipped over;
and they were filthy, too; with their bellies covered in black mud,
they kept grunting all the time as they grubbed in the ground with
their dirty snouts. But Hector assured her that pigs were the nicest
sort of animals and now she was amused to see how they dashed
wildly up to be fed and she loved their fresh pink skin looking like a
silky evening gown, after the rain had washed them clean. The
geese fascinated her, too. Two gaggles of them would often meet at
the end of a lane beside a holeful of dung, coming from opposite
directions. They seemed to greet each other with a click of their
beaks and then joined forces to pick over the vegetable peelings
floating on the surface. One of them would climb majestically on to
the top of the pile, stretching out his neck and opening his eyes
wide; he seemed almost to be strutting as he fluffed out the down on
his breast; with his prominent yellow nose, he looked like a real
king of the castle. Meanwhile the others bent their necks to peck at
the ground, quacking in unison as they did so. Then, suddenly,
the big goose would come squawking down from the top and the
geese belonging to his group would follow him away, all poking
out their necks in the same direction and waddling in time, as if
they all had a limp. If a dog appeared, they would stretch their
necks out even more and start hissing. At this, Estelle would clap
her hands and follow the solemn procession of the two companies
of geese as they made their way home like highly respectable
people intent on important business. Another of her entertain-
ments was to see both pigs and geese going down to the beach in
the afternoon, just like human beings.

On her first Sunday in Piriac, Estelle felt that she ought to go to Mass, something which she never did in Paris. But in the country, Mass was a way of passing the time, and a chance to dress up and see people. Indeed, she met Hector there, reading out of an enormous prayerbook whose binding was coming unstuck. He did not take his eyes off her, peeping over the top of his book while still reading religiously; but the glint in his eye hinted that he was smiling inwardly. As they were leaving the church, he offered his arm to Estelle as they were passing through the churchyard. In the afternoon, after Vespers, there was another spectacle, a procession to a Calvary at the other end of the village. A peasant led the way carrying a purple silk banner embroidered in gold and attached to a red shaft. Then followed two straggling lines of women. The priests were in the middle; the parish priest with his curate and the local squire's tutor were all singing at the tops of their voices. Bringing up the rear, behind a white banner carried by a brawny girl with tanned arms, there came the congregation, tramping along in their heavy clogs like a disorderly flock of sheep. As the procession passed beside the harbour, the banner and the white headdresses of the women stood out against the bright blue sea and in the sunlight, the slow procession suddenly took on a simple grandeur.

The little churchyard made Estelle feel all sentimental, although normally she didn't like sad things. On the day she had arrived, she had shuddered at the sight of all those graves underneath her window. The church was not far from the sea and the arms of the crosses all around it stretched out towards the immense sky and sea; on windy nights, the moisture-laden sea breeze seemed to be weeping on this forest of dark wooden posts. But she quickly became accustomed to this mournful sight, for the tiny churchyard had something gentle and even cheerful about it. The dead seemed to be smiling in the midst of the living, who were almost rubbing elbows with them. As the cemetery was enclosed by a low wall and thus blocked the way through the centre of Piriac, people did not think twice about stepping over the wall and following the paths which were almost invisible in the tall grass. Children used to play there, scampering about all over the granite flagstones. Cats would suddenly leap out from under the bushes and chase each other; you could often hear their amorous caterwauling and see their dark shapes with fur bristling and long tails waving in the air. It was a delightful corner covered with weeds and enormous fennel plants with broad yellow flowers; on a warm day, their heady perfume would come wafting up from the graves, filling the whole of Piriac with a scent of aniseed. And at night, how still and gentle the green graveyard was! The peace of Piriac itself seemed to be emanating from the cemetery. The darkness hid the crosses and people taking a late evening stroll would sit down on the granite benches against the wall and watch the waves rolling in almost at their feet, enjoying the salty tang of the sea carried in on the evening breeze.

One evening as Estelle was going home on Hector's arm she felt a sudden desire to go through the deserted graveyard. Monsieur Chabre thought it was a romantic whim and showed his protest by himself going along the quayside. The path was so narrow that Estelle was obliged to let go of Hector's arm. In the tall grass her skirt made a long swishing sound. The scent of fennel was so overpowering that the lovelorn cats did not run away but remained lying languidly in the undergrowth. As they came into the shadow of the church, she felt Hector's hand touch her waist. She gave a startled cry.

'How stupid!' she exclaimed as they came out of the shadow. 'I thought I was being carried off by a ghost.'

Hector laughed and offered his own explanation:

'It must have been the fennel brushing against your skirt.'

They stopped to look at the crosses all around them and the profound stillness of the dead lying beneath their feet filled them with a strange tenderness. They moved on, full of suppressed emotion.

'You were scared; I heard you,' said Monsieur Chabre. 'It serves you right!'

At high tide, they would amuse themselves by going down to watch the arrival of the sardine boats; Hector would tell the Chabres when a sail was seen making for the harbour. But after seeing a few boats come in, Monsieur Chabre announced that it was always the same thing. Estelle on the other hand never seemed to weary of the scene and enjoyed going out on to the seawall more and more. They often had to run. She would leap over the uneven stones, her skirts flying in the air, and she would catch hold of them to avoid tripping over. When she arrived, she was quite puffed and, putting her hand on her chest, she would throw her head back to regain her breath. With her dishevelled hair and devil-may-care boyish air, Hector found her adorable. Meanwhile the boat had tied up and the fishermen were carrying up their baskets of sardines which glistened in the sun like silver with blue and sapphire, pink and pale ruby-red tints. The young man always provided the same information: a basket contained a thousand sardines which would fetch a price fixed every morning according to the size of the catch; the fishermen would share the proceeds of the sale after handing over one-third to the owner of the boat. Then the sardines would be salted straightaway in wooden boxes with holes to allow the brine to drip away. However, Estelle and her companion gradually came to neglect the sardines. They would still go and see; but they didn't look. They would hurry down to the harbour and then return in silence, lazily gazing at the sea.

'Was it a good catch?' Monsieur Chabre would enquire each time they returned.

'Yes, very good,' they would reply.

And every Sunday evening Piriac put on an open-air dance. The young men and girls of the district would join hands and dance round in a circle for hours on end, droning out the same strongly accentuated refrain, and as these harsh voices boomed out in the half-light, they gradually took on a kind of barbaric charm. As she sat on the beach with Hector lying at her feet, Estelle was soon sunk in daydreams. The sea came lapping in, gently but boldly; as it broke on the sand, it seemed like a voice full of passion suddenly stilled as the sound died away and the water receded with a plaintive murmur like a love that had now been tamed. And Estelle would sit dreaming of being loved by a giant whom she had succeeded in turning into a little boy.

'You must be bored in Piriac, my dear,' Monsieur Chabre would occasionally say, in an enquiring tone, to his wife.

And she would hasten to reply:

'Oh no, not at all, I promise you.'

She was, in fact, enjoying her stay in this remote, dead-and-alive little place. The geese and pigs and sardines had assumed great importance; even the little churchyard was a cheerful spot. This drowsy, unsociable sort of life in a village inhabited only by the grocer from Nantes and the deaf lawyer from Guérande seemed more exciting than the bustling existence of the fashionable resorts. After a fortnight, bored to tears, Monsieur Chabre would willingly have returned home to Paris. Surely the shellfish must have produced their effect by now, he said. But she protested:

'Oh no, my dear, you haven't had enough yet... I'm quite sure you need still more.'

4

One evening, Hector said to the couple:

'Tomorrow there's an exceptionally low tide. We could go shrimping.'

Estelle was delighted by the suggestion. Oh yes, they certainly must go and catch shrimps! She'd been looking forward to this excursion for ages! But Monsieur Chabre had objections. First of all, you never catch anything... Furthermore, it was much simpler to go and buy a franc's worth of shrimps from a local fisherman, without having to get wet up to your middle and scrape the skin off your feet. But in face of his wife's enthusiasm, he was forced to give way.

There were elaborate preparations. Hector undertook to provide the nets. Despite his dislike of cold water, Monsieur Chabre had expressed his willingness to participate and, once having agreed, he was determined to do the job properly. On the morning of the expedition, he had a pair of boots dubbined; he then dressed himself in white twill from top to toe; but his wife could not persuade him to forgo his bow tie, the ends of which he fluffed out as if he were going to a wedding. The bow tie was his protest, as a respectable member of society, against the slovenliness of the Atlantic. As for Estelle, she merely slipped a shift over her bathing costume. Hector was also wearing a bathing costume.

The three of them set off at about two o'clock in the afternoon with their nets over their shoulders. It was more than a mile across sand and seaweed to reach the rock where Hector had promised they would find plenty of shrimps. He piloted the couple towards their goal, taking them in a bee-line through all the rock pools and calmly ignoring the hazards on the way. Estelle followed intrepidly, cheerfully paddling over the cool wet sand. Bringing up the rear, Monsieur Chabre could see no need to get his boots wet before they reached the shrimping grounds. He conscientiously skirted every pool, jumping over the channels of water left behind by the ebbing tide and cautiously picking his way over the dry spots like a true Parisian balancing himself on the tops of the paving-sets on a muddy day in the Rue Vivienne. He was already out of breath and kept asking:

'Is it still a long way? Why can't we start shrimping here? I'm positive I can see some... Anyway, they're all over the place in the sea, aren't they? I bet you only need to push your net through the sand.'

'Go ahead and push, Monsieur Chabre,' replied Hector each time.

So in order to recover his breath, Monsieur Chabre would push his net along the bottom of a pool not much larger than a pocket handkerchief and as empty of shrimps as it was transparent. So he caught nothing, not even seaweed. Then he would set off again, pursing his lips and looking dignified, but as he lost ground each time he insisted on proving that there were shrimps everywhere, he ended by dropping a long way behind.

The tide was still going out, retreating almost a mile from the coast. As far as the eye could see, the rocky, pebbly sea-bed was emptying out, leaving a vast, wet, uneven and desolate wilderness, like some storm-ravaged plain. In the distance the only visible thing was the green fringe of the still receding sea, as if being swallowed up by the land, while long, narrow bands of dark rock slowly emerged like promontories stretching out in the stagnant water. Estelle stopped to look at this immense, bare expanse.

'Isn't it big!' she murmured.

Hector pointed to a number of greenish rocks worn smooth by the waves.

'Those are only uncovered twice a month,' he explained. 'People go there to collect mussels. Can you see that brown spot over there? That's the Red Cow rocks, the best place to catch lobsters. You can't see them except at the two lowest tides of the year. But we must get a move on. We're going to those rocks over there whose tops are just beginning to show.'

When they started to go into the sea, Estelle could hardly restrain her excitement. She kept lifting her feet high in the air and bringing them down with a splash, laughing as the spray shot up. Then, when the sea came up to her knees, she strode along, delighted to feel the water pressing hard against her thighs and surging between them.

'Don't be scared,' said Hector, 'You'll be getting into water up to your waist but it becomes shallower after that. We're nearly there.'

And after crossing a narrow channel, they waded out of the water and climbed up on to a wide rocky platform uncovered by the tide. When the young woman looked round, she uttered a cry of surprise at seeing how far she had come from the shore. The houses of Piriac were just a line of tiny white spots stretching out along the shore, dominated by the square tower of its green-shuttered church. Never had she seen such a vast expanse, with the strip of sand gleaming in the bright sunlight and the dark green seaweed and brilliantly coloured rocks glistening with water. It was as if the earth had reached its uttermost limit in a heap of ruins on the brink of empty space.

Estelle and Hector were just about to start shrimping when they heard a plaintive call. It was Monsieur Chabre stuck in the middle of the channel and wanting to know which way to go. 'How do I get across?' he was shouting. 'Do I keep straight on?'

'Go to your left,' called Hector.

He went to his left but the shock of finding himself in still deeper water again brought him to a halt. He did not dare even to retrace his steps.

'Come and help me,' he wailed. 'I'm sure there are holes round here. I can feel them . . .'

'Keep to your right, Monsieur Chabre, to your right!' shouted Hector.

And the poor man looked so funny in the middle of the water, with his net over his shoulder and his splendid bow tie, that Estelle and Hector could not refrain from sniggering. In the end he managed to find a way through but he arrived in a very nervous state and snapped angrily:

'I can't swim, you know.'

He now began to worry about how to get back. When the young man explained to him how important it was not to be caught on the rock by the rising tide, he started becoming anxious again:

'You will warn me, won't you?'

'Don't worry, I'll look after you.'

They all three started shrimping, probing the holes with their narrow nets. Estelle showed a feminine enthusiasm and it was she who caught the first shrimps, three large red ones which leapt about wildly in her net. She called out to Hector to help her because she was rather scared by their lively behaviour; but when she saw that they stopped moving as soon as you caught hold of them by their heads, she became bolder and had no trouble in slipping them herself into the little basket which she was carrying slung over her shoulder. Sometimes she netted a whole bunch of seaweed and had to rummage through it each time a sound like the fluttering of wings warned her that shrimps were hidden there. She sorted carefully through the seaweed, picking it up gingerly between finger and thumb, rather uneasy at the strange tangle of fronds, soft and slimy like dead fish. Now and again, she would peep impatiently into her basket, keen to fill it.

'How odd,' Monsieur Chabre kept exclaiming. 'I haven't caught a single one.'

Being afraid of venturing between the gaps in the rocks and greatly hampered also by his boots which had become water-logged, he was pushing his net along the sandy beach and thereby catching nothing but crabs, half-a-dozen or even up to ten of them at a time. They terrified him and he wrestled with his net to tip them out. Every so often he would turn anxiously round to see if the tide was still ebbing.

'You're sure it's still going out?' he kept asking.

Hector merely nodded; he was shrimping with all the assurance of a man who knows exactly where to go and as a result he was catching great handfuls of them with each sweep of his net. Whenever he found himself working beside Estelle, he would tip his catch into her basket while she kept laughing and giving a wink in the direction of her husband, with her finger to her lips. She looked most attractive as she bent forward over the long wooden handle of her net or else leaning her blonde curly head over it as she eagerly peered to examine her catch. There was a breeze blowing and the water dripping from her net soaked her bathing costume with spray and made it cling to her, revealing every contour of her youthful body.

They had been shrimping like this for some two hours when she stopped for a rest, quite out of breath and with her honey-coloured curls damp with perspiration. The immense deserted seascape still spread out, peaceful and magnificent; only the sea could be seen shimmering in the distance, creating a murmur that seemed to be growing louder. The sun was blazing in a fiery sky; it was now four o'clock and its pale blue had turned almost grey; but this leaden, torrid heat was tempered and dispersed by the coolness of the water, and a gentle haze dimmed the harsh glare. Estelle was particularly charmed by the sight of a whole host of little black dots standing out very clearly on the horizon; they were shrimpers like themselves, incredibly delicate in outline and no larger than ants, ridiculous in their insignificance in the vast immensity; yet you could distinguish their every gesture, their shoulders hunched over their nets and their arms reaching out and gesticulating feverishly, like trapped flies, as they sorted out their catch, wrestling with the seaweed and the crabs.

'I assure you the tide's coming in,' Monsieur Chabre called anxiously. 'Look over there, that rock was uncovered a moment ago.'

'Of course it's coming in,' Hector retorted impatiently at last, 'and that's exactly the time when you catch most shrimps.'

But Monsieur Chabre was beginning to panic. At his last attempt he had just caught a strange fish, an angler-fish, whose freakish-looking head had terrified him. He had had enough.

'Come on, let's go. We must be going!' he kept repeating. 'It's stupid to take risks.'

'But we've just been telling you that it's the best time when the tide's starting to come in,' his wife replied.

'And it's coming in with a vengeance!' Hector added in an undertone, with a mischievous glint in his eyes.

The waves were indeed beginning to roll in, booming as they swallowed up the rocks; a whole spit of sand would suddenly disappear, swamped by the sea. The breakers were triumphantly retaking possession of their age-old domain, foot by foot. Estelle had discovered a pool the bottom of which was covered in long fronds of seaweed, swirling round like strands of hair, and she was catching enormous shrimps, ploughing up long furrows with her net and leaving behind large swathes, like a reaper. She was thrashing around and determined not to be dragged away.

'All right then,' Monsieur Chabre exclaimed in a tearful voice, 'there's nothing to be done, I'm off. There's no sense in us all being cut off.'

So he went off first, sounding the depth of the holes with the long handle of his shrimping net. When he had gone two or three hundred yards, Hector at last prevailed on Estelle to follow his example.

'We're going to be up to our shoulders,' he said with a smile. 'Monsieur Chabre's going to get a thorough wetting. Look how deep he is already.'

Ever since the start of the outing, Hector had had the slightly furtive and preoccupied look of a young man in love and promising himself to declare his feelings; but he had not been able to pluck up courage to do so. As he had slipped his shrimps into Estelle's basket, he had indeed endeavoured to touch her fingers but it was plain that he was furious with himself for being so timorous. He would have been delighted to see Monsieur Chabre fall into a hole and drown, because, for the first time, he was finding the husband's presence a hindrance.

'I tell you what,' he said suddenly, 'you must climb up on my back and I'll give you a lift. Otherwise you're going to get soaked through. How about it? Up you get!'

He offered her his back but she blushed and declined, looking embarrassed. He, however, refused to take no for an answer, arguing that he was responsible for her safety. Eventually, she clambered up, placing her two hands on his shoulders. He stood as firm as a rock, straightened his back and set off, carrying her as lightly as a feather, telling her to hang on tight as he strode through the water.

'We've got to go right, haven't we?' Monsieur Chabre called out to Hector in a plaintive voice. The water was already up to his hips.

'That's it, keep going right,' the young man called back.

Then, as the husband turned to go on, shivering with fright when he felt the water coming up to his armpits, Hector, greatly daring, kissed one of the tiny hands resting on his shoulder. Estelle tried to draw it away but Hector warned her to keep quite still or else he could not be responsible for what would happen. He started kissing her hand again: it was cool and salty and seemed to be offering all the bitter delights of the Ocean.

'Will you please stop doing that,' Estelle kept protesting, trying to sound cross. 'You're taking advantage of me. If you don't stop, I'll jump off.'

He didn't stop, nor did she jump off. He was keeping a tight hold on her ankles while covering her hands with kisses, not saying a word but also keeping a close eye on Monsieur Chabre's back or at least all that could be seen of his pathetic back, now threatening to disappear beneath the waves at every step.

'Did you say keep to the right?' the husband called imploringly.

'Go left if you like!'

Monsieur Chabre took a step to his left and gave a cry. The water had come up to his neck, submerging his bow tie. Hector gratefully accepted the opportunity of making his declaration:

'I love you. . .'

'You're not to say that, I forbid it!'

'I love you. . . I adore you. . . I haven't had the courage to tell you so up till now because I was afraid of offending you.'

He could not turn his head to look at her and continued to stride along with water up to his chest. Estelle could not refrain from laughing out loud at the absurdity of the situation.

'You must stop talking like that,' she went on, adopting a motherly tone and giving him a slap on his shoulder. 'Now, be a good boy and above all, mind you don't miss your step.'

Feeling the slap on his shoulder, Hector was filled with joy: it was the seal of approval! And as poor Monsieur Chabre was still in trouble, Hector gave a cheerful shout:

'Keep straight on now!'

When they reached the beach, Monsieur Chabre attempted to give an explanation:

''Pon my word, I was nearly caught. It's my boots,' he stammered.

But Estelle opened her basket and showed him it, full of shrimps.

'Did you catch all those?' he exclaimed in amazement. 'You certainly are a good shrimper!'

'Oh,' she replied with a smile, 'this gentleman showed me the way.'

5

The Chabres had only two days left in Piriac. Hector seemed dismayed and furious, yet humble. As for Monsieur Chabre, he reviewed his health every morning and seemed puzzled.

'You can't possibly leave without visiting the Castelli rocks,' Hector said one evening. 'Let's organize an excursion for tomorrow.'

He explained that the rocks were less than a mile away. They had been undermined by the waves and hollowed out into caves which extended for a mile and a half along the coast. According to him, they were completely unspoilt and wild.

'All right, we'll go tomorrow,' said Estelle in the end. 'Are they difficult to get at?'

'No, there are just a couple of spots where you have to wade through some shallow water, that's all.'

But Monsieur Chabre did not want even to get his feet wet. Ever since his experience of almost going under during the shrimping expedition, he had harboured a grudge against the sea and so he expressed considerable opposition to Hector's suggestion. It was absurd to take risks like that: in the first place, he was not going to climb down to those rocks and risk breaking his leg jumping around like a goat; if he were absolutely compelled to, he would accompany them on the cliff path above and even that he would be doing only as a favour.

To make him relent, Hector had a sudden inspiration.

'I tell you what,' he said, 'you'll be going past the Castelli semaphore station. Well, you can call in there and buy some shellfish from the crew. They always have superb shellfish which they practically give away.'

The ex-corn-merchant perked up. 'That's a good idea,' he replied. 'I'll take a little basket with me and I'll be able to have a final feast of shellfish.'

And turning to his wife, he said with a leer: 'Perhaps that'll do the trick.'

Next day, they had to wait for low tide before they set off and, as Estelle was not ready in time, they in fact did not leave until five o'clock. However, Hector assured them that they would not be caught by the tide. The young woman was wearing cloth bootees over her bare feet and a very short and slightly raffish-looking grey linen dress which exposed a slim pair of ankles. As for Monsieur Chabre, he was dressed, most correctly, in a pair of white trousers and a long alpaca coat. He had brought his sunshade and a little basket; he had the appearance of a respectable middle-class Paris gentleman setting off on a shopping expedition.

Reaching the first of the rocks was awkward: they had to walk for some distance over quicksands in which their feet sank. The ex-corn-merchant was soon puffing and blowing.

'All right then, I'll let you go on and I'll go up,' he gasped at last.

'That's right, take that path there,' Hector replied. 'If you come any further, there's no way up. Would you like some help?'

They watched him climb to the top of the cliff. Once there, he opened his sunshade and, swinging his basket in the other hand, called down:

'I've done it, it's much better up here. Now, don't do anything rash, will you? Anyway, I'll be able to keep an eye on you from up here.'

Hector and Estelle began walking over the rocks. The young man led the way, leaping from boulder to boulder in his high boots with the grace and agility of a mountaineer. Estelle followed intrepidly on the same stones and when he turned to ask:

'Shall I give you a hand?' she replied:

'Certainly not! Do you take me for a grandmother?'

They had now reached a vast floor of granite worn down by the sea and hollowed out into deep crevasses. It was like the skeleton of some sea monster whose dislocated vertebrae were protruding from the sand. In the hollows there was flowing water and dark seaweed was dangling like strands of hair. They continued to leap from stone to stone, pausing now and then to recover their balance and laughing each time they dislodged a boulder.

'They're rather tame, your rocks,' said Estelle with a smile. 'They wouldn't be out of place in a drawing-room!'

'Just you wait,' retorted Hector. 'You'll see in a minute.'

They had reached a narrow passage, a sort of gap between two enormous blocks of stone, and the way through was barred by a rock-pool, a hole full of water.

'I'll never get across that!' the young woman exclaimed.

He suggested carrying her but she shook her head: she was not going to let herself be carried again. He then started looking round for some rocks big enough to make stepping-stones; but they kept slipping and sinking to the bottom. Finally, losing patience, she said:

'Give me your hand, I'm going to jump.'

She jumped short and one foot went into the water and this made them laugh again. Then, when they had gone through the passage, she stopped and exclaimed out loud in admiration.

In front of her lay a large round bay full of gigantic tumbled rocks, enormous blocks of stone standing like sentries keeping guard over the waves. All along the foot of the cliffs the land had been eroded by storms, leaving behind vast masses of bare granite, with creeks and promontories, unexpected inlets forming deep caverns and beaches littered with blackish slabs of marble looking like large stranded fish. It was like some Cyclopean town, battered and ravaged by the sea, with its battlements knocked down, its towers half demolished and its buildings toppled and lying in heaps of ruins. Hector showed Estelle every nook and cranny of these storm-wrecked ruins. She walked over sand as fine and yellow as gold dust, with pebbles speckled with mica glinting in the sun. She clambered over fallen rocks where she had, at times, to hang on with both hands to prevent herself from slipping into the crevasses. She went through natural porticos and triumphal archways curved like those in Romanesque churches or soaring pointed arches like those of Gothic cathedrals. She scrambled down into cool deserted hollows a good dozen yards square, charmed by the blue thistles and dark green succulent plants standing out in contrast to the dark grey walls of the rockface on which they grew and delighted by the friendly little brown seabirds fluttering within her reach as they repeated their chirpy little calls. And what amazed her most was that, each time she turned round, she could see the ever-present blue line of the Atlantic stretching out, majestic and calm, between every block of rock.

'Ah, there you are!' cried Monsieur Chabre from the top of the cliff. 'I was worried because I had lost sight of you... Aren't these heights terrifying?'

He was standing a good six yards back from the edge, shading himself under his parasol with his little basket hitched over his arm. He added:

'It's coming in fast, be careful!'

'There's plenty of time, never fear,' replied Hector.

Meanwhile, Estelle had sat down and was gazing, speechless with admiration, at the vast horizon. In front of her three round pillars of granite, made smooth by the waves, were standing like the giant columns of a ruined temple. Behind them, bathed in the golden half-light of the evening, the open sea spread out, a royal blue speckled with gold. In the far distance she could see a brilliant white dot, a tiny sail skimming like a seagull over the surface of the water. The calm of evening was already reaching out over the pale blue sky. Never had she felt so overpowered by such an all-pervading tenderness and exquisitely voluptuous delight.

'Let's go,' said Hector, gently touching her arm.

She gave a start and stood up, full of languor and acquiescence.

'That little house with the mast is the semaphore, isn't it?' called Monsieur Chabre. 'I'm going to get some shellfish, I'll catch you up in a minute.'

Then, in an attempt to shake off the listlessness that had overtaken her, Estelle set off running like a child, leaping over the puddles as she made towards the sea, seized by a sudden whim to climb to the top of a heap of rocks which would be completely surrounded by water at high tide. And when, after scrambling laboriously through the gaps in the rocks, she finally reached the top, she hoisted herself on to the highest point and was delighted to see that she could dominate the whole sweep of the tragically devastated coastline. She stood outlined in the pure sea air, her skirt fluttering like a flag in the breeze.

As she came down, she peered into every little crevice as she passed. In the smallest cranny, she could see tiny slumbering pools whose limpid surfaces were reflecting the sky like shining mirrors. On the bottom, emerald-green seaweed was growing, like some romantic forest. The only living creatures were large black crabs which leapt up like frogs before disappearing without even stirring up the water. The young woman had a dreamy look in her eyes as if she had been granted a glimpse into secret regions of a vast, mysterious and happy land.

When they had come back to the foot of the cliff, she noticed that her companion had filled his handkerchief with some limpets.

'They're for your husband,' he said. 'I'll take them up to him.'

At that very moment, a disconsolate Monsieur Chabre came into sight.

'They hadn't even got a mussel at the semaphore,' he shouted down to them. 'You see, I was right not to want to come.'

But on seeing Hector's limpets, he cheered up; and he was staggered at the young man's agility as he clambered up by a track known only to himself, over a cliff-face that seemed completely smooth rock. His descent was even more impressive.

'It's nothing, really,' Hector said. 'It's as easy as going upstairs once you know where the steps are.'

Monsieur Chabre now suggested turning back: the sea was beginning to look threatening. So he begged his wife at least to find an easy way up to the top of the cliff. Hector laughed and replied that there was no way suitable for ladies; they would now have to go on to the end. In any case, they hadn't yet visited the caves. Monsieur Chabre was compelled to continue along the top of the cliffs by himself. As the sun was now much lower in the sky, he closed his parasol and used it as a walking-stick. In his other hand, he held his basketful of limpets.

'Are you feeling tired?' Hector asked Estelle gently.

'A little bit,' she replied and took hold of the arm which he offered. However, she was not tired; but her delicious feeling of languor was slowly spreading through her whole body and the emotion she had felt at seeing the young man hanging from the cliff-face had left her trembling inwardly. They were walking slowly over a beach composed of broken shells which crunched under their feet like a gravel garden path. Both had again fallen silent. He showed her two wide openings in the rock: the Monk's Hole and the Cat's Grotto. As they walked on over another beach of fine sand, they looked at each other, still without exchanging a word, and smiled. The tide was now coming in, rippling gently over the sand; but they did not hear it. Up above, Monsieur Chabre had started calling to them; but they did not hear him either.

'It's sheer madness!' the ex-corn-merchant was shouting, waving his sunshade and swinging his basket of limpets. 'Estelle! Monsieur Hector! Listen to me! You're going to be cut off! Your feet are already getting wet.'

But they did not feel the cool water lapping round their feet.

'What's the matter with him?' the young woman muttered at last.

'Oh, it's you, Monsieur Chabre,' Hector called out. 'There's no need to worry. We've only got the Lady's Cave to look at now.'

Monsieur Chabre made a despairing gesture and repeated: 'It's sheer madness! You'll both be drowned.'

They were no longer paying attention... To avoid the rising tide, they went along the foot of the cliff and finally came to the Lady's Cave. It was a grotto hollowed out of a vast block of granite that jutted out towards the sea. Its roof, extremely high and wide, was shaped like a dome. Storms had polished its walls until they shone like agate and the pink and blue veins in the dark rock formed magnificent patterns of arabesques like the barbaric handiwork of primitive artists decorating a grandiose bathroom for a sea-goddess. The gravelly floor of the cave, still wet, was glittering like a bed of precious stones while at the far end there was a softer bed of dry yellow sand, so pale as to be almost white.

It was here that Estelle sat down to inspect the grotto.

'It's the sort of place you could live in,' she murmured.

But now Hector at last seemed to become aware of the tide and his face assumed a look of dismay.

'Oh my goodness, we're caught! The sea's cut us off! We're going to have to wait for two hours...'

He went out and looked up at Monsieur Chabre who was standing on top of the cliff, just above the grotto. He told him that they were cut off.

'What did I tell you?' Monsieur Chabre cried triumphantly. 'But you refused to listen to me, didn't you? Is there any danger?'

'None at all,' Hector replied. 'The tide only comes fifteen or twenty feet into the cave. The only thing is that we shall have to wait a couple of hours before we can get out. There's nothing to be alarmed at.'

Monsieur Chabre was annoyed: so they wouldn't be back by dinner-time and he was already feeling hungry! It really was a mad sort of outing! Then he sat down, grumbling, on the short grass, placing his sunshade on his left and his basket of limpets on his right.

'Well, I'm going to have to wait, then,' he called. 'Go back to my wife and make sure she doesn't catch cold.'

Back in the cave, Hector sat down beside Estelle. After a moment, silently, he ventured to reach out and take hold of her hand; she did not try to draw it away. She sat looking into the distance. Dusk was falling and the light of the dying sun was veiled by a gentle haze. On the horizon, the sky was taking on a tender tinge of deepest red and the sea grew slowly darker, stretching out with not a soul in sight. The tide crept gently into the cave, quietly lapping over the glittering shingle and murmuring a promise of exquisite sea-pleasures with its disturbing salty tang of desire.

'I love you, Estelle,' Hector said, smothering her hands in kisses.

Choking with emotion, she made no reply, as though uplifted on the rising tide. She was by now half-lying on the bed of fine sand, looking like some sea-nymph, caught unawares and already at his mercy.

Monsieur Chabre's voice abruptly broke in, faint and hollow: 'Aren't you hungry? I'm ravenous! Fortunately I've got my penknife, so I'll have a first instalment of my limpets.'

'I love you, Estelle,' said Hector again, taking her in his arms.

The night was dark and the pale sea lit up the sky. At the mouth of the grotto, a plaintive murmur was rising from the water while a last gleam of light deserted the top of the domed roof. The sea rippled and a scent of fruitfulness was hanging in the air. Slowly Estelle's head sank on to Hector's shoulder and on the evening air the breeze carried away a murmur of sighs.

Up above, by the light of the stars, Monsieur Chabre was methodically chewing away at his limpets and giving himself indigestion as he ate the whole lot, without any bread.

6

Nine months after her return to Paris, the lovely Madame Chabre gave birth to a bouncing boy. A delighted Monsieur Chabre took Dr Guiraud aside and said proudly:

'It was the limpets that did the trick, I'm absolutely convinced of it! I ate a whole basketful of them one evening, in very peculiar circumstances, by the way. Anyway, never mind the details, doctor, but I never thought shellfish could have such remarkable effects.'

ABSENCE MAKES THE HEART
GROW FONDER

SOMETIMES, as he sat beside the sea, scanning the blank horizon, visions of his past would flit through Jacques Damour's mind: the hardships of the siege, the savage fighting with the Commune and the final brutal wrench which tore him from his home, to land up, broken and bewildered, in this faraway Pacific island of Noumea.* This was no recollection of pleasant times, of love and affection, but the dull brooding of an enfeebled mind returning, again and again, to certain unchangeable, precise facts that alone stood out amidst the general collapse of everything.

At the age of twenty-six Jacques had married Félicie, a tall and beautiful girl of eighteen, the daughter of a greengrocer in the Villette quarter of Paris, from whom he had rented a room. He himself was a metalworker who could earn up to twelve francs a day. At first, she had continued her trade of dressmaking but as they had a son almost immediately, she had no time to do anything but feed him and keep house. The son, Eugène, flourished; and nine years later a daughter Louise arrived who was for a long time so sickly that they spent a great deal of money on medicine and doctors. However, they were not an unhappy family. True, Damour had an occasional binge on payday; but he behaved not unreasonably, went off to bed if he'd had too much to drink and returned to work next day, quite prepared to admit that he'd been a bit of a fool. By the age of twelve Eugène had learnt how to handle a vice and was earning his keep almost before he had learnt to read and write. Félicie was very clean and tidy and a clever and economical housewife, a trifle stingy her husband would sometimes say, when she served vegetables more often than meat so as to be able to put a little money on one side for a rainy day. This was the happiest period of their marriage. They lived in the Rue des Envierges in Ménilmontant,* in a three-bedroomed flat consisting of the couple's bedroom, a bedroom for Eugène, and a dining-room which also served as Jacques' workroom, as well as the kitchen and a closet for Louise. The flat was situated at the far end of the courtyard of a small apartment block; but it was still light and airy enough because their windows looked out on to a demolition yard where cartloads of builders' rubble and old timber were dumped all day long.

When the Franco-Prussian war broke out, the Damours had been living in the Rue des Envierges for some ten years. Although by now nearly forty, Félicie had retained her youthful good looks, although she had put on some weight; and with her plump shoulders and hips, she was acknowledged to be the handsomest woman in the neighbourhood. Jacques on the other hand had become wizened and the eight years' difference in age made him look prematurely old. Louise, no longer sickly but still delicate, was a skinny little girl who took after her father. Eugène, now nineteen years old, was tall and broadbacked like his mother. It was a very united family, apart from the odd payday evening when father and son lingered too long in wineshops. Then Félicie would sulk at the thought of good money being wasted and once or twice they even had a set-to; but this was really quite harmless, just the fault of drinking too much. There wasn't a more stable family in the whole block and they were cited as examples by everybody. When the Prussians began their march on Paris, they had savings of more than a thousand francs, a fine achievement for a working-class couple who had brought up two children.

So the first few months of the siege were not too bad. In the dining-room, even if the workbench lay idle, there was still meat and white bread to eat. Damour was even in a position to help out a less fortunate neighbour, a strapping young fellow by the name of Berru, a housepainter who was starving and whom Damour was kind enough to invite to supper occasionally. Berru was a wag and always ready to crack a joke, so much so that he even managed to disarm Félicie, despite her shock and concern at seeing all the tastiest morsels disappear into his capacious maw. In the evening they played cards and abused the Prussians. Berru talked patriotically of digging mines and underground tunnels, right out into the country as far as Châtillon and Montretout, and blowing their gun emplacements sky-high. Then he'd come back to the government, a bunch of cowards who wanted to open the city gates to Bismarck, so as to put Henri V* on the French throne. He would shrug his shoulders contemptuously at that sort of treacherous republicanism. Republicanism, indeed! And with his elbows on the table, puffing away at his cutty, he would expound his own ideas on government, with brotherhood and freedom and everybody having lots of money, justice and equality for all, from top to bottom.

'Just like '93,'* he'd add firmly, without the least idea of what it meant.

Damour listened solemnly. He too was a republican because from earliest childhood he had heard everyone around him asserting that one day the Republic would bring the triumph of the worker and universal happiness. But he had no firm idea how this would be achieved and this was why he listened so attentively to Berru; and he found his reasoning sound: for sure, the Republic would come about as Berru predicted. He would grow heated and proclaim that if the whole of Paris, women and children as well, had marched against the government in Versailles, singing the 'Marseillaise', the Prussians would have been thrashed, the provinces would have healed their squabbles and a government of the people been set up which would have guaranteed a private income for every citizen in France.

'Look out,' Félicie would say distrustfully. 'That Berru of yours will land you in trouble. Give him food if you like, since you seem to want to. But let him go and be heroic on his own.'

She, too, was a republican; her father had died on a barricade during the revolution of 1848; but instead of stirring her up, this memory of her father made her want to remain calm and reasonable. She used to say that if she were the people her way of forcing the government to show justice would be to be on her best behaviour. Berru's speechifying made her cross and frightened because he seemed to her to be a rabble-rouser. She could see her husband changing, adopting attitudes and using words of which she disapproved. But she was still more concerned by the grim and eager look on Eugène's face as he listened to Berru. In the evening, when Louise had dropped off to sleep with her head on the table, Eugène would sit slowly sipping a little glass of spirits, not saying a word and keeping his eyes fixed on the housepainter who never failed to bring back with him some extraordinary story of treachery in the capital: the Bonapartist supporters were sending signals to the Prussians from Montmartre; sacks of flour and barrels of gunpowder were being tipped into the Seine so that the Germans could win more quickly.

'What a lot of rubbish!' Félicie would say to her son after Berru had finally left. 'Don't let yourself be led astray by all that gossip, will you? You know perfectly well he's lying.'

'I know what's what,' Eugène replied with a frightening gesture.

By the middle of December, the Damours had used up their entire savings. There were announcements issued all the time of the Prussians suffering heavy defeats in the provinces, of a successful sortie which was going to relieve Paris, and so the family were not at first too greatly alarmed, hoping against hope that work would again become available. Félicie was performing miracles and they managed to live from hand to mouth on the black siege bread which only little Louise was unable to stomach. Then, in Félicie's words, Jacques and Eugène finally took leave of their senses. With nothing to do all day, unable to follow their normal routine and flabby from lack of exercise now that they had abandoned their workbench, they were worried and bewildered, with their heads full of wild and bloodthirsty fantasies. They had, in fact, joined an infantry battalion; but, like many others, this battalion had never ventured beyond the fortifications and so they spent all their time in the barrack-room, playing cards. It was in this environment that Damour, with an empty stomach and sick at heart at the thought of the suffering at home, reached the conclusion, listening to reports from various fellow soldiers, that the Versailles government had sworn to exterminate the people and take over the Republic. Berru was right: everyone knew that Henri V was living out at Saint-Germain in a house with a white flag hoisted over it. And that must be stopped. One fine day, those swine who were starving the workers and letting them be shelled merely so as to leave the field free for the priests and the aristocracy, would get a taste of their own medicine. When Jacques and his son came back home in a fever of excitement from the wild talk they had heard outside, all they could do was to talk of taking their rifles and going out to shoot someone. Pale as a sheet, Félicie listened in silence; she was having to look after little Louise, who had fallen ill again because of the poor food.

However, the siege came to an end, the armistice was signed and the Prussians marched down the Champs-Elysées. In the Rue des Envierges, they began eating white bread again, which Félicie had herself gone over to fetch from Saint-Denis. But it was a gloomy meal. Eugène had gone to look at the Prussians and gave details of what he had seen. Brandishing his fork in fury, Damour shouted that all the generals ought to have been guillotined, whereupon Félicie lost her temper and forcibly took his fork away from him. During the following days, as there was still no work being offered, Jacques decided to do some on his own account: he still had a few pieces of cast-iron torch-holders that he could finish off in the hope of selling them privately. Eugène was very restless and gave up after working for only an hour. As for Berru, he had not been seen since the armistice; no doubt he had discovered better free meals elsewhere. One morning, however, he turned up in a state of great excitement and told them how, on the previous night, the army had tried to get back the guns on Montmartre* but had been foiled because the soldiers had refused to fire. All the same, barricades were being set up everywhere. The triumph of the people was at hand and he had come to recruit Damour, for he needed all the good citizens he could find. To Félicie's great dismay, Jacques immediately dropped his tools and left. The Commune had begun.

The fighting continued during March, April and May. When Damour came home tired out and his wife begged him to stay, he would reply:

'What about my one and a half francs? How else can we get bread?'

Félicie looked away: the only money to buy food was the one and a half francs each received by Jacques and his son as members of the National Guard, plus an occasional allocation of wine and salt meat. Moreover, Damour was quite sure he was in the right. He was shooting at the men of Versailles in the same way as he would have shot at Prussians, convinced that he was fighting in defence of the Republic and to bring about the happiness of the people. Following on the hardships and exhaustion of the siege, the turmoil of civil war had thrown him into a nightmare of fear at the prospect of tyrannical government and he saw himself as a hero, however obscure, in the struggle for freedom and was determined, if necessary, to die in its defence. He was not concerned with any fine theoretical considerations of communalistic ideas. In his eyes, the Commune was merely the long-prophesied Golden Age, the beginning of universal happiness. Meanwhile, he held even more obstinately to the belief that somewhere, be it in Saint-Germain or Versailles, there was a king preparing to set up a new Inquisition and bring back feudal rights were he allowed to return to Paris. In his own home, he would not have hurt a fly; but on his barricade, he was eliminating the forces of order without the faintest qualms. When he came back home harassed, covered in sweat and black with gunpowder, he would spend hours at little Louise's bedside, listening to her breathing. Félicie had abandoned any attempt to restrain him but, like the far-sighted woman she was, quietly and calmly waited for the eruption to stop.

However, she did once venture to point out that Berru, the big fellow who kicked up such a fuss, wasn't so stupid as to put himself in the firing line. He'd been clever enough to get himself a cushy job in the commissariat, which did not prevent him, each time he appeared in uniform with plumes and badges of rank, from stoking Damour's ideas with inflammatory talk of sticking all the ministers against the wall, as well as the Parliament and the whole damned lot once they had got to Versailles and caught them.

'Why doesn't he do it himself instead of egging other people on?' Félicie would ask.

But Damour would reply:

'Don't say that. I'm doing my duty. So much the worse for those who aren't doing theirs!'

One morning towards the end of April, they brought Eugène back to the Rue des Envierges on a stretcher. He had been hit by a bullet full in the chest, at Moulineaux.* He died as they were carrying him upstairs. When Damour came home that evening, he saw Félicie standing silently beside their dead son's body. The shock felled him and as he sat sobbing on the floor, propped up against the wall, she looked at him without saying a word because she could find nothing to say and had she spoken it would have been to scream:

'It's all your fault!'

She had shut the door of Louise's closet and was moving about quietly in order not to alarm her. When Jacques eventually rose to his feet, he stood for a long time staring at a photograph of Eugène fixed in a corner of their mirror, which his son had had taken wearing the uniform of the National Guard. Jacques took a pen and wrote along the bottom: 'I will avenge you', adding the date and signing it. This relieved some of his grief.

Next day, in a hearse draped with large red flags, Eugène's body was taken to the cemetery of Père-Lachaise, followed by an immense crowd. His father walked behind, bareheaded, and the sight of those blood-red flags, which made the dark wood of the hearse look even darker, filled his heart with savage anger. Félicie had stayed behind in the Rue des Envierges to keep Louise company. That very evening, Damour was back on the barricades, shooting to kill.

Finally, the May fighting began. The Versailles troops had forced their way into Paris. For two whole days Jacques did not return home, defending each barricade amidst blazing buildings and retreating as his battalion retreated. On the morning of the third day he returned to the Rue des Envierges with his clothes in tatters, bemused and reeling like a drunken man. He had no idea what was happening but had merely kept on firing into the pall of smoke because that was his duty. Félicie helped him to undress and was washing his hands with a wet towel when one of the neighbours came in with the news that the Communards were still holding out in the cemetery of Père-Lachaise and that the Versailles troops were unable to dislodge them.

'I must go and help,' he said simply.

He dressed and picked up his rifle. In his bewilderment he hoped that he might die on his son's grave but these last remaining Communards were not defending the bare upper level of the cemetery where Eugène was lying at rest. In any case, Jacques was not even able to get that far: shells were bursting all around, splintering the tall gravestones. Amongst a clump of elms, hiding behind the gleaming white marble headstones, a handful of National Guardsmen were still firing their last few rounds at the soldiers whose red trousers could be seen as they moved up to the attack. Damour arrived just in time to be taken prisoner. Thirty-seven of his comrades were shot on the spot and it was only by a miracle that he himself was not also summarily executed; perhaps the soldiers spared him because his rifle had not been fired and his hands were not battle-stained, since his wife had just washed them. Anyway, his state of exhaustion and bewilderment was such that he was never able to recall the events of the next few days, which were just one long confused nightmare. He spent hour upon hour shut up in dimly lit places or walking, ready to drop, in the sun; being shouted at and beaten up; marching through gaping crowds. When he at last emerged from this delirium, he found himself in prison in Versailles.

Félicie, still pale and calm, came to visit him. After she had told him that Louise was better, they did not speak, for neither could find anything to say. As she was leaving, in order to cheer him, she mentioned that people were taking up his case and were hoping to get him out. He asked:

'What news of Berru?'

'Oh, Berru's all right,' she replied. 'He made off three days before the Versailles troops came in. No one will even bother him.'

A month later, Damour was on his way to New Caledonia, having been sentenced to deportation. As he had never held any sort of rank in the National Guard, he might have been acquitted had he not calmly confessed that he had been in the fighting from the very first day. At their final meeting, he said to Félicie:

'I'll be back. Wait for me. Look after Louise.'

And amongst all his confused memories, it was those last words that stayed most plainly in his mind as he sat brooding on the beach and staring moodily at the empty horizon. Sometimes he was surprised by nightfall. In the distance, a bright speck still lingered, like the wake of a ship gleaming against the gathering gloom, and it seemed to him that he ought to stand up and walk out over the waves to follow that white trail on the sea, since he had promised he would return.

2

Damour was a well-behaved deportee. He had found employment in Noumea and the authorities held out hopes that he would be pardoned. He was a very gentle person who loved playing with children. He had lost all interest in politics and spent much of his time alone, seeing very little of his companions in misfortune. The only fault that could be found in him was the occasional bout of drinking and even in his cups he remained good-tempered, weeping like a little child and going away to sleep it off of his own accord. Then, one day when he seemed certain to be pardoned sooner or later, he suddenly disappeared and people were amazed to hear that he had escaped with four companions.

During his two years on the island, Jacques had received a

number of letters from his wife, regularly at first, then less often, until finally they had stopped completely. He himself had been writing quite regularly. Three months passed without any news. Then the thought that his pardon might well take another two years to come through had suddenly thrown him into desperation and he had risked everything in one of those ill-considered decisions that you regret the very next day. A week later, some miles along the coast, they found a smashed boat and the corpses, already decomposed, of three of the fugitives, including, they thought, that of Jacques Damour; it was his height and had a long beard. After a cursory inquest, the formalities were concluded and a death certificate was issued and sent to France at the request of his widow, who had been kept informed by the authorities. The press took up the story and a dramatic account of the escape and its tragic outcome was published in newspapers all round the world.

But Damour was not dead. He had been mistaken for one of his companions, the more surprisingly since the two men were not at all alike, their only similarity being the length of their beards. Damour and the fourth man, who had survived almost by a miracle, parted company as soon as they reached British territory* and never saw each other again. This other man no doubt died from yellow fever, to which Damour himself very nearly succumbed. His first thought had been to write a letter to his wife but, having read in a newspaper an account of his escape and subsequent death, it seemed to him to be unwise to do so for the letter might be intercepted, thereby giving the game away. Wouldn't it be far better for him to remain dead in the eyes of the world? Nobody would then bother about him any more, he could find his way back to France without trouble and there await the amnesty before giving himself up. At this point he was struck down by a violent attack of yellow fever and spent weeks in a hospital situated miles from anywhere.

When he finally became convalescent, Jacques was in a state of utter lethargy in which he remained for many weeks; his strength and energy had deserted him; it was as if his fever had completely emptied him of all willpower. He had no wish to do anything since everything seemed equally pointless. His memories of Félicie and Louise had grown dim; he could still see them in his mind's eye but only as if in the far distance, in a sort of fog, where he sometimes had difficulty in recognizing them. Once his strength had returned, he would, of course, go back to them... But then, when he was finally up and about, he thought of another plan: before going back to his wife and daughter, he would make his fortune. What could he do in Paris? He'd probably starve; he'd have to go back to his workbench and there was no guarantee, even, that he would find work, for he could tell that he had aged terribly. On the other hand, if he went to America, he'd pick up a few hundred thousand francs in the space of weeks; indeed, he considered this a modest sum in view of the fantastic tales of millions buzzing all around. On one gold field, the story went, everyone, including the humblest navvy, had been driving about in his coach and six within six months. So Jacques set about replanning his life: he would return to France with his hundred thousand francs, buy a little house in the Vincennes district and live happily with Félicie and Louise on three or four thousand francs a year, a forgotten man, well rid of politics. One month later, Jacques Damour was in the United States.

There followed a life of random adventure, of confused ups and downs that were both strange and banal. He plumbed the depths of poverty and climbed within an inch of the heights of wealth. On three occasions he thought he had at last reached his target but the hundred thousand francs melted in his hands; he was robbed or else, in one final gamble, he was ruined. In a word, he suffered much, worked hard, and ended up without a shirt to his back. After roaming the world, he landed up in England and from there moved across to Brussels, almost on the French frontier. However, he now had no thought of returning home. As soon as he had arrived in the States, he had at last written to Félicie but had received no reply to his three letters. Either they were being intercepted or else his wife had left Paris or was dead. A year later, he had made another equally vain attempt but this time, in order not to give himself away, he wrote under an assumed name, purporting to deal with an imaginary piece of business and relying on the fact that Félicie would recognize his handwriting and understand the position. This complete lack of response had had the effect of dulling his memory: he was dead, alone in the world, and so nothing was of any further importance. For more than a year he worked underground in a coal-mine, away from the sunlight, a nobody living only to eat and sleep.

One evening, sitting in a tavern, he heard a man say that an amnesty* had been granted and all the former members of the Commune were making their way back to France. This news roused him from his lethargy and made him want to leave with his old comrades to return to Paris, to his home. And when he found himself in the train, ideas began to stir in his mind; he started thinking that if he should succeed in finding Félicie and Louise, he might once more be able to live a normal life, win back his place in the sun. Hope was born again: he was a free man now and could look for them openly. In the end, he even found himself imagining them sitting quietly in the Rue des Envierges, with the table laid just as if they were expecting him. Everything would be explained, it would all have been a simple misunderstanding; he'd go to the Town Hall, tell them his name, and he'd return to his old family life.

The Gare du Nord in Paris was packed with a tumultuous crowd. As soon as the returning ex-Communards appeared, there was a tremendous burst of cheering and, amid scenes of extraordinary enthusiasm, men started waving their hats and screaming a name. For a moment, Damour failed to understand and was afraid that all these people had come to boo him; but then he recognized the name which the cheering crowd was shouting: it was that of a famous erstwhile member of the Commune who happened to be on the same train, a celebrated exile who was being greeted with loud applause. Damour saw him walk past, greatly moved, with tears in his eyes at the warmth of his welcome; he had put on a lot of weight. When the hero got into his cab, the crowd thought of unhitching the horse and pulling it themselves. Everybody was jostling and pushing as the wave of humanity surged into the Rue de Lafayette and for a long time the cab could be seen moving slowly forward above the sea of heads, like a triumphal chariot. Squashed and jostled by the crowd, Damour had great difficulty himself in reaching the outer boulevards. Nobody paid the slightest attention to him. He thought of all his sufferings, Versailles, the deportation, Noumea, and gulped with bitterness.

But once he reached the outer boulevards, his mood softened. He forgot the past; it was just as if he was bringing back work from Paris and going quietly home to the Rue des Envierges. Ten years of his life telescoped in his mind into such a rich and confusing pattern that it seemed to him nothing more than part of the pavement along which he was walking. All the same, he did feel some surprise as he found himself reverting so easily to his old habits. Surely the outer boulevards should be wider? He stopped to read some shop signs, surprised to find them still there. Instead of the undiluted pleasure he had anticipated at walking through this corner of Paris which he had missed so much during his exile, he felt a mixture of tenderness, full of echoes of love, and a secret anxiety, the anxiety of facing the unknown, at the sight of all these familiar old scenes. As he came nearer to the Rue des Envierges, this uneasiness grew stronger. He could feel his determination weakening and an increasing desire not to go any further, as if he was expecting some disaster. Why come back at all? What was he doing here?

When he finally reached the Rue des Envierges, he walked past the house three times before plucking up the courage to go in. The coal-merchant opposite had disappeared; in its place was a fruiterer's shop and the woman standing in the doorway seemed so hale and hearty, so aggressively established on her own territory, that he did not dare question her, as he had at first contemplated doing. In the end, he decided to take the risk and made straight for the concierge's lodge. How often in the past had he turned left at the end of the little alleyway and tapped on the little pane of glass...

'May I speak to Madame Damour, please?'

'Never heard of her... No one of that name here!'

He stood frozen to the spot. Instead of his former concierge, who had been enormous, he was facing a cantankerous, wizened little woman who sat watching him suspiciously.

'Madame Damour lived here, at the back, ten years ago.'

'Ten years ago!' exclaimed the concierge. 'Well, there's a lot of water flowed under the bridge since then! We've only been here since January.'

'Perhaps she left an address?'

'No. Never heard of her.'

And when he persisted, she became angry and threatened to call her husband.

'Stop spying about the house, will you? We get a lot of people like you, trying to get in.'

He went red with embarrassment, stammered an apology and retreated, ashamed of his tattered trousers and dirty old tunic. He started to go off down the street with a hang-dog look but then retraced his steps, unwilling to leave like that: it would be too heartbreaking a farewell. Surely there'd be someone to take pity on him and give him some sort of information? He straightened up and started to look more closely at the shop-windows, trying to orientate himself. In these poor districts, where people are being turned out on to the streets all the time, after ten years there would be hardly anyone left whom he had known. In any case, he was becoming wary, even ashamed, and a kind of fear of people was making him scared of being recognized. However, coming back up the street, he at last caught sight of some familiar faces, the tobacconist, a grocer, a laundress and the baker where he used to buy their bread. For a good quarter of an hour, he walked hesitantly up and down in front of these shops, sweating in an agony of indecision and unable to bring himself to act. In the end, with a sinking heart, he decided to try the baker's wife, a sleepy sort of woman who always looked as pale as if she had been dipped in a bag of flour. She looked at him impassively from behind her counter. She certainly didn't recognize him with his long, bristly beard and his face and bald pate tanned by the sun. With his confidence somewhat restored, as he handed her his five centimes for his loaf of bread, he enquired diffidently:

'Don't you have a Madame Damour as one of your customers? She has a little daughter.'

The baker's wife thought for a moment and then said uncertainly:

'Oh well, I may have had in the past, but it must have been a long time ago... I can't honestly remember. I see so many people.'

For the time being, he had to be content with this reply but he went back on other days and plucked up courage to ask more people. Everywhere he met the same lack of concern and the same forgetfulness; and any information he did succeed in eliciting was so contradictory that he was more confused than ever. In general, there seemed little doubt that Félicie had left the district two years after he had been deported, in fact at the very time he was making his escape. Nobody knew her address; some mentioned Gros-Caillou, others thought Bercy.* Nobody even remembered little Louise. So that was the end of that: and one evening, as he sat down on a bench on the outer boulevards, Jacques burst into tears and decided to abandon his search. But what was going to become of him? Paris seemed to have nothing to offer and the few sous he had saved up and which had enabled him to return to Paris were fast running out. For a moment, he thought of going back to Belgium and his coal-mine where he had lived and worked in the dark without any thought of the past, like a contented animal hidden in the gloomy bowels of the earth. Nevertheless, he stayed on, hungry and wretched, for he could not find any work. No employer would look at him: he was too old, even if he was only fifty-five. His sufferings over the last ten years had reduced him to skin and bone; he looked seventy. So he prowled round like a wolf, visiting all the monuments burnt down by the Commune and trying to find the sort of job that you offer children or cripples. A builder working at the Hôtel de Ville kept promising him employment to look after their tools; but he was taking a long time to keep his promise and meanwhile Jacques was starving.

One day as he was standing watching the water flowing under the Pont Notre-Dame,* with the dazed look of some poor miserable wretch contemplating suicide, he suddenly drew back from the parapet with such a violent movement that he nearly knocked down a passer-by, a tall fellow wearing a white smock, who started swearing at him:

'Look out, you clumsy devil!'

Damour's jaw dropped in surprise and he stood staring at him.

'Berru!' he shouted.

It was indeed Berru, a Berru who had changed only to his advantage; he looked younger and bursting with health. Damour had often thought of his former comrade since his return: but how could he hope to find a man who had the habit of doing a midnight flit every fortnight or so? Meanwhile, the housepainter was also staring wide-eyed at Damour and when the latter gave his name in a trembling voice, he refused to believe him:

'It can't be! You're dead! You're pulling my leg!'

Finally, he recognized him and started talking in such a loud voice that all the passers-by began to look round and stare:

'But you're dead!... Well, I never did!... You shouldn't have people on like that!... Honest, are you really alive?'

Damour spoke to him in a low voice, urging him to be quiet, and eventually Berru, who was in fact quite enjoying the situation, seized Jacques by the arm and took him off to a wineshop in the Rue St-Martin, meanwhile still plying him with questions. He wanted to know the truth.

'I'll tell you all about it in a minute,' Jacques said when they were sitting at a table in a private room. 'But first of all, what about Félicie?'

Berru looked at him dumbfounded. Then he said:

'What do you mean?'

'I mean where is she? Have you got her address?'

Berru's amazement was becoming plainer. He said slowly:

'Of course I've got her address. But don't you know what's happened?'

'What do you mean, what's happened?' Damour burst out.

'Well, that's a good one, that is! Do you really mean you don't know anything about it?... Your wife's married again, old chap!'

Damour put his glass down on the table. His hand was trembling so much that the wine was spilling over his fingers. He wiped them off on his tunic and repeated in a flat voice:

'What did you say? Married again? Married again? Are you sure?'

'Good God, man, you were dead, so she married again. There's nothing surprising about that.... Only, of course, it's queer now you've come back to life...'

Poor Jacques sat there, white as a sheet, his lips trembling, while Berru gave him the details. Félicie was very happily married to a widower, a butcher in the Rue des Moines, in the Batignolles district. She was proving very useful in the shop. Sagnard—that was the butcher's name—was a big man, sixty years old but very well preserved for his age. His shop on the corner of the Rue Nollet was one of the busiest in the district; it had fine red-painted iron grills and an ox-head in gilt at each end of the shop-sign.

'Well, what are you going to do?' Berru asked, after he had given all this information.

Bewildered by the description of the shop, the wretched Jacques' only reply was a vague wave of the hand. He'd have to see.

'And what about Louise?' he enquired suddenly.

'Your little girl? Well, I'm not sure... They must have sent her away somewhere to get her out of the way, because I've never seen her with them. Yes, that's true, they could always give you back your daughter, because they're not doing anything for her. But what would you be doing with a fine strapping young girl of twenty? After all, you don't really look all that grand, do you? No offence, mind, but I reckon people'd easily slip you a couple of sous if you were standing on a street corner.'

Cut to the quick, Jacques hung his head, unable to say a word. Berru ordered another carafe of wine and attempted to console him:

'Buck up, old boy! At least you're alive, so make the most of it! All's not lost, everything will sort itself out... What are you going to do?'

And the two men embarked on an interminable discussion, coming back to the same arguments again and again. One thing the housepainter did not reveal was that immediately after Jacques' deportation, he had tried to make up to Félicie, being greatly attracted by her shapely shoulders. As a result, he harboured a secret resentment against her for having preferred the butcher, doubtless because of his money. When the third carafe had been ordered, he exclaimed:

'Well, if I were you, I'd go and confront them, I'd settle in and kick Sagnard out if he got in the way... After all, you're the boss. You've got the law on your side.'

Damour was becoming more and more tipsy and the wine was putting some colour back into his pallid cheeks. He kept saying that he'd have to see, while all the time Berru kept urging him on, slapping him on the shoulder and asking him if he was a man. Of course he was a man! And how he'd loved his wife! And still did and he'd be ready to set the Seine on fire to get her back! Well, what was he waiting for, then? Since she belonged to him, all he had to do was to go and get her back. Now both very drunk, the two men were leaning forward, nose to nose, bawling at each other.

'Yes, I'll go and see her!' Damour said suddenly, rising unsteadily to his feet.

'Good for you! You're no chicken!' exclaimed Berru. 'I'll come with you.'

And they set off for Batignolles.

3

The butcher's shop stood on the corner of the Rue des Moines and the Rue Nollet. With its red grill and its gilt ox-heads, it looked very prosperous. Quarters of meat were hanging over white cloths and rows of legs of mutton were dressed in paper frills, like bunches of flowers. Piles of red meat veined with streaks of fat were heaped up on marble slabs: pink veal, dark red mutton and bright scarlet beef, all cut up into neatly trimmed pieces. The copper basins, the arm of the scales and the hooks on the racks were gleaming. In the bright and airy marble-paved shop there was a feeling of overall abundance and glowing health, with a gorgeous smell of fresh meat that seemed to bring the blood to the cheeks of all the assistants. At the back of the shop, clearly visible in the strong light flooding in from the street, Félicie sat ensconced behind a tall counter, screened from draughts by glass panels. In the cheerful play of light and overall pinkness of the shop, she looked blooming with all the rich, mature vitality of women who have seen their fortieth birthday. Fresh and smooth-skinned, with her well-groomed coils of black hair and immaculate white collar, she had the busy, sober, smiling look of the expert shopkeeper; holding a pen in one hand and giving change from the till with the other, she epitomized the honesty and prosperity of the whole shop. Her assistants were cutting up meat, weighing it and calling out the prices; the women customers were going up to pay at the till; and she was taking the money, not forgetting to exchange a word of local gossip as she did so.

At that moment, a rather sickly-looking woman was paying for a couple of cutlets which she was eyeing with a woebegone expression.

'Seventy-five centimes, isn't it?' said Félicie. 'Things still not quite all right, Madame Vernier?'

'No, I'm still not feeling very well. It's my stomach. I bring up everything I eat. Anyway, the doctor says I've got to have meat. But it's so dear!. . . You know the coal-merchant's died?'

'How sad!'

'With him, it wasn't his stomach, it was his intestines. Seventy-five centimes for a couple of cutlets! It's cheaper to eat poultry.'

'Maybe, but you can't blame us, Madame Vernier. . . Even we have a job to make ends meet. . . What's the matter, Charles?'

Even while chatting and giving change, she had kept her eye on the shop and had just seen one of her assistants talking with two men standing outside on the pavement. As the assistant did not answer, she raised her voice and asked even more loudly:

'Charles, what do they want?'

But she did not wait to hear the reply for she had recognized one of the two, who was leading the way.

'Oh, it's you, Monsieur Berru.'

She did not seem very pleased to see him; she was pursing her lips and looking rather disdainful. On the way from the Rue St-Martin to Batignolles, the two men had made a number of calls at various wineshops; it was a long walk and talking and arguing all the time, as they were doing, was thirsty work. Both were well in their cups. When Berru, from the pavement opposite the shop, had suddenly pointed to Félicie surrounded by the glass panels and said: 'Good Lord, there she is!' Jacques had been touched to the quick at seeing her looking so young and beautiful. It wasn't possible, that must be Louise looking like her mother, because Félicie must surely be much older than that. And the sight of the fine shop with its red meat and gleaming copper and that well-dressed lady looking so distinguished and handling all that money daunted and dismayed him and made him forget his anger. His face went pale and the thought of going into such a grand place made him ashamed of himself. A lady like that would never agree to take him back now, in his dirty tunic and with his long beard and generally brokendown appearance. On the point of taking to his heels, he swung round and was about to dash off down the street to avoid being even noticed when Berru held him back.

'Christ Almighty, haven't you got any guts at all?... Well, let me tell you that if I were you I'd bring that hoity-toity wife of yours down a peg or two! And I wouldn't go away without a fair share-out, yes, half of all those legs of lamb as well as all the rest... So in you go, you chicken!'

He pushed Damour across the street. Then, having asked one of the assistants if Monsieur Sagnard was there and being told he was down at the slaughter-house, he marched in ahead to put an end to the hesitation. Jacques followed, looking and feeling like an idiot.

'What can I do for you, Monsieur Berru?' enquired Félicie in a tone of voice that was far from friendly.

'It's not for myself,' the housepainter replied. 'It's my pal here who has something to say to you.'

He stepped back and Jacques found himself face to face with Félicie. She was looking at him as he stood there terribly embarrassed and staring at the floor in an agony of distress. At first, an expression of disgust and repulsion spread over her normally calm, cheerful face at the sight of this wretched drunken old man, reeking of poverty. But then she looked harder and suddenly, without uttering a word, she went as white as a sheet and with a stifled cry let go of her handful of change which slipped tinkling into the till.

'What's the matter? Aren't you well?' asked Madame Vernier, still standing at the till and watching with curiosity.

Still speechless, Félicie waved people away, rose laboriously to her feet and walked towards her dining-room at the back of the shop. The two men followed her without being asked, Berru with a grin on his face while Damour was still keeping his eyes on the sawdust-covered stone floor, as if afraid of tripping up.

'Well, what an odd thing!' muttered Madame Vernier, left alone with the butcher's assistants.

The latter had stopped cutting and weighing their meat and were exchanging surprised glances. However, anxious not to become involved, they resumed their tasks with an unconcerned air and without replying to Madame Vernier, who left the shop holding her cutlets up in the air and studying them with an aggrieved look on her face.

After reaching the dining-room, Félicie still did not feel sufficiently safe from observation and, pushing open another door, she showed the two men into her bedroom. It was a very neat and tidy room, quiet and private, with white curtains round the bed and at the window, a gilt clock, gleaming mahogany furniture and not a speck of dust to be seen. Félicie dropped into an armchair upholstered in blue rep, mumbling over and over again to herself:

'It's you. . . It's you. . .'

Damour could think of nothing to say. He stood looking round the room, not daring to sit down because the chairs seemed too fine for the likes of him. Once again, it was Berru who spoke:

'Yes, he's been looking for you for the last fortnight. Then he met me and I've brought him here.'

Then, as if feeling the need to apologize, he added:

'I couldn't really do anything else, you understand. He's an old pal of mine and it nearly broke my heart to see the filthy state he's in.'

Félicie was slowly recovering. Being the most sensible of the three as well as the fittest, as soon as she had regained her composure, she realized that she must attempt to find a solution to an unbearable situation and so she prepared to tackle the dreadful subject head on:

'Well, Jacques, what have you come for?'

He made no reply.

'It's true I've married again,' she continued, 'but you know it's not my fault. I thought you were dead and you didn't do anything to let me know that you weren't.'

Jacques found his tongue at last:

'Yes I did. I wrote to you.'

'But I never got your letters, I swear. You know me and you know I never lie. In any case, I've got the certificate in the drawer here.'

She feverishly opened a drawer of her secretaire, took out a piece of paper and handed it to Damour who began reading it with a bewildered look on his face. It was his death certificate. She went on:

'So I was all alone and I accepted the offer of a man who wanted to help me in my distress and my poverty. That's my only fault. I allowed myself to be tempted by the thought of finding happiness with someone else. That's not a crime, is it?'

More embarrassed than his wife, Jacques had been listening to her with his eyes still fastened on the floor. Now he looked up and said:

'What about my daughter?'

Félicie started trembling again.

'Your daughter?... I don't know, she's left home...' she faltered.

'What do you mean?'

'I'd sent her to live with my aunt. She ran away. She got into bad company.'

For a moment, Damour said nothing and remained very calm, as if he hadn't understood. Then suddenly, all his embarrassment vanished and he banged his fist down on the washstand so violently that a shell-covered box jumped about on the marble top. However, he did not have time to say anything because at that moment two children, a little boy of six and a girl of four, burst into the room and ran over to fling their arms affectionately round Félicie's neck.

'Hallo, Mummy, we've just been down to the gardens at the end of the street, but Françoise said we ought to be coming back. Did you know there's a sandpit down there and ducks swimming on the pond?'

'Yes, yes, now that's enough,' their mother replied sharply.

And calling to the maid:

'Françoise, take them away. It's silly to bring them back so early.'

The disappointed children were bundled out of the room by the maid, who was annoyed at having been told off by her mistress. The truth was that Félicie had suddenly been gripped by a wild fear that Jacques might want to take her children away from her and carry them off with him.

Although he had not been invited to sit down, Berru was sprawling comfortably in the second armchair. He had quickly whispered to Jacques:

'Sagnard's children. Don't kids shoot up fast!'

When the door had closed behind them, Damour again thumped the washstand with his fist and shouted:

'No, that's not good enough! I want my daughter and I've come to take you away!'

Félicie's blood ran cold.

'Sit down and let's talk,' she said. 'Making a fuss won't help anybody. So you've come to take me away?'

'Yes, I have and you're going to come with me straightaway, I'm your husband, your only real husband, and I know my rights. Isn't that the case, Berru? So do the proper thing and fetch your hat unless you want everyone to know the truth!'

She was looking at him with an expression of horror on her face, unable to conceal her fear and disgust at the sight of this filthy old man, prematurely aged from poverty and hardship, whom she could no longer love. How could she, so well-fed and pink, accustomed to all the comforts of middle-class life, possibly pick up her former rough and poverty-stricken life with this ghost from the past?

'So, you won't come,' said Damour, reading her refusal in her face. 'Oh, I can understand... You're used to playing the lady behind the till and I haven't got a fine shop and a tillful of money where you can dip in as you like... And then there are those kids we've just seen, you seem to be taking better care of them than of our Louise. Once you've got rid of the daughter, why worry about the father? But that's all one to me, I want you to come with me and you'll come now or else I'll go to the police and get them to take you back to my place... I'm in the right, aren't I, Berru?'

Berru nodded. He was enjoying himself. However, seeing Damour in such a fury, carried away by the force of his own words, and realizing that Félicie was at the end of her tether and on the point of collapse, he felt that a display of magnanimity was called for. So he said sententiously:

'Yes, of course you're in the right but you can't just go ahead without due consideration for others. I've always believed in acting straight, so before deciding on anything, the right and proper thing would be to have a chat with Monsieur Sagnard and since he's not here...'

He broke off and continued in a different tone of voice, trembling with sham emotion:

'But our friend here doesn't want to wait. After all, in his position, it's very hard on him. Ah, Madame Félicie, if you only knew how he's suffered! And now he hasn't a farthing to call his own, he's starving and nobody wants anything to do with him... When I met him a few hours ago, he hadn't eaten for two days.'

Félicie forgot her fears. Her heart melted and tears sprang into her eyes. She was overcome by a feeling of sadness and grief, of disgust with life. A cry burst from her lips:

'Forgive me, Jacques!'

Then, when she had recovered some of her composure, she went on:

'What's done can't be undone... But I can't bear the thought of your being unhappy. You must let me help you.'

Damour made a savage gesture.

'Of course,' Berru interposed swiftly, 'this shop is doing well enough for your wife not to let you starve. Even if you don't want to accept money, at least you needn't refuse a present.

Suppose you only gave him the odd bit of stewing steak, he could make himself a cup of beef broth, couldn't he?'

'Of course, anything he likes, Monsieur Berru.'

At this Jacques began thumping on the washstand top again and shouting:

'No thanks, I'd sooner starve!'

And looking his wife in the eyes, he added:

'You're all I want and I'm going to get you. You can keep your meat!'

Félicie shrank back in her chair, with renewed horror and disgust. Damour's anger was terrifying. He started to heap every kind of abuse on his wife, threatening to smash everything up; he demanded to know his daughter's address, catching hold of his wife and shaking her, screaming that she had betrayed her and abandoned her. Completely overwhelmed by the afternoon's happenings, Félicie made no attempt to defend herself and could only stammer that she didn't know the address but that the police would surely be able to inform him. In the end, having settled himself in a chair, swearing that nothing would make him leave it, Damour suddenly sprang to his feet and, giving a final thump with his fist on the washstand, said:

'All right, blast you, I'm going now . . . Yes, I'm going because I feel like going . . . But don't worry, I'll be back and next time it'll be when your man's here and I'll settle his hash and yours and your kids', too, the whole damn' lot of you! . . . So, just you wait and see what happens.'

He went out shaking his fist, secretly glad to be leaving like that. Delighted to be involved in such a difficult situation, Berru stayed behind and said in a conciliatory voice:

'Don't be afraid, I'll stay with him . . . We must make sure nothing terrible happens.'

He even had the impertinence to take Félicie's hand and kiss it. She did not try to stop him: she was a broken woman and had her husband taken hold of her in his arms, she would have left with him. But now she could hear the two men's footsteps leaving the shop. One of her assistants was vigorously chopping up a loin of mutton; a sum of money was being called out; her business instinct revived and she went back to the till surrounded by the glass panels; she was deadly pale but composed, as though nothing had happened.

'How much?' she asked.

'Seven francs fifty, Ma'am.'

She gave the appropriate change.

4

Next day, Damour had a stroke of luck: the builder found him a job as a night-watchman on the worksite at the Hôtel de Ville, so that he found himself looking after the building which he had helped to burn down ten years earlier, during the Commune. On the whole, it was a pleasant enough job, one of those undemanding mechanical tasks which dull the senses. During the night he would prowl round the various scaffoldings, listening for any suspicious noise and occasionally dropping off to sleep amidst the sacks of plaster. He no longer talked of going back to Batignolles. One day, however, when Berru had offered him lunch, in the course of consuming their third litre of wine, he started shouting that tomorrow was the day; but when tomorrow came, he stayed on the building site. From that time onwards, the pattern was always the same: he would become angry and start demanding his rights only when he was the worse for drink. When sober, he remained gloomy and worried, as though he were ashamed of his behaviour. The housepainter had taken to poking fun at him, saying that he wasn't a man. But Jacques would look grim and mutter:

'I'll have to kill them, then! I'm only waiting till I feel in the mood to do it!'

One evening, he set off and went as far as the Place Moncey,* then, after an hour spent sitting on a bench, he came back to his building site. On one occasion during the day, he thought he had caught a glimpse of his daughter reclining on the cushions of a superb landau driving past the Hôtel de Ville. Berru volunteered to investigate, saying that he was certain that it would only take twenty-four hours to locate her, but Damour refused. What was the point of knowing where she was? All the same, the thought that this beautiful, elegant woman, whom he had seen for a brief second as her fine greys had trotted past, might be his daughter, quite startled him and increased his general feeling of sadness. He went out and bought a knife and showed it to his comrade, saying that he would use it to stick the butcher. The expression appealed to him and he walked about repeating it to himself, laughing as though it were a good joke:

'I'll stick that butcher... Every dog has his day, doesn't he?'

Berru spent several hours with him in a wineshop, trying to convince him that it was wrong to stick anybody, and stupid as well, because you'd end up on the guillotine. He took hold of his hands and made him swear not to land himself in that sort of trouble, although Jacques still kept stubbornly repeating, with a sneer:

'Every dog has his day... I'm still going to stick that butcher!'

But the days went by and he didn't stick anybody.

Then something occurred which seemed likely to precipitate the catastrophe: he was sacked for incompetence: he had dozed off during a stormy night and let someone steal a shovel. So once again he started to go hungry; he would wander round the streets, too proud to beg, peering into cook-shops with feverish eyes. But, far from rousing him, these setbacks made him even more muddled than ever. He slouched around as if completely immersed in his misery, looking as though he would never find the courage to return to Batignolles now that he no longer had a clean shirt to his back.

Up in Batignolles, Félicie was living in a fever of anxiety. The evening after Jacques' visit, she hadn't felt able to tell her husband what had happened; and next day, worried at having said nothing, she felt full of remorse and could not pluck up courage to speak. As a result, she was in a perpetual state of trepidation, with the constant fear of seeing her first husband appear on the scene at any time of the day and anticipating a frightful quarrel. Worst of all, there must have been suspicions amongst the assistants because they were walking around with grins on their faces and each time Madame Vernier came to collect her regular two cutlets, she picked up her change with a very disconcerting expression on her face. In the end, Félicie one day flung her arms round Sagnard's neck and sobbed out her confession. She repeated what she had said to Jacques: it wasn't her fault because when people are dead, they shouldn't come back to life. Sagnard was a good-natured sort of man and still hale and hearty as well, despite his sixty years; and he comforted her. Good Lord! It might not be a very pleasant matter but they'd find a solution eventually. Didn't every problem have a solution? Cheerful and self-assured as he was, with money in the bank, his main reaction was one of curiosity. They must meet this ghost from the past and have a chat. He was so intrigued that when, a week later, Damour still hadn't appeared, he said to his wife:

'Well, what's happened? Is he going to let us down? If you had his address, I'd go and call on him . . .'

Then, when she begged him not to stir matters up, he went on:

'But it's for your own peace of mind, my dear . . . I can see you're fretting. We must clear this thing up.'

And it was indeed true that under the impending threat of trouble and the added stress of having to wait, Félicie was looking thin and worn. Then, one day, as the butcher was telling one of his assistants off for having forgotten to change the water in which a calf's head was soaking, she came running up to him, breathless and white as a sheet.

'He's here!'

'Oh, good,' said Sagnard, immediately calming down. 'Show him into the dining-room.'

And, turning unhurriedly to the assistant, he said:

'Wash it thoroughly, it's stinking to high heaven.'

He went into the dining-room and found Jacques and Berru. Berru had met Damour quite by chance in the Rue de Clichy; he no longer saw him so often because he was tired of his poverty-stricken condition. But when he learned that his friend was on his way to the Rue des Moines, he had started angrily blaming himself, for this was something that concerned him as well as Jacques. He then proceeded to lecture Damour very loudly and asserted that he would certainly not let him go up to Batignolles; he even stood in his way and tried to force him to hand over his knife. Damour merely shrugged his shoulders and looked stubborn; he had certain ideas in mind that he was not prepared to share with anyone. In reply to Berru's remarks, he simply retorted:

'Come along with me if you like but stop nagging me.'

In the dining-room, Sagnard made no move to invite the two men to sit down. Félicie had run off into her bedroom, taking her two children with her; and she was sitting behind the double-locked door with her head throbbing with anxiety, clasping her children in her arms as if defending them and refusing to let them go. She was straining her ears to listen but there was no sound from the next room for the two husbands were eyeing each other in embarrassed silence.

'So it's you,' Sagnard said at last, to break the silence.

'Yes, it's me,' Damour replied.

He was impressed by the butcher's appearance and felt at a disadvantage. With his fresh complexion, clean-shaven face and short hair, Sagnard looked not much more than fifty. In his shirtsleeves and wearing a large, spotlessly clean white apron, he seemed not only young but cheerful.

'However, as a matter of fact,' Damour went on hesitantly, 'it's not you I want to see but Félicie.'

Hearing this, Sagnard completely recovered his composure.

'Look here, my friend, let's put our cards on the table. Damn it all, we're neither of us to blame for anything that's happened. Why quarrel when it's nobody's fault?'

Stubbornly staring at one of the table legs, without raising his eyes, Damour mumbled:

'I've got nothing against you, all I want is for you to go away and leave me alone to talk to Félicie.'

'Well, the answer to that is no,' the butcher retorted very calmly. 'I've no wish for you to make her miserable like you did last time you came here. We can talk it over without her... Anyway, if you're prepared to be reasonable, everything will turn out all right. You claim you still love her so you must try and look at it from her point of view. Think of her happiness...'

'Stop talking like that!' Jacques burst out in a sudden rage. 'Just you keep out of it or there'll be trouble.'

Eager to take the limelight and imagining that Jacques was about to pull out his knife, Berru flung himself between the two men. Damour pushed him away, shouting:

'And you keep out of the way, too, you stupid idiot! What's the trouble with you?'

'Gently does it,' Sagnard said again. 'When people lose their temper, they don't realize what they're doing... Now listen to me. If I ask Félicie to come in, will you promise to be sensible? She's a sensitive woman, you know that as well as I do... We neither of us want to do each other in, do we? Will you behave properly?'

'If I'd come here with the idea of causing trouble, the first thing I'd've done would have been to throttle you, with all your fine talk!'

This was said in such a deeply emotional and sad tone of voice that it seemed to touch Sagnard to the quick.

'All right then,' he replied, 'I'll call Félicie. I'm a fair man, you know, and I can understand you wanting to talk all this over with her... You've got a right to do so.'

He went over to the bedroom door and knocked.

'Félicie! Félicie!'

Then, as nothing seemed to be stirring and Félicie, transfixed with horror at the thought of the impending interview, still sat terrified, clasping her children even more tightly in her arms, he became impatient:

'Now come along, Félicie... You're behaving stupidly. He's promised to be sensible.'

In the end, the key turned in the lock and she appeared, carefully locking the door behind her to keep her children safe from any intrusion. Another embarrassed silence ensued. In Berru's words, the weather seemed set for squalls.

Damour started to speak, slowly and stumbling over his words, while Sagnard stood in front of the window, lifting one of the little white curtains with his finger and pretending to look out, in order to make quite plain how understanding he was.

'Look, Félicie, you know I've never been an unkind man and that's the truth. Well, I'm not going to start being unkind now. At first, I wanted to kill off the whole lot of you here... Then I thought what good would that do me... So I prefer to leave the choice to you. We'll do what you want to do. Since the law can't provide justice for us, it's for you to decide which of us you like best... Now, give us your answer. Who do you want to be with, Félicie?'

Félicie was choking with emotion and quite unable to reply.

'Very well,' Jacques went on after a pause, still speaking in the same flat voice, 'I can see that you want to stay with him... I knew how things would turn out even while I was on my way up here... And I don't bear you any grudge, I've got to admit you're right. After all, I'm finished, I've got absolutely nothing to offer you. You don't love me any more and he's making you happy, quite apart from the two little ones...'

Félicie was weeping distraughtly.

'You're wrong to be crying, I'm not blaming you for anything. Things have just turned out like that, that's all... And so I thought I'd come and see you for the last time, so that you can sleep undisturbed. Now you've made your choice, I'll not bother you any more... It's all over, you'll never hear from me again.'

He made his way towards the door but Sagnard, who had been listening deeply moved, called out and stopped him:

'That's a wonderful thing you've just done! You can't possibly go off and leave us just like that... You must stay and have dinner with us.'

'No, thank you,' Damour replied.

Amazed at what he thought was a very strange ending to the matter, Berru seemed quite scandalized at hearing Jacques refuse this invitation.

'At least you'll stay for a drink,' the butcher went on. 'You'll not refuse a glass of wine, for goodness' sake?'

Damour did not accept straightaway. He was running his eyes round the tidy, cheerful dining-room, with its plain oak furniture, and finally his gaze settled on Félicie who was looking at him beseechingly with her eyes full of tears. He said:

'All right, then.'

Sagnard was delighted. He called out:

'Quick, let's have some glasses, Félicie. We can do without the maid. Bring four glasses, you must join us... My friend, it's very good of you to accept, you can't guess what a pleasure it is for me, because I like people whose heart is in the right place and yours certainly is, I can tell you!'

Meanwhile, Félicie was nervously trying to find the glasses and a bottle of wine but she was so bewildered that in the end Sagnard had to come to her aid. Then, when the wine had been poured, they all clinked glasses round the table:

'Your very good health!'

Sitting opposite Félicie, Jacques had to reach over to touch her glass. Their eyes crossed in a silence pregnant with memories of the past. Her hand was trembling so much that her glass was clinking like the chattering of teeth in a high fever. They addressed each other as strangers, no longer as man and wife. They were dead for each other; only memories were left alive:

'Your health!'

And while all four of them raised their glasses and drank, the children's voices could be heard coming from the adjoining room. They had begun playing and were chasing each other, shouting and laughing. Then they knocked on the door and called: 'Mummy! Mummy!'

'Well, that's that,' said Damour, putting his glass down on the table. 'Goodnight to you all.'

He left. White as a sheet, Félicie stood watching him go while Sagnard politely accompanied him to the door.

5

In the street, Damour started walking so fast that Berru had difficulty in keeping up with him. The housepainter was furious and when they had reached the Boulevard des Batignolles and he saw his companion sink weakly down on to a bench and sit there white-faced, with glazed, staring eyes, he at last let fly and spoke his mind: well, Jacques might at least have slapped that precious couple's faces for them; and he felt revolted at seeing a husband give up his wife without even discussing terms; you had to be a prize idiot, yes, an idiot, if not worse. . . And he quoted the instance of another man who had been in the Commune and had come back to find his wife living with someone else and both men and the woman were now all three living together in perfect harmony! You just had to work things out and not let yourself be made a dummy, because, after all, Jacques was the dummy in all this!

'You don't understand,' Damour replied, 'so just clear off, will you? You're not my friend any more.'

'Not your friend! When I've been doing my utmost. . . Just try and think, will you? What's going to happen to you now? You've got nobody, you're out on the street like a dog and you'll die like one if I don't help you. . . Not your friend! If I desert you now you'll have nothing left to do but crawl into a corner and starve!'

Jacques made a despairing gesture. It was quite true, there was nothing for him to do but throw himself into the river or else give himself up to the police.

'Well,' Berru went on, 'I'm such a good friend of yours that I'm going to take you to a place where you'll get a bit of grub and a roof over your head.'

He stood up as if he had come to a sudden decision and forced his companion to go with him.

'Where are you taking me?' stammered Jacques.

'You'll soon see... As you didn't want to have a meal with your wife, you'll be having dinner with someone else. Just get it into your thick head that I'm not going to let you do two stupid things in one day!'

He was walking down the Rue d'Amsterdam* and when they reached the Rue de Berlin, he stopped in front of a small private house and asked the footman who opened the door whether Madame de Souvigny was at home. Seeing that the footman was hesitating, he added:

'Tell her it's Berru.'

By now utterly bewildered by this unexpected call and the sight of this luxurious townhouse, Damour mechanically followed Berru in. They went upstairs and suddenly he found himself being hugged by a little blonde woman, very pretty and dressed in an extremely revealing lace négligé. What is more, she was exclaiming:

'It's you, Daddy, it's you! Oh, it is kind of you to have persuaded him to come!'

She was friendly and natural and not in the least worried by the old man's dirty old tunic, for in a sudden outburst of daughterly affection, she started clapping her hands in delight. But in his surprise and shock, her father had not even recognized her.

'It's Louise,' said Berru.

'Oh yes,' stammered Jacques. 'It's very kind of you...'

He hadn't the courage to address her less formally. Louise sat him down on a sofa and rang for the footman to tell him that she was not at home to anyone. Jacques meanwhile was looking all round the room which was draped with cashmere and furnished with a richness and elegance that brought tears to his eyes. Berru slapped him triumphantly on the shoulder and said:

'Well, do you still say I'm not your friend? I felt you'd be needing your daughter so I discovered her address and went and told her all about you. She told me to bring you along.'

'Of course I did,' said Louise fondly. 'Oh, I'm sure you know that I can't stand republicanism and those nasty men of the Commune who would ruin everything if they had the chance. But you're different, you're my dear old Dad. I can remember how kind you were to me when I was ill as quite a little girl. You'll see, we'll get along like a house on fire as long as you never talk politics... First of all, we're all going to have dinner together. Oh, isn't it lovely!'

She was almost sitting on the lap of this poor working-class father of hers, her pale eyes shining with laughter and her silky blonde hair floating in loose curls round her temples. He felt exhausted but a delicious sense of well-being was beginning to creep over him. He was tempted to decline, because it hardly seemed right to be sitting down to a meal in this grand house. But the energy which he had felt when leaving the butcher's shop after drinking each other's health had now quite deserted him. His daughter was too sweet and kind, he couldn't resist her tiny white hands which were resting in his own.

'So you won't say no?' enquired Louise again.

'Yes,' he said at last and two tears trickled down his careworn face.

Berru expressed his pleasure that he was being sensible at last. Then, as they were making their way into the dining-room, a servant came to inform Louise that her gentleman had called.

'I can't see him now,' she replied calmly. 'Tell him that I'm with my father but that I can see him tomorrow at six if he wants to call.'

The dinner was delightful. Berru was playing the fool as usual and Louise was in fits of laughter. She felt as if she was back in the Rue des Envierges and it was a real treat. Jacques ate so much that he was quite weighed down by fatigue and food; but each time his eyes met those of his daughter, they lit up with a tender smile. With dessert, they drank a very sweet sparkling wine which went to their heads. Then, after the servants had left, they propped their elbows on the table and talked with tipsy sentimentality about the past. Berru had rolled a cigarette for Louise and she was smoking it with a faraway look in her half-closed eyes. When speaking about her own past, she became very muddled when she reached the subject of her lovers, particularly the first one, a tall young man who had been perfect in all respects. Then she suddenly started to criticize her mother.

'You know,' she said to her father, 'I can't bear to see her any more, she behaved so badly. If you like, I'll go and tell her what I think of the rotten way you've been let down by her.'

But Damour replied solemnly that her mother no longer existed as far as he was concerned. Suddenly, Louise jumped to her feet, exclaiming:

'By the way, I've got something to show you that will please you.'

She disappeared and soon came back, still puffing at her cigarette, and handed her father an old yellow photograph with dog-eared corners. Jacques focused his bleary eyes on the portrait and gave a start.

'It's Eugène, my poor boy Eugène,' he stammered.

He passed the photograph to Berru who was also moved and said in a low voice:

'It's a very good likeness.'

Then it was Louise's turn to look. She held the photograph in her hand for a moment, her eyes brimming over with tears, and as she handed it back, she said:

'I can remember him very well. He was such a nice boy!'

All three suddenly gave way to their emotions and started crying. The photograph went round twice more, to the accompaniment of most touching sentiments. The photograph had faded badly and in his National Guard uniform, he looked like the shadow of a rebel, lost in legend. But turning it over, Jacques read what he had written so long ago: 'I will avenge you,' and waving a dessert knife in the air, he repeated his vow:

'Yes, I'll avenge you!'

'When I saw Mummy going to the bad,' Louise explained, 'I didn't want to let her keep the photo of poor Eugène so one evening, I pinched it... Let me give it to you, Daddy.'

Damour had put the photograph down beside his glass and was still looking at it. However, at long last they came round to practicalities. Her hand pressed to her heart, Louise said she wanted to rescue her father from his predicament. For a moment, it seemed almost as if she thought of suggesting that he might live in her house in Paris; but it would hardly have been feasible. Finally she had an idea: she asked him if he would be prepared to look after a property that one of her gentlemen friends had just bought her not far from Mantes.* There was a little cottage in the grounds where he could live quite comfortably on two hundred francs a month.

'Good Lord! It's paradise!' exclaimed Berru, accepting on behalf of his friend. 'If he gets bored, I'll go and call on him...'

By the following week, Damour had already moved into Bel-Air, his daughter's property. And there he was able to live the sort of quiet life that Providence certainly owed him after all the earlier hardships that he had suffered at her hands. He put on weight and flourished; respectably dressed at last, he had the frank, good-natured look of an old soldier. The peasantry were deferential. He went fishing and shooting. On sunny days, you would see him setting off for a country walk, looking at the wheat growing with the easy conscience of a man who has never robbed anyone and who is living on a hard-earned pension. When his daughter came down with a gentleman friend, he knew his place. His great joy was when she managed to slip away and they could have lunch together in the cottage. On such occasions he would talk baby-talk to her and gaze at her fine dresses with an adoring look in his eyes. They were tasty lunches, with all sorts of good things which he cooked himself, quite apart from the dessert of sweets and cakes which Louise pulled out of her pockets.

Damour never tried to see his wife again. He had his daughter, who had taken pity on her old father and who was his pride and joy. Nor did he ever make any attempt to re-establish his identity. What was the point of putting officialdom to trouble? And this gave him added peace and quiet. He had found his remote little niche where he was quite forgotten, a nobody, and not ashamed to accept his daughter's presents, whereas, had he been brought back to life, certain envious people might well have taken umbrage at his situation and he could well have suffered from them.

Sometimes, there was a lot of activity and noise in the little cottage. That would be Berru coming to spend a few days in the country. In Damour's cottage, he had at last realized his dream: a place where he could really do himself proud. He would go shooting and fishing with his friend and spend days lying on his back beside the river. In the evening the two friends would talk politics. Berru would bring down some anarchist newspapers from Paris and after reading them the two old friends would agree on the radical measures that were necessary: shoot the government, string up the bourgeois, burn Paris down and replace it with a new town, a town that would belong to the people. They still had not gone beyond the stage of achieving universal happiness by means of a general massacre. And finally, just before going to bed, Damour, who had had Eugène's portrait framed, would go up to it, look at it and, brandishing his pipe, shout:

'I'll avenge you!'

And next day, he would go off placidly, with his old man's stoop, to his fishing while, stretched out on the bank, Berru would lie drowsing with his face buried in the grass.

PRIESTS AND SINNERS

I

FATHER PINTOUX had been the parish priest of Saint-Marchal for the last forty years. He was now a little old man of seventy, dried up by his open-air life; with his brick-red, weatherbeaten face and his shabby, threadbare old cassock he looked like a peasant in his smock.

The story of his life was a simple one. He was a woodcutter's son from the neighbouring village of Mériadec. A puny boy, bullied by his brothers, he had had the good fortune to be taken up by a patroness who arranged for him to be admitted to the little seminary of Guérande. Physical labour had always been anathema to him and the thought of wielding an axe to cut down trees scared him so much that he would have preferred to become a tramp. He had moreover always possessed a childlike faith which persisted at the seminary, together with an equally blind submission to authority. He believed everything his teachers told him and, never having been very bright, he avoided the need for thought by telling himself that God would do his thinking for him. He had taken holy orders with the same unquestioning submissiveness and with one single idea in mind: to exercise his ministry undisturbed. At first, the bishop of Nantes sent him round to a couple of smaller parishes and, finally realizing his simple-mindedness, innocence and complete lack of initiative, he had packed him off to Saint-Marchal and thought no more about him.

Saint-Marchal is a tiny hamlet in the wilds of Lower Brittany. The Nantes to Brest railway did not pass within twenty-five miles of it; it was real wolf country, set on a high plateau battered by storms raging in from the Atlantic, which can be seen as a thin green line on the horizon. Saint-Marchal had almost four hundred inhabitants and poverty was widespread, for the soil is stony and there is a great shortage of water. The wretched villagers seemed to belong to quite a different world from that of the average Frenchman. And it was in this poor hamlet that Father Pintoux had grown old.

Little by little, the priest had settled into his narrow round of routine, like some old riding-school hack. Mass in the morning, catechism in the afternoon; and in the evening, a game of cards with a neighbour. Since it was quite impossible to live on the few hundred francs he received from the parish, he had been forced to overcome his distaste for hard work and take to wielding a mattock in the vegetable garden at the back of his presbytery, where he grew beans and cabbages. He could be seen in his shirtsleeves, bareheaded in the sun, grappling with a stony soil far too hard and heavy for his puny arms. Afterwards he would put on his cassock and go off to hear confession from the girls of the village, still out of breath from his exertions and searching his memory for the Latin formulas which he trotted out automatically.

Father Pintoux had a whole collection of ready-made phrases and gestures which he had been using for the last half-century and from which he never deviated. For him, religion had become purely a matter of outward observance. His services went like clockwork. His devotion of earlier days had turned into mere empiricism and found satisfaction in the repetition, at every opportunity, of the same details culled from his missal. Had he returned to earth in the shape of one of those peaceful oxen lumbering stolidly through their pastures, he would have bowed down to the sun with the same conviction that he showed in kneeling before the figure of Christ.

Meanwhile, over the last forty years, he had officiated at the weddings of most of the villagers and baptized a whole generation of children. He was the patriarch of Saint-Marchal. At church festivals, they would bring him gifts of eggs and butter. It was he whom they consulted on any matter of importance; he conducted lawsuits, reconciled families and shared out inheritances. There was, indeed, nothing more natural than this regal status of the priest, for he alone was capable of reading the books, he alone was in communication with science and with God. He represented authority even more than the mayor, for he spoke in the name of the Lord whereas the mayor spoke only in the name of the government; and Heaven, which metes out hail and thunder, is the only power feared by peasants, the only one before which they would bend the knee.

In the whole village, there was not one single unbeliever. On Sundays, the church was packed, with the women on one side and the men on the other. When the priest came in carrying the chalice, he could see at a glance if everyone was present. As soon as one of his flock was an absentee, he would be required to offer an excuse, such as an illness preventing him from leaving the house; otherwise the priest would call down God's wrath upon the head of the lost sheep. From the pulpit, he would fulminate dire threats against the ungodly, conjuring up the horrors of hell-fire, with cauldrons of boiling oil and souls in torment roasting on red-hot iron bars. Strong men and women would blench and after the service little children would be haunted by nightmares for the whole week. In fact, the priest would not have harmed a fly; but he was repeating sermons that he had heard from others and he himself lived in awe of the divine wrath of a jealous God; he really believed these cruel and miraculous tales and legends. So Saint-Marchal lived in a state of humility and terror, like a primitive tribe prostrating itself beneath a cloud streaked with lightning and always on the point of loosing its thunderbolts.

One Sunday, having noticed that Marianne Roussel was not in her usual place beside the font, Father Pintoux set off after lunch to find out if Marianne was ill. He had the stiff, halting gait of an old man; the only signs of life now left in his stolid, leathery old face were his tiny grey eyes, as sharp and innocent as a child's. On the way, a few peasants stopped him to ask him what the weather would be like tomorrow and he looked up at the sky, wagged his head and finally promised that it would be fine. A few steps further on a woman's washing caught his eye; then he went into a backyard to look at a brood of chicks. For everybody in the village he was one of the family. The only thing which differentiated him from the other villagers was his cassock; he shared their ideas and their speech and he, too, looked as if he was walking in his sleep.

Finally, he reached the Roussels' cottage. Marianne was outside, looking perfectly well and chatting to her tall neighbour Nanette.

'Well, Marianne, what's all this about? You missed Mass this morning!'

And without giving her a chance to explain, he launched into his attack: it was wrong, the Devil was always lying in wait and she would certainly end up in Hell if she didn't go to church. In the end, Marianne managed to explain:

'It's my little girl, Father... She's very poorly. This morning I thought we'd lost her... So I had to stay at home.'

'Little Catherine isn't well?'

'Yes, Father, we've put her in our bed. Come and take a look.'

In a large bed at the far end of the gloomy room, a little girl about ten years old was lying with flushed face and closed eyes shivering with fever. The whole of her poor little body was trembling under the sheet. The priest went over and looked at her silently for a moment. Then he said slowly:

'It's the good Lord punishing you, Marianne. You've offended Him by your bad example and He has laid His hand upon you.'

He jerked his chin to emphasize each word, as if to indicate his approval of such divine vengeance. And Catherine had not been a very good girl, either. The previous Thursday during catechism, he had been obliged to send her out of church because she had been laughing and disturbing the other children. It happened to have rained very heavily that afternoon and, not daring to go home for fear of being scolded, the little girl had been drenched to the skin in a shower.

'She must have caught it last Thursday,' her mother murmured. 'She came home in a dreadful state.'

'God is punishing her as He is punishing you,' the priest went on. 'Do you think He is happy when He sees a naughty little girl making fun of Him in His own house? Everything must be paid for, you know.'

Nanette crossed herself and old Roussel, who was eating a bowl of soup at a table, nodded his head in approval. Yes, everything had to be paid for. If there had been a hailstorm last April, it was because the people of Saint-Marchal had displeased the Virgin Mary by not offering such fine bunches of flowers as in previous years, on the feast of the Assumption. If old Lazare's mare had died, it was because the old man had forgotten to make the sign of the cross as he walked past the Calvary.*

However, as the Roussels had no recollection of having given any cause for God's anger, they hoped that their young daughter would recover, with the help of the angels. And if things were no better after a couple of days, they could even send for the doctor who lived at Pontenac, some fifteen miles away. Nanette gave a shrug; as far as she was concerned, doctors were of no use at all. Once Heaven had passed judgement on someone, there was certainly no doctor who could save him. And besides, the doctor at Pontenac was a heathen; everybody knew that you could see the Devil standing at the foot of the bed of any dead man whom he'd been treating and who had his medicine inside him.

'Rub her temples every hour with holy water,' said the priest, 'and say three Paternosters and two Ave Marias.'

Then he knelt down and mumbled a quick prayer. The Roussels and Nanette said 'Amen' with him and crossed themselves vigorously.

'It's not going to be anything much,' said the priest as he left. 'The child's body must cast out all its wickedness... I'll be back tomorrow.'

But when Father Pintoux came to see the Roussels next day, he was greatly agitated and in a voice trembling with emotion he recounted the appalling story that he had just been told by his bell-ringer: Catherine had committed an act of sacrilege. On Thursday, after being sent out of the catechism class, she had slipped off to play for a moment in the sacristy, where the bell-ringer had seen her take off the crown of the large plaster statue of the Virgin Mary and put it on her own head, making several curtsies all by herself as she did so, doubtless in order to make fun of the Mother of God. The priest could not understand why Heaven had not struck her down on the spot. But now she was surely doomed. Her illness had come from on high.

'But she did come home soaked to the skin on Thursday,' Marianne said again. 'Perhaps, after all, if we were to get her into a good sweat...'

'Oh, she's ill, very ill,' old Roussel said in a low voice, sitting in a corner with his hands on his knees.

And the poor little girl seemed indeed on the point of death as she lay in the large bed with her short blonde hair all dishevelled, gasping feverishly for breath through her burning lips; behind her half-closed lids, her eyes were glazed and staring and in her fever she kept moaning: 'Oh, it's hurting me, it's hurting dreadfully!' It was pitiful to see this tender young girl in such pain, clenching her tiny fists in her lonely struggle against death.

Meanwhile the story of the sacrilege had spread through the village and all the neighbours had come flocking to the house. It was rumoured that Father Pintoux was going to attempt to chase out the Devil who had got into the body of the Roussel girl. Soon there were a dozen people gathered in the front room. They were all whispering together and recalling other well-known incidents of the same sort. Three years before, another little scamp had stolen a holy wafer and pinned it to a tree for fun; the tree had immediately started to groan and red liquid had begun to stream out of its trunk while large drops of blood had dripped from every branch. Nanette swore that she had seen it happening, adding that at any rate her sister had seen it. But the group of villagers were even more impressed by another story: on one Shrove Tuesday, some young lads from Saint-Nazaire were walking round with cardboard masks on their faces and when a priest had gone by carrying extreme unction, one of the young rascals had decided not to remove his mask which had then stuck so tightly to his face that he had started screaming with agony and they had been forced to tear the mask off piece by piece, pulling the skin away with the cardboard.

After listening to these examples, no one was surprised that Catherine had been struck down with a dreadful illness for having dared to put the Virgin Mary's crown on her own head. A feeling of anxiety mingled with awe filled the room. Although it was broad daylight, the men felt rather uneasy and the women kept glancing apprehensively over their shoulders, half expecting to see a cloven hoof and a pair of horns.

'She was such a quiet well-behaved little girl,' said her father. 'Something must have got into her, that's for sure.'

The priest had started praying. He walked round the room, reciting his Latin prayers and, dipping a box twig into a plateful of holy water, each time he reached the child he sprinkled some over her, making a sign of the cross in the air. Catherine was still moaning, writhing and arching her back while she babbled incoherently in her delirium, laughing and sobbing simultaneously. Suddenly she started up with staring eyes, calling out to the people she saw around her; then she fell back, singing a children's song until her voice died away into silence.

The men and women in the room shrank back trembling, afraid of seeing a monster spring out of the poor feverish girl's open mouth. She must certainly be possessed by the Devil if she started like that as soon as a drop of holy water touched her. Surely the Devil was going to throttle her and put an end to it all.

At the foot of the bed, Marianne was in tears: Catherine was all she had and now she was going to lose her without even knowing what had caused her death. Once more, she mentioned a doctor and begged her husband to drive quickly over to Pontenac; but old Roussel was still slumped stupidly in his corner and merely shook his head apathetically in reply. He was resigned to the death of his daughter, like all old peasants who submit to higher powers which they cannot understand. Why bother to send for a doctor when Father Pintoux had announced that God wished to take away their child? Father Pintoux certainly knew better than anyone. All you can do is to submit; your turn will come, too, and the best thing was to be always on your best behaviour.

When he saw that the holy water was making the little girl suffer and not bringing her any relief, Father Pintoux clapped his hands lightly, as he did in church when he wanted the congregation to kneel. They all fell on their knees. He remained standing for a moment, saying:

'Let us pray together and ask our Lord to perform a miracle.'

His brown leathery face lit up with the radiance of his faith and, despite his stoop and his weatherbeaten peasant-like appearance, he had a majestic look as he fell on his knees and, with all the fervour of his seminary days, prayed God to show mercy on the poor sinner. The murmur of prayer grew louder and the anxious atmosphere in the room was filled by the icy chill of superstition, the helpless ignorance of people crushed by life's adversity. The little girl gave one final convulsive shudder and then lay flat in the bed, gasping as if in relief. Then, all at once, she gave a deep sigh and lay still. She was dead.

'*Requiescat in pace*,' said the priest, raising his voice.

'Amen!' came the response from the villagers.

And they all rose to their feet and left, greatly affected by the scene, while Marianne stifled her sobs in her apron and old Roussel, utterly bewildered and unable to realize what he was doing, opened his clasp-knife and cut himself a slice of bread.

When Father Pintoux left he was greeted by the whole village as the representative of the dread Master who can exercise his power of life and death at any time. It so happened that municipal elections were being held on the following Sunday and the villagers clustered round him to ask him how they should vote. He repeated the instructions which he had received from the bishop's palace the previous day. Next Sunday, not one of the villagers failed to attend Mass and the bishop's candidate was elected without a single dissenting voice. Father Pintoux ruled in Saint-Marchal like God himself, like some old rough-hewn, wooden idol with power to dispense thunderbolts and horrible diseases.

II

Every Friday, Father Michelin would hear confession from his lady clientele in the Dominican chapel in a little street in the Faubourg St-Germain. It was a very cosy little chapel, more like a large drawing-room, scented and intimate in its dim light from the stained-glass windows. It was considered the acme of good taste for ladies not to go to confession in their own parish but to come here instead, far from the common crowd of penitents. It placed them on another plane; they could imagine that God was offering them a more elegant absolution of their sins.

Father Michelin was a tall, fine-looking man of thirty, brown-haired and white-skinned, who was at that time enjoying a considerable vogue in high society. The son of a glass and china dealer in the Rue du Bac and born in that aristocratic quarter, he was now confessing the daughters of the countesses and marchionesses who had been his father's customers. This fact had not, however, gone to his head; he had succeeded in striking the exact balance of manner between the deference of an inferior and the all-powerful authority of the priest; this had given a special piquancy to his exercise of his ministry.

His schooldays were obscure but he was said to have been a good student at his seminary. He was basically a pleasant young man, fully determined to enjoy life and to be adaptable. While still a youth he must have had dreams of forcing an entry, in a position of authority, into those aristocratic drawing-rooms which he had till then been able to glimpse only through half-closed doors. His ambition was to move in select circles where he could satisfy his taste for fine things, choice meals and elegant women, everything that smelt nice. As far as religion was concerned, he looked upon it as a decent veil to throw over human ugliness. Without religion, polite society was impossible.

On that Friday, Father Michelin was hearing confession from the young Countess de Marizy, an adorable blonde as yet barely twenty-two years old, whose beauty had become proverbial in the social columns of all the newspapers. It was she who set the tone and no party was complete without her. The priest had become a friend of the family after a stay in the count's country seat of Plessis-Rouge in Normandy.

The countess was kneeling as she waited her turn. Her dainty little chin was resting on her clasped hands and she was pondering while gazing vaguely in front of her at the pale pink light from the stained-glass window. It did not take her long to examine her conscience: she had only one major confession to make and she was merely deliberating with herself how best to make it. She briefly toyed with the idea of not revealing her lapse, because it was a very difficult matter to speak about; however, it was that very difficulty which attracted her; she felt a feminine urge to relate to this tall handsome young priest how, unfortunately, she had been so far forgetful of her wifely duty as to yield to the solicitations of the Marquis de Mauroy, a sort of cousin of hers whom she had been in love with before her marriage.

Meanwhile, her turn had come. She stood up and went over to the confessional with a slight involuntary curl on her lips which provided a charming foil to the contrite expression which she had felt it proper to assume. No doubt she had found the appropriate approach and turn of phrase needed to make her task easier. She knelt down slowly and stayed there for a good half hour. Nothing could be heard, no voices were raised, there was not even a creak from the woodwork. Then she came out of the confessional, her eyes demurely cast down, and it was impossible to read anything from the expression on her face; she still had the slight involuntary curl on her lips which brought dimples to her pink cheeks.

Father Michelin confessed his men in the Dominican chapel on Mondays. So, on the following Monday, the Marquis de Mauroy was kneeling in exactly the same place as the countess had knelt, similarly awaiting his turn. The marquis was a slightly built and delicate-looking young man, with a rather pretty face. Despite his dissipated way of life, he had never stopped regularly practising his religion, considering it as forming part of his duty to society.

While kneeling, he was, like the countess, pondering and at the same time watching the pale pink light from the stained-glass window. He was wondering whether it would be wise to reveal his relationship with Madame de Marizy to Father Michelin. No doubt the secrets of the confessional were sacrosanct; but the priest might unwittingly betray what he knew by certain pointed glances in the count's presence. The marquis decided on a middle course: he'd confess his lapse while keeping the lady's name secret. Having set his mind at rest by this decision, when he reached the confessional, he went briskly down on to his knees.

Monsieur de Mauroy took less than five minutes to put his conscience in order but he came out looking extremely cross. The priest had refused to let him finish his rigmarole and had informed him very sternly that it was extremely remiss of him to have taken advantage of a gentleman who had welcomed him to his home as an old friend of the family. He had mentioned the count by name and shown that he knew all about the whole affair. To hell with all women! They couldn't go to confession without blurting out their whole story and often even embroidering on it!

Every Tuesday, Father Michelin dined with Monsieur de Marizy, a small party to which only a few friends were invited. So, the day after hearing the young marquis's confession, the priest was sitting in the small drawing-room of the count's Paris residence, with the countess and a few other guests. It so happened that the marquis had also been invited on this occasion. He came in smiling, greeted the countess and held out his hand to the priest with the bland assurance of a man impervious to embarrassment in any situation, however awkward.

It was now seven o'clock but the count had still not come in; they waited for a good quarter of an hour longer. The countess apologized for her husband's late arrival: he had so many important commitments. Everyone nodded understandingly although they all knew that the count's only commitments were the self-imposed ones which he undertook with the better-known amongst the actresses playing in Paris's smaller theatres. Indeed, his friends considered him too incompetent to go into politics.

'Monsieur de Marizy must have been delayed by the ministerial crisis,' said Father Michelin. 'No doubt he's being consulted.'

'Yes, that must be the reason,' murmured the marquis, looking at the countess with a sly smile.

She was playing with a scent-bottle and seemed completely unmoved. Father Michelin's remark had been made purely out of politeness, for he too knew quite well where the count must have been delayed. He even knew the name of the little singer at the Italian opera whom Monsieur de Marizy had just presented with a house in town. This actress, who went by the name of Bianca, was a Bordeaux girl who would gobble up the count in three months if she didn't show him the door before. The priest had caught a glimpse of her once in the Bois de Boulogne. A really lovely little creature... And, still thinking of her to himself, the priest said out loud:

'Yes, Monsieur de Marizy will certainly be at the Ministry.'

Eventually the count appeared. Although barely fifty years old, he had a grey, careworn face, receding hair and a morose expression which made him look like a distinguished statesman, prematurely aged by the burden of public office. He made his excuses, complaining that he was snowed under with work. They moved into the dining-room.

The food was delicious. At table, the conversation continued in an undertone but, during the second course, one very old gentleman raised his voice to ask the count who was going to be the new minister. The count did not hear him; he was looking worried and anxious. The old gentleman had to repeat his question.

'Well, as a matter of fact they haven't yet come to any decision,' stammered the count finally. 'It's a serious situation, very serious indeed.... We've never been in such a serious situation.'

Everyone had stopped talking to listen to him and he was obliged to go on talking, which he found great difficulty in doing.

'Yes, it's a very dangerous situation. There's been some very violent disagreement... I expect they'll be able to patch things up.'

Looking at the count, Father Michelin thought to himself that little Bianca must have got hold of the fire-tongs and sent him packing. That would be the violent disagreement to which the count had referred. At this same moment, the priest overheard the countess and the marquis, sitting close to him, exchanging rapid whispers.

'Why didn't you come?'

'I couldn't get away.'

'I waited for you all day. You don't love me any more, Laura!'

'Be quiet! I'll come and see you tomorrow at two o'clock.'

The countess had noticed that the priest was listening to their conversation. She turned towards him with an engaging smile: after all, he was in the secret too and wasn't it his duty to show sympathy towards human frailty?

'Father, I know you're fond of game... Jean, offer Father Michelin some more partridge.'

The priest remained calm. He would certainly know how to deal with the countess as she deserved next time she came to confession; but here, in her own dining-room, he was merely a guest and he was too much a man of the world to show the slightest trace of sternness, which would have been a gross breach of manners. And so dinner continued with the priest still hearing whispers on his left while at the same time looking at two pink spots he had just noticed, two little scratch marks beside one of the count's eyes. Meanwhile the wines were perfect, the dining-room was filled with the fragrance of fresh fruit, the whole meal was being served with the utmost elegance and decorum.

'Are you not preaching at Ste-Clotilde* next Saturday?' an old lady enquired from the priest during dessert.

'Yes, Madame de Beauvoisin. I'm preaching in aid of the charitable institution of Our Lady.'

The conversation turned to this organization whose aim was to save the souls of orphan girls who were in moral danger. The countess was one of the lady patronesses.

'We're doing all we can,' she said. 'There are so many poor girls who go wrong because of the lack of a sound religious upbringing. Once a woman has learnt to know God, she is safe from all danger.'

The Marquis de Mauroy gave wholehearted approval to the countess's remarks. Without religion, morality was impossible. Even the count rose to the occasion with a splendid homily:

'As I was saying to two senator friends of mine only the other day, if you want to raise the moral level of the masses, you must force them down on their knees in the churches. And they agreed with me. They're intending to introduce a bill making the observance of the Sabbath Day compulsory. We must set an example, gentlemen, we must set an example!'

Exhausted by the effort of making this speech, the count seized the opportunity, as they were leaving table, to take his hat and slip discreetly away. Work is such a hard taskmaster!

The party was drawing to its close. The two old ladies were the first to leave, followed by the other guests. Finally, only Father Michelin and the marquis remained with the countess. The countess was sitting on the left of the fireplace, the marquis on the right, with the priest in the middle. Conversation became desultory and monosyllabic. Father Michelin realized that he was balking the two lovers but he was tactless enough to want to make his presence felt in order to discipline the young couple and recall them to their sense of duty. He made no reference to the matter but he had promised himself not to leave before the young man.

Half an hour dragged by. The priest's situation was becoming more and more embarrassing. In the end, the man of the world won the day over the priest. Father Michelin stood up to take his leave. At this the countess and the marquis became extremely affable and, as he was going through the door, they called out to him:

'Good night, Father! You know we'll be there to hear you on Saturday.'

On the following Saturday, the church of Ste-Clotilde was full of flowers and draped overall in red velvet. In the pulpit, Father Michelin had taken as his text the supreme virtue of the holy state of virginity, a theme of considerable delicacy which he handled in the choicest and most subtle terms. Amongst the congregation, the Count and Countess de Marizy could be seen sitting in the front pews, together with the young Marquis de Mauroy. After the sermon, at the consecration of the host, all three went devoutly down on to their knees. And Father Michelin could congratulate himself on having risen from his father's china-shop to the choir-stall from which he was now able to look down on these reverently bowed aristocratic foreheads. But there was one thought which tempered his elation: he knew that in his church religion was above all a matter of pomp and ceremony and that although these pious attitudes were his to command, he had little power over the souls of his congregation.

III

There was a small private dinner party at the Robinots', a wealthy middle-class family. No more than four people were present: Monsieur and Madame Robinot, their daughter Clémentine, and the parish priest, Father Gérard.

'Do help yourself to a piece of sole, Father,' urged Monsieur Robinot. 'I know you're fond of fish, so you can't refuse.'

'Now Father, you must have some mushrooms,' said Madame Robinot in a confidential undertone. 'Do me the pleasure of taking these two.'

And even Françoise the maid, busily uncorking a bottle, whispered into the priest's ear:

'Some Chambertin,* Father?'

And Father Gérard beamed affably to his left and right at his host and hostess and made polite replies; he even gave a sly friendly wink to thank Françoise. He was being spoilt, really he was. But the sole was superb and he'd be very happy to have a few more mushrooms. Then he leant back in his chair and drained his glass of Chambertin with half-closed eyes.

Father Gérard was fifty years old. He was fat but he was so ready to poke fun at his paunch himself that nobody would think of blaming him. He boasted a large, round, pink face and a fresh complexion which bore witness to his level-headed, peaceful and happy existence. The son of well-to-do lower middle-class parents he had gone into the church with a gentle smile on his lips rather than with any passionate faith in his heart; he had shrewdly weighed up the pros and cons and come to the conclusion that the life would suit him. Some of the very best livings had fallen to his lot and his superiors had never failed to further his advancement, and were still furthering it, for they saw in him one of those affable and tolerant sorts of priest who, in that day and age, could do more for religion than any apostolic zealot.

He had enjoyed considerable success in Tours for, like many middle-class provincial towns, Tours liked peace and quiet. The women were generally pious while most of the men rarely set foot in church. Father Gérard had realized that his most import-ant task was to cause no disruption of family life and had shown unerring skill in achieving that goal. He was made welcome wherever he went; he heard the wives' confessions and played a hand of piquet with their husbands.

'Now, Father, what's your opinion of this chicken?' enquired Madame Robinot.

'Quite delicious... I'll take a little salad.'

After dessert, coffee and liqueurs were served. Madame Robinot and her daughter withdrew. Father Gérard cheerfully downed a small glass of Chartreuse and, as he was alone with Monsieur Robinot, they both started chatting about an event that was the talk of the town: the elopement of a Tours lady with a young man from Paris.

'A very pretty young woman,' said the priest. 'Tall, good figure, lovely teeth.'

'You were her confessor, I believe?' asked Monsieur Robinot.

But Father Gérard did not seem to have heard the question. His voice took on a fatherly tone: at the family's request, he'd no doubt have to make up his mind to go to Paris to call on the lost sheep and bring her back into the fold. With a sly grin on his face, Monsieur Robinot was trying to embarrass the priest, who finally exclaimed jovially:

'Now! Now! You're just a heathen. There's nothing would give you greater pleasure than to make me say something foolish... Let's drop the subject.'

In fact Monsieur Robinot tried to tease Father Gérard at every opportunity. He enjoyed bringing the conversation round to scabrous subjects and was always looking for new ways to pull his leg in an attempt to make him lose his temper. But the priest always remained imperturbable, exchanged quip for quip and was prepared to discuss any topic, women or anything else, like a man quite untroubled by fleshly desires. In these skirmishes, it was usually Monsieur Robinot who came off second best.

Madame Robinot and Clémentine were waiting in the drawing-room. As soon as the priest came in he went over and sat down between them, while Monsieur Robinot walked outside on to the terrace to smoke his cigar. The priest's manner became quite different and more unctuous as he talked with the ladies about a big procession which was due to take place the following Sunday. He was the confessor of both the mother and the daughter. Lolling back in his comfortable armchair, he toyed with his gold snuff-box as he explained that it would be a most moving ceremony.

Then Madame Robinot turned towards her daughter:

'Clémentine, do show Father Gérard how your needlework is getting on.'

Clémentine went to fetch a chasuble that she was embroidering for Father Gérard: it showed mystical green and red flowers on a gold background; the workmanship was superb and the priest exclaimed in admiration as he complimented the girl, who was overcome with delight and confusion. Both women were huddling round him, hanging on his slightest word. When Monsieur Robinot came back, having finished his cigar, he exclaimed:

'And there's Father Gérard leading our ladies astray again!'

But the priest intended to have the last word.

'We were talking about you, Monsieur Robinot,' he said with his sly smile. 'We were saying that you'd be joining in our Sunday procession.'

'Me? Good Lord no!'

Without saying anything more, the priest wagged an admonishing finger at him. A few friends now arrived and the drawing-room filled up; as in all provincial drawing-rooms, the ladies had not changed out of their everyday clothes. There was a registrar of mortgages, who was an elderly eccentric and a rabid anti-Jesuit; a rich wheat-merchant who prided himself on his liberalism; and a principal secretary in the Prefecture, a pretty young man who took very seriously his role of sceptical young Parisian male. However, they all shook hands with the priest in a very friendly manner. As for the ladies, they clustered rapturously around him to enquire after his health and to express the hope that his gout was not proving too troublesome. He was able to reassure them and then agreed to have a game of piquet with the registrar of mortgages.

The conversation became general, with Father Gérard interjecting the odd remark between two hands of piquet and carefully avoiding any mention of religion. When one of the men was tactless enough to refer to his cassock, he smiled without saying a word and refused to be drawn. The whole town was still talking about an incident that had just occurred in someone's house, when a priest had lost his temper with the registrar of mortgages who was accusing the Jesuits of fostering the use of tobacco in order to stupefy the masses. Father Gérard would certainly have never allowed himself to be provoked into departing from his exquisite manners by anything like that; on the contrary, he would have been greatly amused, for these little fantasies of the registrar of mortgages had the knack of arousing his mirth.

However, the priest could not always avoid being drawn into discussion. When his game of piquet was over, Monsieur Robinot and the rich grain-merchant managed to corner him in a window and brought the conversation round to the part played by religion in a modern society.

'Seriously, Father,' Monsieur Robinot exclaimed, 'I'm not so fanatically anti-religious as you may think but I am an unbeliever and so I prefer not to go to church. I'd rather be a heathen than a hypocrite... Aren't I right?'

The priest bowed but said nothing.

'However,' Monsieur Robinot went on, 'I do fully recognize that religion is an excellent guardian of morality and as such an indispensable form of discipline for our wives and daughters... For example, I prefer my wife to have God on her mind rather than some young cavalry officer.'

The principal secretary in the Prefecture, who had joined the group, thought this remark delightful and exploded in a loud guffaw.

'And you do teach them many valuable things—their marital obligations, obedience and so on, and you threaten them with fire and brimstone if they misbehave... that sort of thing is very helpful to husbands...'

'In a word, we're a police force ensuring that your honour doesn't come to any harm,' Father Gérard interrupted.

Once again the principal secretary in the Prefecture went into ecstasies.

'Oh, that's delightful,' he murmured.

'Well, as far as I'm concerned,' the wheat-merchant exclaimed, 'that's the sort of police force I could well do without... You must excuse me, Father, I've no desire to offend you, but if my wife spent less time on her knees in church, she'd spend more time at home with me. And it's not really so very admirable, from the moral point of view, to do your duty merely because you're afraid of hell-fire.'

'Now you're going too far,' said Monsieur Robinot. 'As long as everything is running smoothly at home, you don't need to worry about anything else.'

'No need to worry about anything else? Do you think it's a good thing for your wife to spend every day and all day on her knees? It quite upsets my wife and when she comes back from church, all she can think about is the next world!'

'But the important thing is that when she comes back from church she's not coming back from anywhere else.'

The priest had prudently withdrawn, leaving the wheat-merchant and Monsieur Robinot to fight it out alone; they became quite abusive. Then, when they had calmed down, the priest came back and said in his usual bland voice:

'I don't suppose you know about it but you really ought to take part in the procession next Sunday. Just to set a good example, of course, in support of those guardians of morality Monsieur Robinot was talking about a few moments ago.'

These two pillars of bourgeois society laughed and declined: it would really be too funny for words to see them carrying candles through the streets of Tours when everyone knew their liberal views. . .

'I won't insist on any candles,' the priest retorted in the same joking tone. 'Just think of yourselves as taking a stroll behind the canopy and I can assure you that you'll be in very good company for all the local authorities will be there as well as representatives of the town's most distinguished families.'

The two men continued to treat the matter as a joke: it was very kind of Father Gérard to invite them but religious processions were really against their principles and they couldn't accept. Courteous as ever, the priest did not insist and as it was striking ten, he took his leave. All the ladies went with him to the door, whispering amongst themselves and following him fondly with their eyes.

'Goodnight, Father, sleep well!'

And then Madame Robinot seemed to have remembered something and ran downstairs after him. They could be heard talking together very quietly for some ten minutes.

On the following Sunday, Monsieur Robinot and the corn-merchant were in the front rank of the procession behind the canopy. Father Gérard must have given Madame Robinot the task of persuading her husband, who had, however, agreed only out of sheer middle-class snobbery: he felt very proud at being a member of one of the most distinguished families of the town.

But he still intended to maintain his independence and vote against the bishop's candidate at the next municipal elections.

Father Gérard noticed him and gave him a smile, with a glint of triumph in his tiny eyes. For a moment he could imagine himself as the real master of Tours. Not only did he reign over that flock of wives walking along in the procession with downcast eyes and clasped hands; his power even extended to the husbands of Voltairean persuasion who in the privacy of their homes continually made fun of religion. No doubt the reverend father was too intelligent to cherish any hopes of converting them but it was sufficient satisfaction for him to see them paying lip-service to Catholicism. When churches are growing emptier every day, you need to bring every possible means into play to fill them.

IV

In the Rue de Charonne, in the heart of the Faubourg Saint-Antoine,* a common-law couple was living on the sixth floor of a large and dilapidated old tenement building, housing exclusively manual workers. Every evening the man, a bricklayer called Lambert, came home the worse for drink. The woman, Lisa by name and a stitcher by trade, was so lazy that one by one all the workshops had refused to employ her. They had been living—and fighting—together for the last three years. But their fighting did not prevent them from being fond of each other, in their own way. If they kept continually knocking each other about, this was merely because it was a good way of keeping warm in winter and passing the long summer evenings. The neighbours had ceased to be concerned about them.

However, last winter had been a difficult one. After a more than usually vigorous battering by Lambert, Lisa had been forced to spend six weeks in bed. There had been unemployment and Lambert had not had any work for the last two months. They were without food or heating. One evening in January, Lambert, certainly not a sensitive person, had been reduced to sitting on the floor with his face in his hands, weeping like a little girl.

Without saying anything, Lisa, who was only just recovering, dressed and went downstairs. She was going to beg in the streets to see if she could collect enough money to buy a loaf of bread. So, keeping a sharp lookout for the police, she sidled along in the shadow of the houses, stopping any passers-by who seemed to have kind faces. It was a bitterly cold night and the passers-by were reluctant to take their hands out of their pockets; they quickened their pace and made no response. Crying with cold and shame, Lisa was on the point of giving up when she saw a young priest walking quickly along, wearing such a threadbare cassock that his face and hands were purple with cold. Well, she felt pretty certain that he wouldn't give her anything but, having no great liking for priests, she held out her hand purely to see what sort of face he would pull.

He stopped, fumbled in his pocket, blushed and said in a hurried voice:

'Take me back to your place, but you must be quick, I'm in a hurry.'

When Lambert saw her come into the room with this 'black beetle', he shot angrily to his feet; he too was not fond of priests. But although he immediately recognized Lambert's indignant reaction, the priest did not seem to be put out by it. He cast a rapid glance round the garret: there was no doubt of their abject poverty. He put his hand into his fob-pocket and pulled out an old silver watch attached to a silk ribbon and handed it to Lisa, saying in the same hurried voice:

'Here you are, take this to the pawn shop straightaway. Please be quick. I'll wait here till you come back.'

Although bewildered by this strange turn of events, Lisa ran quickly down the six flights of stairs. All the time she was gone, the priest remained standing, pale and deep in thought, in the middle of the room, while Lambert went back to squat in his corner, supporting his head in his hands and glaring at him with burning eyes.

A quarter of an hour later Lisa returned with ten francs. The priest took only the pawn ticket.

'Keep the money,' he said. 'If you need me, come and ask for Father de Villeneuve at St Margaret's.'

Thereupon he left and went shivering back to his own home to eat his usual evening meal of two slices of bread and butter. Then he settled down to work in his unheated room, wrapping his legs in a blanket.

Father de Villeneuve was tall and thin and his long pale face already bore two deep creases, although he had been born only twenty-eight years ago, in the south of France, into a family of small country gentry, completely ruined. Left an orphan at the age of ten, he had become deeply religious and had entered the seminary with such burning enthusiasm that his teachers had felt compelled to restrain his potentially dangerous fervour; they saw in him one of those excitable spirits who would be incapable of sensible compromise. Later on, he had passed through a period of appalling spiritual struggle: outstandingly intelligent, he had become obsessed with a desire for knowledge and been assailed by doubts. He argued with his teachers and wrestled with his grave misgivings concerning his faith. In an attempt to overcome these doubts, he had imposed on himself the most rigorous acts of penance. But he had remained inwardly torn and unhappy, still harrowed by the violence of his feelings under the mask of serenity which he had forced himself to present to the world. In the diocese, he had been marked out as a young priest on whom a watchful eye would have to be kept and who must be disciplined should the need arise to avoid scandal.

This was why such a highly intelligent man had remained a humble parish priest attached to the church of St Margaret in a poor inner Paris suburb. He himself had accepted this kind of exile with complete equanimity, his consuming desire being merely to reconcile the modern world and Catholicism. He was anxious to reject neither science nor the new society, while continuing to hold to Catholic dogma. He was, indeed, glad to be living in this essentially working-class district, for he felt convinced that the main task of religion should be to win back the hearts and minds of the urban population. He would mingle constantly with the crowds of workers, studying their needs, seeking to convert them with an apostolic fervour and offering them aid and comfort. He had met with deep hostility and, till now, nothing but resentment. He described this situation as a monstrous misunderstanding; but it pierced him to the quick.

He had been deeply moved as well as shocked by the sight of Lisa begging in the streets for a crust of bread and by her look of hatred, starving though she was. A week later, he went back to the Rue de Charonne and found Lisa alone, just about to put a saucepan of potatoes on to the stove. She offered him a lukewarm sort of welcome but he sat down and chatted to her. Lisa made no bones about telling him the truth of her situation: she was not married to Lambert; they had come together one evening and it'd last until it came to an end...

'But that's all wrong!' the priest exclaimed. 'You must get married.'

Lisa laughed and shrugged her shoulders.

'We're better off as we are,' she said. 'At least, if things don't work out one day, we can leave each other without any fuss... Would we have any more money in our pockets if we were married? The answer to that is no, isn't it? So there you are and it's not a matter of being decent or indecent at all.'

When he still kept telling her she ought to think it over and talked about morality and the bad example they were setting, Lisa shook her head.

'Look, sir, there's a married couple on our landing. Well, they knock each other about more than we do and they've got a daughter of fifteen who they're already trying to turn into a bad lot... Marriage doesn't really make people more respectable, that's for sure.'

And when, as he was going out, the priest tried to leave a five franc piece on the table, Lisa asked him not to: Lambert had found work, and charity was for when you were starving and didn't know which way to turn. She pointed down the corridor, where a poor old sick woman lived who hadn't got the money to buy the medicines she needed. He could give his five franc piece to her, it'd be very welcome...

After this, the priest often came for a chat with Lisa. He had sensed that this fallen woman was good at heart and he desperately wanted to persuade her to marry Lambert. Later, he would persuade Lambert to agree to get married. He felt that he would be conducting a sort of propaganda on behalf of religion and for the revival of religious beliefs in the hearts of the populace. But reality had always led to rude awakenings...

He soon became known in the tenement block in the Rue de Charonne, an enormous stuccoed building in which more than a hundred families were crammed, in cramped little lodgings. Each time he walked through the courtyard and went up the six flights of stairs, eyes would follow him with a malicious gleam. Of the two or three hundred tenants, not one ever went to Mass. So, as he went through, the priest ran the gauntlet of a beguiling commentary. Women would say: 'What on earth does he think he's doing here?' Or: 'Ah well, today's not my lucky day, I've just seen something that'll do me no good.' Or: 'Well, well, a priest. I suppose he might be going to pay a visit to that curly haired blonde on the first floor. He might at least have had the decency to change out of his cassock . . .' As for the men, they were even more outspoken. They would enquire if it wasn't a real pity to see such a well set-up young fellow, a strapping young man like that, spend his life just gourmandizing and doing damn all.

Nor did their comments stop there: they started accusing the priest of calling on Lisa for very uncanonical reasons: she still had very nice teeth and hair. And it was not only the bad workmen, the drunkards and loafers who placed this interpretation on his visits. Even the good tenants, the respectable workmen, decent fellows, made jokes about him as loudly as all the rest. The more broadminded amongst them said that priests were no different from anyone else, there were good ones and bad ones, but they ought to be made to marry to prevent them from disrupting other people's families.

In the end, after a brawl in the courtyard, a locksmith who had just received a black eye from Lambert shouted to him:

'Go and pick up your handout from the priest! Your Lisa's robbing the poor-box with what that black beetle of hers keeps giving her!'

The builder stormed upstairs and started knocking Lisa about, swearing that if he ever caught the priest up to his tricks, he'd do for him. And the very next day, the priest arrived just as Lambert was finishing his supper.

'Don't you touch him!' cried Lisa, terrified at the thought of a scandal. 'This gentleman doesn't mean any harm, he just wants us to get married, he says it would be more respectable.'

Lambert was too infuriated to listen.

'Clear off and don't you ever come here again,' he yelled. 'What the hell do you mean by interfering and trying to stop people from living the way they want!'

The priest waited calmly for a chance to reply and, speaking in a very quiet voice, tried to appeal to the better nature of this half-demented man: what would become of their children if they ever had any?

'Please listen to me, think of the future and get married.'

Lambert cut him short:

'Why not start by getting married yourself? Get yourself a

woman, but not mine, do you understand? And now clear off and sharp's the word!'

Father de Villeneuve hung his head and left. As he went downstairs, he could hear laughter all around: the neighbours had been listening to the row and were amused to see him beating such an ignominious retreat.

And as he went on his way, the priest imagined all the passersby looking at him and laughing, as if they knew of his discomfiture. Yes, the whole district disliked him and he could feel how completely all these city dwellers lay outside the influence of the church. His dream of reviving the faith of ordinary people and building the new society on it lay shattered. Dear God, were these the modern times that had already come? Would he have to look elsewhere for truth than in Catholic dogma, where he had always tried to find it hitherto? As his doubts increased, his inner struggle grew fiercer. He felt himself already launched on that slippery slope with other fervid and intelligent priests beset by religious scruples and unable to become Christian soldiers supporting the onward march of progress. And so, bruised and bleeding from their struggle, they eat out their hearts in pain and sorrow...

V

Monsignor was sitting in his study hidden away in the remote depths of the episcopal palace. He had announced that he would not be in for anyone, as he had a great deal of work that day. His secretary Father Raymond, a young priest of twenty-six, was alone with him, sitting at one end of the big rosewood desk on which the bishop was writing in his large, sprawling handwriting.

'Raymond,' he said, without looking up, 'take that batch of proofs and correct them. It's an article for *La Religion* that must be sent off to Paris at once. It's due to appear tomorrow.'

And he went back to his work. He was writing a pamphlet attacking the materialistic theories of a philosopher with whom he had been waging almost constant war for nearly a decade. He had a vigorous, biblical style; but he made a rather excessive use of anathema.

'Raymond,' he said again, after a long pause, 'will you find me the word "neurosis" in the medical dictionary... Yes, pass it to me.'

He dropped his pen and buried himself in the weighty tome. He read the article on neurosis which covered several pages. A whole section of his pamphlet revolved round the authenticity of certain miracles. Then, having acquired sufficient knowledge of the technical terms, he once again put pen to paper and scratched vigorously on. This scratching pen was the only sound to be heard; the town was plunged in wholesome provincial slumber.

Monsignor was a tall, athletic-looking old man of sixty, as thin as a rake, with a ravaged face to which his narrow nose added a note of implacable determination. He had shapely hands, with long tapering fingers suggesting his aristocratic origins: on his mother's side, he was descended from an old Auvergne family; but his father, a man of peasant stock who had risen in the world through his success in industry, had bequeathed him a far from aristocratic name which he was moreover quite happy to bear, taking pride in having raised it to its present eminence. His determined hands were being elegantly employed in the service of a superior class.

Monsignor had taken orders relatively late in life; he had originally been a colonel in the dragoons. It was not until the age of thirty-six that he had lost his taste for the military life, which had doubtless failed to provide him with the satisfactions he had expected. In the space of a few years he had joined the ranks of the most distinguished doctors of divinity and ever since he had been conducting his fierce and unrelenting struggle against the spirit of his age. He had been immediately acknowledged as an outstandingly vigorous polemicist and had swiftly risen to the upper hierarchy of the Church. If truth be told, he was now feverishly waiting to receive his red cardinal's hat, an ambition which he had fondly nursed ever since he had been ordained.

Monsignor had not disappointed the expectations of his superiors. This ex-colonel of dragoons seemed to think that he was still on the field of battle, smiting his enemies hip and thigh with his crozier. He fought in the newspapers, he fought with broadsheets, he used every weapon, including the most worldly ones. Above all, he should have been seen in his diocese, where he filled everyone with fear and trepidation. He had vanquished the whole *département*. He waged pitched battles against the civil authorities and would conduct a three months' campaign in order to obtain the dismissal of a gamekeeper to whom he had taken a dislike. For him, God was a policeman and nothing else; and he would threaten to call Him in at the slightest sign of insubordination amongst the rank and file.

Monsignor had in his study a large ivory figure of Christ on a cross of ebony, somewhat in the same way as you keep a bust of the reigning monarch in a town hall, purely as a symbol of authority. Monsignor rarely went down on his knees before his Christ; he preferred merely to make a rapid sign of the cross. But if there was any sign of revolt amongst the troops, the bishop would hold up his hand to the Christ on the cross as though appealing for help from the armed forces.

Meanwhile, Father Raymond had finished correcting the proofs of the article intended for the newspaper *La Religion*. Monsignor cast a quick eye over the article, put it in an envelope, rang his bell and had it sent straight off to the post.

'Tell me, Raymond,' he said after a moment's thought, 'which of these two titles do you prefer: *Judas discomfited* or *The Stupidity of Science*?'

But he did not give Father Raymond time to reply before making up his own mind, as he wrote *Judas discomfited* in large capitals at the top of his manuscript. Then he rang again and gave instructions for it to be sent off to the printers, 'and without delay', he added loudly to his usher.

'Excuse me, Monsignor,' the latter said, 'there are a number of people waiting who are very anxious to speak to you.'

'They can wait. If I'm free, I'll see them before lunch . . . Oh, and if the Marquis de Courneuve calls, show him in straightaway.'

Monsignor stood up and took a few paces round his study. Then he sat down briskly and said:

'Pass me my correspondence, Raymond. I'd like you to help me with it.'

His secretary placed an enormous bundle of letters on the table and picking them up one by one he opened them with a paper-knife and handed them to Monsignor, who ran his eye rapidly through them; he always insisted on seeing everything for himself. He sorted the letters as he read them, screwing up and throwing on the floor those which he considered unimportant and placing the others in piles.

This voluminous correspondence contained a little of everything: requests for aid, letters relating to diocesan affairs, letters
from every corner of France as well as overseas, concerning
the propagation of the faith. Occasionally Monsignor would
become absorbed in a letter and his sallow face would reflect
the complicated calculations of a statesman hatching vast schemes
of conquest. The threads of every possible clerical intrigue
would end up in this study and decisions affecting the most
substantial issues would be reached, questions of war or peace
between nations or matters of internal policy in which the
material and spiritual welfare of France was constantly at
stake.

But on this particular morning, the principal business was
happily not a European upheaval but merely the question as to
who should have the upper hand on an educational issue, the
préfet or Monsignor. The *préfet* who, although not a republican,
prided himself on his liberalism, had set up a lay school in the
little town of Verneuil; and Monsignor had sworn to replace it by
a Catholic denominational school. The battle had been raging for
six months now and both the *préfet* and Monsignor were digging
in their heels. There were already a good score of letters on the
subject in the file.

'The Marquis de Courneuve,' the usher announced.

Monsignor hurried over to greet the newcomer.

'Well?' he enquired anxiously.

'I'm just back from Paris,' replied the marquis. 'I saw the
Minister but I didn't want to broach the matter openly. If we
succeed, the *préfet* is talking of tendering his resignation and that
makes it rather a sensitive issue.'

'Anyway, what's the situation?'

'I wasn't able to have a categorical answer but I've asked my
mother-in-law to see what she can do and she has promised to let
you know as soon as a decision is reached.'

Monsignor could not refrain from making a gesture of impatience: he should have gone to Paris himself, for abominable
things were taking place in that school.

'Just look at these letters,' he said to the marquis. 'They've
given the children books to read in which religion is attacked...
I'm told that the schoolmaster has a sister who lived in sin with a
man for ten years before marrying him... I'm assured that at the

last municipal elections, that same schoolmaster was a member of a committee of troublemakers... Isn't all that enough?'

He went on to attack the *préfet*. This question of a lay school was an excellent opportunity of getting rid of an official completely lacking in any sort of religious feeling. It so happened that he had just received letters from a number of the town notables, all deeply religious people, who were acting in concert with him against the *préfet*. He showed the marquis their letters.

Madame de Saint-Luce, whose brother was a member of the *Chambre des Députés*, had written to say that her brother had been sending her excellent news. Monsieur Baudoin, a local lawyer with a great deal of influence in the town, had assured Monsignor that 'anyone who was anybody' was solidly on his side. Monsieur de Mortal quoted the following statement by the *préfet*: Clericalism is a cancerous growth in the *département*—dangerous and incautious words that could well be of use if conveyed to the proper government quarters... In fact, the *préfet* seemed all set to take a fall. It would be the third *préfet* in two years whom Monsignor had succeeded in unseating.

At that moment, the usher came in to inform the bishop that the parish priest of Villeneuve, an old man, had come sixteen miles on foot to present a petition to him.

'Tell him I can't see him now, he'll have to wait!' the prelate cried.

But the door had been left open and the priest himself came in. He was a poor old country priest in a threadbare cassock and wearing heavy dust-covered shoes. He came forward and said in a humble, quavering voice:

'Monsignor, you must please forgive me, I shouldn't have come to trouble you on my own behalf, but it's a matter that concerns our dear Lord, Monsignor. Our church at Villeneuve is so old that the recent storms have damaged the roof, the windows are all broken and the doors won't close, so that now the rain comes in on the chancel. The other day we had to put up an umbrella over the altar while I was saying Mass, so that the host shouldn't get wet... It's a dreadful state of affairs, Monsignor.'

'Well, what do you expect me to do about it?' retorted the bishop, visibly bored by the priest's longwinded explanation.

'You need only to say the word, Monsignor, and they'll repair our church. You have the authority.'

'That's where you're wrong, there are endless formalities involved... Draw up a proper report and we'll send someone to look at the damage and the matter will be dealt with through the appropriate channels.'

He rose to his feet to indicate that the interview was over but the old priest stood his ground, with tears in his eyes.

'Monsignor, I beseech you to help, it's not for my sake, it's for the sake of our dear Lord.'

The bishop lost his patience.

'I'm telling you I can't do a thing. Now, stop troubling me, you can see that I'm very busy.'

And in the unmistakable voice of a former colonel of dragoons, he snapped:

'Our dear Lord won't melt in the rain, for heaven's sake!'

Completely disconcerted and dismayed by Monsignor's wrath, the old priest backed out of the room, apologizing as he went, with his head trembling like a man in his dotage. He would have to walk the sixteen miles all the way back to Villeneuve, haunted by the thought that the rain would be pouring into his leaking church all that winter.

Meanwhile the usher had brought in a letter.

'It's my mother-in-law's handwriting!' exclaimed the Marquis de Courneuve glancing at the envelope.

Victory was theirs! In great excitement, standing by the window, Monsignor reread the letter in which the countess announced that she had seen the Minister and the lay school would be closed. She also informed him that the *préfet* had sent in his resignation.

'I shall be lunching with the Marquis de Courneuve, Raymond,' said the bishop. 'Tell the printers that I want the proofs of my pamphlet by tomorrow morning at the latest. We'll read the proofs together.'

And as he was making his way towards the door, his eyes happened to fall on his large ivory figure of Christ. He had almost forgotten to associate Him with his victory. So, as he bowed, he spoke these simple words to Monsieur de Courneuve, in the joyful tones of a soldier who has faith in the flag beneath which he serves:

'Marquis, by this sign we shall always defeat our foes!'

FAIR EXCHANGE

EVERY Saturday, as regular as clockwork, Ferdinand Sourdis would come into old Morand's shop to stock up on paints and brushes. The shop, which was nothing more than a damp and gloomy ground-floor room, overlooked a tiny square in the town of Mercoeur and stood in the shadow of a former convent, now converted into the local school where Ferdinand had been working for the last year as a very junior assistant master. Ferdinand, who was rumoured to have come from Lille, was an enthusiastic painter and spent all his spare time shut away in his room pursuing his hobby, although he never revealed the results of his work. He usually found himself dealing with old Morand's daughter Adèle who was herself a painter of delicate watercolours which aroused much comment in Mercoeur. He would place his order: 'Three tubes of white, please, one of yellow ochre and two of Veronese green,' and Adèle, who knew all about her father's business, would serve him, never failing to enquire:

'Do you need anything else?'

After the ritual 'That's all for now, thank you,' Ferdinand would slip his little package into his pocket and pay her with the sheepish look of a poor man always afraid of being snubbed. He would then leave the shop. This transaction had proceeded uneventfully on these lines for a whole year.

Old Morand's customers could be counted almost on the fingers of both hands. Mercoeur, a town of some eight thousand souls, was noted for its tanneries but the fine arts were not greatly cultivated, although there were four or five youths who daubed away under the pale eye of a lean Pole with a profile resembling that of a sick bird. The Lévèque girls, daughters of the local solicitor, had indeed taken up 'oils' but this was considered quite scandalous behaviour.

The only customer of note was the well-known painter Rennequin, a native of Mercoeur, who had achieved enormous success in the capital, winning many medals and commissions, and had recently been decorated. When he came to spend a month in Mercoeur in the summer, he caused an upheaval in the tiny shop in the Place du Collège. Morand would take endless trouble, even having paints sent specially from Paris. He would greet Rennequin hat in hand and enquire deferentially about his distinguished client's latest triumphs. The painter, a large, jovial man, had ended by accepting invitations to dinner and would cast a friendly eye over Adèle's watercolours which he declared to be a trifle pale but as fresh as a daisy.

'You might just as well do that as embroidery,' he would say, tugging her ear. 'And it's not too bad, either, there's a sort of astringency and determination in them that almost adds up to a personal style... So keep at it and let yourself go, just paint as you feel.'

Old Morand did not, of course, make his living from his shop. For him it was an inveterate hobby, a secret artistic bent that had never broken through but was now emerging in his daughter. He owned his house and he had benefited from a series of legacies; people reckoned he had an income of six or eight thousand francs a year. Despite this, he still sold artists' materials in his poky little ground-floor drawing-room whose window was the window of his shop: a narrow shop-window full of tubes of paint, sticks of Chinese ink and brushes and where occasionally some of Adèle's watercolours would appear, sandwiched between small sacred pictures painted by the Pole. Days would go by without a sign of a customer. All the same, old Morand's life was a happy one, surrounded by the smell of turpentine and varnish, and whenever Madame Morand, an ailing old woman who spent most of her time in bed, advised him to get rid of the shop, he would take offence, as a man dimly aware of fulfilling a mission in life. Though a middle-class reactionary at heart and strictly pious, his feeling of being a failed artist kept him attached to his paltry little shop. Where else would the townspeople be able to buy their paints? If the truth be known, nobody did buy any; but it was always possible that they might want to do so. He refused to abdicate.

Mademoiselle Adèle had grown up in this environment. She had just celebrated her twenty-second birthday. Short and a trifle plump, she had a pleasant-looking round face with narrow eyes; but she was so pale and sallow that nobody thought of her as pretty. She seemed like a little old woman; her complexion already had the faded look of a schoolmistress aged by the secret stresses of spinsterdom. However, Adèle was not looking to be married. There had been suitors but she had turned them all down. People thought that she was being haughty; no doubt she was waiting for some Prince Charming to come along; and there were unpleasant stories circulating with regard to the liberties which Rennequin, an old reprobate of a bachelor, might be taking with her. Very 'withdrawn', in common parlance, but in fact a thoughtful and taciturn girl, Adèle seemed quite unaware of such scandalmongering. Quite unrebellious by nature, she was used to living in the drab, damp atmosphere of the Place du Collège, having become accustomed since childhood to looking out at all hours of the day on to the same moss-covered paving sets and the same gloomy street crossing which nobody ever crossed; twice a day only, the pupils jostled and scurried along outside the school gates. It was her sole entertainment. Yet she was never bored. It seemed as if she was steadfastly pursuing a plan of action for her life drawn up by herself long ago. She was strong-willed, very ambitious and possessed inexhaustible patience, which led people to fail to understand her true nature. Gradually, they began to speak of her as an old maid. She seemed likely to be spending the rest of her days painting watercolours. However, when the famous Rennequin called and talked about Paris, she would listen in silence, pale-faced but with a sparkle in her tiny eyes.

'Why not send some of your watercolours in for the Salon?'* the painter asked her one day, in the unceremonious tone* he always used as an old friend of the family. 'I'll see to it that they're accepted.'

She gave a shrug and said without false modesty, though not without a touch of bitterness:

'Oh, it's woman's painting... It's not worth the trouble, you know!'

The coming of Ferdinand Sourdis had been quite an important event for old Morand's business. It meant an extra customer and an extremely valuable one, for no one in Mercoeur ever disposed of so many tubes of paint as he. For the first month, Morand gave the young man a great deal of attention, surprised to see such a passionate interest in art in one of those 'ushers' whom, after observing them going past his front door for nearly half a century, he had come to despise for their grubbiness and sloth.

But, according to what he heard, this one came from a good family which had come down in the world, so that after his parents' death he had been forced to accept any situation he could find in order not to starve. He was continuing to study painting with hopes of becoming independent, going to Paris and perhaps becoming famous. But a year went by and Ferdinand seemed to have become resigned to being stuck in Mercoeur by the need to earn his daily bread. Old Morand had become used to seeing him around and no longer paid him any special attention.

However, one evening his daughter asked him a surprising question. She had been busy drawing under the lamp, trying to reproduce, with mathematical accuracy, a photograph of a Raphael and after a lengthy silence, without looking up, she said:

'Why don't you ask Monsieur Sourdis to let you have one of his pictures, so that we could put it in the shop window?'

'My goodness, that's right!' exclaimed her father. 'What a good idea. I've never thought of asking to see what he does. Has he ever shown you anything?'

'No,' she replied. 'It was just a thought . . . At least we'd see the sort of thing he can do.'

Adèle had begun to be obsessed by Ferdinand. She had been greatly taken by his youthful good looks and his superb head of fair hair, which he wore very short, though his beard was long and silky, the colour of gold, and you could see his pink skin underneath. He had very gentle blue eyes while his dainty hands and fingers and dreamy, tender expression suggested a soft, sybaritic temperament. He would seem unlikely to be capable of exercising much will-power, except spasmodically. Indeed, on three previous occasions he had failed to come to work for three weeks; he had dropped his painting and rumour had it that the young man was behaving in a most deplorable manner in a certain house that was the shame of Mercoeur. As he did not return home for two nights running and was dead drunk when he did return one evening, there was talk for a while of dismissing him; but he was so charming when he was sober that they kept him on despite these escapades. Old Morand avoided mentioning these things to his daughter: these 'ushers' were all birds of a feather, a completely immoral lot; and as such conduct scandalized his middle-class sense of propriety, he had adopted a distant manner towards the young man, while still keeping a soft spot for the artist.

Nevertheless, thanks to the indiscreet gossip of their maid, Adèle knew all about Ferdinand's dissipated habits. However, she, too, said nothing although she thought a good deal about such matters and had felt so angry with the young man that she had made herself scarce as soon as she saw him coming towards the shop, so that she would not have to serve him. It was at this time that Ferdinand had begun to preoccupy her and all sorts of vague ideas had started stirring in her mind. He had become interesting. Each time he went by, she would follow him with her eyes and then, with her head bent over her watercolours, she would remain meditating for the whole day.

'Well, is he going to bring you a picture?' she asked her father one Sunday, having arranged the day before for her father to serve Ferdinand when he had called to make his purchases.

'Yes, he is,' replied Morand, 'but he took a lot of persuading. I don't know whether it was false modesty or not but he kept making excuses and saying that they weren't worth exhibiting. He's letting us have the picture tomorrow.'

Next day when Adèle came back from a visit to the old ruined castle of Mercoeur where she had gone sketching, she stopped in front of an unframed canvas placed on an easel standing in the middle of the shop and examined it closely. It was Ferdinand Sourdis's picture. It showed the bottom of a wide moat whose high green bank formed a horizontal line against the blue sky; in the moat, a group of schoolboys out for a walk were playing together, while the master in charge of them was lying in the grass reading. The painter had obviously drawn the subject from life; but what Adèle found quite disconcerting was a certain vibrancy of colour and a boldness of line which she herself would never have dared to attempt. In her own work she had reached such an extraordinary mastery of technique that she could achieve the elaborate effects of Rennequin and of some other painters whose work she admired; but in this unknown painter's temperament there was a new personal touch which took her by surprise.

'Well, what do you think of it?' asked her father who was standing behind her waiting to hear her opinion.

She was still looking. Finally, with some hesitation but finding the work none the less attractive, she murmured:

'It's interesting... It's very nice...'

She went back to look at the picture several times, with a serious expression on her face. Next day, as she was examining it again, Rennequin, who happened to be in Mercoeur, came into the shop and gave a slight exclamation:

'Goodness me! What's that?'

He was gazing at it in amazement. Then, drawing up a chair, he sat down in front of the painting and examined it in detail, with growing enthusiasm.

'It's very odd... There's such delicacy and truth in the tones... Just look at the white of those shirts against the green... And there's originality, too, a really individual note! Tell me, little girl, it can't have been you who painted that, surely?'

Adèle was listening, red in the face, as if these compliments were being addressed to herself. She replied hurriedly:

'Oh no, it's that young man, you know, the schoolteacher next door.'

'Really? It's a bit like your work,' the painter went on. 'Your work, but with more force... Oh, so it's that young man. Well, he's got talent, bags of talent. A picture like that would have a lot of success at the Salon.'

Rennequin happened to be dining with the Morands that evening, an honour he paid them each time he visited Mercoeur. He talked painting the whole evening, returning several times to the subject of Ferdinand Sourdis, whom he was promising himself to call on and encourage. Without saying a word, Adèle sat listening to him talking about Paris, and his life and triumphs in the capital. A pensive furrow was creasing her pale, girlish forehead, as though an idea was slowly creeping into her mind and refusing to go away.

Ferdinand's picture was framed and put on exhibition in the shop window; the Lévèque girls came to look at it but found it lacking in 'finish', while the very anxious Pole spread the rumour through the town that it represented a new school of painting which rejected Raphael. However, the picture was successful: people found it 'nice' and families flocked to identify the schoolboys depicted in it. Ferdinand's situation in the school was, however, not thereby improved. Some of the senior masters were scandalized by the stir caused by the 'usher' who had unscrupulously used as models the children placed in his care.

Nevertheless, the school agreed to keep him on, on condition that he promised to be more careful in future. When Rennequin called on Ferdinand to offer his congratulations, he found the young man very downhearted, almost in tears and talking of giving up painting altogether.

'Cheer up,' he said in his blunt, jovial way. 'You've got talent enough to snap your fingers at all those idiots. And don't worry, your day will come and you'll be able to escape from your present troubles, just as other fellow painters have done. In my time, I've worked as a bricklayer, you know. Meanwhile, the main thing is to keep on working.'

A new life now opened up for Ferdinand. He gradually became a friend of the Morands. Adèle had begun to copy his picture *The Walk*. She was determined to give up watercolours and try her hand at oils. Rennequin's comment had been very discerning: as an artist, she had the graceful qualities of the young painter but she lacked his masculinity; in any case, her style of painting was already similar to Ferdinand's with an even greater skill and flexibility which made light of technical difficulties. Her slow careful copying of his picture brought them closer together. Adèle took Ferdinand's technique to pieces, as it were, and soon mastered his methods so successfully that he was amazed to see this sort of artistic double who interpreted and gave a literal reproduction of his work with a completely feminine discernment. It was like him, full of charm but in a minor key. In Mercoeur, Adèle's copy had much greater success than Ferdinand's original. Meanwhile, all sorts of scandalous gossip was beginning to circulate about the couple.

In fact, Ferdinand gave little thought to such things. Adèle did not tempt him in the slightest; he had his own vicious habits which he was able to satisfy abundantly elsewhere and this left him completely cold towards this conventional middle-class girl whose sallow complexion and poor figure he found most unattractive. He treated her purely as a fellow painter. Their only conversation was about painting. His imagination was becoming fired; his talk was full of dreams of going to Paris and he would refer bitterly to his poverty that kept him stuck in Mercoeur. Ah, if only he had enough to live on, how he'd love to get away from schoolmastering! He felt sure he'd be successful. That miserable question of money and the need to earn his living threw him into a fury of anger. She would listen solemnly, seeming to be examining the question and weighing up his chances of success. Then, without going into any explanation, she would tell him not to be downhearted.

Suddenly, one morning, old Morand was found dead in his shop, struck down by apoplexy while unpacking a case of paints and brushes. A fortnight went by. Ferdinand had avoided intruding on the daughter's and her mother's grief. When he next called, nothing seemed changed. Adèle, dressed in black, was painting; Madame Morand was dozing in her bedroom. So they resumed their former habits, their conversations about art and dreams of triumphant success in Paris. However, the two young people now enjoyed a greater measure of intimacy, though a purely intellectual one, for no word of love or tenderness or over-familiarity ever came to disturb their friendship.

One evening, Adèle, more solemn than usual, after looking long and searchingly at Ferdinand, made up her mind to come to the point, doubtless feeling that by now she knew him well enough and that the time of decision had arrived.

'Listen, Ferdinand,' she said, 'I've been wanting to talk to you for a long time about a plan of mine. I'm alone in the world now, my mother hardly counts. So I hope you'll forgive me if I speak to you directly...'

Somewhat surprised, he sat waiting for her to continue. Then, quite without embarrassment, she reminded him how he was always complaining about his lack of money, that he could become famous in very few years if only he could find the initial backing which he needed to work independently and make his mark in Paris.

'Well,' she said finally, 'let me come to your rescue. My father has left me an income of eight thousand francs a year and I can have it straightaway because he also made provision for my mother. She doesn't need me.'

Ferdinand started protesting: he couldn't accept such a sacrifice, he couldn't possibly deprive her of her money. She stared at him, realizing that he had failed to understand.

'We would go and live in Paris,' she continued slowly, 'we could look forward to the future together.'

Then, seeing the scared look on his face, she smiled and, stretching out her hands, said to him in a frank, friendly voice:

'Ferdinand, will you marry me? You'd be doing me a favour, because you know I'm ambitious, I've always had dreams of becoming famous and I shall be, through you.'

He was at a loss for words, unable to recover from the shock of this sudden proposal, while she meanwhile calmly finished explaining the plan that she had been working out for so long. Finally, she adopted a motherly tone: she would require only one thing as part of her bargain: he must swear to behave properly. Genius was useless without orderliness. And she gave him to understand that she knew about his wild habits and though this did not deter her, she intended to reform him. Ferdinand understood the bargain she was offering him perfectly well: she was putting up the money, he would have to provide the fame for both of them. He didn't love her, he even felt at that moment repugnance at the thought of having to sleep with her. However, he went down on his knees to thank her, although he could find only these words to say to her, which sounded insincere to him as soon as they were uttered:

'You'll be my good angel . . .'

Then, despite the coldness of her nature, she felt a sudden surge of emotion: she hugged him and kissed him on the face. Her hitherto dormant passions were awakening; she was captivated by his blond good looks and the bargain she was striking was also providing a release for her long pent-up desires. She was in love.

Three weeks later, Ferdinand Sourdis had ceased to be a bachelor. He had capitulated, not as a premeditated scheme but because he had been driven to it by necessity and a set of circumstances from which he was unable to escape. The goodwill of old Morand's shop had been sold to a small local stationers'. Madame Morand was used to being alone and had accepted everything with great placidity. And so the young couple had set off at once for Paris, taking *The Walk* with them in their baggage and leaving Mercoeur in a state of shock at this sudden dramatic ending to its speculations. The Lévèque girls went about saying that Madame Sourdis would arrive in the capital just in time to have her baby.

2

It was Madame Sourdis who saw to the setting up of their home. It was a flat in the Rue d'Assas with a big bay-windowed studio overlooking the trees of the Luxembourg gardens. As the couple's resources were limited, Adèle performed miracles in producing a comfortable home without excessive expense. She wanted to keep Ferdinand close at hand and provide him with a studio that he would like. And indeed, in the beginning, their life together in the heart of the great capital was delightful.

Winter was drawing to an end. The fine days in early March were most agreeable. As soon as he learnt of the presence of the painter and his young wife, Rennequin hurried round to see him. Their marriage had not surprised him, although he was usually very critical of such matches between artists; according to him, they always turned out badly, for one of the two was bound to gobble up the other. So Ferdinand would gobble up Adèle and that would be that; and good luck to him, since he needed the money. He might as well have a rather unattractive girl in his bed as have to eat bad meals in cheap restaurants.

When Rennequin went in, he saw *The Walk*, elaborately framed, on an easel standing in the middle of the studio.

'Ha, ha!' he exclaimed jovially, 'I see you've brought the masterpiece with you!'

He sat down and once again launched into an admiring commentary on the delicacy of the tones and originality of conception of the picture. Then, suddenly:

'I hope you'll put it in for the Salon. It's bound to be a great success... You've come just in time.'

'That's exactly what I've been advising him to do,' said Adèle quietly, 'but he can't make up his mind, he'd like to make his début with something bigger and more complete.'

On hearing this, Rennequin became very annoyed. Youthful works were born under an especially lucky star. Ferdinand might perhaps never again find the freshness of impression, the boldness and lack of sophistication of this first work. Only an idiot could fail to realize that. Adèle smiled at the violence of his tone. Her husband was surely destined for great things and she had every hope that he would go on and paint something better; but she was delighted to hear Rennequin taking such a strong stand against Ferdinand's strange last-minute qualms. So it was agreed that *The Walk* should be submitted the very next day; the final entry date for the Salon was only three days off. There was no doubt that the picture would be accepted, for Rennequin was one of the judges and extremely influential.

The Walk was indeed accepted and had enormous success. For six weeks, the public thronged in front of the painting and, as often happens in Paris, Ferdinand became famous overnight. He

Fair Exchange

even had the luck to arouse controversy, which doubled his success. While there were no outright attacks, some people criticized certain details which others passionately defended. In a word, *The Walk* was deemed to be a minor masterpiece and the official authorities immediately offered to buy it for six thousand francs. It had the necessary spice of originality to whet the jaded appetite of the majority of the public without any outrageous display of temperament on the part of the painter which might have offended some people: in a word, the exact mixture of novelty and vigour that the public required. It was a magical balance of pleasant qualities and people acclaimed the advent of a new star in the artistic firmament.

While her husband was suddenly enjoying such rapturous praise from the press and the general public alike, Adèle, who had submitted a few of her Mercoeur works, some very delicate watercolours, received no notice whatsoever, either from the visitors to the Salon or in the newspapers. But she was not envious and did not even feel hurt in her artistic pride; her pride was entirely bound up with her handsome Ferdinand. This withdrawn girl who had been mouldering away in the damp and gloomy depths of the provinces for twenty-two years, this frigid, sallow-faced, conventional little miss had suddenly turned into an extraordinarily passionate woman, in heart and mind. She worshipped Ferdinand's golden beard, his pink flesh, the grace and charm of his whole person; she was jealous of him and unhappy when he was away for even a short time; she kept constant watch over his movements, for fear that some other woman might steal him from her. When she looked at herself in the mirror, she was acutely conscious of her inferiority, her dumpy figure and her already fading complexion. It was he, not she who provided the beauty in their marriage and she even felt she owed him what she should have claimed herself. Her heart melted at the thought that everything came from him. She would reflect in admiration on his masterly skill as a painter and would be filled with boundless gratitude at the realization that she was an equal partner in his talent, his success, his celebrity and that she would be able to rise to dazzling heights of fame at his side. All her dreams were coming true, not now through herself but through another self whom she loved as a disciple, as a mother and as a wife. And even, in her heart of hearts, her pride would whisper to her that Ferdinand would be her creation and that, after all, everything was owed to her.

During these first few months, life in the studio in the Rue d'Assas was sheer magic, day in, day out. Despite her feeling that so much of what she had came from Ferdinand, Adèle did not feel in the least humiliated, for the thought that it was she who had been instrumental in bringing all this to pass was sufficient. With a tender smile on her lips, she watched the blossoming happiness which she had sought and engineered. Without pettiness or meanness of any sort, she could say to herself that it was her money and her money alone which had made this happiness possible. So she kept her place, realizing that she was necessary. Her admiration and worship was a tribute freely given by a person glad to abdicate her personality in support of a work that she looked on as her own and on which she intended to live. In the Luxembourg gardens, the tall trees were putting on green leaves, the twittering of birds floated into the studio on the warm breezes of the lovely spring days and every morning fresh newspapers would arrive, full of praise. Ferdinand was being photographed and his painting was being reproduced by every possible process and in every possible format. And so with childlike joy, the young newly-weds basked in this blaze of publicity, in the knowledge that, as they sat eating together at their little table in their charming quiet retreat in the Rue d'Assas, Paris, that great and glorious capital, was interested in them.

Meanwhile Ferdinand had not yet begun working again. He was living in so great a fever of excitement that he claimed he was incapable of handling a brush as he would have liked. Three months went by and still he kept putting off his studies for a large picture which he had long had in mind to paint: a painting which he had baptized *The Lake*. It would depict an avenue in the Bois de Boulogne, seen at the time of day when the long queue of carriages drives slowly along in the golden light of the setting sun. He had already been to make a few sketches but he no longer seemed to feel the divine spark that had inspired him during his hard times as a poverty-stricken usher. His present well-being seemed to have quenched his ardour; also, he was enjoying his sudden fame too much to want to risk forfeiting it in a fresh work. For the moment, he was always out and about, frequently vanishing in the morning and not reappearing until evening. On two or three occasions, he came home very late. He was always finding different pretexts to go out and not come back: he would be visiting a studio or a show by some contemporary artist; he had to collect material for his future work; above all, he was dining out with friends. He had run across a number of his old Lille friends, he was already a member of several artistic groups; all these activities launched him on a continual round of pleasure and he would come home in a state of feverish exhilaration, with shining eyes and talking very loudly.

As yet Adèle had refrained from making any protest. Although extremely unhappy at his growing self-indulgence which was depriving her of her husband and leaving her constantly alone at home, she was trying to stifle her jealousy and fears: Ferdinand had to manage his own affairs; an artist wasn't a grocer who could stay comfortably by his own fireside; he had to go out into society, he owed it to himself to further his reputation. She almost felt remorse at her secret resentment when Ferdinand put on his act of a man worn out by social obligations, swearing that he was 'fed up' and that he would have given his right arm to be able to stay at home with his darling little wife. Once it was even she herself who sent him off when he was pretending to be reluctant to go to an exclusively male luncheon party where he would be introduced to a very wealthy collector. Then, left alone, Adèle would cry. She was trying to be brave and yet she was continually imagining her husband with other women; she felt that he was being unfaithful and this made her so unwell that sometimes she had to take to her bed as soon as he had left the flat.

Rennequin would often call to pick up Ferdinand and she would try to joke about it:

'Now, you'll be good little boys, won't you? You know, I'm putting him in your charge...'

'Don't worry,' the painter would laugh. 'If someone tries to make off with him, I'll be there.... In any case, I'll bring back his hat and stick, at least.'

She trusted Rennequin. Since he, too, was going out with Ferdinand, the outing must be justified. She'd get used to it. But she would sigh when she remembered their first few weeks together in Paris, before all the upset caused by the Salon and they used to spend their days happily together in the studio. Now she was the only one working there, for she had gone back to her watercolour painting with frantic energy, to while away the time. As soon as Ferdinand had disappeared round the corner of the street with a final farewell wave, she would close the window and settle down to her task. He was gallivanting about all over the town, God alone knew where, visiting all sorts of shady haunts and coming home dog-tired, with bloodshot eyes, while she sat patiently at her little table, all day and every day, doggedly painting the studies for pictures that she had brought with her from Mercoeur, sentimental little landscapes that she was painting with an increasingly impressive skill. She described it, with a wry smile, as her embroidery.

One evening she had stayed up late waiting for Ferdinand, absorbed in a pencil drawing of an engraving, when she was startled to hear a dull thud just outside the studio door. She called out and then decided to open the door, where she discovered her husband slowly getting to his feet, with an inane laugh. He was drunk.

As white as a sheet, Adèle helped him to his feet and half dragged, half lifted him into their bedroom. He kept apologizing; his speech was slurred and incoherent. Without a word, she helped him to undress. Then, when he was drunkenly snoring in bed, completely dead to the world, she spent the rest of the night, wide awake in an armchair, her pale forehead furrowed in thought. Next morning, she made no mention of his scandalous behaviour of the previous night. He was deeply embarrassed and still bemused, with swollen eyes and a bitter taste in his mouth. His wife's silence increased his embarrassment and for two whole days he stayed at home and shamefacedly set to work on his painting, like a schoolboy eager and anxious to be forgiven for some misdemeanour. He set about laying out the main lines of his picture, consulting Adèle and trying hard to show how much he valued her judgement. At first, she remained coldly silent, as a living reproach, although still making not the slightest reference to what had occurred. Then, seeing how contrite he was, she became her natural, kindly self again; everything was tacitly forgiven and forgotten. But on the third day, Rennequin came to pick up his young friend to take him to dinner at the Café Anglais* to meet a well-known art critic. Adèle had to wait up until four o'clock for her husband and when he did eventually come home, he was bleeding from an open cut over his left eye, caused by a bottle in the course of a brawl in some low haunt. She put him to bed and dressed his wound. Rennequin had left him on the boulevards at eleven o'clock.

From now on, the pattern was set. Ferdinand could never accept an invitation to dinner or a party or stay out in the evening on some pretext or other without coming home in a revolting state. He would be frightfully tipsy, black and blue from bruises, with his clothes in disorder and reeking to high heaven of spirits or the cheap scents favoured by street-walkers. He had got into a vicious rut from which his spineless character made it impossible for him to escape. Adèle maintained her stony silence; each time it happened she would tend him with icy indifference, never questioning him, never even slapping his face for his abominable behaviour. She would make him tea, hold a bowl for him to be sick into, clean up after him, refusing to wake the maid in order to keep his condition to herself, since it was too disgusting for a decent person to reveal to anyone. Anyway, what would have been the point of questioning him? Each time it took place, she could easily reconstruct the scene: a few drinks with friends to set him going, a wild rampage through the unsavoury night haunts of the capital, drunken debauchery, crawling from bar to bar with stray drinking companions, picking up women on the streets, brawling with soldiers for their favours and finally satisfying his squalid lust in some filthy little attic room. Sometimes she would discover strange addresses stuffed into his pockets and unmentionable objects, all sorts of disgusting evidence which she would hastily burn in order not to learn about such things. When one of his women had scratched him with her nails or he had come home filthy and injured, she would merely take a tighter hold on herself and wash him in such scornful silence that he did not dare to utter a word. Then, the day after these spectacular nights of riotous living, he would wake up and find her as tight-lipped as ever; as neither of them mentioned it, it seemed to them that they had both lived through a bad dream. And so life would begin again as before.

Only once, in a fit of uncontrollable tenderness, Ferdinand had suddenly flung both arms round her neck when he woke up. He was sobbing as he gasped brokenly:

'Forgive me, oh please forgive me!'

Obviously disconcerted, she had pretended to be surprised and pushed him away, saying:

'What do you mean, forgive you? You haven't done anything to forgive. I'm not grumbling.'

And this dogged refusal to acknowledge his shortcomings and her female superiority in self-control and mastery of her emotions had made Ferdinand feel like a naughty little boy.

In fact, Adèle's attitude was concealing agonized disgust and anger. Both her religious upbringing and her sense of decency and human dignity were completely outraged by Ferdinand's behaviour. Each time he came home stinking of vice and she had to touch him with her hands and spend the rest of the night smelling his breath, she was filled with nausea and contempt. But beneath the contempt, there lay a dreadful jealousy directed at his friends and at the women who sent him back to her so soiled and degraded. She would have enjoyed seeing those women dying in the gutter; she thought of them as monsters and could not understand why the police didn't shoot them on sight. But her love was undiminished. When, on certain nights, the man himself filled her with disgust, she would console herself by her admiration for the artist; and this admiration became in a way purified, for with her conventional middle-class notion of the typical man of genius fated to live a wild bohemian life, she had ended by accepting Ferdinand's conduct as being the dunghill on which alone great works of art could flourish. Indeed, if, as a woman, she was shocked by his callous disregard for her own affection and delicacy of feeling, she blamed him perhaps even more strongly for his failure to fulfil his obligations as an artist, for breaking the pact they had made whereby she would supply the material means in return for which he would provide the fame. It was a breach of faith which she deeply resented and she began to cast about to find ways and means of rescuing the painter even should the man sink without trace. It was up to her to be strong for it was she who now had to be the master.

In less than a year, Ferdinand felt himself reduced to the level of a little boy; he had fallen completely under Adèle's thumb. In this survival of the fittest, she had proved to be the male. Each time he had fallen by the wayside and, sternly but without uttering a word of blame, she had condescended to care for him, he had hung his head in shame and humiliation, sensing her contempt. There was no room for lies between them: she represented sweet reasonableness, decency and strength while he was the epitome of weakness and degradation. The thing which he found most painful and made him utterly powerless in her presence was the fact that her implacable condemnation was based on full knowledge of his guilt and her cold contempt was capable of forgiving without feeling the need to reprimand him. It was as if any explanation would destroy their dignity as a couple. She was maintaining her silence in order to remain high above him and not abase herself, with the risk of being sullied by his filth. Had she lost her temper, had she flung his despicable one-night amours in his face like any frantic, jealous wife, he would certainly have suffered less. If she had been prepared to come down to his level, she might have raised him up; but how small he felt, how immeasurably inferior, when he woke up, ashamed and fully aware that she knew all but would never lower herself to utter one word of reproof!

Meanwhile, his picture was progressing, for he had realized that his only superiority lay in his painting. When he was working, Adèle would once again become the tender-hearted wife and bring herself down to his level; she would stand respectfully behind him and study his picture and the better his day's work had been, the more deferential she would become. At such times, it was he who was the master; the male was asserting his proper role in the family. But he was now becoming subject to paralysing fits of laziness. When he came home exhausted, as if drained of energy by the sort of life he was leading, his hands felt weak, he was full of hesitation, he could no longer paint decisively. Some mornings, his whole being seemed gripped by an overwhelming feeling of impotence. At such times, he would fritter away the whole day in front of his easel, picking up his palette only to fling it down again a moment later, fretting and fuming with rage and unable to do anything at all; or else he would lie down and sleep like a log on the settee, not waking up until evening with an appalling migraine. On these days, Adèle would watch him in silence, creeping around on tiptoe in order not to irritate him or scare away the inspiration that would surely come. She believed in inspiration, that invisible flame that would dart in through the window and settle on the chosen artist's brow. And then she, too, would be seized by discouragement and anxiety at the thought, as yet not clearly formulated, that Ferdinand might fail her, like a defaulting business partner.

It was February and the Salon was approaching. *The Lake* was still not nearly completed. The main part had been done, inasmuch as the canvas was entirely covered; but apart from certain sections that were quite well advanced, all the rest was blurred and unfinished. It was barely more than a rough sketch and could certainly never be submitted in that state. It needed to be pulled together, it lacked the highlights and the finish which gives a work its value as a painting. Ferdinand was now making no progress whatsoever, losing himself in finicky details, undoing in the evening what he had painted during the day, spinning helplessly like a frenzied top. One evening as dusk was falling, when Adèle returned from a distant shopping excursion, she heard the sound of sobs coming from the darkened studio and was moved to see her husband sitting slumped on his chair in front of his easel.

'You're crying!' she exclaimed. 'What's the matter?'

'No, nothing's the matter,' he replied brokenly.

He had sunk into his chair and for the last hour had sat gazing vacantly at his canvas, even when the failing light had made it invisible. Everything was dancing in front of his blurred eyes. His work seemed to him an absurd, pitiful and chaotic mess and he felt paralysed, as weak as a child, powerless to bring any sort of order into this confused mass of colours. Then, when darkness had gradually hidden the canvas and even the brighter colours had been obliterated, he had been overcome by an immense sadness which seemed to be throttling him. It was then that he had burst into sobs.

'But you are crying, I can feel it,' said Adèle, running her hands over his cheeks bathed in warm tears. 'Are you in pain?'

He was choked by a renewed burst of sobbing and was unable to reply. Then, forgetting her resentment and giving way to her compassion for this poor, failed creature, she gave him, in the darkness, a motherly kiss. He was bankrupt.

3

Next day Ferdinand had to go out after lunch and when he came back a couple of hours later, as he was standing as usual absorbed in front of his painting, he suddenly gave a muttered exclamation:

'Well I'm damned! Someone's been touching my picture.'

Part of the sky and a small section of foliage on the left had been finished. Adèle was bending over her table busily concentrating on one of her watercolours and at first made no comment.

'Who on earth can have taken such a liberty?' Ferdinand went on, more surprised than annoyed. 'Has Rennequin been in?'

'No,' said Adèle at last, 'it was me, I did it just for fun. It's not at all important, I only did some of the background.'

Ferdinand gave an embarrassed laugh.

'So you want to collaborate with me, do you? Well, I think you've got the general tone very nicely, only there's one highlight there that needs toning down a bit.'

'Where's that?' she enquired, getting up from her table. 'Oh yes, I see, it's that branch.'

She picked up a brush and made the necessary alteration, while he stood watching her. After a pause, he began to make other suggestions, as though speaking to a pupil, while she went on painting the sky. Without anything being said, it became understood that she would undertake to finish off the backgrounds. Time was short and they had to hurry... And he pretended that he was not feeling very well, a statement that she accepted without demur.

'As I'm not very fit at the moment,' he would say, 'your help is going to come in very useful. The backgrounds aren't all that important...'

From that moment, he was completely reconciled to the sight of her standing in front of his easel. Now and again he got up from the settee with a yawn and came over to have a look and pass a brief judgement on the work, sometimes making her go over some of it again. As a teacher, he was very strict. Next day, still complaining that he was feeling even more under the weather, he told her that she should first go ahead with the backgrounds before he finished the foregrounds himself; he felt that that would make the work easier, the situation would be clearer and they would progress more rapidly. So he was able to enjoy a week of utter idleness, spending long periods asleep on the settee while his wife stood all day painting in silence. Then he bestirred himself and tackled the foregrounds. However, he did not want her to go far away and whenever he grew impatient, she would calm him down and herself complete the details as he pointed them out to her. She would often send him off into the Luxembourg gardens to take a breath of fresh air: as he wasn't feeling very well, he must take care of himself; it was doing him no good at all to get excited like that. Her concern was very affectionate. Then, once he was out of the way, she set rapidly to work with feminine determination, not hesitating to get on with the foregrounds as quickly as possible. He had reached such a state of enervation that he did not even notice how much she had done while he was away or, at any rate, he made no comment on it; he seemed to think that the painting was going ahead all on its own. Within the fortnight, *The Lake* was completed. But Adèle herself was not satisfied. She still felt that something was definitely lacking. When a relieved Ferdinand declared that the picture was very good, she shook her head unenthusiastically.

'What on earth do you want, then?' he snapped angrily. 'We can't kill ourselves doing it!'

What she wanted was for him to give the picture his own personal touch and, by dint of patience and willpower, she managed to perform the miracle of infusing him with sufficient energy to do it. For one more week, she nagged at him and encouraged him. He never left the flat; she aroused him with her caresses and intoxicated him with her admiration. Then, once she felt that he was sufficiently stimulated, she thrust his brushes into his hand and kept him standing for hours in front of his picture, talking, discussing and generally putting him into such a state of excitement that he was like a giant refreshed. In this way he reworked the whole picture, going back over what Adèle had done and adding the vigorous individual touch which it lacked. It might not have seemed much but in fact it was everything: the entire painting had come to life.

Adèle was overjoyed. Once again, the future looked rosy. Since working long hours tired her husband, she would help him. It would be a more private mission, a secret happiness which filled her with hope. But she jokingly made Ferdinand swear not to reveal her part in the painting: it wasn't worth mentioning, it would embarrass her. He expressed surprise but made his promise. He felt no jealousy towards Adèle as an artist; he always went about saying that she knew the painter's trade better than he, which was true.

When Rennequin came to see *The Lake*, he stood looking at it for a long time without saying a word. Then he offered his young friend his very sincere congratulations.

'It's certainly more finished than *The Walk*,' he said. 'The background's incredibly light and delicate and the foreground's very spirited and vigorous... Yes, it's really good, really original.'

He was obviously surprised but he did not reveal the reason for his surprise. This young fellow-me-lad had nonplussed him; he would never have thought him capable of such skilful technique; he also found something new in his painting. All the same, although he did not say so, he preferred *The Walk*, for although certainly more slipshod and less polished, it was more personal. So, despite the surer, broader, treatment of *The Lake*, he still found it less attractive because he could detect in it a more conventional, deliberate, approach, with a hint of prettiness and over-elaboration. This impression did not prevent him from saying as he left:

'Remarkable, my dear boy... You're going to be a tremendous success.'

His prophecy came true. The success of *The Lake* was even greater than that of *The Walk*. The women particularly raved about it: it was exquisite. The carriages with their flashing wheels gliding along in the sunshine, the tiny fashionably dressed figures, the bright specks of colour bringing out the vivid greenery of the Bois, charmed those members of the public who look upon painting as a decorative art similar to that of a goldsmith. But even severe critics, those who expect vigour and logic from a work of art, were attracted by its painterly skills, an excellent understanding of overall effect and its rare level of execution. But the predominant impression, the one which finally won the total approval of the general public, was the graceful, slightly finical, individuality of the style. All the critics agreed that Ferdinand Sourdis was 'coming on well'. Only one of them, notoriously outspoken and heartily disliked for his imperturbable way of speaking the truth, dared to write that, should the painter continue to elaborate and emasculate his style, he would give him less than five years to ruin his precious gift of originality.

In the Rue d'Assas, there was great satisfaction. This was no longer the unexpected success of a tyro but a definitive recognition that Ferdinand ranked among the best painters of the age. What is more, he was becoming prosperous: commissions were beginning to flow in from every quarter, and buyers were competing, cash in hand, for the little canvases left lying about in his studio. He had to get down to work.

Amidst this new-found prosperity, Adèle kept her head. She was not miserly but she had been brought up in that provincial tradition of economy which, as they say, knows the value of money. As a result, she showed herself a strict manager and saw to it that Ferdinand never failed to honour his commitments. She would make careful note of his commissions, ensure that they were completed on time, and invest the proceeds. Above all, she exercised relentless pressure on her husband and ruled him with a rod of iron.

She had laid down his way of life: so many hours' work before he could relax. However, she never lost her temper; she remained, as always, dignified and sparing of words; but he had behaved so badly in the past and had allowed her to assume such an ascendancy over him that he was now terrified of her. This was certainly the greatest possible service that she could have done him, for without her willpower to sustain him, he would have let things slide and not produced the works which, in fact, he now managed to produce over a number of years. She was his greatest strength, his guide and support. This fear which she inspired in him did not, however, prevent him from sometimes relapsing into his former disorderly ways; as she refused to pander to his vicious habits, he would break out and launch into wild bouts of debauchery, returning home ill and in a state of stupor that would last three or four days. But each time this happened, he was providing her with fresh ammunition to use against himself. She would look at him with eyes full of an even greater and more pitiless contempt which would chain him to his easel for a week. She suffered too much as wife and woman whenever he betrayed her for her ever to want him to indulge in these escapades from which he returned in such a repentant and obedient state; all the same, whenever she recognized the symptoms, his pale eyes, his restless, urgent gestures, and realized that he was racked by lust, she could hardly wait to see him come reeling back off the streets, a nerveless jelly of a man who would be like wax in her determined, stumpy hands. With her plain face, her dull complexion, her leathery skin and big bones, she knew that she was indeed no beauty and so she took her revenge on this handsome man, who belonged to her, as soon as his fancy women had bled him white. Moreover, Ferdinand was ageing rapidly; he had been afflicted by rheumatism, and by the age of forty his manifold excesses had already turned him into an old man. Age would inexorably clip his wings.

After *The Lake* there was a tacit agreement between husband and wife that they should collaborate. They still kept it a secret but behind closed doors, they would set to work on the same picture and make it a joint effort. Ferdinand supplied his masculine gift of inspiration and construction; it was he who would choose the subject, divide it into the appropriate parts and establish the general layout. The execution of the project would then be handed over to the feminine talent of Adèle, although Ferdinand would keep certain vigorous passages for himself to paint. Indeed, at the beginning, he did most of the painting himself and made a point of not letting his wife help him except in minor parts of the picture; but as his strength decreased and he gradually lost heart in his work, he gave up the struggle and let Adèle take over. So, in the nature of things, her collaboration inevitably increased with each new work, without any intention on her part to replace his painting by her own. What she primarily wanted was for the name of Sourdis, which was now hers as well, not to disappear ingloriously, for his fame, which had been this plain, deprived girl's constant dream, not to decline; and, furthermore, she wanted not to let their customers down, to deliver the pictures on the promised date, like an honest business woman whose word is her bond. The result was that she inevitably found herself forced to complete the paintings in a hurry, to fill in the gaps left by Ferdinand and finish the work off when she could see him fuming with impotent rage and unable to hold his brushes in his trembling hands. However, she never gloated and always maintained the pretence of being the pupil, of restricting her task to that of a journeyman working under her husband's instructions. She still respected him as an artist and genuinely admired him, with the instinctive intuition that, despite his degradation, he was still the master without whom she would never have been capable of producing such large-scale paintings.

Rennequin was following with growing surprise and incomprehension this slow supplanting of the male by the female temperament in their work, although they kept their secret from him as from all their other fellow painters. Rennequin felt that Ferdinand could hardly be considered to be strictly on the wrong track since he was, after all, continuing to produce and keep his head above water; but his painting was evolving in a direction that seemed out of line with his earlier work. His first picture, *The Walk*, had revealed a lively, witty individuality; this had vanished from his later work which was now increasingly swamped in a soft, fluid *impasto*, very easy on the eye but more and more banal. And yet it was the same hand at work; at least, Rennequin would have sworn that it was, so adept had Adèle become at imitating her husband's technique. She had a genius for taking other people's methods to pieces and adapting herself to them. On the other hand, Ferdinand's paintings were now taking on a kind of vaguely puritanical middle-class feeling of propriety which the old painter found offensive. In the beginning he had welcomed the very great freedom of spirit shown by his gifted young friend and he was now irritated to see this new formality, a sort of starchy prudishness, in his later painting. One evening, in a group of fellow artists, he could no longer restrain himself.

'That fellow Sourdis is turning into nothing more than a preacher!' he exclaimed. 'Have you seen his latest painting? It's sheer milk and water. All those tarts of his have squeezed him dry. It's the old, old story: you let some stupid female gobble you up... Do you know what makes me really mad? The fact that he can still paint quite well. You may laugh, but I mean it! I'd always imagined that if he went off the rails, he'd do it on a grand scale and finish up an utter shambles, like a man sunk without trace. Not a bit of it! He seems to have found a sort of clockwork mechanism which he can wind up every day and it enables him to churn out his boring stuff *ad infinitum*. It's a disaster! He's finished; he can't even paint badly!'

They were used to Rennequin's paradoxical outbursts and merely laughed. But he knew what he meant and, being fond of Ferdinand, he felt sad about it.

Next day he called in at the Rue d'Assas. Seeing the key in the door, he took the liberty of going in without knocking and stopped short in amazement. There was no sign of Ferdinand and Adèle was standing in front of the easel, deftly finishing off a picture which the papers had already started talking about. She was so completely absorbed in her work that she did not hear the door opening and did not realize that when the maid had come in, she had left the key in the door. Rennequin was thus able to stand watching her for a good minute. She was carrying out her task with a sureness of touch indicative of long practice and putting on the paint with the fluency and facile mechanical perfection which he had been berating the day before. All at once, he understood what had happened and the shock was so great that, realizing the full extent of his indiscretion, he was on the point of going out and knocking on the door before coming in again. But at that moment, Adèle looked round.

'Good gracious, it's you!' she exclaimed. 'How did you get in?'

And she went very red in the face. Rennequin, equally embarrassed, replied that he had only just arrived; but, realizing that if he made no reference to what he had seen the situation would be even more embarrassing, he added in his most hearty manner:

'Well, well, I can see that we've been running short of time! You've been lending Ferdinand a hand...'

Her complexion had returned to its normal waxen pallor. She replied calmly:

'Yes, this picture should have been handed over last Monday and as Ferdinand has been suffering from his pains again... Oh, it's just a couple of glazes, nothing of any consequence.'

But she was not deceiving herself; she knew that it was impossible to fool someone as expert as Rennequin. Nevertheless, she made no move but merely stood where she was, still holding her palette and brushes in her hands. He felt obliged to say something:

'Don't let me disturb you, just keep going.'

She gazed at him for a few seconds before making up her mind what to do. What was the point of further pretence, now that he knew everything? And as she had given her word that the picture would be ready that evening, she quickly set to work again, with a completely unfeminine firmness and boldness of touch. Drawing up a chair, Rennequin followed her work. At this moment, Ferdinand came in. At first he seemed shocked to see Rennequin sitting behind Adèle and watching her at work on his picture. But he looked very tired and hardly capable of any strong reaction. He sank on to a chair beside the older painter, with the sigh of a man whose only need is sleep. Silence fell. Ferdinand did not feel that any explanation was required: that was how things were and he didn't mind. However, after a moment, when Adèle was reaching up and slashing bold strokes of vivid colour on to her sky, he leaned over towards Rennequin and said in a voice full of pride:

'You know, old man, she's better than me! How about that technique, eh? Isn't she stylish!'

Later, when Rennequin left, perplexed and quite upset, once he was alone on the staircase he gave vent to his feelings out loud:

'There's another good man gone west! She may stop him from going under but she'll never let him reach the top! He's buggered!'

4

Years went by. The Sourdis had bought a little house in Mercoeur, with a garden looking out on to the Esplanade. At first they came to spend a couple of months there every summer to escape from the stifling Paris heat in July and August. It was a sort of permanent retreat. But, gradually, they lived there more and more. As they settled in and made themselves a home, they felt less and less need for Paris. Since the accommodation was rather cramped, they had a very spacious studio built in the garden and soon enlarged it with further additions. Now they found themselves going to the capital during the winter, two or three months at most; they lived in Mercoeur and kept only a small flat in Paris, some rooms in a small house which belonged to them, situated in the Rue de Clichy.*

This withdrawal to the country had thus taken place gradually, with no particular foresight on their part. When people expressed surprise, Adèle would talk about Ferdinand's poor health and give the impression that her hand had been forced by the need to provide her husband with a peaceful open-air environment. But the truth was that she was fulfilling at last a long cherished dream. As a girl she had sat for hours looking at the wet cobble-stones of the Place du Collège and she had indeed dreamt of a brilliant future in Paris, amid the plaudits of the crowd, basking in the fame of the name of Sourdis; but now her dream did not extend beyond Mercoeur, in a quiet little corner of the tiny town surrounded by the respectful admiration of its surprised inhabitants. It was here that she had been born and here that she had felt the continual spur of her ambition to succeed, so much so, indeed, that the amazement of the good women of Mercoeur gossiping on their doorsteps, as she walked by arm-in-arm with her husband, meant more to her than all the praise of the sophisticated denizens of Paris drawing-rooms. At heart, she had remained a provincial middle-class woman concerned at how her little town would view each new triumph; every time she went back there, her heart would beat faster and she would purr with inner satisfaction at the thought of the way in which her obscure beginnings had blossomed into the fame which now surrounded her. Her mother had died some ten years ago and she was merely coming back to recover her lost youth which had been dormant and repressed in her earlier years.

By now the name of Sourdis could hardly have been more famous: at fifty, the painter had received every conceivable award and honour, all the obligatory medals and crosses and titles. He was a Commander of the Legion of Honour and had been a member of the Academy for a number of years. The only thing that was still expanding was his wealth; newspapers had long since run out of superlatives. There were now ready-made formulas of praise which were trotted out at every opportunity: he was the 'prolific master'; he had 'exquisite charm which won every heart'. But such things no longer seemed to interest him; he was becoming indifferent and wore his halo like an old suit which he had ceased to notice. When the inhabitants of Mercoeur saw him go by, with his eyes glazed, already terribly round-shouldered, their respect was strongly tinged with astonishment for they found it difficult to conceive how this weary, withdrawn old man came to be so famous in the capital.

In any case, by now everyone knew that Madame Sourdis used to help her husband in his painting. She had the reputation of being a most capable woman, although she was so tiny and very stout. Indeed, this was another cause for astonishment in Mercoeur, that such a plump lady could stand all day in front of an easel without her legs giving way by the evening. Must be just a question of habit, opined the worthy citizens of Mercoeur. This collaboration from his wife had had no adverse effect on

Ferdinand's reputation, indeed quite the reverse. With her infallible tact, Adèle had realized that she must not openly expose her husband as a man of straw; he still signed the paintings, like a constitutional monarch who reigns but does not rule. Works by Madame Sourdis would have impressed no one, whereas works by Ferdinand Sourdis retained all their old power over critics and public alike. For this reason, she always showed the greatest admiration for her husband and, strangely enough, this admiration was perfectly genuine. Although he had reached the stage where he very rarely picked up a brush, she still looked on him as the real creator of the pictures now painted almost entirely by herself. In this exchange it was her character which had forced its way into their joint work, to the point of dominating it to the exclusion of her husband; but she nevertheless still felt dependent on his initial impulse; she had replaced him by dint of assimilating him, adopting, as it were, his sex. The result was freakish. Whenever she was showing their works to visitors, she would always say: 'Ferdinand did this, Ferdinand's going to do that', even when he had not provided nor would be providing a single brushstroke. She would flare up at the slightest criticism and would not allow anyone to question his genius. Her blind faith in her husband was superb. Her anger at his squalid adulteries, her disgust and contempt, had never managed to destroy her high opinion of him as the great artist whom she had loved and gone on loving even when that artist had declined and she had been forced to step into his shoes to avoid failure. It was a charming touch of blind simplicity, based on her mingled pride and affection, which enabled Ferdinand to live with his secret sense of impotence. His moral decay did not cause him to suffer excessively; he, too, would speak of 'my picture', 'my work', without thinking how little of his work had gone into the pictures he was signing with his name. And all this had come about so naturally between the two of them and he felt so little jealousy towards this woman, who had even robbed him of his individuality, that he could not talk for more than a few minutes without starting to praise her. He would keep repeating all the time what he had once said to Rennequin one evening:

'I assure you, she's more talented than me... I have the devil of a job with my drawing whereas she does it in a jiffy, as easy as falling off a log... You just can't imagine how clever she is! It's a gift. You've either got it or you haven't. I haven't and she has.'

People would smile discreetly and see it as a compliment from a loving husband; yet should anyone show that they thought highly of Madame Sourdis as a person but had no great opinion of her as an artist, he would take umbrage and launch into a long theoretical disquisition on the artistic temperament and the mechanics of painting, always finishing up by asserting:

'And I'm telling you that she's better than I am! People must be mad not to see it!'

They were a very united couple. Latterly, age and ill-health had greatly subdued Ferdinand. He could no longer drink, for the slightest excess upset his stomach. Only women were still capable of enticing him into his old habits of debauchery, bouts that would last two or three days. But when the couple finally settled in Mercoeur, the lack of opportunity forced him to become almost completely faithful. After this, Adèle's only danger would be if he took a sudden fancy to one of her maids. She had accepted the fact that she must employ only very ugly ones but that still did not prevent Ferdinand from chancing his arm, if he could persuade the maid to cooperate; in certain moods, he had a pathological urge to satisfy his sexual appetites and gratify his perversions, an urge which he was quite incapable of controlling, however unpleasant the consequences. Adèle merely changed her maids each time she thought she detected too intimate a relationship between master and servant. Then Ferdinand would be contrite for a whole week and, even in their old age, this would rekindle their love. Adèle still worshipped her husband with the same savage jealousy which she had always managed to conceal from him; and he, faced by one of her terrifying silences when she had had to dismiss a maid, would try to obtain forgiveness by a display of cringing affection. At such times, she would dominate him like a little boy. His sallow face was by now fearfully ravaged and deeply lined; but he still had his golden beard, paler but with no trace of grey, so that he looked like some venerable god still possessing the golden charm of youth.

Then one day, in their Mercoeur studio, Ferdinand was suddenly overcome by a deep dislike for painting, a sort of physical revulsion. The smell of turpentine, the feel of the oily brush on the canvas, threw him into a state of nervous exasperation; his hands started to tremble and he was attacked by dizziness. No doubt it was a consequence of his own incapacity, the result of an acute crisis in the breakdown in his artistic faculties, which had been bound to end in this sheer physical impotence. Adèle was very sympathetic and comforted him by assuring him that it must be a passing indisposition from which he would soon recover. She insisted that he should rest and as he was now doing absolutely no work at all on his pictures, he became gloomy and anxious. She thought up a compromise: he would produce the sketch plans in pencil and she would square them up on the canvas and paint them, under his instructions. Henceforth, that was the procedure that they followed and in every work he signed, there was now not one single brushstroke of his own. All the actual painting was undertaken by Adèle while he merely provided the inspiration, the ideas and the pencil sketches, which were sometimes incomplete and even wrong, so that she was forced to correct them, without, however, informing him.

Following his great success in France, orders had poured in from abroad, particularly from America and Russia, and as the art collectors from those distant lands were not very demanding, all that was required was to send off crates of pictures and cash the money, with no questions asked. Gradually, the Sourdis had gone over completely to this convenient form of production. Moreover, sales in France had dropped. When, at rare intervals, Ferdinand sent a picture to the Salon, it was still given the same enthusiastic reception by the critics, for, being a recognized and established painter of undisputed talent, he had been able slowly to slip into the mass production of mediocre pictures without disturbing the habits of either the critics or the public. For the majority of people, the painter was still the same, only, as he grew older, he had given way to younger, more controversial, painters. Buyers were, however, beginning to lose their taste for his paintings and, though he was still considered a contemporary master, his pictures now sold rather poorly. His whole production was going overseas.

However, one year, one of Ferdinand Sourdis's pictures made a great stir at the Salon. It was a kind of counterpart to his first Salon painting, *The Walk*. In a cold, white-walled room, schoolboys were working, exchanging sly grins and watching flies, while the assistant master in charge of them was absorbed in a novel, seemingly oblivious to everything. It was entitled *The Preparation Room*. Everyone found it charming and there were critics who, comparing the two works painted at an interval of thirty years, spoke of the progress achieved, of the 'prentice quality' of *The Walk* and the mastery of *The Preparation Room*. Almost all of them contrived to discover extraordinary finesse in the second picture, exquisite artistry and a perfection of technique that would never be surpassed. However, the great majority of artists protested, Rennequin most vigorously of all. Although by now a man of seventy-five, he had remained young and was still passionately interested in painting.

'For God's sake!' he exclaimed. 'I'm very fond of Ferdinand but it really is idiotic to prefer his present works to those he painted as a young man. He's got no spunk, no bite, no originality of any sort. Oh, I grant you it's pretty, it's easy on the eye. But you'd have to be a grocer to enjoy that unimaginative technique, tarted up and titivated into a tawdry mish-mash of every possible style and even the perversion of every style... It's not the Ferdinand I used to know who's painting that sort of rubbish.'

Yet, although he knew their secret, he still held back from telling the truth about the Sourdis's paintings. You could, however, sense in the bitterness of his remarks the hidden resentment he had always felt against women, those 'noxious animals' as he sometimes called them. So he contented himself merely with repeating angrily:

'No, that's not the old Ferdinand, definitely not!'

He had been following and analysing with curiosity the way in which Adèle had slowly taken over from Ferdinand. With each new picture, he had noted the slightest changes, recognizing the parts painted by the husband or by the wife and realizing that the former were steadily and increasingly being superseded by the latter. It was such an absorbing phenomenon that he forgot to be angry and merely enjoyed watching the interplay of personalities, as a man fascinated by life's oddities. He had been conscious of every tiny change in the mutation and he now sensed that this psychological and physiological drama had been played out. The ending, represented by *The Preparation Room*, was there in front of his eyes. Adèle had gobbled up Ferdinand and that was that...

As in July of every year, Rennequin now decided to go down and spend a few days in Mercoeur. Indeed, ever since the Salon, he had been feeling an irresistible desire to meet the couple again. It would give him the opportunity of seeing for himself whether his reasoning was correct.

When he called on the Sourdis, it was a scorching hot afternoon and the garden was drowsing in the shade. The house and even the flowerbeds looked neat and tidy, the hallmark of middle-class orderliness and peace. Not a sound from the little town could penetrate into this remote corner; all that could be heard was the humming of bees in the climbing roses. The maid told him that the mistress was in the studio.

When Rennequin opened the door, he saw Adèle standing in front of the easel in the same attitude as he had once seen her many years before. Today, however, she was making no secret of the fact that she was painting. She gave a quiet exclamation of pleasure and was about to put down her palette when Rennequin protested:

'If I'm disturbing you, I shall go away... Hang it all, I'm a friend of the family. Off you go, keep working!'

She let herself be persuaded; she was a woman who knew that time is money.

'Very well, then, since you insist! You know, one never has time to turn round...'

Despite increasing age and obesity, she was still tackling her work with determination and extraordinary deftness of touch. Rennequin watched her for a minute then asked:

'Is Ferdinand out?'

'Of course not, he's over there,' replied Adèle, pointing with her brush towards a corner of the studio.

Ferdinand was indeed there, lying stretched out on a divan. He had been dozing and Rennequin's voice had woken him up; but his mind had become so feeble and sluggish that he did not at first recognize him.

'Oh, it's you, what a nice surprise,' he said eventually.

He made a great effort to sit up and held out a flabby hand. The day before, his wife had caught him out with the little girl who came in to do the washing-up and he was in a very contrite mood; he looked scared and worried, not knowing what to do to be forgiven. Rennequin found him more drained and subdued than he had expected. He had become a complete wreck and Rennequin felt pity for the poor man. Wishing to see if he could perhaps rekindle some of his former spirit, he mentioned the great stir that had been created by *The Preparation Room* at the last Salon.

'Well, young fellow, you can still excite the public. Everybody's talking about you in Paris. It's just like the old days.'

Ferdinand gazed at him blankly and then, making an effort to find something to say:

'Oh yes, I know, Adèle's been reading me the papers. It's a very good picture, isn't it? Oh, I'm working, I'm still doing a lot of work... But I'm telling you, she's better than me, she's got a fantastic technique!'

He blinked his eyes and gave a wan smile towards his wife. She had come up to them and she gave a good-humoured shrug of her shoulders as she said:

'Don't listen to him! You know that crazy idea of his... To hear him speak, you'd think it was I who was the great painter... All I do is to help him, and not very well at that... Well, since it gives him pleasure to say so...'

Rennequin watched without a word this game of pretence which they were playing with each other, no doubt in good faith. But what he saw in the studio told him plainly that Ferdinand's talent had sunk without trace. He was not even producing the little pencil sketches; he had reached the stage of not feeling any need to preserve his self-respect by lies; in his mind it was now enough to be merely Adèle's husband and it was she who composed, sketched and painted the pictures, without asking any advice from him. Moreover, she had, as an artist, entered so completely into his skin that she was able to continue his work without leaving the slightest indication to show where the break had occurred. Now, it was all her own work and all that remained of her female personality was the earlier imprint of Ferdinand's male personality.

Ferdinand gave a yawn.

'You'll stay to dinner, won't you?' he said. 'I'm fagged out... Can you understand that, Rennequin? I've done damn all today and I'm still completely fagged out!'

'He says he hasn't done anything,' interrupted Adèle, 'but he works from morning to night. He'll never listen to me and take a good long rest.'

'That's true enough,' Ferdinand said. 'If I take a rest, I don't feel well, I have to keep busy.'

He had stood up and wandered about the studio for a minute before sitting down again at the small table on which his wife used to paint her watercolours. He was examining a sheet of paper on which someone had started putting the first washes of a watercolour painting. It was a sort of schoolgirlish subject, a stream turning the wheel of a mill, with a screen of poplars and an old willow. Rennequin leaned over his back and started to smile as he saw the childish clumsiness of the drawing and the colours. It was an almost laughable daub.

'How odd,' he murmured to himself.

He stopped short when he saw Adèle give him a sharp look. With a vigorous flourish, not bothering to use a maulstick, she had just dashed off a whole figure in her picture, roughing it in with a quite masterly boldness of brushwork.

'Don't you think that's a really pretty mill?' said Ferdinand, still bending over his sheet of paper. He sounded just like a little boy pleased at the progress he was making. 'Of course, you know, I'm only a learner, nothing more.'

Rennequin stood there in stunned amazement. It was Ferdinand who was now painting watercolours.

THE HAUNTED HOUSE

ABOUT two years ago I was cycling down a deserted country lane near Orgeval, up-river from Poissy, when I caught sight of a building, set slightly back from the road, of such striking appearance that I jumped off my bicycle to examine it more closely. Under the lead-grey November sky, in the middle of a vast garden planted with ancient trees whose leaves were swirling about in the bitterly cold wind, there stood a brick-built house, quite ordinary-looking in itself; but the thing which made it so remarkable, so weird, grim and distressing, was the appalling state of disrepair into which it had been allowed to fall. As one of the iron gates had fallen off and a large placard announced, in letters almost completely obliterated by the weather, that the property was for sale, impelled by a curiosity not unmixed with an uneasy feeling of apprehension, I went into the garden.

The house must have remained unoccupied for possibly thirty or even forty years. The crumbling brick cornices and architraves, disintegrating under the effect of the weather, were overgrown with moss and lichen, and the front of the house, while sound enough, even though badly neglected, was furrowed with cracks like a prematurely wrinkled face. Covered in brambles, the steps leading up to the terrace in front of the entrance were broken up by frost and sprouting nettles from every crack. It was completely desolate, like the threshold to a house of the dead. Particularly terrifying was the melancholy sight of the bare, livid green windows, smashed in by stones thrown by urchins and opening on to dismal, deserted rooms, like the dull, staring eyes of a lifeless corpse. The vast garden surrounding the house was a scene of sheer devastation with its flower beds swamped in weeds and barely recognizable, predatory plants that had run riot and obliterated the paths, arbours which had degenerated into a jungle, rank growth such as you find in an abandoned cemetery, under the dank shade of giant hoary trees, over which, on this late autumn day, the winds were singing their mournful dirge as they stripped off the last leaves.

For a long time I stood there lost in thought, gazing at this melancholy sight and listening to this universal, despairing lament, oppressed by secret fears and a growing distress, yet gripped by a deep compassion, a need to know and sympathize with the misery and suffering which I sensed all around me. So when I at last made up my mind to leave, catching sight of what seemed like an inn on the other side of the lane where the road forked, a wretched sort of hovel where you could buy a drink, I walked over to it, determined to see what I could find out from the local inhabitants.

Inside there was only an old woman who served me a glass of beer. She was full of moans, complaining that her inn was too far off the beaten track and that she would be lucky if she saw a couple of cyclists a day. She went on to tell me the story of her life: her name was Toussaint and she was a widow. She had come from Vernon to take over the inn with her man; at first, things hadn't gone too badly but ever since her husband had died everything had been going downhill. When her stream of words had subsided and I started to question her about the property across the way, she suddenly became very wary and looked at me suspiciously as if I were trying to extract some dreadful secret from her.

'Oh yes, you mean *The Wilderness*, the haunted house, as people call it round here. Well, I don't know anything about it, it wasn't during my time, I'll have been here thirty years come Easter and all that happened nearly forty years ago. When we came here, the house looked more or less like it does now... Summers come and go and winters come and go and nothing much changes except that a few more stones fall off.'

'But why hasn't it been sold, since it's up for sale?' I enquired.

'Ah, why not, why not? How can I know? People say so many things...'

No doubt I was beginning to gain her confidence. What was more, she was dying to tell me all those things that people said. To start with, she told me that not one of the girls from the neighbouring village would ever dare to go into *The Wilderness* after dark because of the rumour that there was a poor soul who returned from the dead at night. And when I expressed surprise that there were still people who believed that sort of thing, so close to Paris, she shrugged her shoulders and, after professing to be sceptical, admitted that she herself had sneaking fears.

'Facts are facts, sir. Why can't they sell it? I've seen buyers come along and they've all gone away faster than they came and not one of them has ever come back. Well, one thing's certain and that's that as soon as anyone is bold enough to go into that house, strange things begin to happen: doors fly open or slam shut by themselves, just as if there's a terrible wind blowing; cries and groans and sobs can be heard in the cellars and if people still persist they hear earsplitting screams of: "Angeline! Angeline! Angeline!" so sad and mournful, they'd freeze the blood in your veins. I'm telling you, it's been proved and nobody can deny it.'

I confess that I was beginning to be passionately intrigued myself and even feeling a slight shiver run down my own spine.

'And who was this Angeline?' I enquired.

'Ah, sir, I'd have to tell you the whole story... But I must say again, I don't know anything.'

But she ended by telling me everything. Forty years before, around 1858, at a time when the Second Empire was at its height and life was one long celebration, Monsieur de G***, who held a post in the Emperor's household in the Tuileries, was widowed and left with his young daughter Angeline, about ten years old and an amazingly beautiful little girl, the living image of her mother. Two years later, Monsieur de G*** married again, a general's widow and another celebrated beauty. It was said that after this second marriage, Angeline and her stepmother became dreadfully jealous of each other, the little girl being heartbroken at seeing her mother so quickly forgotten and replaced by an outsider while the stepmother was obsessed and even terrified by the continual presence of this living image of a wife whom she could never entirely replace in her husband's affections. *The Wilderness* belonged to the new Madame de G*** and one evening, seeing her husband passionately kissing his daughter, she was said to have been so carried away by her insane jealousy that she had struck her stepdaughter so hard on the back of her head that the poor little girl fell dead. There was a horrible sequel: in order to protect the woman who had murdered his daughter, the father agreed to bury Angeline himself in one of the cellars and the little body lay there for years while the couple gave out that the girl was staying with an aunt. Later a dog was seen scratching at the earth and howling, so the crime came to light, but it was all hushed up by the Emperor's entourage to avoid scandal. Now both Monsieur and Madame de G*** were dead but Angeline still came back to earth every night as a mournful voice called out to her from the mysterious regions of the other world.

'Everybody knows the story,' said old Madame Toussaint in conclusion. 'It's as true as two and two makes four.'

I had been listening to her tale with bated breath, gripped, despite its improbabilities, by the strange violence of this sinister drama. I had heard of this Monsieur de G*** and I seemed to remember that he had remarried and that a domestic tragedy had cast a shadow over his life. So was it all true? What a tragically sad story it was! The clash of passions exacerbated to the point of madness, the most terrifying of *crimes passionels* imaginable, a little girl of unearthly beauty, deeply loved, yet killed by her wicked stepmother and buried by her own father in the corner of a cellar! The emotion and the horror were both on an unspeakably grand scale. I was just about to question the old woman further and start a discussion, when I stopped and asked myself: what's the point? Why not go away with this frightful tale, such a superb figment of the popular imagination, still fresh and unspoilt in my mind?

As I remounted my bicycle, I cast one final glance at *The Wilderness*. Night was falling, the unhappy house was watching me through its blank, murky windows, like the eyes of some dead woman, while the autumn winds kept up their moaning through the ancient trees.

2

How was it that this story impressed itself so firmly on my mind as to become a nagging obsession that refused to go away? Such things are problems of psychology that are difficult to solve... I kept telling myself that legends of this sort are to be found in every country district in France and that this particular one could have no direct interest for me; yet despite this, I was haunted by the thought of this little dead girl, that entrancing, tragic, little Angeline who every night for the last forty years had been called to by a mournful voice echoing through the empty rooms of that deserted house.

So, during the first two months of the following winter, I started investigating. Obviously, even if such a spectacular disappearance had never become widely known, the newspapers of the time must still have made some reference to it. I went through the relevant issues in the Bibliothèque Nationale* without discovering anything: there was not one word about any such story. Then I questioned contemporaries, members of the Emperor's household: nobody could give me any firm answer and the only information that I succeeded in gathering was so contradictory that although I was still tantalized by the mystery, I had given up all hope of getting at the truth. And then, one morning, quite by chance, I struck another track...

Every two or three weeks, I used to go and pay my respects to a fellow writer, the old poet V***, for whom I had great admiration and affection; he died last April, just short of his seventieth birthday. For many years he had been paralysed in his legs and confined to an armchair in his little study in the Rue d'Assas, overlooking the Luxembourg gardens. He had long lived in his imagination, cut off from reality in his ideal ivory tower, where he had loved and suffered; this life of dreams was now drawing gently to its close. Who amongst us can fail to remember his pleasant, delicate features, his white hair, as curly as a child's, and his pale blue eyes that had never lost the innocence of youth? He could not be described as an inveterate liar; but it was true that his mind was so continually inventive that you could never really tell where, for him, reality ended and dreams began. He was a most charming old man who had long been living in a world of his own. I found that his conversation frequently had the effect of opening up a vague, discreet and yet thrilling vision of the Unknown.

So that day, I was chatting with him, sitting by the window of his tiny little room, always heated by a blazing fire. It was freezing hard outside and the vast Luxembourg gardens stretched out immaculately white as far as the eye could see. I don't remember how I came to mention *The Wilderness* and the story that I still couldn't banish from my mind: the father remarrying, the stepmother insanely jealous of his little daughter with her uncanny resemblance to her mother, and her sinister burial in a corner of the cellar. He listened to me with the quiet smile which was always on his lips even when he was sad. There was a pause and, as his pale blue eyes became lost in contemplation of the vast white Luxembourg gardens, he gave a little shudder and a sudden aura of dream seemed to be hovering round him.

'I knew Monsieur de G*** very well,' he began slowly. 'I knew his first wife, whose beauty was truly preternatural... I knew his second wife, a prodigiously lovely woman. I was even in love with both of them, without ever divulging my feelings. I knew Angeline, who was even lovelier and who, had she lived, would have had every man at her feet. But her death did not occur quite as you say...'

I was completely dumbfounded. Was this going to be the revelation of the truth that I had despaired of ever learning? Would I finally know the whole story? At first unsuspecting, I said:

'My dear V***, you can't imagine how great a kindness you'll be doing me! At last I shall be able to have peace of mind... Tell me everything, quickly!'

But he was not listening to me and his pale blue eyes were still gazing into the distance. Then he started speaking in a dreamy voice, as if creating the people and things he was conjuring up from the past.

'By the time she was twelve, Angeline had already blossomed into womanhood and was capable of feeling all its transports of love as well as its pangs of suffering. It was she who became jealous, madly jealous, of this new wife whom she saw every day in her father's company. She felt it as a monstrous betrayal and it caused her untold anguish; it was not only an affront to her mother but a heartrending torment for herself. Every night she could hear her mother calling to her from her tomb and one night, tortured by her immense love and unable to bear her sufferings any longer, she determined to join her mother beyond the grave. She stabbed herself to the heart with a knife.'

I uttered a cry.

'Gracious Heavens! Is that possible?'

'You can imagine all the terror and the horror,' he went on, not heeding my exclamation, 'when, on the following morning, Monsieur and Madame G*** found Angeline in her little bed with a knife thrust up to the haft in the middle of her chest. They were leaving for Italy the following day and there was only one other person left in the house, a maid who had brought Angeline up. Terrified lest they might be accused of the crime, they enlisted her help and did indeed bury the little girl's body, but in a corner of the conservatory at the back of the house, at the foot of a giant orange tree. And it was there it was found when, after her parents' death, the old housemaid told her story.'

Doubts were beginning to arise in my mind and I uneasily scrutinized his face in the suspicion that he might be inventing the whole story.

'But do you too really think,' I asked him, 'that Angeline may be coming back as a ghost every night when she hears that earsplitting cry of the mysterious voice calling to her?'

This time he looked at me and gave an indulgent smile.

'Come back as a ghost? My dear boy, everybody comes back... Why shouldn't the soul of that dear little girl still be haunting the place where she had loved and suffered? If a voice is heard calling to her, you can be sure that it's only because life hasn't yet begun again for her. Everything begins again, nothing is ever lost, whether it be love or loveliness... Angeline! Angeline! Angeline! And she'll be born again and return to the sunshine and the flowers...'

I was definitely neither convinced nor reassured. My poetic, childlike old friend had in fact thrown me into still greater confusion. He must have been making it all up. All the same, he had perhaps, like all seers, divined the truth.

'And what you've just been telling me is completely, genuinely true?' I ventured to ask him, with a laugh.

He gave a gentle laugh in reply.

'Of course it's true! Isn't everything true that is part of the Infinite?'

That was the last time I met him, for some time later I had to leave Paris. I can still see him now, with his rapt look as he gazed absently out over the white expanse of the Luxembourg gardens, so quietly certain of the truth of his endless dreams, whereas I was consumed by the need to nail down the constantly elusive truth.

3

Eighteen months went by. I had been forced to travel and my life had been caught up in a passionate web of joy and sorrow in the storm of life which whirls us all away towards the great Unknown. But at certain times, I could still hear in the distance that piteous call: Angeline! Angeline! Angeline! It would transfix me and I would remain trembling, once again tortured by doubt and the need to know the truth. I found it impossible to forget; uncertainty is my private hell.

I can't remember exactly how it came to be that on one splendid June evening I found myself once more cycling along that remote little lane past *The Wilderness*. Had I made a conscious decision to go back? Or had I unthinkingly left the main road to go off in that direction? It was nearly eight o'clock but at that time of the year when the days are so long, the sky was still aglow with the triumphant splendour of a sun setting in a cloudless sky, an infinite prospect of gold and azure blue. A delicious lightness filled the air, a rich scent of trees and grasses and an immense peace and joy spread out tenderly over the meadows. It was bliss to be alive.

As on the first occasion, it was amazement which made me spring off my bicycle at the sight of *The Wilderness*. For a moment, I felt uncertain: was this really the same property? A fine new gate was gleaming in the sun, the boundary walls had been rebuilt and the house itself, which I could barely discern amongst the trees, seemed to have been rejuvenated: it was gay and cheerful. Could this be the promised resurrection? Had Angeline come back to life in response to the calls from the mysterious, distant voice?

I had remained standing in the lane, greatly puzzled, when I was startled to hear shuffling footsteps coming up behind me. It was the old widow Toussaint bringing her cow back from a nearby field of lucerne.

'So they weren't put off, were they?' I said, pointing towards the house.

She recognized me and brought her cow to a halt.

'Ah well, there are people, you know, sir, who'd walk over the good Lord! The property was sold more than a year ago. But it was an artist who bought it, the painter B***, and artists'll do anything.'

And she went on her way, taking her cow with her and adding, with a shake of her head:

'Anyway, we'll have to wait and see how it turns out.'

The painter B***, that clever, sensitive artist who'd painted all those attractive Parisian women? I knew him slightly, we used to exchange greetings at the theatre, at art exhibitions, at all those other places where people meet. Suddenly, I was seized by an irresistible urge to go in and confess my obsession to him and beg him to tell me anything he might know about the mysterious *Wilderness* that was preying so insistently on my mind. So, without further ado, and ignoring my dusty cycling get-up, which people were, by now, beginning to accept in any case, I propped my bicycle up against the moss-covered trunk of an old tree. When I pulled the bell-chain that was dangling beside the gate, a servant appeared. I gave him my card and he went away, leaving me alone in the garden.

As I looked around me, my surprise increased. They had restored the front of the house; the cracks and loosened bricks had gone; the entrance terrace, gay with rose-bushes, had become friendly and welcoming, while the windows, hung with cheerful white curtains, bespoke happiness within. The garden had been cleared of its nettles and brambles, the flower beds had re-emerged, full of colour and fragrance; even the century-old trees looked younger, basking peacefully in the golden rays of the spring-like sunshine.

When the servant came back, he showed me into the drawing-room, explaining that his master had gone into the village but that he would not be long. I should have been prepared to wait for hours, so I settled down patiently and started to examine the room into which I had been shown, luxuriously furnished with deep-pile carpets and cretonne curtains at the windows and doors, matching the immense divan and the deep armchairs. The window curtains were so voluminous that I was surprised by the sudden arrival of dusk; night began to fall and soon the room was almost completely in the dark. Once again I had started to day-dream and go over the whole tragic story in my mind. Had Angeline been murdered? Had she really stabbed herself in the heart? And I must confess that, sitting all alone in this deserted house, now completely plunged in darkness, and waiting for what seemed many hours for someone who never came, I began to be gripped by a strange fear, a fear that, starting as a feeling of unease, a slight shiver down the spine, gradually grew stronger and stronger until my blood began to freeze and I was filled with a panic terror.

Why had no one brought me any light? Why had I been forgotten? And now vague sounds seemed to be coming from somewhere: soft moaning, stifled sobs, heavy ghostly footsteps.

Were they in the cellar? The sound increased and came nearer and the whole gloom-filled house seemed to be in the grip of some fearful anguish. Then, suddenly, the dreadful cry rang out: Angeline! Angeline! Angeline! in such a wild crescendo that I could almost feel its cold breath on my face. With savage violence, one of the drawing-room doors was flung open and Angeline came in and ran across the room without seeing me... I recognized her in the light which streamed in through the door from the hall outside. There could be no doubt: there was the little dead twelve-year-old girl of whom I had heard so much, marvellously lovely, with her long fair hair flowing over her shoulders, dressed in a white frock and herself all white from the earthy grave from which she rose every night... She dashed wildly past and disappeared through another door while the same cry came again, further away this time: Angeline! Angeline! Angeline! I stood there bathed in perspiration, with every hair on my body bristling with terror at the sight of this mysterious flashing apparition.

I think it must have been almost at once, just as the apologetic servant at last brought me a lamp, that I became aware that the painter B*** must have come into the room and was shaking my hand and apologizing, too, for having kept me waiting for so long. Any false pride I might have had had evaporated and, still trembling from head to foot, I immediately poured out my story. You can imagine his amazement as he listened to me and you can imagine mine as he suddenly broke into a great guffaw and hastened to reassure me:

'You probably don't know, my dear fellow, that the second Madame G*** was my cousin. Poor woman! Fancy accusing her of the murder of that little girl whom she loved and mourned as if she had been her own. You see, that's the only true part of your story: the poor little girl did die, not by her own hand, Heaven's above, but from a sudden attack of fever. It was such an unbelievable shock for her father and stepmother that they refused to go on living in a house where such a terrible thing had happened. That explains why it remained unoccupied during their lifetime. After their death, there were endless lawsuits which prevented the property from being sold. I had always wanted to buy it and had kept my eye on it for years. I can assure you that up till now we've never seen a single ghost!'

Another little shiver ran down my spine.

'But I've just seen Angeline here only a moment ago,' I stammered. 'I heard a strange voice calling her and she went through here, I saw her myself running across the room.'

He looked at me again in bewilderment as though I had taken leave of my senses. Then his cheerful face broke into a broad grin.

'That must be my daughter,' he exclaimed with a laugh. 'Her godfather was Monsieur de G*** who gave her the same name in memory of his own daughter. I expect her mother was calling her and she ran through here.'

He opened a door and himself called out the familiar name: 'Angeline! Angeline! Angeline!'

The little ghost came in, bubbling over with life and high spirits. She stood there in her white dress with her long fair hair streaming over her shoulders, so lovely, so radiantly full of hope, the epitome of a budding spring rich with the promise of a lifetime of love and happiness.

What a darling ghost she was, this new little Angeline, reborn from the dead one! Death, where is thy victory? My old friend, the poet V***, was right: nothing is ever lost, everything begins again, love and loveliness alike. Mothers' voices call to their daughters, those little girls of today who are the sweethearts of tomorrow, and they live again in the sunshine and the flowers. It was the hope of this child's awakening that had been haunting this house, now once more joyful and renewed, happy at last in the rediscovery of the secret of eternal life!

EXPLANATORY NOTES

THE GIRL WHO LOVES ME (*Celle qui m'aime*) is from *Contes à Ninon*, a collection of five short stories. Published in November 1864, it is Zola's first publication. The first-person narration frequently appears in Zola's early *chroniques*; it would be dangerous to assume that such stories are accurately autobiographical.

    4 *the Friend of the People (l'Ami du Peuple')*: this increasingly grotesque figure of a hypocritical would-be humanitarian takes his name from Marat's revolutionary news-sheet; it was also the title of an influential left-wing republican periodical in the period leading up to the 1848 Revolution. At this stage, Zola's pity for the poor showed no political leanings.

  10 *in their own way*: the contrast between the beauty and grandeur of nature and the sordid bustle of the crowd is typical of young Zola's early works where he is striving, as an idealist, to come to terms with reality. There are echoes of Baudelaire's *Petits Poèmes en Prose* here.

RENTAFOIL (*Les Repoussoirs*): first published 1866 as part of a volume containing a short novel and three other tales grouped under the title *Esquisses parisiennes*: it is an amusing and sadly cynical story about a cynical and erotic epoch, the declining years of the Second Empire.

  19 *Walter Scott*: a constant source of ridicule for French writers as providing fuel for the sloppy romanticism of silly young women, and even some less silly: Madame Chabre takes to reading Scott's novels (see 'Shellfish for Monsieur Chabre').

DEATH BY ADVERTISING (*Une Victime de la réclame*): this caricaturally satirical and chilling tale, first published in *L'Illustration* in 1866, was reprinted with various changes, some considerable, in other periodicals in 1868, 1869 and 1872; we have mainly followed the text of the first version. The original idea occurs in a similar tale by a fellow journalist, Philarète Chasles.

  23 *'the best of all possible worlds'*: echoing, of course, the philosopher Pangloss's optimistic belief in Voltaire's *Candide*.

STORY OF A MADMAN (*Histoire d'un fou*): first published in *L'Événement illustré* in June 1868. Forcible internment in asylums of allegedly mad people was a topical issue and then, as now, it aroused strong feelings. The story has similarities of plot with Zola's novel *Thérèse Raquin* published the year before and adumbrates parts of the later Rougon-Macquart novel *La Conquête de Plassans* of 1874.

25 *Belleville* is in the XIXth arrondissement in the north-east of Paris.

27 *Charenton*: a psychiatric hospital to the south-east of Paris, near the Bois de Vincennes.

BIG MICHU (*Le grand Michu*): first published in March 1870 in *La Cloche*, for which Zola wrote a number of *chroniques* from 1870–2; these have a marked anti-Second Empire tone. In 'Big Michu' sympathy for republicanism and student protest is quite plain: its idea was based on actual happenings in two Paris *lycées* in 1869. 'Big Michu' was reprinted in 1874 as part of a collection of fifteen stories entitled *Nouveaux Contes à Ninon*.

30 *Var*: part of Provence.

   the Maures: a low range bordering the Mediterranean.

THE ATTACK ON THE MILL (*L'Attaque du Moulin*): appeared in Russia in June 1877, and in three French periodicals before publication, with five other stories by five friends and admirers, in 1880 under the title *Soirées de Médan*, from the name of the village near Paris where Zola had bought a country property after the huge success of *L'Assommoir*. The stories, anti-militarist in tone, all dealt with the Franco-Prussian war of 1870–1; they were intended as a naturalist manifesto. Apart from Zola's story, of the others only Maupassant's *Boule de Suif* has survived; in any case, Maupassant soon went his own way. Despite the clichés (the harsh Prussian officer, the dashing French commander, the heroic refusal to betray), the story has dramatic suspense, a touching love interest, an intriguingly eccentric main character (in old Merlier), and a finely anti-climactic climax, but a reader untouched or bored by French chauvinism may prefer other more down-to-earth but subtler tales.

53 *endearingly*: this 'endearing' tone represents, in the French, the first time she had addressed Dominique with the intimate 'tu' instead of the formal 'vous'.

CAPTAIN BURLE (*Le Capitaine Burle*): the last of Zola's stories for *Vestnik Evropy*, it appeared in Russia in December 1880. It was published twice separately in French periodicals before giving its title to a collection of six short stories from *Vestnik Evropy* published in a single volume in 1882; they included 'The Way People Die' (*Comment on meurt*) and 'Coqueville on the Spree' (*La Fête à Coqueville*). A further volume of six *Vestnik Evropy* stories followed in 1884; it took its title from *Naïs Micoulin* ('A Flash in the Pan'), and included 'Dead Men Tell No Tales' (*La Mort d'Olivier Bécaille*), 'Shellfish for Monsieur Chabre' (*Les Coquillages de Monsieur Chabre*) and 'Absence Makes the Heart Grow Fonder' (*Jacques*

Damour). We have in our selection followed the order laid down by Zola, not the order of publication as separate stories.

If 'Captain Burle' is possibly the most squalid of all Zola's short stories, it is perhaps, through its paucity of light relief, one of his most disturbing. There is little comfort for optimists in this tale of family pride leading a mother to instigate her son's death and drive her grandson to an early grave and of military honour bringing about the death of an officer at the hands of an old friend.

67 *Solferino*: an Italian village in the province of Mantua, the scene of a victory of Napoleon III's army over the Austrians in June 1859.

72 *absinthe*: a wormwood-flavoured French rot-gut liqueur; its sale was later banned.

THE WAY PEOPLE DIE (*Comment on meurt*): the third of Zola's stories for *Vestnik Evropy*, published in August 1876. The convenient formula of treating the same theme in a series of dramatic sketches grouped according to social class had already been used by him in a story entitled *Comment on se marie* in the Russian magazine in January 1876. Zola used a similar technique on other occasions, notably in 'Priests and Sinners' (see below).

98 *Academy of Moral and Political Sciences*: one of the five Academies, which include the famous Académie française, that together form L'Institut français, housed in the seventeenth-century Palais Mazarin on the Left Bank.

Conseil d'État: the highest administrative court of France; originally set up by Napoleon I to advise on the drafting of regulations, it gradually developed judicial functions to protect citizens against abuse of such government regulations.

103 *Montparnasse cemetery*: in the XIVth arrondissement in the south of Paris.

105 *the Marais*: a district in the IIIrd and IVth arrondissements, containing many superb old townhouses.

110 *Père-Lachaise cemetery*: XXth arrondissement, north-east of Paris.

111 *Rue de Clichy*: IXth arrondissement; quite a good address.

113 *Auvergne*: a poor and harsh, though lovely, province in the Massif Central. Its inhabitants (Auvergnats) have a reputation of being hard workers and dour; thus they are supposed to make good concierges.

Saint-Cloud: just east of Paris, it has a fine park and a former Imperial palace.

114 *Melun*: a little country town on the Seine south-east of Paris.

117 *Montmartre cemetery*: in the XVIIIth arrondissement in the north of Paris, not far from the Rue de Clichy.

Batignolles: in the less fashionable eastern part of the XVIIIth arrondissement.

122 *Rue Nollet*: round the corner from Rue Cardinet. Zola took pains to be accurate in his topography of Paris.

123 *Angers*: some 180 miles south-east of Paris and the former provincial capital of Anjou.

COQUEVILLE ON THE SPREE (*La Fête à Coqueville*): published in *Vestnik Evropy* in August 1879, in French in May 1880. This story shows flashes of optimism of a sort rare in Zola: it seems to be suggested that man's natural goodness, here released by massive doses of free alcohol, can rise above influences of history and environment. But Zola obviously has tongue in cheek, and the only glimpse into the future shows the downtrodden Monsieur Mouchel tanning the hide off the acerbic Madame Veuve Dufeu.

130 *Louis XIII*: takes us back to the period 1610–43.

132 *Brisemotte*: French for a 'clod-crusher', a sort of harrow; but an earlier familiar meaning of *motte* was the *mons Veneris*.

La Queue... Louis-Philippe: Louis Philippe reigned from 1830–48, long after pigtails (French, *queue*) were out-moded.

134 *the Emperor*: strange to have been so called because he had served under a king, but nicknames are like that, and anything imperial is military. Charles X reigned from 1824–30.

sous-préfet: for administrative purposes, France is divided into ninety odd *départements*, each under a *préfet*, and each *département* is subdivided into *arrondissements* of which the head is a *sous-préfet*. Father Radiguet, despite certain similarities to Father Pintoux in 'Priests and Sinners', is far less bigoted and thus more humane and intelligent, just as the Normans are less superstitious and more hard-headed than the Bretons.

143 *ratafia*: a liqueur flavoured with almond, peach, apricot or cherry kernels.

150 *tuica calugaresca... Serbian slivovitz*: Zola obviously enjoyed dredging up the names of very exotic spirits and liqueurs: even in our well-travelled, affluent age, while Serbian (or Yugoslavian) slivovitz is not unfamiliar to many, Romanian tuica calugareasca (misspelt by Zola)—also a plum-brandy—is less likely to be widely known. 'Calugareasca' tells us that, like trappistine (made by Trappist monks), this tuica is made by monks.

A FLASH IN THE PAN (*Naïs Micoulin*): published in *Vestnik Evropy* in September 1877 and in France two years later. For its publication in volume form, see note to 'Captain Burle' (above). Zola wrote this story on holiday at L'Estaque and Frédéric and Naïs's desire is closely linked to the ambience of warmth and natural beauty; there is also an obvious contrast between the sophisticated townsman and the country girl. Zola was able to bring his familiarity with Provence acquired as a boy to good use in the portraits of old Micoulin and his wife. The landscapes of the story were much painted by Zola's schoolfriend, Paul Cézanne.

162 *Durance*: one of the main tributaries of the Rhone into which it flows south of Avignon.

Cours Mirabeau: the magnificent tree-lined main street of Aix.

170 *La Joliette*: the modern port of Marseilles.

DEAD MEN TELL NO TALES (*La Mort d'Olivier Bécaille*): published in *Vestnik Evropy* in March 1879 and in France a month later (see note to 'Captain Burle' above). The story reveals an underlying morbidity in Zola.

187 *Rue Dauphine*: in the VIth arrondissement, on the Left Bank near Saint-Germain-des-Prés.

210 *my sense of direction*: Bécaille must have been buried in the Montparnasse cemetery, like the Comte de Verteuil in 'The Way People Die'.

SHELLFISH FOR MONSIEUR CHABRE (*Les Coquillages de Monsieur Chabre*): published in *Vestnik Evropy* in September 1876; section IV appeared separately in France in July 1881, and the whole story appeared in the collection of stories published under the general title of *Naïs Micoulin* in 1884 (see note to 'Captain Burle' above).

Zola wrote that the chief character in this story was the sea (he had holidayed in Piriac, on the Atlantic coast south of Nantes, in 1876, and many personal memories of the landscape have been incorporated). It is also an excellent manual of seduction for the use of males and females.

ABSENCE MAKES THE HEART GROW FONDER (*Jacques Damour*): published in *Vestnik Evropy* in August 1880, in France in April/May 1881; included in the *Naïs Micoulin* volume of 1884 (see note to 'Captain Burle' above).

246 *Noumea*: the capital of the French colony of New Caledonia, to which convicted members of the Commune uprising in 1871 were transported.

Ménilmontant: a working-class district in the XXth arrondissement in which lies the Père-Lachaise cemetery, on a site originally belonging to Father de la Chaise, one of Louis XIV's confessors.

247 *Berru . . . Henri V*: in Berru we see Zola once again (as in the Friend of the People in 'The Girl Who Loves Me') taking a hard look at deviousness and hypocrisy in republicans. Félicie who, like Big Michu, has a father who fought in the heroic ranks of the 1848 or

360 — Explanatory Notes

1851 republicans, is far more sympathetic. Zola seems to prefer heroic actions to words.

Henri V, who lived from 1820 to 1883, was the grandson of the last Bourbon King of France, Charles X (reigned 1824–30), and in direct line of descent from the deposed and guillotined Louis XVI. Henri took the title of Henri V in 1843. The French royalist flag was white, and his refusal to accept the tricolor was to be a major factor in stopping any restoration.

248 *'93*: the year 1793 was, in fact, the most bloodthirsty of the French Revolution and saw the height of Robespierre's Terror.

250 *guns on Montmartre*: the newly-elected, largely conservative French government, fearing trouble from subversive elements in Paris, had decided to sit in Versailles. When the Parisians, who also thought that the government had not prosecuted the war against the Prussians besieging Paris with sufficient vigour, learned that the 'men in Versailles' proposed disbanding the National Guard, they removed one hundred and seventy guns from the Place Wagram in the XVIIth arrondissement, ostensibly to prevent them from falling into Prussian hands, and hauled them by hand up to the heights of Montmartre. Rioting broke out when government troops were sent to recover the guns; elections were held in Paris, and in April 1871 an independent Paris government, the Commune, was set up.

251 *Moulineaux*: in the south-west of Paris. The red flag was the Commune's flag.

254 *British territory*: the nearest would be the British New Hebrides.

256 *amnesty*: the amnesty for ex-Communards was issued in July 1880, so Zola's story was topical.

258 *Gros-Caillou...Bercy*: Gros-Caillou, in the VIIth arrondissement on the Left Bank; Bercy in the XIIth, on the Right Bank.

259 *Pont Notre-Dame*: joins the Right Bank to the Ile de la Cité, just east of the Hôtel de Ville, the City Hall of Paris.

269 *Place Moncey*: in the IXth; Damour still had a long way to go.

276 *Rue d'Amsterdam*: in the IXth, runs north from the Gare Saint-Lazare. All the streets in this district are named after European capitals or major cities.

278 *Mantes*: now know as Mantes-la-Jolie; it lies on the Seine north-west of Paris.

PRIESTS AND SINNERS: no title in Zola's lifetime. It was published in *Vestnik Evropy* in January 1877, and in French in August/September 1877, with a short introductory paragraph by Zola in which he claims to be writing as an observer rather than a moralist.

284 *Calvary*: Brittany is renowned for its sculpted roadside crucifixion scenes.

292 *Ste-Clotilde*: the then recently built church of Ste-Clotilde stands in the Rue Las-Cases in the heart of the aristocratic Faubourg Saint-Germain, near the French Chamber of Deputies.

294 *Chambertin*: a red Burgundy, however fine, would hardly be considered today a fit accompaniment for sole.

299 *Faubourg Saint-Antoine*: an essentially working-class district, east of the Place de la Bastille.

FAIR EXCHANGE (*Madame Sourdis*): published in *Vestnik Evropy* in April 1880, and in French only in May 1900. It has been suggested that this unusually long gap may be explained by the fact that Ferdinand Sourdis's debauched life offers similarities with that of Alphonse Daudet, Zola's friend and fellow author, and that since it was also rumoured that Madame Daudet had a hand in the writing of Daudet's books, it would have been inappropriate to publish the story during Daudet's lifetime; he died in 1897.

312 *the Salon*: the annual official art exhibition in Paris.

unceremonious tone: Rennequin uses the familiar 'tu' towards Adèle, as though she were still a child.

323 *Café Anglais*: a fashionable boulevard café.

335 *Rue de Clichy*: IXth arrondissement; more fashionable but less charming than the Left Bank Rue d'Assas.

THE HAUNTED HOUSE (*Angeline*): written during Zola's English exile (see Chronology), first published in the London *Star* in January 1899, and in French the following month. Monsieur Ripoll in his excellent Pléiade edition of Zola's short stories points out that the obsessive search for truth by the narrator of 'The Haunted House' may be likened to the author's call for the revelation of the truth in the Dreyfus case.

347 *Bibliothèque Nationale*: in Paris, the equivalent of the British Library.

THE WORLD'S CLASSICS

A Select List

HANS ANDERSEN: Fairy Tales
Translated by L. W. Kingsland
Introduction by Naomi Lewis
Illustrated by Vilhelm Pedersen and Lorenz Frølich

ARTHUR J. ARBERRY (Transl.): The Koran

LUDOVICO ARIOSTO: Orlando Furioso
Translated by Guido Waldman

ARISTOTLE: The Nicomachean Ethics
Translated by David Ross

JANE AUSTEN: Emma
Edited by James Kinsley and David Lodge

Northanger Abbey, Lady Susan, The Watsons,
and Sanditon
Edited by John Davie

Persuasion
Edited by John Davie

WILLIAM BECKFORD: Vathek
Edited by Roger Lonsdale

KEITH BOSLEY (Transl.): The Kalevala

CHARLOTTE BRONTË: Jane Eyre
Edited by Margaret Smith

JOHN BUNYAN: The Pilgrim's Progress
Edited by N. H. Keeble

FRANCES HODGSON BURNETT: The Secret Garden
Edited by Dennis Butts

FANNY BURNEY: Cecilia
or Memoirs of an Heiress
Edited by Peter Sabor and Margaret Anne Doody

THOMAS CARLYLE: The French Revolution
Edited by K. J. Fielding and David Sorensen

LEWIS CARROLL: Alice's Adventures in Wonderland
and Through the Looking Glass
Edited by Roger Lancelyn Green
Illustrated by John Tenniel

MIGUEL DE CERVANTES: Don Quixote
Translated by Charles Jarvis
Edited by E. C. Riley

GEOFFREY CHAUCER: The Canterbury Tales
Translated by David Wright

ANTON CHEKHOV: The Russian Master and Other Stories
Translated by Ronald Hingley

JOHN CLELAND:
Memoirs of a Woman of Pleasure (Fanny Hill)
Edited by Peter Sabor

WILKIE COLLINS: Armadale
Edited by Catherine Peters

JOSEPH CONRAD: Chance
Edited by Martin Ray

Victory
Edited by John Batchelor
Introduction by Tony Tanner

NORMAN DAVIS (Ed.): The Paston Letters

CHARLES DICKENS: Christmas Books
Edited by Ruth Glancy

Sikes and Nancy and Other Public Readings
Edited by Philip Collins

FEDOR DOSTOEVSKY: Crime and Punishment
Translated by Jessie Coulson
Introduction by John Jones

ARTHUR CONAN DOYLE:
Sherlock Holmes: Selected Stories
Introduction by S. C. Roberts

TOBIAS SMOLLETT: The Expedition of Humphry Clinker
Edited by Lewis M. Knapp
Revised by Paul-Gabriel Boucé

ROBERT LOUIS STEVENSON:
Treasure Island
Edited by Emma Letley

ANTHONY TROLLOPE: The American Senator
Edited by John Halperin

GIORGIO VASARI: The Lives of the Artists
Translated and Edited by Julia Conaway Bondanella and Peter Bondanella

VIRGINIA WOOLF: Orlando
Edited by Rachel Bowlby

ÉMILE ZOLA: Nana
Translated and Edited by Douglas Parmée